STUDY GUIDE

Irving M. Copi
UNIVERSITY OF HAWAII

INTRODUCTION TO
LOGIC

SEVENTH EDITION

Prepared by
Richard W. Miller
UNIVERSITY OF MISSOURI, ROLLA

MACMILLAN PUBLISHING COMPANY
NEW YORK
Collier Macmillan Publishers
LONDON

Macmillan Publishing Company
866 Third Avenue, New York, New York 10022

Collier Macmillan Canada, Inc.

ISBN 0-02-381310-5

Printing: 1 2 3 4 5 6 7 8   Year: 6 7 8 9 0 1 2 3 4 5

How To Use This Book

This **Study Guide** is designed to aid you as you work your way through Irving Copi's **Introduction to Logic**, 7th edition, whether on your own or as part of a course in logic. In most cases Professor Copi's explanation of material is substantially more detailed than what will appear here, so it makes sense to read sections of his book before you tackle them here. However, since the two books do complement each other, reading the Study Guide first should cause you no real problems. After studying the material in both books thoroughly, you should find few difficulties in doing the many exercises Professor Copi provides in the **Introduction to Logic**. You will also find that Professor Copi's explanations and mine (and those of your classroom teacher, if you have one) occasionally will approach material from slightly different perspectives. That is not a sign of disagreement, but a display both of different teaching styles and of the diversity of philosophic viewpoint. Nevertheless, we all hope that one approach or other will communicate the critical ideas to you in a manner that you find easily understandable.

Notice that Professor Copi marks about one fifth of the exercises in the **Introduction to Logic** with a star. That is a sign that there is a solution to that exercise in the back of his book. About another one fifth of the exercises are solved, frequently in somewhat more detail, in this **Study Guide**. The difference in explanation lies in the fact that this book will use many of Professor Copi's exercises as means of showing how solutions are reached, what the purpose of specific terminology is, and why you may find material you are studying useful to you. Professor Copi's solutions, then, provide you with answers to problems (as is appropriate, since the "how-to's" are presented in his text); the solutions here are designed to supplement, expand upon, and clarify what is presented in the text. Also, from this point on, the **Introduction to Logic**, 7th edition, will be referred to as "Copi," as opposed to "Professor Copi," which will refer to the author himself.

R. W. M.

Contents

Acknowledgements

I would like to thank Professor Irving Copi for his helpful comments about the earlier edition of this **Study Guide** and for advance copies of his suggested answers to new sections of his 7th edition. I also appreciate the patience of Ms. Helen McInnis of Macmillan. Special thanks are also due Mrs. Alberta Olsen for her skillful typing of the entire **Study Guide** to the 6th edition onto diskettes, so that my revisions could be done more easily.

Early versions of some of the material in this work were prepared under the auspices of the University of Missouri Center for Independent Study Through Correspondence and with the aid of its Coordinator of Curriculum, C. Alex Phillips. I am grateful for the opportunity that they gave me to get my ideas on paper. I also appreciate the comments that I have received, both from teachers and from students who used the earlier edition of this **Study Guide** and from those many students who have had examples and expressions tried out on them.

Sufficient thanks cannot be given to my teenagers Mark and Morna, whose acceptance of the impact of this revision on our family life and of Dad's need both for the computer and for reduced stereo volume, was mature beyond their years.

My greatest debt, however, is to my wife Margaret, who taught me that writing is more than using words to put ideas on paper.

I owe as much to these people, and others too numerous to identify, for what appears here, but I accept as my responsibility alone any errors and infelicities that remain.

Last, but in no way least, I would like to dedicate this book to the man who taught me that, no matter what its liabilities, the best life one can have is on a university campus, my father, M. Warner Miller.

R. W. M.

PART ONE
LANGUAGE

1
Introduction

1.1   What is Logic?

Part of the reason that such multiple approaches to logic are possible is that logic is both a skill and an art. It is a skill in that anyone who is willing to devote a bit of effort to its study ought to be able to operate in it comfortably. It is an art insofar as there are some people for whom it seems to "just come naturally." If you are one of the former, then your study should help you acquire logical skills; if you are one of the fortunate latter group, the work should fairly fly past. In either event logic can be more than just a learning experience. If you think of logic as a sort of sophisticated game of solitaire or as a great puzzle, you should find the working of the problems more interesting.

There is some wise advice that you ought to hear before beginning this, or any other work in logic. It comes from the celebrated Englishman D. L. Dodgson, from the Introduction to his book <u>Symbolic Logic</u>. (By the way, Dodgson was better known by the pseudonym under which he wrote <u>Alice</u> <u>in</u> <u>Wonderland</u>: Lewis Carroll.)

The Learner, who wishes to try the question <u>fairly</u> whether this little book does, or does not, supply the materials for a most interesting mental recreation, is <u>earnestly</u> advised to adopt the following Rules:--

(1) Begin at the <u>beginning</u> and do not allow yourself to gratify a mere idle <u>curiosity</u> by dipping into the book, here there. This would very likely lead to your throwing it aside, with the remark "This is <u>much</u> too hard for me!", and thus losing the chance of adding a very <u>large</u> item to your stock of mental delights. This rule (of not <u>dipping</u> is very <u>desirable</u> with <u>other</u> kinds of books--such as novels, for instance, where <u>you</u> may easily spoil much of the enjoyment, you would otherwise get from the story, by dipping into it further on, so that what the author meant to be a pleasant surprise comes to you as a matter of course. Some people, I know, make a practice of looking into Vol. III first, just to see how the story ends: and perhaps it <u>is</u> as well just to know that all ends <u>happily</u> the much-persecuted lovers <u>do</u> marry after all, that <u>he is</u> proved to be quite innocent <u>of</u> the murder, that the wicked cousin is completely foiled in his plot and gets the punishment he deserves, and that the rich uncle in India (<u>Qu.</u> Why in <u>India</u> <u>Ans.</u> Because, somehow, uncles never <u>can</u> get rich anywhere else) dies at exactly the right moment--before taking the trouble to read Vol. 1. This, I say, is <u>just</u> permissible with a <u>novel</u> where Vol. III has a <u>meaning</u> even for those who have not read the earlier part <u>of</u> the story; but, with a <u>scientific</u> book, it is sheer insanity: you will find the latter part <u>hopelessly</u> unintelligible, if you read it before reaching it <u>in</u> regular course.

(2) Don't begin any fresh Chapter, or Section, until you are certain that you <u>thoroughly</u> understand the whole book <u>up</u> <u>to</u> <u>that</u> <u>point</u>, and that you have worked, correctly, most <u>if</u> <u>not</u> <u>all</u> of the examples which have been set. So long as you are conscious that all the land you have passed through is absolutely <u>conquered</u>, and that you are leaving no unsolved difficulties <u>behind</u> you, which will be sure to turn up later on, your <u>triumphal</u> progress will be easy and de-

lightful. Otherwise, you will find your state of puzzlement
get worse and worse as you proceed, till you give up the
whole thing in utter disgust. [Of course, if Professor Copi
has promised to more fully explain a concept later in the
book, you ought not be disturbed at not fully understanding
it before that later explanation is given.]

(3) When you come to any passage you don't understand,
read it again if you fail, even after three readings, very
likely your brain is getting a little tired. In that case,
put the book away, and take to other occupations, and the
next day, when you come to it fresh, you will very likely
find that it is quite easy.

(4) If possible, find some genial friend, who will
read the book along with you, and will talk over the difficulties with you. talking is a wonderful smoother-over of
difficulties. When I come upon anything--in Logic or in any
other hard subject--that entirely puzzles me, I find it a
capital plan to talk it over aloud, even when I am all
alone. One can explain things so clearly to one's self!
And then, you know, one is so patient with one's self: one
never get irritated at one's own stupidity!

If, dear Reader, you will faithfully observe these
Rules, and so give my little book a really fair trial, I
promise you, most confidently, that you will find Symbolic
Logic to be one of the most, if not the most, fascinating of
mental recreations!

If you follow this advice, you will have no trouble in your
study of logic. Now you are ready to begin. Just a few more words
from Carroll:

Once master the machinery of . . . Logic, and you have a
mental occupation always at hand, of absorbing interest, and
one that will be of real use to you in any subject you may
take up. It will give you a clearness of thought--the
ability to see your way through a puzzle--the habit of
arranging your ideas in an orderly and get-at-able form--
and, more valuable than all, the power to detect fallacies
and to tear to pieces the flimsy illogical arguments, which
you will so continually encounter in books, in newspapers,
in speeches, and even in sermons, and which so easily delude
those who have never taken the trouble to master this fascinating Art. Try it! That is all I ask of you!

As was suggested earlier, you should begin by studying Professor
Copi's book (hereafter, for brevity, referred to as Copi). In particular, now, you should begin with sections 1.1 and 1.2.

After reading the first two sections in Copi you should understand that the task of logic is to evaluate arguments.

The 19th-century American logician Charles S. Peirce (pronounced
"purse") once claimed that the whole business of logic was to toss
arguments into two piles: good ones and bad ones. In general that
does summarize what this book is designed to do. It points out, too,
that the fundamental element in logic is the ARGUMENT. No matter
what else a logician may study, it is done so as to be better able to
analyze arguments.

1.2 Premisses and Conclusions

An ARGUMENT is always composed of at least one premiss and exactly one conclusion. The premisses provide (or are claimed to provide) support, evidence, justification, etc., for the conclusion. It is the logician's business to determine just how good that support is.

As Professor Copi suggests, one of the great difficulties in sorting out premisses and conclusions is the fact that their being identified as either premiss or as conclusion is always relative to some context. And, curiously enough, his example of the analogous employer/employee realtivity can be extended to show the property of circularity, which arguments, too, sometimes possess: If your gardener happens to be a stockholder in the company for which you work, then, at least in an indirect or partial sense, not only is he your employee, but he is also your employer.

A second significant problem in your sorting out is that on some occasions premisses and/or the conclusion may go unstated. Particularly in contexts where some of the evidence needed for support of the conclusion is part of the generally accepted knowledge of both the arguer and the "arguee" this will occur. And conclusions that the arguer takes to follow obviously often will go unstated. It's important, therefore, as you analyze an argument that you look for such omitted premisses and conclusions.

When there are problems available to work, you should always attempt them. It is only through such "hands-on" experience that you come to know whether or not you really did understand the information that you have so carefully studied. As Profesor Copi tells you at the beginning of 1.2's exercises, he has provided answers to roughly 20% of the exercises (and has starred them). In this study guide roughly another 20% are solved--usually the ones following the starred ones.

Two words of caution in working logic problems: first, in deciding that you do understand, don't be lulled to sleep by working only the first few problems (usually the easiest); try the later, tougher ones too. And, second, try to work the problem BEFORE you look at the answer; most magic tricks, too, seem obvious ONCE YOU KNOW THE SOLUTION. Try 1.2's exercises and then go on to check your work with the following answers. Please note that in some cases the solutions here involve paraphrases of the original text. Also be aware that, given the different backgrounds that each of us brings to analysing such problems, different interpretations of the materials may result in different answers to the same problem.

(2)   PREMISSES: [1] Cutting wage rates may enable one employer to hire more workers.
[2] Workers [being paid less, even if there are more of them] would have less to spend on goods.

CONCLUSION: Cutting the wages of all workers may lead to fewer jobs [than leaving wages at current rates].

Note that the second premiss, in this case, is set off by the premiss-indicator "since." It might also be reasonable to claim that the first premiss is not a premiss at all, just information to clarify the context of what would be normally expected.

(6) PREMISS: The advanced technologies applied in super-
computers tend to quickly permeate the entire
computer industry.

CONCLUSION: The nation that leads in supercomputer
development tends to have the jump on other
countries in producing more powerful--and more
lucrative--lower-level computers.

Here you find the conclusion identified by the conclusion-
indicator "so."

(11) PREMISS: There are no mental diseases.

CONCLUSION: There can be no treatment for mental diseases.

Here the premiss is very clearly flagged by the "since."

(16) PREMISSES: [1] If an opinion that is suppressed is
right, then people can't correct their errors.
[2] If an opinion that is suppressed is
wrong, then people lose the chance to strengthen
their own belief by defending it against error.

CONCLUSION: Suppression of any opinion, whether right
or wrong, is harmful to humanity.

Here there are no clues given to you. The only way to determine
what is premiss and what is conclusion is to read the argument with
understanding, trying to give the author's reasonability the benefit
of the doubt whenever possible.

(21) PREMISSES: [1] The study indicates that in the future
engineers will have to function on interdisci-
plinary teams and will be subject to greater
governmental and public scrutiny.
[2] [One of the responsibilities of a
University is to prepare its students for changing social and political climates affecting
their fields of study.]

CONCLUSION: The Colorado School of Mines should help
students develop a "broader view of the social
and political implications of [their] actions,
better communicative skills, more intellectual
mobility, better management capabilities, and a
commitement to the preservation of the environ-
ment."

The conclusion is marked by the conclusion-indicator "accor-
dingly," and, thus, is not too hard to pick out. What may seem
strange, however, is the second premiss. It is set in square brackets to indicate that it was not stated as part of the original
argument. It might be that the argument should be viewed as claiming
that ③ follows directly from ① , but, whether it is explicitly
stated or not, that second premiss (or something very like it) is
needed for the argument to be plausible.

(26) PREMISS: Citizens who do not enroll in a political
party abandon their chance to help chose the
candidate.

CONCLUSION: Citizens who do not enroll in a political party forfeit rather than protect their
political independence.

Here the rather the common premiss-indicator "because" makes the
structure clear.

1.3   Diagrams for Single Arguments

In the study of logic, as in many areas of life, we must "walk
before we can run." The reason for this is simple: if one masters a
set of skills in its least complicated occurrences, then, when it
meeds to be applied in a complex situation, the skills come naturally
and without much effort. This is exactly the idea underlying the
ordinary teaching of life-saving and first aid skills (as, for
example by the Red Cross, Boy Scouts or Girl Scouts). It is also the
reason for fire drills in schools, businesses and homes. If you
repeat an action or behavior pattern **consciously** many times in varied
simple (or non-stressful) situations, then it is far more likely
that, when you encounter a complex (or stressful) occasion on which
the earlier-practiced skills are needed, the skill will come to you
unconsciously. It is for this sort of reason that Professor Copi has
you begin your analysis of arguments by representing the "flow" of
premiss(es) to conclusion in single arguments.

The procedure is quite straight-forward: you draw arrows down-
ward from a premiss to the conclusion which it supports. In the
event that you have a group of premisses which provide such support
only in combination and not individually, then you join them with a
brace and draw the arrow from the brace to the conclusion. As an
abbreviation of the diagrams, to focus attention upon the "flow" and
not the words of the various sentences, he suggests that each proposition be numbered sequentially and the circled numbers replace the
sentences in the diagram. In cases, like exercise 21 in 1.2, where a
proposition is not stated, the "understood" character of that proposition is represented by making the circle around the number be a
broken (or dotted) one.

With these tools in hand you ought now to try the problems
following 1.4, then check them with his answers and these:

(2)   ① ...we often learn about causes from cures: ② if
ingesting a chemical cures a disease, we may learn that
the disease was caused by a lack of that chemical.

In this case there are no premiss- or conclusion-indicators, but
the intent seems to be to infer the general principle--causes can be
learned from cures--from the specific case--curing of a chemical
deficiency.

(6)   ① Hunting, ... particularly the hunting of large
animals, is so complicated, difficult and hazardous
that the cooperation of numerous individuals is needed.
② [There is good evidence that Peking man hunted large
animals, particularly deer.] ③ It can be inferred,
therefore, that Peking man was more likely to have been
living in a group than in solitude when he began to
hunt deer.

Here the lengthy conclusion-indicator "It can be inferred, there-fore" identifies 3 as the conclusion.   The reason that ① and ② must be joined is that neither alone really supports ③. ② is needed by ① to establish that Peking man needed social hunting. ① is needed by ② to show that size of prey was in any way relevant to social structure.   Interestingly, one might claim that the added premiss was unnecessary, that the premisses and conclusion actually should have been identified:

> ① Hunting, ... particularly the hunting of large ani-
> mals, is so complicated, difficult and hazardous that
> the cooperation of numerous individuals is needed. ②
> It can be inferred, therefore, that Peking man was more
> likely to have been living in a group than in solitude
> ③ when he began to hunt deer.

This way of looking at the argument reads the last clause of what appears to be the conclusion as the second premiss.   In this case the diagram would be:

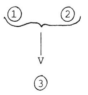

(11) ①To say I believe in spanking children implies that
     spankings are in some way essential to their proper
     upbringing.   ② I do not hold that opinion; ③ there-
     fore, I do not believe in spankings.

The conclusion-indicator "therefore" clearly marks the conclu-sion.   But, since neither premiss, if taken alone, would provide sensible support for the conclusion, they must jointly imply it.

(16) ① Furthermore, if you look at the history of the
     death penalty in this country, you'll find that its
     application has been arbitrary, capricious and discri-
     minatory. ② ... The poor and minorities tend to be
     overrepresented on death row. ③ Blacks who kill
     whites are overrepresented in relation to blacks who
     kill blacks. ... ④ People who can afford expensive
     lawyers can beat the system when it comes to the death
     penalty as well as other kinds of punishment.

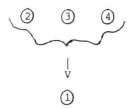

Again the first statement is the generalization for which each of the following ones provides evidence. Note that the sentence "That tells us something about the way the system works" is not treated as a premiss. In a significant sense it serves a role like a premiss-indicator. It is telling the reader that the information just given should be considered to be but one of many similar cases.

(21)   ① Over the past quarter century...the average work week in industry has increased moderately. ② The standard work week has declined but his has been more than offset by increased demand for overtime work and the companion willingness to supply it. ③ During this period average weekly earnings, adjusted for price increases, have nearly doubled. On the evidence, one must conclude that, ④ as their incomes rise, people will work longer hours and seek less leisure.

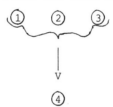

No one of these premisses would provide adequate (or even reasonable) support for the conclusion. The three of them, taken together, do, however, plausibly argue for it.

(26) ① [Interest] rates can't fall much, for several reasons: ② The economic recovery is spurring credit demands, ③ the federal budget deficit is large, ④ inflationary expectations remain fairly high and ⑤ the Federal Reserve Board's commitment to fighting inflation will work against rates falling too far.

The phrase "for several reasons:" serves as both a premiss- and conclusion-indicator. It says that what preceded it is conclusion and that what follows are premisses. The greatest difficulty here is deciding whether the premisses must work together to support the conclusion or whether they can function separately in the inference. For an argument like this one, the decision is probably a reflection of the reader's own economic philosophy and the difference is unlikely to be of major significance.

Having mastered this material, you ought to go on to study 1.4.

1.4   Recognizing Arguments

Before you can analyze an argument, you must be able to recognize it. In the ordinary daily discourse this is no mean feat. The
key to identifying a group of propositions as an argument is whether
or not they can be divided into a set of premises which are asserted
and a conclusion which is asserted to follow from them. Often you
find clues in the language: "since," "because," and the like are
premisses-flags; "thus" and "therefore" are marks of the conclusion.
These are not, unfortunately, infallible guides. They can all be
correctly used in non-argumentative ways. They do, however, provide
a point where you can begin looking for an argument.

Most commonly confused with arguments are conditional statements. They indicate an "if - then" sort of relationship, usually
between propositions, but assert nothing beyond the conditional relationship. In the following examples, the "a" line is an argument;
the "b" line is not:

1a.   Since racism is un-American, the federal government
      cannot tolerate bias in hiring.
1b.   If racism is un-American, then the federal government
      could not tolerate bias in hiring.

2a.   Logic is easy; therefore, you should do well.
2b.   Logic is part of intelligent thought; therefore, take
      it.

3a.   Since college is good training for life, college
      graduates should live good lives.
3b.   Since attending college, John has had seven different
      jobs.

Number 1a asserts that that racism **is** un-American and that from
the evidence we may correctly infer that the federal government
cannot tolerate hiring bias; 2a asserts that logic is easy and
asserts that, on that basis, it is justifiable to infer that you will
do well; 3a infers that college graduates can be expected to live
good lives from the assertation that college is good training for
life. By contrast, 1b says that IF racism is thus, THEN the government, etc., but clearly admits even the possibility that racism might
not be un-American; 2b is directive, telling you what to do, but this
imperative does not follow in any clear sense from logic's nature; 3b
describes a time sequence, not an inference. From these you can see
that there are no simple ways to tell whether a passage is or is not
an argument; you simply have to think about each case individually.

One of the most difficult elements in analysing arguments is
deciding how much to "add to" the argument as stated. How can you
know whether the added material was really intended? The answer
surely is not clearcut. However, the basis for decision, usually, is
analogous to the judicial "innocent until proven guilty" principle:
unless there's good evidence to the contrary, assume that the arguer
is being as reasonable as possible.

The sort of thing that gets omitted from an argument is socalled
"common knowledge." That's the sort of information that your teachers told you did not have to be footnoted, "since anyone with a
reasonable education would have know it." The difficulty is that
there is no standard as to what should count as a reasonable education or as common knowledge. Some things are obvious. For example,
look at the following argument.

                 Horses are mammals.
                 [Mammals bear their young alive.]
                 Therefore horses bear their young alive.

People who have had enough science to know some biology would be insulted if told that the assumed premiss, "[Mammals bear their young alive.]," had to be stated for them. On the other hand, a child who had no knowledge of the essential properties of mammals would find it indispensible for evaluating the argument. It is all, as Professor Copi says, a matter of understanding the context in which the argument is proposed.

At the end of 1.4, Professor Copi says that there is a significant difference between an argument and an explanation. It is well to notice that followers of one rather clearly defined philosophic view of explanation, the so-called deductive-nomological model, would claim that anything that serves as a satisfactory explanation after-the-fact of an occurrence would also serve well before-the-fact of an occurrence as a prediction of it (or argument that it will occur).

It also is a defensible, although not self-evident, position that any explanation does in fact constitute an argument. In the case of the explanation by Dyson what one might argue is that you are not dealing with an argument, but the conclusion of one. The missing premisses of the argument would deal with people's disinclination to get excited about technological issues, while being quite easily stirred up about human ones. Professor Copi is correct when he indicates that the "because" in Dyson's statement is not a standard premiss-indicator. In this regard, Professor Copi's description of the importance of knowing what the writer (or utterer) intended the passage to do is particularly significant. The issue which causes the difficulty in this area, that is, whether or not explanations are arguments, is not one that you should expect to see resolved in an introductory logic text. It is one on which there is significant, reasoned difference among professional philosophers who have devoted substantial portions of their lives to studying. You will encounter further discussion of explanation in chapter 14, and, if you are particularly interested in the topic, you might wish to look at R.B. Braithwaite's <u>Scientific Explanation</u>, Ernest Nagel's <u>The Structure of Science</u>, Pap's <u>An Introduction to the Philosophy of Science</u>, or any of the standard philosophy of science texts.

To test your ability to sort out arguments and non-arguments, you should work your way through the exercises after 1.4, checking your results with Copi and these:

(2)   ① Houseflies, for example, have become resistant to DDT. ② Because of random mutations of genes that affect the sensitivity of flies to insecticide, some flies were more resistant and some less. ③ When DDT was widely applied, the sensitive flies and their genes were lost, while the resistant forms survived and reproduced, so their genes were passed on to future generations. ④ Thus, the species as a whole became resistant to DDT.

A good case can be made for claiming that this is an explanation of the flies' resistance, but the above interpretation, too, seems plausible. The rather unusual representation of this argument is because the first sentence and the last one really repeat the same proposition.

(6)   This explains the human element in the U.S. early warning system, but offers no argument.

(11) ① ... the number of strategic warheads on each side far exceeds the number of significant nonmilitary targets, so ② the majority of the weapons must be aimed at military targets if they are aimed at anything at all.

This argument is simple in structure, but the simplicity masks the complexity of the issue it argues. [It is, of course, possible that weapons are aimed at insignificant nonmilitary targets or that more than are needed for total annihilation are aimed at those nonmilitary targets.]

(16) This explains why the Russians use unusual orbits for their communications and early-warning satellites, but argues nothing as it stands. It could, of course, be converted into an argument by inserting issues relating to the pragmatic purposes of such devices.

(21) ① New orders for hardgoods rose briskly in that month [November]. ② This trend should continue, since ③ business plans to increase plant and equipment spending through the first half of the year and into the second.

OR

New orders for hardgoods rose briskly in that month [November]. 1 This trend should continue, since 2 business plans to increase plant and equipment spending through the first half of the year and into the second.

(26) Despite the sometime conclusion-indicator "thus," this can be read as an explanation of why governments "all over the world" place greater emphasis on combatting inflation than on remedying unemployment. **If** you read it as an argument, it would be :

The costs of unemployment are important... But we should recognize that ① these costs, however large, do not seem as significant to the American people as the costs or threats of inflation, however exaggerated. The reason is easily understood. ② The costs of unemployment are borne by a small minority of the population--as we shall see, a minority without much political voice. ③ But the effects of inflation are felt by everyone. Thus ④ it is not surprising that all over the world, the need to hold back inflation has been regarded by governments as being of much greater urgency than the need to remedy unemployment.

The right-hand representation results from trying to read the passage as an argument and trying to take the "Thus" in the last sentence very seriously. [Doing so, however, makes this argument more complex than Professor Copi intended it to be when he placed it in this section.] One of the strengths (and weaknesses) of the human mind is its ability to take the very simple and straightforward and convert it to the very complex and tortuous. It's sometimes called making a mountain out of a molehill. I recall once having been told by an excellent undergraduate teacher that he could watch a bright student taking a true/false test and, without looking at the answers, tell which problems the student had wrong. His theory was that every time the student paused to ponder a true/false question the answer was going to be wrong, that with a little creativity a bright student could always manage to read something into the question that wasn't intended to be there. That same sort of "creative complication" can afflict your analysis of arguments, too. Probably the best advice I can give you is to try hard to unpack arguments, but not too hard. [That advice is rather like the adage: If at first you don't succeed, try, try again, but quit before you make a complete fool of yourself.]

Now that you have achieved enough skill to recognize a simple argument and then diagram it, you are ready to study 1.5 in Copi in order to learn how to sort out the component arguments from passages in which the arguments are intertwined.

1.5 Passages Containing Several Arguments

Multiple-argument passages are basically of three types. Simplest are those where two (or more) separate arguments are mixed together, rather like playing cards which are shuffled. All that is necessary in analyzing these is to "unshuffle" them, much as you would sort a shuffled deck of cards according to number or suit.

Only slightly more complex are sequential arguments. These function much like dominoes that fall in order: the first's falling leads to the second's also falling, but the second results in the third, and so on. In a sequential argument, a conclusion is supported by one (or more) premiss(es) but in turn serves as premiss for a further conclusion. In such cases it is often easiest to identify the ultimate conclusion, then its premisses, then theirs (if any) and so on.

Most complicated are arguments which involve overlapping premisses, where the same propositon serves as support for more than one conclusion. In such cases, it usually is easiest to sort out the several conclusions, then identify what serves as premiss for each of them without regard for its previous use as premiss for something else.

If you look carefully at the examples that Professor Copi presents, you will see that he is continually increasing the level of complexity and interconnection among premisses and conclusions. Of course, if you wished to seek some sort of ultimate complexity, you

could mix three approaches together, but even then the sorting out
could be done by applying the identification techniques one-by-one.
First you would untwist those arguments whose elements had just been
shuffled.   Then, within each of those you would lay out sequences.
Finally, within all of these you would note the elements which are
shared.   In such a case, as you will find so often in the study of
logic, the key to success is patiently handling difficulties one step
at a time.

Now that you understand how arguments that are interconnected
can be sorted out and diagrammed, work the exercises following 1.5
and check your results here and in Copi.

I   (2) ① Education is as old as man, for ② in all ages and
        all societies some provision has always been made to
        pass on to succeeding generations the knowledge and the
        values which were fundamental to the culture. ③ Al-
        ways there have been difficulties, for ④ no society
        has ever perfected an educational system which fully
        and completely satisfied its dual needs--the conserva-
        tion of sound traditional values, and the encouragement
        of innovation and the creation of new concepts suffi-
        cient to serve the needs of a growing, changing cul-
        ture.

Although the entire passage deals with the history of education,
the first part, ① and ② , argues from the drive for imparting
knowledge to the existence of education, while the latter part, ③
and ④ , argue from the specific inadequacies of education to the
generalization that education has always been plagued with difficulties.

One of the problems with analyzing arguments written in one of
our natural languages is that it is frequently possible for two
people to read the same set of words quite differently.   Differences
in background can provide radically different contexts for two people
encountering the same passage.   It is possible, therefore, to interpret the conclusion of the second argument as a second premiss for
the first conclusion.   That is, since there have always been difficulties in achieving educational goal, there must always have been
education for there to have the difficulties.   This would require the
argument to be represented as follows:

(6) ① Shielding against radiation is not the only prere-
quisite for an adequate shelter. ② Once the attack
has occurred, people must remain inside the shelters
untilthe outside fallout decays to a safe level, a
period that may exceed one month if the intensity of
the fallout has been great. Therefore, ③ the shelter
must have adequate ventilation and sanitation facili-
ties and ④ it must be stocked with sufficient food,
water, and other supplies.

In problem 6, identifying the last sentence as conclusion is
simple. Deciding that it really is two separate conclusions is
little more difficult and may not be altogether necessary. However,
the role of the first sentence is far more problematic. Ultimately
the way to decide its function may be to ask either "So what?" or
"Why?" If a response to "Why is this the case?" springs to mind,
then it is reasonably clear that you were considering a conclusion.
If the response is to the "So what?" then it is likely that it served
as a premiss. The diagram above seems to be what comes to mind when
asking those questions about sentence ① . With this argument,
however, it is possible to have responses to both questions come to
mind. In that case, one might claim that ① is both conclusion of
② and evidence for ③ and ④ .

When you confront what is actually being said, however, the
simplest interpretation may also be the best. That would treat the
sentences marked above as ③ and ④ as a single element ③ . The
representation, then, would be the simple chain:

(11) ① Over the decade 1961 average smoke concentrations in urban areas in Britain fell by 60 percent, and SO_2 (sulfur dioxide) concentrations fell by 30 percent, despite increasing population and inductrial output.. And ② these are averages of <u>all</u> urban areas, so ③ they include those towns that have not yet taken advantage of the powers conferred on them under the Clean Air Acts to introduce smokeless zones. Hence, ④ the reduction in air pollution in some major cities, such as London and Sheffield, has been much greater than the above figures indicate.

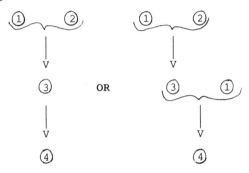

The left-hand representation is probably adequate, but it can be reasonably argued that ③ alone would not yield ④ , while the reintroduction of ① together with ③ would. This concept of reusing an element in an argument will be raised again in the chapters 8 to 11, on formal logic. The point is that, once you have asserted something to be true, you should be able to rely upon its remaining true in that context.

(16) While ① savings may be hoarded rather than channeled into productive investments, ② the demand generated by increased consumption necessarily induces increased investment, and hence ③ promotes the greatest possible utilization of a society's resources. [④ A government's responsibility is to promote the greatest possible utilization of the society's resources.] Hence, ⑤ rather than encouraging individual thrift, the appropriate economic role for government is to generate consumption through such devices as public works programs, ⑥ which put money in the hands of the poorer classes ⑦ (whose lack of surplus wealth gives them a greater "propensity to consume" than the wealthy).

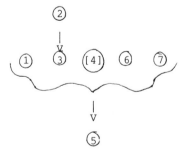

The 4th (added) premiss might be left out, but without some sense of governmental responsibilities (which we tend to add to the argument without realizing we have done so) the connection between the economic "realities" and the conclusion is unclear.

(21) ① Hunting was a valuable adaptation to the environ-
ment since ② meat could supply more calories and
protien than a vegetarian diet. ③ Peking man was
evidently able to compete successfully with large car-
nivores as a hunter. ④ An abundance of fossil bones
of mammals of various sizes found in the cave indicates that ⑤ Peking man not only hunted small game
but also ⑥ was capable of killing large animals.

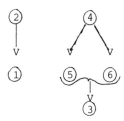

A reasonable case can be made for claiming that statements   5
and 6 should be considered as one, since they both are derived from
the same premiss and they function together to yield the conclusion
3.   It might also be claimed that the initial argument, from 2 to
1, is really an explanation used to put the later "real" argument in
context.

(26) ① The motivations behind this set of sanctions are
puzzling.   ② The Western Eurpoean concern doesn't
appear to be humanitarian; ③ if it were, the Common
MArket presumably would have placed sanctions on Libya,
Syria, and Iraq in 1975, when those nations assisted in
dismembering Lebanon, or it would have agitated for an
arms embargo against Syria when that nation occupied
Lebanon with a 25,000 man "peace-keeping force." [4]
[The Common Market didn't put sanctions against these
nations in those circumstances.] ⑤ The sanctions
would not seem to be a defense of democratic rights,
for ⑥ Israel is the only nation in the region remotely resembling a democracy. And ⑦ it would be difficult to construe the Common MArket's insistence that
Israel negotiate with the PLO as a matter of principle,
since ⑧ the PLO has never agreed that Israel has any
right to exist.

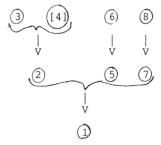

The added premiss is needed to make the argument from ③ and ④
to ② one called **Modus Tollens,** a formal argument that you will
study in chapter 9.

1.6   Problem Solving

All of us spend most of our lives solving problems. One of the
simplest ones is figuring out what we did with the car keys the night
before. A reasonable way to solve the problem is to think "when was
the last time I specifically recall having had the keys and what did
I do immediately thereafter?" More complex problems range up to
finding a means to achieve world peace (which, to my knowledge, is
yet to be solved). There is one element, however, that virtually all
successful problem solutions have in common: the organized application of whatever background information is available. In many cases
there is a general approach that is usually both helpful and fairly
simple to apply. Sherlock Holmes frequently told Dr. Watson that the
best way to solve a problem was to lay out all the alternatives, then
proceed to eliminate all those that cannot be the case. When only
one remains, no matter how unlikly it seems, it is the solution.
That dictum is the guide for solving almost all the problems in this
section. In some cases the best approach is to lay out a grid which
includes all possible combinations of properties in the problem.
Exercise number 4, among the Exercises in Reasoning, is a good
example of this sort.

	Cash	Clerk	Manager	Asst Mgr	Steno	Teller
Miss Ambrose						
Mr. Black						
Mrs. Coffee						
Miss Earnshaw						
Mr. Kelly						
Mr. White						

If you label all of the information given in the problem (for
ease of reference), you can sequentially eliminate all but one space
in each column and row, thus deciding who holds each job. Below is
one possible eliminative sequence.

    a.   The asst. magr. is the manager's grandson.

    b.   The cashier is the steno's son-in-law.

    c.   Mr. Black is a bachelor.

                                                                     Given

    d.   Mr. White is 22 years old.

    e.   Miss Ambrose is the teller's step-sister.

    f.   Mr. Kelly is the manager's neighbor.

1.   Since the asst. mgr. is male, he is not A, C, or E
    (from a).

2.   Since the mgr. has a grandson, s/he (he or she) is
    married, and thus is not A or E (a).

3.   The cashier is male (b), and thus not A, C, or E.

4.   The steno has a son-in-law (b), and thus is not A or E.

5.   Given (c) and (1) and (2) we know that B is not the
    mgr. or steno.

6. Given the ages of the children of the mgr, and steno. (a & b), and W's age (d), W is not mgr. or steno.

7. A is not the teller (e).

8. Since the only job left for A is clerk, she is clerk and no one else can be.

9. Since only the teller's job is left for E, she is the teller and no one else is.

10. K is not the mgr. (f).

11. C is the only one left who can be mgr., so she and no one else is.

12. K is the only one left who can be the steno., so he is and no one else can be.

13. The cashier is married (he's a son-in-law, b), and since B is a bachelor (c), B can't be the cashier.

14. By elimination W must be the cashier and B the asst. mgr.

In the second form of the grid (below) you can see what it looks like with all of the steps (above) filled in. The reason for using the numbers rather than just crossing out squares is that, should you make an error and find one column or row completely eliminated or someone with two jobs, you would be unable to check back to see why you had performed each elimination without some sort of specific referencing method. With the numbers as a reference tool you can look at any specific job/person intersection and determine how it was that you decided either to eliminate that option or to assert it.

	Cash	Clerk	Manager	Asst Mgr	Steno	Teller
Miss Ambrose	3	XXXX	2	1	4	7
Mr. Black	13	8	5	XXXX	5	9
Mrs. Coffee	3	8	XXXX	1	11	9
Miss Earnshaw	3	8	2	1	4	XXXX
Mr. Kelly	12	8	10	12	XXXX	9
Mr. White	XXXX	8	6	14	6	9

Please notice that there is a slight difference in the way this grid and the one in Copi. Professor Copi suggests that you place "N" and "Y" in the intersections of the grid as you solve or eliminate. The grid you have just looked at replaces the "N" with the letter or number of the elimination sequence on which you based the elimination, and it replaces the "Y" with "XXXX." If you don't make a mistake, Professor Copi's approach and mine are, for all practical purposes, the same. If you should find, however, that you have some person or job completely eliminated (or forced into two roles), the approach I suggest will let you check specific eliminations to find your mistake. If you have used "N" and "Y" then you'll have to scrap your effort and start from scratch. Your choice of approach should be guided by your own propensity for mistakes.

Exercise number 2 in the same set may also be solved by a process of elimination, but a different approach may prove more effective. If we lay out all possible hat color combinations for the three prisoners, we get the following:

	Blind	One Eye	Two Eyes
Case 1	White	White	White
Case 2	White	White	Red
Case 3	White	Red	White
Case 4	White	Red	Red
Case 5	Red	White	White
Case 6	Red	White	Red
Case 7	Red	Red	White

Note that there is no Red/Red/Red case, for there are only two red hats.

After hearing both companions admit that they could not tell the color of their hats, the blind prisoner infers his hat color. The likely process is, again, elimination:

1.   Had the two-eyed prisoner seen two red hats, he would have known that, there being no more red hats, he wore white. Since he did not know this, case 7 must be eliminated.

2.   Had the one-eyed prisoner seen red hats on both of his companions, he would have known his hat was white. Since he did not know this, case 6 must be eliminated.

3.   The tricky piece of reasoning is that the one-eyed prisoner can infer that there are two possible cases here he would see a red hat on the blind man and a white one on the two-eyed man: cases 5 and 7. The one-eyed man would eliminate case 7, as in step 1. Thus, if the one-eyed man saw the blind/red, two-eyed/white combination (knowing case 7 could not be), then he would have inferred that case 5 obtained. Since the one-eyed man did not reason in this way, the blind man can infer that case 5 can be eliminated.

4.   When the blind man reasons that cases 5, 6, and 7 are to be eliminated, he can "see" that the remaining possibilities ALL require that he be wearing a WHITE HAT.

In this example, you can see that, despite the apparent difference in approach, the underlying technique is still a process of elimination.

A third sort of approach can be applied to a problem like exercise 8. In this case it is easiest to lay out the men and their statements (in an abbreviated form), then eliminate where possible.

Otto: 1. Otto in Chicago during murder.
         2. Otto innocent.
         3. Kid guilty.
         4. Otto & Mickey are pals.

Curly: 1. Curly innocent.
           2. Curly never owned a gun.
           3. Kid knows Curly.
           4. Curly was in Detroit on March 17.

Slim: 1. Curly owned a gun.
           2. Murder was on St. Pat's Day.
           3. Otto in Chicago during murder.
           4. One of 5 is guilty.

Mickey: 1. Mickey innocent.
           2. Kid was never in Pontiac.
           3. Mickey never saw Otto before.
           4. Curly was in Detroit on March 17.

Kid: 1. Kid innocent.
           2. Kid was never in Pontiac.
           3. Kid does not know Curly.
           4. Otto lied when he said Kid guilty.

The key datum to keep in mind is that each man made three true and one false statement. A possible reasoning sequence is:

1.   Since K-1 and K-4 (the Kid's 1st and 4th statements--note that, for brevity, the initial and statement number will be used for references) amount to the same statement and only one statement can be false, it must be true that the Kid IS innocent.

2.   Since the Kid is innocent, O-3 must be false and O-1, O-2 and O-4 must be true.

3.   S-2 and S-4 are part of the premisses of the problem, so must be true. S-3 is the same as O-1, a known true statement, so must be true. Thus S-1 must be Slim's false statement.

4.   Since M-3 is the denial of O-4, a known true statement, M-3 must be false and M-1, M-2, and M-4 must be true.

5.   Since K-2 is the same as M-2, a known true statement, and step 1 says K-1 and K-4 are true, then K-3 must be the Kid's false statement.

6.   Since S-1 is the denial of C-2 and S-1 is false, C-2 must be true. Since K-3 is the denial of C-3 and K-3 is false, C-3 must be true. Since M-4 is true and the same as C-4, C-4 must be true. With C-2, C-3, and C-4 true, C-1 must be Curly's false statement. If it is false that Curly is innocent, Curly must be the guilty party.

     One of the most satisfying things about working such problems is that they are, in a sense, self-checking. In general, if you get an answer that you can retrace to your conclusion, you are likely correct. With these hints about ways to approach various types of such "Exercises in Reasoning" in hand, you should be ready to tackle them on your own. You have seen exercises 2, 4, and 8 above; solutions to 1, 5, and 10 are in the back of Copi; and solutions to 6 and 11 are below.

(6)   This problem works most easily as an elimination grid, with a few inferences on the side. Below is the grid, with the sequence of inferences beneath it.

Item/Person	Adams	Baker	Catt	Dodge	Ennis	Fisk	FLOOR
BOOK	XXX	a/j	a/j	a/j	a/j	a/j	1 (j)
DRESS	a/d	XXX	h/c	n	f/c	d/g	3 (d)
HANDBAG	a/j	h	XXX	h/c	h/c	h/c	2(h)
HAT	a/j	m	h/c	m	f/1	XXX	6(m)
LAMP	a/f	f/1	h/c	f/1	XXX	f/1	5 (f)
NECKTIE	a/c	8	c	XXX	f/1	m	2 (c)
floor	1 (a)	3 (D/n)	2(c)	2(c/o)	5(f/1)	6 (g)	

a.   Adams stayed on 1st floor, all others got on elevator.

b.   2 men got on the elevator, too.

c.   Catt and the tie-buyer got off on 2.

d.   Dresses are on 3.

e.   The men got off on 4.

f.   The lamp-buyer got off on 5.   GIVEN

g.   Fisk was left alone on 6.

h.   Baker got the bag as a surprise from a 2nd floor person.

i.   Baker's husband got the tie, but not from Baker.

j.   Books are on 1.

k.   Ennis got out 6th.

l.   5 women and 2 men got on (a,b)

	Number Off
Carr and tie-buyer off on 2 (c)	0 2
Dress-buyer off on 3 (d)	3
Men off on 4 (e)	5
Lamp-buyer off on 5 (f)	6 Ennis ,(k,l)

m.   Books are on 1 (j)
     Ties and bags are on 2 (c,h)
     Dresses are on 3 (d)
     Lamps are on 5 (f)
     Since Fisk was on 6, the only thing left for her is the
     hat.

n.   Since the only item left in Baker's column is the dress,
     it must be hers.

o. Since the only item left in Dodge's column is the tie,
     it must be hers.

(11)   This problem looks hard, but solves directly using the
     grid approach. Begin by laying out the information given.

a. The 3 VP is the pampered grandson of the Pres, but is
     disliked by Mrs. Brown and ATell.

b. The ATell and 2 S shared equally in their father's
     estate.

c.   The 2 VP and the ATell wear the same style of hats.

d.   Mr. Grant told Miss Hill to send him a steno at once.

e.   The Pres's nearest neighbors are Mrs. Kane, Mr. Grant, and Mr. Long.

f.   The 1 VP and the Cash live at the exclusive Bachelor's Club.

g.   The Jan, a miser, has occupied the same garret room since boyhood.

h.   Mr. Adams and the 2 S are leaders in the social life of the younger unmarried set.

i.   The 2 VP and the Book were once engaged to be married to each other.

j.   The fashionable Tell is the son-in-law of the 1 S.

k.   Mr. Jones regularly gives Mr. Evans his discarded clothing to wear, without the elderly Book knowing about the gift.

l.   There are 6 men and 5 women. by a, f, g, and j, we know that 1-VP, #-VP, Cash, T and J are men.   Thus, from this and c we know tht 2-VP and ATell are women.

m.   Since 2-VP is a woman (l), from i Book must be a man.

n.   Since Book is the 6th man (l&M), Pres, 1-S and 2-S must be women.

o.   The only person left to be Pres is Mrs. Ford.

p.   The only person left to be 2-S is Miss Dale.

q.   Since ATell and 2-S are sisters (b) and Miss Dale is 2-S, ATell must be married (or they share a name). This means, be elimination, that ATell is Mrs. Kane.

r.   The only person left to be 1-S is Mrs. Brown.

s.   The only person left to be 2-V is Miss Hill.

t.   Since Mr. Grant gives Miss Hill orders (d), he must be her superior, thus must be 1-VP.

u.   Since Grant is among the Pres's nearest neighbors (e) and he and the Cash live at the Bachelor's Club, then Long (another near neighbor) must be Cash.

v.   The only job left for Adam is 3-VP.

w.   The only job left for Jones is Tell.

x.   The only job left for Evans is Jan.

y.   The only job left for Camp is Book.

Person Job	Mr. Adam	Mrs. Brown	Mr. Camp	Miss Dale	Mr. Evans	Mrs. Ford	Mr. Grant	Miss Hill	Mr. Jones	Mrs. Kane	Mr. Long
Pres	a/g	a	n	a	n	XXX	e	a	n	e	e
1 VP	t	f	t	f	t	f	XXX	f	t	f	t
2 VP	l	r	l	p	l	o	l	XXX	l	q	l
3 VP	XXX	a	v	a	v	a	t	a	v	a	u
Cash	u	f	u	f	u	f	t	f	u	f	XXX
Tell	h/j	j	w	j	w	j	t	j	XXX	j	u
ATell	l	a	l	p	l	o	l	q	l	XXX	l
Book	h/k	m	XXX	m	k	m	t	m	k	m	y
1 S	n	XXX	n	p	n	o	d	d	n	q	n
2 S	g	h	n	XXX	n	o	d	d	n	h	n
Jan	g/h	f	x	f	XXX	f	d	f	k/g	f	u

Since, between Copi and this book, so many of the Exercises in Reasoning have been worked, a few more of that type of problem are included below.

1. Adams, Brown and Clark have for pets a dog, an elk and a fox. The men's hobbies are golf, hockey (on ice) and ice-fishing. Clark never has anything to do with ice, even in his drinks. Adams and the dog owner watched the hockey player as he received his league's Most Valuable Player award. The hockey player then rode the bus back to town with the elk owner. Determine the pet and hobby of each man.

2. Abe, Boz and Cal are the best students in their class, ranking first, second and third (not necessarily in that order). Their favorite fruits are apricots, bananas and cantaloupes (again not necessarily in that order). Only bananas are yellow; only apricots are fuzzy; and only cantaloupes are rich in vitamin C (at least among the three). The top ranked student likes only fruit rich in vitamin C. Abe was ranked above Cal but below the cantaloupe lover. Cal gave away the apricots on his salad because he hated them. Identify the class rank and favorite fruit of each person.

3. Robbery of the Eleventh National Bank of Polkatoo was followed by prompt police actiton. Three suspicious characters were brought in immediately. Only one of them could be indicted for the one-man robbery. Brought before the District Attorney and questioned about his activities, each man made four statements, three of which were true and one false. These were the statements:

Frank: Chester did it. I'm as innocent as a new-born babe. Nor had Gerald anything to do with it. Chester was once found guilty of burglary.

Gerald: Frank is your man. I'm not involved at all. As for Chester, he was seen leaving the bank yesterday. He served time for burglary, you know.

Chester: I was never near the place. Gerald is the man you want. I did not rob the bank. I never arrested by the police before.

Now it's up to you to decide--Who robbed the bank?

4. Williams, Xavier, Yates and Zeldon have 1, 2, 3, and 4 children. Their hobbies are archery, bowling, chess and darts. Xavier's children play one-on-one with some of Zeldon's. The bowler asked Yates to be the godfather of his only child. Zeldon feared a scratch from one of Yates' or Xavier's hobby devices. The chess player had two more children than Yates. Xavier took his children to the archer for lessons.

How many children and what hobby did each man have?

5. Jacobs has recently completed a study of European nobility. He judges that the key kings were Karl I, Charles II, Carlos III and Karol IV, absolute rulers of German, England, Spain and Poland. One was a hemophiliac, one a diabetic, one an alcoholic and the fourth addicted to morphine. Kark I and the German played whist, but the Spaniard and the alcoholic didn't. The hemophiliac and the Pole formed an alliance against Karol IV. The Englishman, the diabetic and Karl I sahred a grandfather. The diabetic, the German and Karol IV were noted horsemen. Charles II married the Spaniard's daughter.

Identify each king with his country and ailment.

CHAPTER ONE SUMMARY

I.   The business of logic is the analysis and appraisal of ARGUMENTS.

II. The "things" of which arguments are formed are PROPOSITIONS.

   A. Propositions are the sorts of things that are true and false.

   B. Propositions are independent of the language they appear in.

   C. Propositions are usually expressed by sentences.

III. There are two roles for propositions in arguments.

   A. PREMISS--
      1. Premisses are asserted as evidence or support for a conclusion.

      2. Every argument must have at least one premiss.

   B. CONCLUSION--
      1. Conclusions are derived from, supported by or inferred from premisses.

      2. Every argument has exactly one conclusion.

IV. One or more arguments may occur within a given passage, but none has to.

V.   Arguments differ from non-arguments that resemble them because arguments not only assert the relationship between premisses and conclusion but also assert the truth of both premisses and conclusion.

VI. Arguments, whether simple or complex, may be diagrammed with arrows showing the "flow" of information (or support) from premisses (or groups thereof) to a conclusion.

VII. Most "problems" in reasoning can be solved, or at least simplified, by using an evident (usually mechanical) means of laying out what you do and do not know.

2

The Uses of Language

2.1   Three Basic Functions of Language
2.2   Discourse Serving Multiple Functions
2.3   The Forms of Discourse

You may recall that, in the early days of your learning English, you were taught that sentences were declarative, exclamatory, imperative, and interrogative. The first three of these seem, roughly, to correspond to Professor Copi's classifications of informative, expressive, and directive, but there is obviously nothing like a question included. This is because he is concerned essentially with the sort of sentences that are used to convey information of some sort. If you think that a sentence could be pigeon-holed very neatly, you would probably be over-simplifying. In general, the sentences that Professor Copi wants to consider are ones that have informative, expressive, and directive elements all at the same time.

Since the analysis of the Burns passage ("O my Luve's like a red, red rose . . .") is in the section in which he is differentiating the functions, you might have the impression that it is solely expressive. While the directive element of this passage seems to be negligible, Burns surely means metaphorically to inform the reader of the beauty and delicacy of his love. What Professor Copi has done is to show you as "chemically pure specimens" of simple function as are likely to be found in ordinary usage. But, as he points out at the beginning of 2.2, even these seem to serve multiple functions. Natural language, having evolved over centuries of use, seems to have grown too sophisticated for "real" simple functions to occur.

One of the greatest problems you will encounter in your attempts to "sort out" what you hear and read will be the use of what appears to be one kind of discourse but really is another. A few examples might make this a little clearer.

1. A young man and an attractive young woman are talking when a very large football player comes up and says to him, "That's my girlfriend."

2. A teacher, disgusted by a student's poor performance on a test, comes into class, gives the student the graded exam and says, "What kind of idiot are you?"

3. A mother says to her teen-aged son, "Would you like to take the trash out?"

In case 1 prudence would suggest that they young man make his farewells rapidly, for what looks like a simple declarative sentence, an information-conveyer, is surely a directive (possibly with a veiled threat thrown in for good measure).

In case 2, if the student were to reply, "Type Six, subgroup Alpha-3, sir," the teacher would probably be the most surprised one in the room. Although the teacher's utterance sounded like a question, undoubtedly including the appropriate rising inflection at the end, it was actually either a "cute" way for the teacher to **assert** that the student was an idiot or an unpleasant way of expressing feelings of anger and frustration.

Case 3 actually happened to me. Without thinking, I foolishly responded, "No, I wouldn't" and got a verbal blast that I can recall after a thirty-year interval. Had I thought for a moment I would have realized that my mother's apparent question was, in fact, her way of politely giving an order.

What if you encountered a case similar to # 1, but with a couple of critical differences? Suppose, instead that you are sitting at a college commencement ceremony and as, they are announcing the award of a major graduate fellowship to one of the female graduates, the young man sitting next to you says, "That's my girlfriend." The utterance was identical, but the intent surely wasn't. In the altered situation you have surely encountered an expression of happiness and pride, with only the minor informative element and probably no directive properties at all.

There simply is no currently-known way to mechanically determine the function of a sentence. In fact that difficulty has been one of the sources of great embarrasment to workers in the field of so-called Artificial Intelligence. Twenty or so years ago AI reseachers were routinely predicting that a "Natural Language Parser" [that is, an AI program that could "understand" language as it is commonly spoken] was to be available **Real Soon Now.** Despite the phenomenal hardware and software revolution of the past decade, there is still no functional, general natural language parser (nor does one appear to be on the near horizon). What it takes to sort out language is a sensitivity to meanings, shadings, distortions and context that come from long years of using it. You have to listen or read carefully and then ask yourself **"What did she/he mean to say?"**

It may be instructive to examine a few of the exercises after 2.3.

I. (2)   This clearly has the information function of telling the reader that criminal rehabilitation is an area in which we have no definitive knowledge. Also, this statement almost surely expresses frustration at our inability to deal effectively with problems of rehabilitative techniques, to pleas for understanding for unrehabilitated former convicts, or, perhaps, to reprimand those who have criticized judges' decisions.

(6)   This is an argument for the conclusion that pleasure is often sought only by seeking something else. As such it is primarily informative, telling you the conclusion and evidence for it. There are, however, significant directive and expressive elements in it. The tone is rather condescending, indicating some scorn for persons who did not understand the importance of indirectly seeking pleasure. And, probably, Blanshard is encouraging the reader to focus more upon the activities which give him or her pleasure, thereby increasing the likelihood that she or he will experience pleasure.

(11)   Machiavelli in informing you that bearing arms results in your being respected, expresses scorn for the unarmed, and (probably) directs or at least suggests that you bear arms.

(16)   Shaw is informing you that patriotism is the cause of the unrest in the world, indicating his disgust for it and suggesting that it ought to be eliminated.

(21)   Butler is explaining that the pleasure derived from the satisfaction of an appetite or passion by a by-product of the appropriateness of the thing that does the satisfying to the need to be satisfied. He seems to be expressing a pleasure at that harmony (probably as a manifestation of Divine Harmony). And it is likely that he wished that his parishoners would thus seek appropriate means to satisfy their appetites.

II. (2) Will is asserting that the government has foolishly
included ice in its category of "food products." He would
probably like you both to oppose such a classification and
to be wary of the government as an authority. He has a
good, but caustic, sense of humor and an eye for the ridiculous, and is not bound by authority.

(6) Spinoza is asserting that he has tried to understand
human action, despite the times when it seemed humorous,
lamentable or detestable. He would very likely wish that
others follow his lead, and accept the sincerity and accuracy of his analysis of human action. The passage would
indicate that Spinoza was earnest, objective and, probably,
rather humorless.

(11) Cecil is asserting that the primary cause of current
social unrest is the middle class, that this is not what we
would have expected, and that we are unduly proud of the
middle class. He would like to redirect social antipathy
from the lower to the middle class, (In fact, in an appropriate context, this could almost be taken as an incitement
to revolution.)
   This probably provides evidence that Cecil is a member of
neither the middle class nor the lower class, thus letting
him take such an "objective" stance. It may also indicate
that he has had some rather unpleasant dealings with representatives of the middle class.

(16) The assertation is that keeping your mouth shut is a
good way to appear to be wise. The goal is to persuade
people that they will be better off listening more and
talking less. The author is a bit sarcastic, impatient
with those who talk too much, and quite sure of himself.

(21) Mill's assertation is that if your material needs are
met and you are still not happy, then the cause is probably
that you are too self-centered. His goal is to get the
reader to think more of the wants, needs and aspirations of
others, to become outward-directed. One would infer from
this that Mill was socially conscious and aware of the
emptiness of a self-centered life.

2.4 Emotive Words
2.5 Kinds of Agreement and Disagreement

The entire subject of emotional language and its impact could be
(and has been) the topic for a very extensive work. Essentially, the
point Professor Copi wishes to make is that most words have some
emotional associations, ones which incline us to favor or oppose,
frequently without our being aware of that effect. One TV critic,
belittling the mentalities of television executives, pointed out that
shows about dogs, babies, doctors, and Abraham Lincoln always do well
and suggested that most networks would jump at the chance to produce
a series about Lincoln's doctor's baby's dog. The positive associations with those four subjects is surely not, as the supposed executives would hope, additive. As a matter of fact, it is quite likely
that each would tend to offset or dilute the effect of the others.
Professor Copi mentioned the more positive associations we have with
a can of tunafish than one of horse mackerel. A similar, very conscious, alteration of name was made within the last few years. New
Zealand had long grown a fruit with a fuzzy brown coat, with roughly
the size and shape of a duck egg and with a bright green interior.
It had, for many years, been called a Chinese gooseberry. [I assume
the name came in part from the similarity in color of the flesh of
these fruit and that of standard gooseberries.] The fruit is tangy
but sweet, rich in vitamin C and attractive when peeled and sliced,

but the name "turned people off." Some bright marketing person recognized that difficulty, then noticed that there was a (very) modest similarity between the appearance of the coat of the fruit and the appearance of New Zealand's national bird. And thus started the sale of the now-fashionable and popular Kiwi fruit.

The emotional meaning of a word can have quite subtle effects on our values and ideas, too. One of the great battles of the movement for women's rights (a movement called by its supporters "Women's Liberation) has centered on the so-called "generic" use of masculine pronouns. Strong advocates of Women's Lib have argued, with some justification, that the use of "he" and "his" in documents, for example, about human rights or social order subconsciously educates us to think of these as issues relating more to men than to women.

I became aware of a similar sort of "verbal discrimination" when, as a teenager, I sought to annoy my younger sister. While taking Latin I learned that the Latin word for lefthanded is "sinis-ter" ("dexter" means righthanded). Since she is lefthanded, for an unreasonably long time I delighted in referring to her as my "sinis-ter sister." But the negative impact of "sinister" is not only terminological unpleasantness. A person who uses both hands effec-tively is said to be ambidextrous (having two right hands) while someone who is clumsy is said to have two left feet. If you were to tell someone that, for a fat person, they didn't sweat much, you would be offering a "lefthanded compliment." And, in medieval heral-dry, a diagonal ribbon across a coat of arms was a sign that the bearer was the son on the man whose arms were there--the bar dexter (righthanded ribbon) was carried by the legitimate son, the bar sinister (lefthanded ribbon) by the bastard son. There is little question but that we were conditioned by our vocabulary to regard lefthandedness unfavorably. Words have power beyond their "objec-tive" meanings.

The purpose of the presentation of Russell's "conjugations of irregular verbs" is to familiarize you with the ways in which a single person, object, or event may be described so that the reader has a positive, negative, or neutral response. The emotional atti-tude we have toward something affects the way we choose to describe it. Thus it is possible for two people to observe the same occur-rence but describe it in what seem to be radically different terms (as a result of their opposed attitudes toward that occurrence).

There are times when we claim that we wish that our language could not express emotional attitudes. It would appear that that would free us from the "loaded" appeals, for example, of advertising. But, unless we like such a language we're totally without emotions, it would be quite likely that the emotion would creep in through the way in which we SAW what happened. That is to say, our emotional attitudes can strongly affect the way in which we see the world. For example, assume that you and I both have known Jane for many years. We both know that she is strong, decisive, impatient, very self-confident and that she served a tour of duty in Vietnam as a para-medic. Let us further assume that my experiences with her have been uniformly positive--she has been a good friend, a staunch defender, and once in my presence saved a heart attack victim's life. But finally let's assume that your experiences with her have not been good--she has butted in when she did not understand the circum-stances, has seemed conceited, and once in your presence almost killed a man when she tried to use the Heimlich maneuver on him when she thought he was choking but wasn't. Your attitude toward her is that she is boorish, conceited and prone to rash and irresponsible actions; mine is that she is realistic, self-assured and heroic. If both of us were to come into a room and were to see her cutting at the throat of a man who was lying on the floor, our "unemotional" descriptions of her actions would probably be quite different: you would likely say she was cutting his throat, while I would probably

say she was performing surgery. Neither is a terribly emotional
loaded description, but mine conveys information which approves of
Jane's action while yours does not. And, if pressed, I would claim
that I saw her trying to save his life while you would assert that
you saw her trying to end his life. For this reason it is important
to realize that even the most sincere effort to be "objective" (including the most neutral of languages) may fail.

It is clear that there are two ways in which persons can agree
and disagree--with regard to the "facts" and with regard to their
feelings about what they take to be the facts. Thus, there are four
combinations of complete disagreement. If you put in a sort of chart
form you'd have:

I	Agree in Belief (Fact) Agree in Attitude	III	Disagree in Belief Agree in Attitude
II	Agree in Belief Disagree in Attitude	IV	Disagree in Belief Disagree in Attitude

All four cases are relatively common. If you and your next-door
neighbor each see a third neighbor's dog in your shared garden,
digging holes, and each judge the third to be irresponsible in allowing his dog such freedom, then you agree in belief (the "fact"
that the dog was allowed loose and damaged the garden) and in attitude (the "wrongness" of it being allowed).

If you and the neighbor both see the third neighbor's two-year-
old son toddling nude across the back yard, you might think it "cute"
and the neighbor think it "immoral." Here the two of you agree in
belief (that the child was outside unclad) but disagree in attitude
(yours being positive, your neighbor's negative).

If you see the third neighbor as a political opportunist, who
has been picketing a local factory with a pollution problem only (you
judge) because she believes it will get her elected mayor, and your
neighbor sees her as a dangerous-but-sincere fanatic who overlooks
certain economic realities, then you both will probably oppose her
election. Here you disagree in your beliefs (you that she is a fake,
he that she is sincere) but you both agree in the attitude that she
is an undesirable political option.

Of course you are used to encountering the fourth case. If you
and your younger brother each have Mrs. Jones for an advanced biology
class, you may think that she is the most inventive, instructive
teacher you have ever had while he sees her as very strange and
totally incapable of following the text. Here you disagree in belief
(you that she is a responsible teacher, he that she is not) and in
attitude (you like her, he does not).

Ultimately, the reason you want to be able to sort out such
differences in attitude and belief is so that, in trying to communicate with another person, you can discover where and how (if at all)
you differ. If you disagree in belief, you may have the chance to
change another's mind by presenting additional information. But the
sad truth is that, if you differ in attitude (especially attitude
only) it is most likely that no amount of information or argument
will resolve your differences.

You now are well-prepared to analyze the exercises following
2.5. The key is to try to decide whether the two statements could
reasonably be made by different persons in describing the same situation. If so, then there is agreement in belief; if not, then there
is disagreement in belief. Similarly, try to decide whether both
statements are positive or both negative. For example, if both refer
to a person, could both speakers be used as character witnesses (pro
and con) together in a court trial? If the same side would subpoena
both, then there probably is agreement in attitude; if not, then not.

(2)   Both agree that Mr. Blank thinks his own thoughts (agree
in belief) but the speaker of a. thinks that's good and the
speaker of b. that it's bad (disagreement in attitude).
[Case II]

(6)   They differ about how much Ms. Roe talked (disagreement in
belief) but each disapproves of her behavior (agreement in
attitude). [Case III]

(11) They disagree in belief: the speaker of a. thinks your
first chance is your only chance while the speaker of b.
thinks more will come. Attitudes here are harder to sort
out. If both were said after an opportunity had passed,
then the first would indicate some remorse and the second
(probably) none. If both were uttered before you knew
you'd had a chance, then the first would indicate some
tension and/or pressure while the second (probably)
wouldn't. Thus, although you probably wouldn't want to
characterize the attitudes as positive and negative, there
does seem to be a difference in the attitudes expressed
here. [Case IV]

(16) Clearly Rice and Lombardi differ about the importance of
winning (disagreement in belief). Again, here, there is
some fuzziness about the attitude. Obviously, if their
attitude toward winning is the issue, they disagree. But,
if at stake is each man's attitude toward his own (or the
other man's) position, then Rice has a positive attitude
toward concern for playing as best you could and Lombardi
has a positive attitude toward winning. Without a resolution of which of these "targets" of attitude you are discussing, you can't decide whether they agree or disagree in
attitude. [One sportsman suggested that an attitude like
that of Tevye (in Fiddler on the Roof) would be a good com-
promise, that is, losing is no sin but it's no great honor
either.]

(21) Washington and Russell seem to disagree about the status
of agriculture, but there is genuine reason for doubt. If
you look carefully at what each says you will see that
they are not actually addresing the same issue. Washington
is discussing the importance of agriculture to a society;
Russell is discussing the effect of working in an agricultural society upon the people themselves. It is possible
that something can be of great social value and yet be
awful for the person who has to do it. If you interpret
Washington's statement as an endorsement of the agricultural life, then they would disagree in belief. On the
other hand, it is fairly clear that Washington's attitude
toward the patriotic service rendered by the agriculturist
is positive, while Russell's toward the conditions people
live under in an agricultural society are negative.

(26) In distinction to problem 21, this one is fairly obvious.
Stobaeus sees agriculture as futile and dull, while Jef-
ferson sees it as rewarding and delightful. They disagree
completely. [Case IV]

2.6   Emotionally Neutral Language

One great difficulty we are likely to encounter in our attempts
to avoid emotional distractions, whether in what we read and hear or
what we write and say, is our difference in background. If I had
been raised in and had accepted a very conservative religion and you
had been raised in and had accepted atheism, it is likely that terms
to which you relate negatively (such as "divine," "prayer," "devout")

are ones to which I relate quite positively. Similarly, if you have studied medieval history and I have not, use of the phrase "yoke of serfdom" (such as in The Communist Manifesto will probably strike you as quite emotionally loaded while it will be not only unemotional but probably meaningless to me. In general, the best we can hope for is to try to be sensitive to the sort of emotional impact our choice of words have.

The other significant problem in our trying to "neutralize" our language is the difficulty we have in separating the emotionality of the langugage from the emotional elements of the situation per se. Quite evidently the language is emotional if I say that Herb split Hank's head open in the best tradition of the mad axe-murderers, If I re-write the idea unemotionally (as best I can) I might get something like: Herb vertically bifurcated Hank's cranium in the manner usual to those who are unable to understand why they ought to behave in certain acceptable ways when they bring about the non-vital state in others by means of an implement usually reserved for the felling of trees. This "talks around" the event sufficiently to seem to accomplish the goals of preserving the factual content and deleting the emotional. But, once you wade through the mass of words, seeing what the sentence says, you have an intense emotional reaction (like "Good Heavens, he's talking about an axe-murderer"). It seems fair, here, to claim that the language was neutral, it was the situation that wasn't. You have to be very careful not to confuse the two.

CHAPTER TWO SUMMARY

I.   For our purposes language has three primary functions:

    A.   Language is informative; it conveys information.

    B.   Language is expresive; it conveys emotional reactions and intensities.

    C. Language is directive; it conveys orders, suggestions and instructions.

II.   In most cases language performs all three functions at the same time.

III. In some cases the apparent linguistic form. e.g., a question, is not a reliable indicator of the primary function being performed, as in a rhetorical question.

IV.   Some words and phrases are particularly evocative of emotion.

V.   There are different ways to agree or disagree.

    A. You may agree or not in belief, that is, concerning the "facts" involved in a situation.

    B. You may agree or not in attitude, that is your emotional reaction to what you perceive to be the "facts."

VI.   Emotionally neutral language tries to eliminate the expressive element from discourse as far as possible.

    A.   Perception of a word or words as emotional may be a function of experience, making it hard to tell whether or not a given location will be emotional to a given person.

    B.   A situation may itself be so emotionally charged that any description of it, no matter how bland and round-about, will appear emotional.

3

Informal Fallacies

3.1 Classification of Arguments
3.2 Fallacies of Relevance

You will find that the explanations of the logical fallacies are quite straightforward and clear. This commentary will indicate a few additional characteristics of some fallacies, characteristics that may make it a bit easier for you to distinguish between related fallacies. In real life, of course, it becomes slightly less important to be able to apply the correct "label" to a fallacious argument; what is important is that you be able to identify an argument as fallacious and that you be able to put your finger on what it is about that argument that makes it problematic. What is critical is that you be able to see how it is that the so-called fallacies tend to persuade you.

The fallacies of relevance generally create the impression of leading straightforwardly from premises to conclusion. Their problem is that, when you carefully look at the relationship, the premises do not really provide evidence that supports the conclusion. The **Ad baculum** (or appeal to force) gives a "practical" reason for doing whatever is specified in the conclusion--the threat of physical, emotional, or financial violence for non-acceptance. If I tell you that you ought not block a doorway and the reason is that you are creating a fire-escape hazard, then I have given evidence justifying the assertion that you ought to move; if I tell you that you ought to move because if you don't move I will tear your arm off and beat you with it, then I am threatening, not reasoning. In a sense, the first argument might be rewritten as follows:

Premiss 1. (Explicit) If one stands in a doorway, one is creating a fire hazard.

Premiss 2. (Explicit) You are standing in a doorway.

Conclusion 1. (Intermediate) You are creating a fire hazard.

Premiss 3. (Implicit) If you create a fire hazard, you are endangering others.

Conclusion 2. (Intermediate) You are endangering others.

Premiss 4. (Implicit) If you are a moral person you do not wish to endanger others.

Premiss 5. (Implicit) You are a moral person.

Conclusion 3.(Intermediate) You do not wish to endanger others.

Premiss 6: (Implicit) If you are doing something that results in your endangering others when you do not wish to endanger others, then you ought not to be doing it.

Conclusion 4.(Explicit) You ought not be standing in that doorway.

Notice how much "unpacking" the argument underwent, making explicit the assumed premises and the intermediate conclusions. In contrast, the ad baculum argument would become something like this:

Premiss 1.   (Explicit) You are standing in the doorway.

Premiss 2.   (Explicit) If I do not want you to be in the doorway then if you are in the doorway then I will forcibly remove you. (Assumes the threat actually made is meant to be metaphoric.)

Premiss 3.   (Implicit) I do not want you to be in the doorway.

Conclusion1. (Intermediate) If you are in the doorway then I will forcibly remove you from it.

Conclusion2.(Intermediate) I will forcibly remove you from the doorway.

Premiss 4.   (Implicit) If you do not like to be forcibly removed, then you must not stand in the doorway.

Premiss 5.   (Implicit) You do not like to be forcibly removed.

Conclusion3.(Intermediate?) You must not stand in the doorway.

Premiss 6.   (Implicit) If you are doing something that results in your being forcibly removed when you do not wish to be forcibly removed, then you ought not to be doing it.

Conclusion 4. (Explicit) You ought not to be standing in the doorway.

Notice that the second argument has been unpacked in as similar a manner to the first as seems possible, but the argument thus generated just doesn't follow in the same way. In a sense, the real conclusion of the argument may be found in the "Intermediate?" conclusion 3. But that conclusion is solely the result of IMPLICIT premisses 4 and 5. It seems to be a questionable way to reason when what are explicitly stated as premisses and what is explicitly stated as a conclusion are only incidental to what we claim the argument "really means."

Ad hominem arguments direct one's attention to the person who has asserted something rather than whatever it is that he or she has asserted. The attack on the person sometimes takes the form of abuse or criticism of that person's character. When William O. Douglas was a Justice of the Supreme Court, some elements of the populace would argue that his opinions ought to be discounted because he was a "dirty old man." Their evidence was his marriage to a woman almost 50 years his junior, his fathering a child by her, and his authoring an essay on the evils of consorship, even of pornography, which was published in **Eros** (a magazine edited by Alan Ginsberg, who was convicted of distributing pornography--**Eros**--through the mails). While this evidence might be used as a way to call into question his objectivity on an obscenity issue--at least the last item might--it appears in no way relevant to his competence and objectivity in ruling, for example, on the constitutionality of a newly-imposed poll tax in Montana. And, of course, even if one granted the assumption that he was a dirty old man, that still does not show that any decision in particular is wrong.

A second sort of ad hominem, for example, involves an attack on the persons because they are in some sort of special circumstances. If one rejects an argument for the defeat of hand-gun registration legislation because the arguer is a member of the N.R.A., you are not focusing on the argument but on the arguer. Certainly it would be expected that such a person is predisposed against registration of firearms, but that in no way proves that the ARGUMENT offered in defense of the position is in any way objectionable.

Ad ignorantiam arguments derive some sort of assertion from a lack of evidence of any sort. One person might argue that the lack of hard physical evidence of a reliable sort for the existence of flying saucers is proof of their nonexistence. A second could as easily argue that any species advanced enough to build such vehicles would be skilled enough to hide all such traces of their visits, and thus the combination of many "sightings" but no hard data (like a wrecked saucer with the squashed remains of little green people) is justification for asserting their existence. And, of course, the point is that we really ought to say that we just don't know, that the data so far is insufficient to draw any reasonable conclusions.

In our society, where each of us is taught from earliest child-hood that we are responsible for the welfare of others, the Ad mise-ricordiam fallacy is quite common. It is the basis of most of the advertising of such worthwhile organizations as C.A.R.E., the U.S.O., Save the Children, and so forth. The mere facts that people abroad are hungry, that young servicemen away from home are lonely, or that many children need some sort of minimal aid to become functional adults do not entail your sending money to these causes. The en-tailment is a product of a whole series of additional premises about social responsibility and being one's brother's keeper. In this case, as in all fallacious arguments, the conclusion may be altoge-ther an objectionable one; the problem, logically, is that it does not follow from the premises that are given.

One extraordinarily clever use of an ad populum occurred in 1962 at Colorado State University. The student council, in the attempt to overcome what they saw as the "apathy" of the student body, invited George Lincoln Rockwell to speak. Rockwell, the founder of the American Nazi Party, had been frequently featured in the media as a result of his vocal opposition to the then-growing civil rights movement. Over 1000 students had come to hear him. He entered the hall wearing a conservative suit, white shirt, and narrow tie, rather than the Nazi uniform that had been expected. He stepped to the microphone and said something like "Good morning. I imagine some of you are disappointed, having come to watch the monkey in the funny suit scream, shout, and offer to hit an old woman with a club to entertain you. Well, if you think for a minute, you will realize that that is the sort of thing that I have to do to get any sort of news coverage. And I have to have such coverage so that people will know that National Socialism is an option for patriotic Americans. But I don't have to resort to that sort of thing with you. You are all intelligent, fair-minded people. I can present my ideas and you will give them a hearing, then discuss them in a mature, rational fashion." At that point he already had the entire audience, if not on his side, at least no loger hostile to him. He had appealed to their prejudices about themselves: what college student would fail to recognize the intelligence of a man who saw that he or she was intelligent, fair-minded, mature, and rational? He had skillfully used their emotions to "argue" that his position was one that de-served their serious attention.

It has often been claimed that 99-44/100% of all we know is a product of our accepting what-someone-else-tells-us-is-the-case as if it is the case. In that way each of us does not have to rediscover gravity, the spherical shape of the earth and that hot things burn. As a matter of fact, what you are learning in this course you are accepting, as it were, on faith--the faith that neither Copi nor any other logician would deliberately misinform you about logic. That faith, hopefully, is not misplaced. If, however, this study guide were to have a section telling you which political party to join, what religion to follow, or where to seek employment, and you were to do what it said, then you would have accepted an <u>ad verecundiam</u> argument. Authorities ought only to be consulted and/or accepted when they **are genuine authorities.** Joe Namath's expertise on the football field in no way makes him an authority on popcorn poppers, french friers, hamburger cookers, or pantyhose. In each case, his endorsement of the product is merely playing upon the supposed warm associations the viewing audience has with him as a person.

The fallacies of accident and converse accident (hasty generalization) deal with what might be called a class-member relationship. Since classes are usually identified by some set of properties that its members have in common, it is natural to expect that, once you know what those properties are for a certain class and know that an individual is a member of that class, that individual will possess all of those properties. Similarly it is normal to expect that some prominent feature of an individual will be shared by the other individuals with which it shares class-membership. Usually these inferences are fine. The only problem is that you have to check to make sure that there are not special circumstances that affect the situation. Thus, while it is true that Americans can say what they want to say when they want to say it (as a Constitutional Right), there really needs to be the qualifier "usually" added. For example, you may not lie under oath in a court of law without incurring the risk of being found to be a perjurer. To apply the freedom of speech generalization to the special circumstance of being under oath in a court would be to commit a fallacy of accident.

When you place a chunk of zinc in a beaker of sulphuric acid, the colorless gas that bubbles off is hydrogen. Doing this experiment once would incline anyone familiar with scientific processes to make the following generalization: when I put this zinc in that acid I got hydrogen; thus, when anyone puts any zinc in any sulphuric acid they get hydrogen. Given the way one piece of zinc tends to be pretty much like any other and the way all sulphuric acids tend to be pretty much alike, the generalization is reasonable. If you had hired a philosopher as a bodyguard and he had failed to protect you from an assault, then you might generalize that all philosophers make incompetent bodyguards. (You might even go so far as to infer that all philosophers are incompetent at whatever they try to do). But you have had no reason to infer that that individual was in any way representative of philosophers, taken as a group. People, generally, tend to be far more individual than lumps of zinc. Without some evidence that the sample from which you are generalizing is truly representative of its class, and that the property that you are inferring is generally true of members of that class, you have no reason to infer that the particular property is a property that is somehow related to being in that class. You might find some characteristic of philosophers that made them incompetent bodyguards, thereby supporting the inference. Had you noted that the individual had a mole on his left hand but not his being a philosopher, you might have drawn the analogous conclusion that all people with moles on their left hands are incompetent bodyguards. However, it seems unlikely that you will be able to find any relevant connection between moles and incompetence. The key, in both the case of accident and that of converse accident, is that of relevance: fallacies of accident ignore relevant circumstances which exempt a member of a class from a generalization that usually holds for such members; a hasty generalization does not establish the relevance of a property to the class of which an individual is a member before inferring that all members of that class share that property.

Arguments about causation are quite difficult to handle. Later (in Chapter 13) you will study one of the major attempts to discover causal relationship. Here, however, you will note that many arguments which claim to uncover causes fail to do so. Most obvious are <u>post hoc ergo propter hoc</u> (commonly called <u>post hoc</u>) arguments. They are the basis of most superstition. If you happen to notice that you did better than you had expected to do on your last three exams and that you were wearing your red-and-green-striped socks each time, it is no long step to thinking of them as your "lucky" socks. The problem is that, the way we usually think of causes, causes must precede effects, but the mere fact that one event happens before another is not enough to show that the first caused the second. It was post hoc reasoning that led the rooster to believe that he had to crow every morning to make the sun rise.

Another common causal fallacy, which Professor Copi does not discuss in detail, is that of confusing conditions and causes. Oxygen (or something which serves as an oxidizer), a combustible material, and heat, all taken together, might be seen as the "cause" of fire. If two of the three were already present, we might be led to say that the introduction of the third "caused" the fire. But, being more critical, we would probably perfer to say that each of the three is a NECESSARY CONDITION for a fire, that the three together provide SUFFICIENT CONDITIONS for a fire.

Circular arguments (begging the question or petitio principii) come in all shapes and sizes. Simplest are arguments like: "Aspirin relieves pain since it is an analgesic." Of course, to say that something is an analgesic is just to say that it relieves pain. More complex arguments might resemble:

A.   The Bible is the Revealed Word of God.
B.   How do you know?
A.   Jesus said so.
B: How do you know what Jesus said is true?
A.   He is the Son of God.
B.   How do you know that?
A.   The Bible says so.
B.   How do you know that what it says is true?
A.   Because it is the Revealed Word of God.

The circularity is obvious. Unfortunately, these are not the only forms that such arguments may take. Entire books have been written to argue an idea, only to have that idea be one that must be assumed to make the argument understandable. There is no question but that if you assume some datum, say X, as an element in your argument, then you will have no trouble showing how it is that X follows from your assumption—it is a very unusual logical system in which X does not follow from X. Thus, while the proof of X from premiss X is easy, it is neither particularly valuable or interesting, and it surely does nothing to **establish** X's independent truth .

Many of us have had a smile from obvious complex questions like "Have you stopped beating your wife?" (Although, when you think of it, there is nothing at all funny about wife-beating), but have never thought about the serious implications of such questions. Most of us, if asked apart from the context of a course in which we were on guard, would reply that we believe that a person's "taking the Fifth Amendment" (refusing to answer from fear of self-incrimination) really is an admission of guilt, that you could not incriminate yourself unless you had something to incriminate, that is, unless you were guilty. During the "witch-hunt" period of the investigations of the House UnAmerican Activities Committee, however, the questioning frequently was:

> Just give a simple "yes" or "no" for an answer, we don't want any speeches. Did you really believe that you could hide your communist affiliations from the government forever?

If you say "yes" then you have admitted such affiliations, but if you answer "no" you have still admitted them. If you are not allowed to give the answer that you have no communist affiliations, then (assuming that you do not have them) your only option is to "take the Fifth."

In a sense, the _ignoratio elenchi_ fallacy is a catch-all. It, and the related _non sequitur_, which Professor Copi does not include, could probably be used to describe any fallacy of relevance. In general, however, it is best to classify a fallacy as one of the more specific forms (if possible) so that you more precisely indicate what is wrong with the argument. Ignoratio elenchi arguments are frequently used, as a sort of misdirection approach, when one does not have adequate support for a position in which one deeply believes. The very heated debate over the Equal Rights Amendment during the mid-70s generated a wealth of such arguments. Proponents of the amendment would frequently claim that the ERA had nothing to do with the drafting of women (that being a charge frequently leveled against the ERA). They would point to the text of the amendment, showing that it made no mention of the draft. The problem is that from the fact that the amendment does not specifically mention the draft it does not follow that it has no implications regarding the ammendment. As a matter of fact, the provisions of the amendment are such that if Congress reinstated the draft then women could not be exempted from it simply because they are women. The term _non sequitur_ means "it does not follow." Thus this argument is a "textbook" example of a _non sequitur_ fallacy. The information may be relevant to the conclusion, but the conclusion simply does not follow from the premises as they are presented.

Opponents of the ERA made equally fallacious arguments. One common one was that if the federal government forced all children to spend their formative years in state day-care centers, then the core of family life would be destroyed. The conclusion drawn from this would be that the ERA ought to be defeated. Few would doubt the undesirability of **compulsory** state-run nurseries for all children, but that is irrelevant to the issue of support for or rejection of the ERA. At least it would be necessary for an opponent of ERA to show that it would entail such state action.

All of the arguments that are classed as fallacies of relevance share a common characteristic: they mislead by misdirection. In that way they resemble the "patter" of a stage magician: by calling attention to the fact that there is "nothing up his sleeves" he gets you to focus on his sleeves and ignore his pockets. In either event you have been misled: in the case of the magician you are watching the wrong thing; in the case of the argument you are thinking about the wrong issues. And, even when you are aware of the potential for misdirection, it is easy to err anyway. For the next 30 seconds don't think about monkeys! See? Once you were told NOT to do it, you couldn't avoid it. Even if you haven't thought of monkeys for months, you are now. Once the misdirection is offered, most of us "bite."

You should now be able to recognize the common fallacies of relevance and should be able to explain briefly why any argument which you judge to be fallacious is so. Please be careful of two pitfalls of such explanations. To repeat a definition of a fallacy as explanation does not show why that particular argument is a case of that particular fallacy. Also, to repeat the argument as explanation does not explain: it actually constitutes a claim that the fallaciousnes of the argument is self-evident. But, of course, had it been so obvious that the argument was bad, its author, we hope, would not have used it.

(2)   Ignoratio elenchi (irrelevant conclusion). The fact that the sage's timing is good says nothing about where his emotions are located.

(6)   Petitio Principii (Begging the question). One might have thought that this was an appeal to authority, but one would hope that the head of the Bullfight Association would be properly acknow-

ledgeable relative to bullfighting. Instead, note that the premiss "...a bullfighter is and should be a man" amounts to the same thing as the conclusion "women shouldn't fight bulls...."

(11) Argumentation and Misericordiam (Appeal to Pity). All of the information about the cost of the ticket, the condition of his wife, and the cost of the operation are quite sad, but they are not what's at issue. The law specifies tickets for speeding, and all the tale of woe has nothing to do with the question of whether or not he was speeding.

(16) Converse Accident (Hasty Generalization). The wartime invasion of privacy took place under quite special circumstances. Without added evidence that they still are in effect, one wouldn't want to yield all one's right to privacy.

(21) False Cause. Evidently, according to the joke, Fernandez took membership in the Republican Party as a causal condition for wealth. All that had probably been intended was the assertion that, in the mind of the person who spoke with him, the policies of that party tended to be allied with the interests of the rich.

(26) Argumentum Ad Ignorantiam (Appeal to ignorance). The "alarmists's" success or failure in their attempts to prove nuclear hazards has no bearing upon the existence of such risks. All it does is tell us how good they are at coming up with evidence.

II (2) Petitio Principii (Begging the question). The ultimate evidence given for believing that the men of old were offspring of the gods is the last sentence: "How can we doubt the word of the children of the Gods?" But that assumes that they are what you were trying to prove they were.

(6) Petitio Principii. The one man's getting three pearls is justified immediately by his being the leader, but that depends upon his getting the three pearls. Thus, you conclude where you began.

(11) Argumentum Ad Ignorantiam (Appeal to Ignorance). The lack of evidence of a scandal could just as easily be taken for proof that he is rotten to the core, but very good at covering his tracks.

(16) Ignoratio elenchi (Irrelevant conclusion). The fact that these are the Soviet theories does not entail that they are correct or that any action taken by the Soviet Union is in accord with their theories.

(21) False cause. The fact that you know how hard you will have to work to replace money you spend does not necessarily affect your spending. You may still buy on impulses, or thoughtlessness, or even simple irresponsibility.

(26) Petitio Principii (Begging the question). Although this circle is longer, the conclusion and last premiss are the same.

3.3   Fallacies of Ambiguity

The second group of fallacies arises not so much through a conscious (or unconscious) desire to misdirect, but through the "slipperiness" of the language. The problems they cause result from words and phrases with multiple meanings being treated as if they each had but one meaning, or from the use of vague or imprecise terms being used as if they were not so. Often this sort of fallacy is more pronounced in the words of children or those who are not native speakers of the language.

One of the most common of this sort of fallacy is equivocation. In the early 1960s people in Colorado were shocked when, in the defense arguments of a divorce suit where the wife charged her husband with beating her with a whip from a willow tree, the attorney for the husband read to the court an 1898 law making it a misdeameanor for a man "to beat his wife with a willow whip any bigger around than the base of his smallest finger." The whip the man had used was in evidence, was measured and found to be smaller than the base of his smallest finger. Conclusion -- the divorce was denied. (She immediately re-sued on different grounds and won.) The point is that this case raised a hue and cry about the need to have laws periodically reexamined and to repeal those that were causing problems. One small town newspaper editor (who favored space exploration, but evidently understood little science) offered "Einstein's Laws" as an immediate candidate for repeal. He argued that "since Einstein's Laws prevent us from developing a faster-than-light space drive, we can't get to the stars. And since we want to get there, we ought to repeal them as soon as we can." His problem was an unintentional equivocation: he didn't realize that the laws we can repeal are those that men choose to put into effect, and that laws like Einstein's are observed physical regularities that will be there whether or not we acknowledge them.

Amphibolies are usually the result of sloppy grammar. When English teachers point out problems of reference, agreement or dangling phrases, they are generally identifying amphibolies. A want-ad appeared several years ago saying, "For sale, a piano by a woman with carved legs." Don't you wonder, as many readers did, why she ever had her legs carved? Phrases can also be amphibolous when they involve a series of ideas in which strict parallelism has not been maintained. Television advertisements have recently been appearing, asking for volunteers "to work in care of the aged, rehabilitation of drug offenders, and child abuse." Caring for the aged and rehabilitating persons with drug problems are certainly worthwhile activities, but isn't it questionable whether one wants people to volunteer to abuse children? Had the third classification of volunteers been listed as "counsellors for child abusers" or as "foster parents for abused children" not only would the original request have been more rhetorically correct, but the amphiboly would not have occurred.

The fallacy of accent has its most common occurrences in relation to the language as we speak it. Oral communication is very fragile because it is so dependent upon the tone, inflection and stress of the voice. This makes it particularly hard to transfer the full import of what someone says into a written record. That was the basis of Richard Nixon's attorney's arguments when they tried to prevent public access to the so-called White House Tapes. Their contention was that, in a written transcript, one could not identify irony, sarcasm, and the like. Thus, a statement like "I can solve the financial problems of New York City except for one minor problem: how to keep the nuclear fallout from drifting into New Jersey" could be said in the attempt (rather tastelessly) to describe humorously how completely frustrating NYC's problems are, In its literal written form, however, it sounds like the ravings of a madman.

A consciously misleading case of accent occurred in the advertisement of a movie. A major newspaper (let's call it the DAILY
PLANET) had reviewed the film saying: "Except for wooden acting,
incompetent direction, an infantile plot, raucous music, and unimagi-
native camera work, the movie is great." Obviously, the critic was
not pleased with the show. The movie company, however, included part
of the revieiw in their ads, saying "'...The movie is GREAT,' says
the DAILY PLANET." Those words, in that order, had as a matter of
fact occurred in the review; so the movie company could not be
accused of misquoting, only of quoting out of context. (Incidentally, the newspaper sued and the film maker had to run corrective ads
everywhere the original had appeared.)

The fallacies of composition and division often cause students
difficulties because there seems to be so much similarity between
them and the fallacies of accident and hasty generalization. Roughly, the difference between them is that accident/converse accident
deal with the relationship between classes or sets and their members
while composition/division concern part/whole relationships. If we
were to sample randomly ten of the thousands of members in the American Philosophical Association, find them to be impoverished, and then
to infer that all members of the Association were poor, we would be
hastily generalizing. Instead, if we were to make a rather larger
sampling, find the same results, and then to infer that the Association is itself financially hard-pressed, we would be committing a
composition (although the conclusion would happen to be true). Even
if several of your favorite dishes happen to be sauerkraut, sardines,
lime sherbet, pizza, and corn flakes, it is unlikely that a sardine
pizza, topped with a layer of sauerkraut, a scoop of lime sherbet,
and a sprinkling of corn flakes, would be high on your list of
gourmet delights. Tasty as you may find each of the parts, the whole
would probably spoil any appetite; the inference is a composition.
Similarly, misapplication of statistics can be fallacious. It is the
case that every fifth child born in the world today is Chinese. If,
however, you anticipate gloating over your racially prejudiced neighbor's distress when his expected fifth child is born, figuring that,
as a fifth, it will be Chinese, then you are due for a disappoint-
ment. One child out of five, on the whole, will be Chinese, that is,
1/5 of the total number of babies born will be Chinese, but no matter
how many children a black Congolese couple or a white Danish couple
give birth to, they'll never get a Chinese child. The statistic
doesn't transmit down from the whole (of the human race) to the part
(represented by any one couple).

You are now prepared to identify and analyze the fallacies of
ambiguity. The same cautions, about repeating the argument and about
stating a definition, apply here as they did in the fallacies of
relevance.

I   (2)   Composition. It may well be that every "thing" in
            the Universe had to be as it is for the Universe
            to exist. In that event, relative to the existence
            of the Universe, every part of it is essential.
            But there may also be infinitely many possible
            Universes and the one that we happen to have may
            have been arrived at purely by chance.

     (6)   Amphiboly. Knight has misunderstood Daye's state-
            ment. Daye intended to say that he was unaware of
            any good reason for taking the trip; Knight heard
            Daye to say that there were good reasons but that
            he didn't know what they were. If you were to
            claim that the gram- matical structure here was
            unambiiguous, then you would have to claim that
            the problem is equivocation on the phrase "I do
            not see any good reasons...."

(11)   Amphiboly. The premiss of this argument is multi-
         ply ambiguous. The fact that the president is
         talking in the gym doesn't mean that the job
         opportunities have anything to do with physical
         education. Also it is possible to talk about job
         opportunities and be saying that there are none,
         as in "I am writing to tell you about employment
         opportunities as a department store Santa; since
         it is April there are none."

II (2) Composition. Part of the difficulty here comes
         from Pascal's use of the word "affinity." Today
         we tend to use it to mean something like "attrac-
         tion" as in "he had an affinity for trouble."
         Pascal's uses here, however, are more like "kin-
         ship." And, as our knowledge of tadpoles and
         frogs or caterpillars and butterflies indicates,
         resemblance in one area does not require resem-
         blance in others.

(6)   Accent. Emphasis here is put upon the necessity
         of paying more to get people to do dirty or dan-
         gerous work. However, the conclusion is stated in
         terms of what OUGHT to be. If you had had free
         choice of all the fallacies, you might quite rea-
         sonably have argued that this was an ignoratio
         elenchi.

(11)   This is a reasonable argument. If understanding
         is the crucial difference between man and the
         beasts, it is of importance, for example, in argu-
         ments about abortion and mercy killing. Thus, it
         ought to be worth our efforts to try to understand
         understanding.

(16)   Amphiboly. The purpose of the second statement is
         to point out where the misunderstanding occurred.
         The grammar was such that, if you took this liter-
         ally, you would have to take the properties of
         leaking badly and being manned by a skeleton crew
         as belonging to the infirmities. And, of course,
         the original author intended to claim these pro-
         perties for the ship not its infirmities.

(21)   Equivocation (probably). The phrase "improbable
         event" has a meaning shift. In the former use, it
         meant that some one member or another of the class
         of things which are improbable occurs almost
         every day. In the latter case it meant that each
         specific event happens almost every day. If you
         preserved the meaning of the first in the occur-
         rence of the second, you'd get as a con- clusion
         something like "it is very probable that some
         improbable event or other will occur." And that,
         given the premiss, is quite a reasonable conclu-
         sion.

Perhaps the single most important thing to remember in all this
analysis of informal fallacies is that there is NOT a necessary
relationship between truth and fallaciousness. The fact that an
argument does NOT mean that its conclusion is false, All that you
prove about the conclusion of a fallacious argument is that the
information offered as premisses for its support is insufficient to
support it.   Don't forget that if you were to infer that a statement
was false because it was the conclusion of a fallacious argument, you
would be guilty of an ad IGNORANTIUM fallacy yourself.

If you can find a copy of Max Shulman's book **The Many Loves of Dobie Gillis,** you will find it both profitable and fun to read the chapter entitled "Love is a Fallacy." In it you will have a humorous review of several of the fallacies and will see the pitfalls in the unthinking application of what you have learned in this chapter. In particular you will see how Dobie, who supposes himself to be a proficient logician, lapses into fallacious reasoning when pressed emotionally. The only thing left for you to do is to try to work exercises where you don't already know whether they are fallacies of relevance or of ambiguity. The problems following 3.4 are of that sort. Try them and check your results here and in Copi.

(2)   Argumentum Ad Hominem (abusive). Calling his opponent a quibbler in no way provides evidence for or against Scotus's conclusion in favor of self-evidence. It merely draws your attention away from the argument and toward the opponent.

(6)   Petitio Princippi (Begging the question). Premiss (justice can be achieved only by ... order) is basically the conclusion (justice finds order indispensible).

(11)   Argumentum Ad Hominen (abusive). Feyerabend is not supporting his realism; he's attacking those who do not see his point as self-evident as being unreasonable.

(16)   Accident, or Ignoratio elenchi. If you take the premiss (about the long tradition of cooking) to mean that they have done their job well, then you still have no reason to suppose that your cook does, making the argument accident. If you take it literally, the premiss speaks only of the duration of cooking, never anything about quality. Perhaps the cooks have been being made to "do it again until they get it right."

(21)   Argumentum Ad Hominem (circumstantial). The fact is that there are a number of ways in which "business sense" can benefit a college, for example in its business dealings with the "outside world." Thus the accusation that his background is not academic is not entirely relevant.

(26)   Equivocation. The phrase "are seldom found" shifts from meaning "arae an uncommon breed" to meaning "are difficult to find when lost."

(31)   Converse Accident (Hasty Generalization). The special circumstances under which the Professor let Bill miss class (and which were the prof's reason for allowing Bill the privilege of missing class) are ignored in the generalization.

(36)   Converse Accident. Again there are special circumstances which hold for the individiual but not for the nation as a whole.

(41)   Converse Accident (Hasty Generalization). Again the special circumstances of being a prize fighter prevent generalization to all times and places.

(46)   Ignoratio elenchi (irrelevant conclusion). This presumes that we can intelligiibly express the question, which may well not be the case.

CHAPTER THREE SUMMARY

I.   There are fallacious reasoning patterns which tend to distract us from the parts of arguments that ought to be most significant.

    A.   Argumentum Ad Baculum substitutes overt or covert threats for reasons.

    B.   Argumentum Ad Hominen (abuse) distracts by attacking the opponent rather than his/her argument.

    C.   Argumentum Ad Hominen (circumstantial) points to special circumstances surrounding an arguer to shift attention to her/him instead of her/his argument.

    D.   Argumentum Ad Ignorantium tries to draw conclusions without evidence.

    E.   Argumentum Ad Misericordiam distracts you from the argument to someone's sad plight.

    F.   Argumentum Ad Verecundiam tries to use as authority those who are not authorities **in this area.**

    G.   Accident applies general principles in cases where special circumstances render them inapplicable.

    H.   Converse Accident seeks a general conclusion from evidence which is not known to be representative.

    I.   False cause sees causal links where, at best, there are only simultaneous or sequential occurrences.

    J.   Complex question derives its conclusion by smuggling the real issue in as a presupposition of an, apparently, innocent question.

    K.   Ignoratio elenchi misdirects completely, deriving the conclusion from evidence which is logically irrelevant.

II. Improperly used grammar and reference can result in misunderstanding (or misleading) inferences.

    A.   Equivocation occurs when words or phrases are
treated as if they meant the same thing when, in
fact, they do not.

    B.   Amphibolous arguments occur when the grammar is
used in a sufficiently loose or incorrect manner
to result in multiple or erroneous interpretations
of what is said.

    C.   If the intent of an argument or a statement is
altered by shifting the emphasis within it, then a
fallacy of accent has occurred.

    D.   Composition results from inferring that some whole
(or composite) has the same properties as do its
elements.

    E.   Division results from inferring that the indi-
vidual elements of a composite whole have the
same properties as the whole itself.

III. The distinction drawn in identifying the various kinds of
fallacious argument all have imprecise (or fuzzy) edges: depending upon how you read an argument, you may reasonably attribute
several different fallacious characters to it.

4

Definition

Most of us tend to think of definitions as the strings of words that we can look up in a dictionary that explain, clarify or describe how and when we ought to use some specific word. It is also the case that definition can be looked upon as "the act of defining." Viewed this way, definition is an activity, something that people **do**.

4.1   Five Purposes of Definition

If you think of THE ACT OF DEFINING as the source of definitions, then Professor Copi's discussion of the purposes of definition becomes an analysis of WHY we do what we do when we define. If you ask a surgeon WHY he cuts open people's bodies, he will answer by telling you the purpose of the surgery. If you ask a carpenter WHY she puts foam padding around a door, she will answer by telling you the purpose of weatherstripping. Similarly, if you ask someone WHY he/she is defining a word, he/she will tell you the purpose of the definition.

In many ways the simplest reason to use definition is to add to your vocabulary. There are many ways to make such additions, but not all are reliable. Persons who read a great deal tend to add to their vocabulary by reading unfamiliar words and figuring out from the context what the word must have meant. I recall having occasionally read of persons becoming LIVID with rage. Although I have never read a definition of "livid," I inferred, since all the people whom I had seen being enraged got red in the face, that "livid" must mean "red in the face." Imagine my surprise when I took the time to check a dictionary and found the definition was either "discolored, as by a bruise," or "ashen, pallid, as in livid with rage." Had I first checked the dictionary, I would have avoided years of misconception.

An old joke runs: "You ought to just sit down and read 20 pages of the dictionary every night; it has a wonderful vocabulary, although the plot is awfully thin." As a matter of fact, there are teachers who do recommend doing almost that. They suggest that you try consciously to add 10 (or 20 or some other magic number) new words to your vocabulary daily. Usually their technique is to have you note unfamiliar words that you encounter in ordinary communication, but, if you don't find the required number that way, you are usually told to thumb through a dictionary until you find enough new words to fill your quota. It's hard to tell whether this activity is worthwhile in any abstract sense, but it probably does make crossword puzzles easier.

If you recall the example of equivocation from chapter 3 (p. 38 above) you should remember how definitions were used to clarify a misunderstanding. The core of the equivocal argument had been:

> All laws which have undesirable social effects ought to be repealed.
> Einstein's laws say we can't get to the stars and that has such effects.
> Thus, Einstein's laws should be repealed.

The explanation of why this was considered to be a fallacy of equivocation involved defining the two senses of "law." The first meant "product of the legislative process" while the other meant "observed (or hypothesized) physical regularity."

When a word or phrase has multiple meanings, one which in an appropriate context could be confused, then definition has great value. If you carefully define terms as you use them, then you significantly reduce the chance of an equivocation occurring. The second purpose, then, of definition is to avoid ambiguity.

A closely related function of definition is to reduce vagueness. In fact, some lists of synonyms will give "uncertain" both as a synonym of "vague" and of "ambiguous." Professor Copi, however, does not treat the latter terms as synonymous. His position is that a term is ambiguous when it has two (or more) clear meanings which can, in the right circumstances, be confused. A term is vague insofar as it is fuzzy or indefinite in meaning. In the example of equivocation from chapter 3, the term "law" is, in Copi's sense, ambiguous: it has two distinct, easily separable meanings. Similarly, the word "right" can be ambiguous: one use meaning "correct or appropriate" while another might be "that which is due one by law, tradition or nature."

But both meanings of "right" can also be vague. Social niceties suggest that it is sometimes RIGHT to lie (as to avoid needlessly hurting another's feelings), but persons of good will can (and do) debate endlessly about the correctness of applying this exemption from honesty. And, unless some authority is recognized as being capable of (or responsible for) defining the term "right," we will have to struggle along with our intuitions about what is RIGHT and what is not.

The That-which-is-due sense of "right" is also vague. During and after the war in Vietnam the entire debate about the government's right to obtain and maintain records of the domestic political activity of citizens vs. the citizen's right to privacy and freedom from governmental meddling hinged upon the vagueness both of those rights and of the language in which we discuss them. What was finally required to clear up that vagueness was a series of Supreme Court decisions which spelled out the nature and extent of the rights both of the government and of the individual. These decisions functioned as at least partial definitions of the terms "privacy" and "national interest."

Thus, in the case of vague terminology, definition may serve to eliminate the vagueness. One needs to recall, however, that for vaguenesss to be so eliminated there needs to be some authoritative structure that puts a seal of approval upon such clarifying definitions.

A fourth reason one would want to offer a definition is to clarify the exact limits of usage of a term relative to some theory. Terms in science are frequently derived from our ordinary usage of a term relative to some theory. Terms in science are frequently derived from our ordinary usage. However, frequently the "scientific" use of the term becomes far more precise than was that use it had had in ordinary usage. A good example of this is the term "valid" as used by logicians. In everyday language, one would use "valid" to mean "supportable, well-grounded, or cognent." As you recall, the logician is far more specific when defining the term (see the discussion of validity in Chapter 1 above and in Copi. above). In this way, the logician restricts the usage of the term to the area in which it serves the most significant function for his purposes.

The fifth purpose which Professor Copi suggests for definition is to persuade, or to alter someone's attitude. In many ways this use of definition resembles the AD POPULUM fallacy. It usually involves playing upon the emotions of the reader or listener. For example, in the very emotional area of the discussion of abortion those who believe in the so-called "right-to-choice" might be found defining "abortion" quite differently than those who believe in the so-called "right-to-life." Respective definitions might look like:

    Abortion : The removal of parasitic tissue from the uterine
                       wall of the human female.

    Abortion : The murder of an innocent child for the selfish
                       convenience of his/her mother.

It would be a rare person who could accept the first definition as
correct and still say they opposed abortion (for wouldn't that entail
that it would be equally wrong to remove leeches, tapeworms, and
harmful bacteria?). Similarly one would question the sanity of
anyone who agreed with the second version and still claimed to favor
abortion (for wouldn't that suggest that, if you had trouble finding
a babysitter, then it would be ok to strangle your children instead?). Thus, you see, in some cases three-quarters of the battle
is getting someone to accept your definition.

4.2   Verbal Disputes and Definition

You should recall Professor Copi's discussion of agreement and
disagreement in belief and attitude. In chapter one his analysis of
actual and verbal disputes is a quite straightforward way of uniting
that discussion with the question of ambiguity in definitions. He
points out that, in this area, he is not discussing the obvious case
of simple attitude-disagreement. Rather, he divides the question of
possible verbal dispute into three realms: real differences, verbal
differences, and real differences that appear to be only verbal. It
may seem to you that there ought to be a fourth area, that is, verbal
differences that appear to be real (to "round out" the combinations).
The reason that it is not included is that such a group IS what is
meant by merely verbal differences; they would not be significant
unless they gave the impression of being real.

In the case that two people genuinely differ about the facts,
whether those facts be things, words, or whatever, there is a real
difference. If we disagree about who won last year's Super Bowl, or
about the spelling of the word "premiss" (or, as some would have it,
"premise"), or even the attitude of the person-in-the-street toward a
full-blown free market economy, then our differences can be resolved
by the appropriate research into the facts. In the first case, we'll
go to an NFL record book (or some other appropriate reference tool);
in the second, we would consult dictionaries, logicians and etymo-
logists; in the last, we would need to see if such a survey had been
done recently and if so consult it and if not do it ourselves. In
any event, in each case our resolution would be made by checking out
the facts. We might be left with a further difference in belief
about the reliability of the consulted source, but, insofar as we
could get "the facts," we would no longer disagree.

If our dispute were strictly verbal, then it would have to hinge
upon the occurrence of some ambiguous term in the discussion. There
is a puzzle often given astronomy students after they have, they
believe, come to know the parts of our solar system. It asks: What
planet is closest to Pluto (the outermost in the Solar System)? The
answer is not, as we expect, Neptune (the next-outermost) but Mercury
(the innermost). When the answer in explained, it seems that it is
based upon the fact that Pluto's "year" is almost 250 of our Earth-
years, Neptune's is almost 165 and Mercury's is 88 days. This means
that, if you AVERAGE the distance between the planets when they are
closest AND farthest from each other, then the average distance
between Pluto and Neptune is about 4.5 billion miles while the average distance between Pluto and Mercury is about 3.6 billion miles.
In this case the surprise occurred because the idea of being "closest
to" was ambigous. There is no real disagreement about the facts:
clearly, when their orbits are properly aligned, the planet that

passes closest to Pluto is Neptune (in fact Pluto's orbit swoops
inside Neptune's on rare and brief occasions); while the planet **whose
average distance to Pluto is smallest** is obviously Mercury.

You ought now to be ready to work the problems following 4.2,
then to check them in Copi and here.

(2)   Here there is a genuine dispute between Daye and
        Knight. Daye's criterion for relevance is dealing
        with "eternally recurring problems," while
        Knight's is having something to "say about the
        pressing and immediate issues of our time." Since
        Knight's focus is upon what is unique to our time
        and Daye's is upon what is not unique to our
        time, they have a genuine dispute.

(6)   In this case Daye and Knight clearly have dif-
        ferent attitudes toward Ann. There is used, how-
        ever, an ambiguous use of the phrase "excellent
        student." By it Daye means a lively, interested,
        questioning student, while Knight means someone
        who completes assignments promptly.

(11)   This is a verbal dispute. Reasonable walking
        speed is between two and four miles per hour; that
        would put Helen's house between four and eight
        miles away by Daye's calculation. But one could
        drive four miles in ten minutes at 24 mph and
        eight at 48 mph, thus Knight's assertions are also
        reasonable. Once they have compared modes of
        travel, they can probably agree that Helen lives
        a-long-way-by-foot but not-too-long- by-car.

(16)   This is verbal in a way quite like the Pluto/
        Neptune/Mercury problem in the discussion above
        (p. 49). Daye's interpretation of the phrase "The
        average intelligence of college freshmen" is that,
        if one took the average intelligence of all col-
        lege graduates and compared that with the average
        intelligence of all entering college freshmen, the
        graduate average would be higher than the freshman
        average. Knight's is that, if you compared the
        intelligence of each individual who graduated with
        THAT SAME INDIVIDUAL'S intelligence as a freshman,
        there would be no difference. What has occurred,
        in effect, is a fallacy of division.

4.3   Five Types of Definition

To further his discussion of definitions, Professor Copi introduces two "technical terms" of logic: DEFINIENS and DEFINIENDUM.
There is a mnemonic (memory device--like "I before E except after C")
which defines: If you were "dumb" (meaning not very bright rather
than mute), then you'd have to ask to have people define things for
you frequently; thus, the definienDUM is the thing to be defined.
One statement of a definiendum and a definiens would be:

A **circle** [definiendum] is **a plane closed curve all of whose
points are equidistant from the same point** [definiens].

Another device, which some logic teachers use, is the use of
"=df" as a sign to indicate the occurrence of a definition. It is
particularly useful in the case of what he calls a stipulative definition. Thus, if a situation came about in which I wished to introduce a new term (or specify some new use for an old term), I might
use this symbol to show that I did not consider this definition to be

an area for discussion, that I was asserting that this was how it was to be used. I might, for example, invent a machine that served a function similar to that of a helicopter, but did so by using bird-like wings. In essence I would have made a passenger-carrying hum-mingbird. Now, the word "helicopter" comes from two Greek words (HELIKO- and PTERON) meaning "spiral" and "wing." I might reason (as a matter of fact, several science-fiction authors actually have done so) that, since my machine's motion imitates a bird rather than a pinwheel, I ought to replace HELIKO- with ORNITHO- (meaning "bird") thus calling the machine an ORNITHOPTER. If I adopted the "=df" sign, then my stipulative definition would be

Ornithopter=df A heavier-than-air flying machine capable of
                flight in any direction and of hovering by the use
                of wings which imitate in form and function those
                of a bird (particularly those of a humming-bird).

Once such a stipulative definition is made, ethics of the use of terminology ought to compell everyone to use the term in the way stipulated (or at least to acknowledge deviation from that use).

A type of definition that strongly resembles the stipulative one is lexical definition. It is the vocabularly-building form which is used to report (and sometimes clarify) a definition which has already been stipulated, either by common usage or by some authority. Professor Copi discusses such definitions as being true or false, but it might really be better not to make them appear quite so clear-cut. Perhaps a preferable way to characterize such lexical definitions would be on a broadly divisible "good" to "bad" scale. That would mean that the definition "A chair is a thing for one person to sit upon" could be discusses as being better than "A chair is something to sit on" but worse than "A chair is a (usually four-) legged artifact (usually) with a back and (usually) designed to have the feet of its single occupant reach the floor." Note that in this case the presence of the "(usually)'s" indicated that there is some vari-ability in what we will accept as an example of a chair.

In any event, the definitions of a lexical definition is inten-ded to report the generally-accepted meaning (or meanings) of the definiendum.

When the difiniendum is vague, rather than ambiguous, you need to use a precising definition. In some ways it seems to lie some-where between the stipulative and lexical types. It involves an already-accepted term as definiendum (like the lexical type), but it specifies more explicit detail than was understood by the earlier use of that term (somewhat like the stipulative type).

It seems likely that as long as we have had language we have had some word for death. If you look at any standard dictionary you will find a lexical definition much like: the act of dying, termination, the cessation of life, the final stoppage of all vital functions. And, for centuries, these surely seem adequate. However, with the development of modern medical technology, we have come to see such as too vague. One can hook a drowning victim to a respirator and that person's chest will continue to rise and fall as long as the machine pumps. The function is just like pushing air into and out of a balloon. Traditionally, a person's chest rising and falling would be taken as a vital sign, but this seems inadequate in the case of respirator-use. And, of course, artificial hearts, kidneys, and the like make the "vital signs" test seem less and less definitive. The term "death" has become vague and is in need of precising definition in order that, for example, surgeons who wish to perform transplants will have some basis for deciding when someone is dead (so that a recently-deceased person can be used as a donor to the still-living). It is just this sort of case that has led both state and federal legislators to hold lengthy hearings (consulting doctors, lawyers,

philosophers, theologians, and anyone else they can think of) to try
to make the definition of death substantially more precise.

Theoretical definitions are part and parcel of the action of
theorizing. Usually, when you offer a theoretical definition, you
are trying to explain or expound a theory. Theories are developed
generally as a means of explaining some set of occurrences which
could not previously be well-explained. In the older, Ptolemaic,
Earth-centered view of the Solar System, the Earth was defined as the
immovable central object in the Universe. When the newer, Copernican, sun-centered view was theorized, a new theoretical definition of
"Earth" was needed. Since part of the earlier definition had been
Earth's immovability, without a definition that dropped that element,
anyone who supported the Copernican view could rightly have been
treated as being a candidate for a padded room: Only a madperson
would talk of the motion around the sun of an immovable object (the
Earth). The theoretical definition, then, will likely be no more
satisfactory than the theory for which it is being introduced.

Persuasive definitions are just what their name implies--defini-
tions whose purpose is more to bring others to accept your point of
view than it is to inform. The earlier discussion of persuasion,
using the definitions of "abortion," (on p. 43) show how one might be
persuaded by definition.

4.4   Various Kinds of Meaning

There are two basic ways in which you can work out the meaning
of a term: (1) list the things to which you would apply it (or the
occasions on which you would use it), and (2) list the sort of things
you could claim to know about an object (or occasion) to which the
term was applied. Thus, if you listed **Chariots of the Gods, Secret
Forces of the Pyramids, The Mystery of Atlantis,** and **Our Mysterious
Spaceship Moon** as the things to which you wanted to apply a single
term I would guess that the term you had in mind was something like
"pseudoscientific books." If this were the term you were trying to
clarify by your list, then what you did was list part of the EXTEN-
SION, or denotation. The problem, of course, with using denotation
as a method of defining is that the lists tend to be both too long
and not unique. In the case suggested above, this surely is not a
complete list of such books. In fact there have been times in the
last few years that books of this sort seem to be being published
faster than they can be listed. But it is also the case that the
same four titles could have been used as samples of books first
published in paperback, or even copyrighted titles for movies. Thus,
you see, extensions or denotiative definitions, although occasionally
helpful, are usually not precise enough to make them reliable.

It would be easier, if you wanted to define what you meant by
the term "pseudoscientific books," to list the characteristics you
saw as common to such publications. You might include unsupported
hypotheses, questionable interpretations of data, avoidance of the
simplest explanations, the introduction of speculations which will
later be treated as if they were proven facts, inconsistency with
currently accepted scientific theory, and so on. Such a listing of
the properties or characteristics of the things (or occasions) to
which a term is applied is usually called the INTENSION, or CONNOTA-
TION, of the term. One of the most valuable assets of defining by
intension os that when you encounter a new object or occasion you are
in a good position to see if it "fits" the definition--if it has the
properties on the connotative list then it does, if not then it
doesn't. It is also convenient that, as you learn more and more
about the things to which you apply your term, you can add to the
list of properties which are part of the term's connotation. And, if
you find that some groups of properties adequately separate off
identifiable sub-groups of the original extension of your term, then

you are able to identify the connotation of the new sub-groups in
contrast to the original. An example of this kind of increasing
specification might occur as you learned more and more about cooking.
You might, early on, encounter the term "thickening." The first way
you would probably be introduced to what a thickening is would be by
being given examples of thickenings (like flour and cornstarch).
This is, of course, extensional. In time, however, you would learn
that there are many more things that serve this function. This ought
to lead you to identify the intension of the term. Particularly if
you are a novice cook, and adequate intensional definition will be
"having the property of making a liquid more dense or viscous (i.e.,
thicker)." As you become more skilled, however, you learn that
cornstarch and flour, when added to cheese liquids, tend to cause a
grainy texture, but that potato starch does not. Further you may
find that flour, corn- and potato starch, and other fairly common
thickenings make the liquids into which they are stirred become
rather cloudy, while arrowroot starch results in a clearer, more
glistening liquid. However, you will also learn that arrowroot loses
its thickening property if the liquid into which it is stirred is
then boiled. With all this information you are in a position to
identify the intensions of several kinds of thickening, all of which
share the original intension, but which do not share simple intension
suggested for "thickening" are part of the extension of the term.
And, as the intension is increased, for example by adding "results in
a clear liquid," the extension (in this case) decreases. This happens unless the addition to the intension is in a sense parallel to
the already given intension. In the case, for example, of "clear"
thickenings the further addition of "cannot be boiled without losing
its thickening property" would, obviously, entail an increased intension, but, since arrowroot was already identified as the "clear"
thickening, would not reduce the extension. You'd still be talking
about arrowroot.

It is also important to remember that terms can have intensions
without having extensions. Almost any schoolchild can give you a
very detailed intensional description of Superman--faster than a
speeding bullet, more powerful than a locomotive, able to leap high
buildings at a single bound, vulnerable only to kryptnite in its
various forms and magic, champion of truth, justice and the American
Way, and so on. Unfortunately, except for orthopedists in hospital
emergency rooms, children sometimes do not realize that being able to
so fully characterize Superman does not mean that there is anyone who
possesses those qualitites. That is why numerous children each year
break various assorted bones trying to fly like Superman. It makes
perfect sense, at least to those of us familiar with the Superman
myth, to discuss his assorted powers in detail, but expressing a
desire to meet him (or, worse, claiming to have already done so)
would suggest a need for intense psychiatric care.

You ought, now, to try the problems following 4.4 and to check
your results in Copi and here.

(2)   Beverage, alcoholic beverage, wine, white wine,
        fine white wine, champagne. Except for certain
        American versions, the name "Champagne" is re-
        stricted to the carbonated white wine that is
        naturally fermented and carbonated in the Cham-
        pagne region of France. Each term in the list
        reduces the kinds of liquids which might be in-
        cluded by its predecessor in the list. Thus,
        "alcoholic beverage" eliminates milk which is a
        beverage, "wine" eliminates beer which is an alco-
        holic beverage, "white wine" eli- minates claret
        which is a wine, fine white wine eli- minates most
        restaurant house wines, and "champagne" eliminates
        even Savignon Blanc.

4.5   Techniques for Defining

As was suggested earlier, denotative definition is not a very satisfactory approach. In the event that you try to list the extension of a term, unless the term has almost trivially few things to which it ought to be applied, you will be unable to complete your listing in a useful length of time.

Even if you try to generate your list more rapidly by listing not the things to which it applies but the SORTS OF THINGS (like recliners, rockers, folding ones, overstuffed ones and so on to identify "chairs") the list will probably also be too long to be useful. But even it it is not, you must be extremely cautious, for one extension may be shared by several intensions.

We do find, however, that there are occasions on which it seems quite useful to explain a term by "pointing." This sort of definition, which is called an ostensive definition, has problems quite like the other forms of denotative definition, especially those of shared intension, and, additionally, has great probability of misunderstanding. We see this most frequently when we try to explain the meanings of words to children by pointing. Children, particularly, are inclined to take things quite literally. When a child asks, "What is the Moon?" and I reply "That is the Moon" and point skyward, she is just as likely to believe that my outstretched finger or the television antenna which she sees beyond it (from her perspective) is the "Moon" to which I referred.

Thus, although we do learn much of vocabulary through experience, the use of denotative definition is not a very reliable approach. This can be further understood by trying the problems on p. 161 and then comparing your answers to Copi's and those here.

I   (2)   boxer: Mohammad Ali, Sugar Ray Leonard, Michael Spinks.

     (6)   flower: Rose, Lily, Daisy

II   (2)   Olympic Gold Medal winners

     (6)   Women's names

In discussing connative definition, Profesor Copi first introduces the idea of definition by synonym. As he suggests, this is particularly useful for lexical, stipulatiive or (perhaps) persuasive definitions, but not for precising or theoretical ones. One of its commonest uses is in trying to develop vocabulary in a second language. In this case, rather than a lengthy denotative or connotative definition, all that most of us require is identification of the word in our native language that "means the same" as the foreign one.

Whether across languages or within them, however, this approach is not altogether reliable. Some words do not have exact synonyms (or, in some cases, any at all). The German words ESSEN and FRESSEN may both be rendered in English as EAT. However, the former is used in German to refer to the eating done by people and the latter that is done by animals. Thus, to use them interchangeably (as a native English-speaker might do when venturing into German) could be a terrible social blunder. Similarly, in referring to an apple which was of ideal proportion but was 20% larger than the average apple, few would hestitate to call it a very big apple. In the case, however, of a woman who was ideally proportioned but stood six feet, six inches tall, most of us would feel some reluctance to call her a very big woman. The reticence would probably stem from the fact that the term "big" when applied particularly to women tends to carry an overtone of meaning overweight. And in a third case, where we encountered a man who stood over seven feet tall but was again ideally proportioned, we would again be reluctant to call him a very big man, but for different reasons. The phrase "big man" has become colloquial for a man of importance, regardless of his size physically. It is therefore clear that the use of synonyms as a method of defining is useful only as a first approximation of meaning and ought to be used with caution.

As Professor Copi suggests, the function and application of operational definitions is fit material for another book (or two or more). For a fuller understanding of operational definitions, you might find it interesting to search out a course in the philosophy of science.

Another way of defining is by grouping things into classes, subclasses, and so on. This is usually referred to as species/genus classification. The third century Neoplatonic philosopher Porphyry is credited with originating the diagramming of such relationships and with noticing that they somewhat resemble trees, hence their commonly being called the Trees of Porphyry. An example of such a tree (with many branches missing) is below:

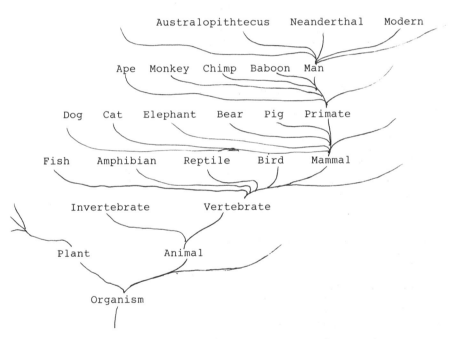

Of course, a term must have some complexity to its connotation or this approach will not work. "Organism" is the base of this tree, but could be a branch relative to inanimate matter. Those things that rest as ultimate bases, however, would not be definable by this technique because they could not be branches on any more general "tree." Such ultimate bases are so rare that we do not need to worry greatly about their occurring as limitations for this method.

Below are answers which you may wish to compare with your own after you have done the exercises following 4.5.

I   (2)   Buffoon: clown (although "buffoon" has a somewhat
            more negative connotation).

(6)   Feast: banquet (although "feast" sometimes car-
        ries the additional connotation of celebrating
        some specific occasion, as in "a harvest feast").

(11)   Kine: cattle (although "kine" is generally consi-
        dered old-fashioned, romantic or Biblical).

(16)   Panaca: cure-all (although "panacea" frequently
        is taken to have the connotation of not being able
        to bring about what is claimed).

II (2)   Banquet -- 4. meal -- 5. very large

    (6)   Foal   -- 2. horse -- 7. young

    (11)   Girl   -- 8. woman -- 7. young

    (16)   Mother   -- 5. parent - 1. female Note here that
            you could have selelcted 8. woman from the first
            column, but then would have found nothing in the
            second column to characterize "son" fully.

    (21)   Son   -- 1. offspring - 2.   male Note that
            here, too, you could have selected a different
            first column term "man" but they would have had no
            choice in the second column to characterize "son"
            fully.

4.6   Rules for Definition by Genus and Difference

Language "works" as a way to communicate because, consciously or
not, we all agree to use each work in the same way. In general we
simply reject the approach of the caterpillar in ALICE IN WONDERLAND
when he tells Alice that words mean whatever he wants them to mean at
the moment. In defining terms, then, we have an obligation to include in the definition those characteristics which native speakers
of the language would usually agree are the essential, important, or
defining properties of things to which the definition is usually
applied. Thus the first rule for definition by genus and difference
is

Rule 1: A definition of a term ought to include all the properties
    normally attributed to things to which that term is usually
    applied by persons familiar with the term.

Note, please, that this formulation of the definition is not the one
given in Copi. Since you are fully capable of reading the rule as it
is stated there, it seems more useful to have an alternative way of
stating it (and the other four, too) here.

There is an old joke about the man who gets onto a race track by
mistake while trying to drive downtown. When his wife suggests that
they pull off the track and try to find their way back to the road,
he refuses, saying "How can you ask me to do that when I'm making
such terrific time?" He fails to see that making great time but
going nowhere is of questionable value. You should recall the Petitio Principii fallacy and all of the reasons that it was undesirable.
For the same sorts of reasons, a definition which uses a synonym or
another form of the term to be defined in the definiens will not take
you far in understanding the definiendum.

Rule 2:   A definition of a term ought not include the term being
    defined (in any form) or any synonym or antonym of it.

Since one of the primary purposes of defining terms is to increase vocabulary, any definition which might reasonably result in

misusing the term is obviously defective. Sometimes in the interest
of simplicity or convenience we omit from definitions elements that
ought to have been included. This can result either in the definition's admitting things to its extension that we would have wished to
exclude or in omitting things that we would have wished to include.
If you think back to Professor Copi's mentioning that a traditional
species/genus definition of "man" is that man is a rational animal,
then you will see a definition that is both too broad and too narrow.
It is too broad because, if current research with dolphins, porpoises
and whales proves that cataccians are thinking beings (which some
researchers think likely) then such aquatic mammals must be men
according to this definition. It may well be that we ought to treat
them as people, but they don't seem to be men. It is too narrow
because, if the natural offspring of a man and a woman--for whatever
traumatic or genetic reason--is incapable of rational thought, then
this definition would deny that that offspring is part of the class
"man." Again, it may be well that we do not confer the same sorts of
rights and responsibilities (voting, for example) on that individual,
but that seems no reason to deny such an unfortunate's humanity.
Caution, therefore, is necessary in formulating definitions.

Rule 3: A definition of a term ought not exclude appropriate
individuals from or include inappropriate individuals in the
extension of that term.

If you keep in mind the communication-purpose of most definitions, then you will see that it is important that the language
employed in stating a definition ought to really communicate. If the
words used in stating a definition are unclear to the reader or
hearer, for whatever reason, then the effort expended in defining
brought no benefit and may have done harm. If you are reading Hamlet's famous "To Be or Not To Be" soliloquy and encounter the term
"fardels" in the question "Who would the fardels bear?" then you may
seek a definition. If the one you encounter is "fardel: A sheaf of
staves," then the definition may have proven worthless. Of course,
if you knew that a sheaf was a bundle resembling the way grain in the
fields used to be bundled and that a stave was a small strip or piece
of wood, then you might have figured that a fardel was the large
bundle of sticks that peasants used to gather and carry home at night
to fuel their fires. Chances are you were baffled.

Similarly, the use of figurative, metaphoric, so-called poetic
language is generally to be avoided in setting forth a definition.
There is a delightful children's book called **Amelia Bedelia** by Peggy
Parrish that every adult ought to read. It tells the story of a new
maid who takes all of her instructions VERY literally: she dusts the
furniture by spreading bath powder on it, she dresses the chicken by
making little clothes for it, she changes the towels by cutting them
into odd shapes, and so on. The humor, for adults, in the book
results from our knowing what was intended by the mis-followed directions. In the case of a new (to us) term's being defined, however,
the humor might not be so evident were we the ones to take metaphoric
definition literally. Thus, the language of a definition ought to be
as straightforward as possible.

Rule 4: A definition of a term ought to be presented in clear,
simple, understandable language.

There is such variety in the universe that there are surely
infinitely many things that any given thing is not, but only a few
things that it is. If you owned a car painted the color of the sky
at noon on a cloudless day in the Rocky Mountains, then there would
be a very limited range of shades of blue in which your car's color
would have to fall. The entire remainder of the spectrum of precision and in the interest of being able to finish the job, then,
negative definitions ought to be avoided.

Rule 5:   A definition of a term ought to be presented positively whenever possible.

The exercises at the end of Chapter 4 in Copi should provide you with good practice in developing and analyzing definitions.   After you have worked them, you can check your answers in Copi and here.

II   (2)   This violates rule 3.   It is too broad because it would allow, for instance, the conclusions drawn by a palm reader (if they happened to be correct) to be counted as knowledge.   It is usually thought that knowledge must also involve some justification of the true opinion.   [That might make this a breech or rule 1 also.]

       (6)   This violates rule 2.   Since deceiving is an antonym for being honest, no real knowledge gain has occurred.

       (11)   This violates rules 1, 3, and 4.   It omits the fact that wars must be waged by political units (countries or the like) and this makes it too broad.   For it this social aspect is ignored, the compulsion of the weak by a bully would seem to count as a war.   And the language is figurative, not conveying the usual violence and destruction image which we usually associate with wars.

       (16)   The primary problem here is the violation of rule 4, but there may be some broadness difficulty, too.   Tolstoi (or Tolstoy) is not differentiating between art and the sciences or art and religion either.   In the attempt to transmit his sense of awe at the endeavor of the artist, he has lapsed into poetry himself.

       (21)   Since Mao uses "analyzing" to define "analysis," he is violating rule 2.

III. (2)   This probably violates Rule 1.   The traditional view of knowledge is that it, at least, includes "true belief."   James' "folksy" definition ignores the fact that if one **knew** something to be false, that would entail a true belief that it was false. One could not, then, also believe (have faith) that it was true.   [Unless, of course, you want to claim that James means to assert that faith is intrinsically self-contradictory.]

       (6)   Wilde is being metaphoric and, thus, violates rule 4. One who did not already know what a cynic was might well think that Wilde was describing a strange breed of economist.

       (11)   Keynes has made a very sharp turn to come back upon himself.   One could have just as well said: "Slabulonics is the science which treats of the phenomena arising out of the slabulonic activities of men in society."   In this case you must now find out what slabulonic activity is; in Keynes' case you need to know what economic activity is. [Slabulonic actvity, incidentally, is what a teething child goes through--it's drooling.]

(16)   For a philosopher writing an article in a series
        on the logic of science in **Popular Science
        Monthly,** Peirce is being very poetic. The figura-
        tive language is a clear violation of rule 4.

(21)   So is a rock. The negative definition is clever
        but applies also to all inanimate matter. It's a
        clear violation of rule 5.

(26)   There may be several minor problems with this, but
        most critical is the omission of the fact that
        female intuition is SUPPOSED TO BE based upon no
        real evidence at all. Greer is actually trying to
        overthrow the stereotypic view of women's rea-
        soning process, however, and perhaps this ought to
        be treated as a sort of stipulative definition,
        or maybe a theoretical one.

CHAPTER FOUR SUMMARY

I. Definitions have several purposes

   A.   They increase vocabulary

   B.   They eliminate ambiguity when terms have multiple meanings.

   C.   They reduce vagueness when the application of a term is not clear.

   D.   They show the place of a term within a theory.

   E.   They influence attitudes.

II. Some disputes are genuine and some are not.

   A.   If a disagreement can be resolved by appealing to the facts, then it was genuine.

   B.   If a disagreement can be reduced to agreement about the facts and difference about attitude toward them, then it is genuine.

   C.   If a disagreement can be resolved by agreeing upon how the terms ought to be used, then it is verbal.

   D.   If a disagreement about how terms ought to be used cannot be resolved, then there probably is a genuine disagreement.

III. There are five types of definition which closely correlate with the purposes of definition.

   A.   Stipulative definitions introduce new terms and state how they ought to be used.

   B.   Lexical definitions state how a term is usually used.

   C.   Precising definitions pinpoint how a term ought to be used, particularly within specific contexts.

   D.   Theoretical definitions lay out the way in which terms are intended to be used within (usually) proposed theories.

   E.   Persuasive definitions try to alter the hearer's (or listener's) point of view by altering the way key terms are understood.

IV. There are two different kinds of meaning.

   A.   Extensional meaning (or denotation) lists all the things to which a term may be correctly applied.

   B.   Intensional meaning (or connotation) lists all the properties possessed by things to which a term may be correctly applied.

V.   There are several approaches to defining.

    A.   Denotative definitions are usually impractical.

          1.   There is usually too little time to complete the list.

          2.   Lists of things to which one term applies are not precise enough to prevent another term from being correctly applied to them also.

    B.   Ostensive definitions have the same flaws as denotative ones and are subject to ambiguous understanding too.

    C.   Synonymous definitions are of variable value.

          1.   In learning a new language they are helpful.

          2.   In increasing vocabularly they are helpful.

          3.   For words without synonyms they are useless.

          4.   For words with imprecise synonyms they can be deceptive.

    D.   Definition by species and genus lays out connotation nicely.

          1.   Terms which are ultimately basic cannot be defined this way.

          2.   There are five rules for defining by species and   genus.

               a.   Include essential elements in your definition.

               b.   Don't define by using the defined term.

               c.   Include and exclude all and only what you want to.

               d.   Use clear, understandable language when defining.

               e.   Say what things are, not what they are not.

PART TWO

DEDUCTION

5

Categorical Propositions

5.1 Categorical Propositions and Classes

The approach to logic developed by Aristotle was a product of his philosophical structure. He claimed that things fell into natural categories. For our purposes what he called a category we usually call a class. Whether one adopts the Aristotelean view, called realism, that such classes are natural or what philosphers call a nominalistic position that the limits of classes are just agreed upon conventionally, it is clear that a class is a clearly identifiable group of things, ideas, actions, or the like.

Given the convention that we will only examine the relationships of classes pairwise, then it turns out that there are only four ways in which two specific classes can relate to each other. Their relationship AS CLASSES will be extensional, that is, it will be one of inclusion or exclusion is either total or partial. If these possibilities were put in a grid form, like you used for the exercises in reasoning in chapter 1, the result would look like:

	Total	Partial
Inclusion	All A is B	Some A is B
Exclusion	No A is B	Some A is not B

Statements which relate classes (or categories) in the above ways are called **Categorical Propositions**. They are **Propositions**; that is, they are informational sentences which are either true or false, and they involve the relationship between two **Categories**. Traditionally, the property which was described above as total or partial relation has been referrred to as the number (or universality and particularity) of the proposition; the property above identified as inclusion or exclusion has been called affirmation or negation. The classes identified in the grid above as "A" and "B" would traditionally have been "S" and "P," standing for the subject category and the predicate category respectively of the proposition. That grid, re-written in the more traditional format, would be:

	Universal	Particular
Affirmative	All S is P	Some S is P
Negative	No S is P	Some S is not P

Whatever S and P may be, the universal affirmative proposition asserts that anything you encounter which is included within class S will also be included within class P. The universal negative propositions asserts that anything that is within S will lie outside P (or, alternately, nothing is both in S and in P). The particular affirmative proposition claims that at least one thing in S is also in P. And the particular negative asserts that at least one thing within S is outside P.

The intension of the terms used as A and P may become far more complex than the simple structure implies, but the nature of the assertions made in each of the categorical proposition-forms remains the same. If, for example, you encountered the complex-looking categorical proposition "All tall, dark, and handsome men are vain, shallow or boring," you might be tempted to pass it by as too complicated for you to analyze. But it's far simpler than it appears.

67

Since it refers to ALL such men, you know that it is universal. Since it asserts that they ARE that way, you know that it is affirmative. Its form, then, is "All S is P." What are "S" and "P"? "S" is the class of all persons who are simultaneously tall, dark, handsome and male. "P" is the class of all persons who are vain or shallow or boring or any of the combinations of those characteristics. The proposition asserts that all of the members of the former class are also members of the latter one.

You should now work the problems following 5.2 and then check your answers in Copi and here.

(2)   S = Athletes who have ever accepted pay for participating in sports.

P = Amateurs

Form: Universal negative -- No S is P. The assertion is that, for an athlete, the properties of being paid to play and being an amateur are incompatible.

(6)   S = Paintings produced by artists who are universally recognized as masters.

P = Works of genuine merit that either are or deserve to be preserved in museums and made available to the public.

Form: Particular negative -- Some S is not P. The assertation that at least one work by a universally recognized master is excluded from those that should be hung in a museum, preserved, etc.

5.2   The Quality, Quantity, and Distribution

The four sorts of proposition represented on the grids in section 5.1 (above) are traditionally identified as A, E, I and O propositions. Professor Copi explains the origin of these names at the beginning of section 5.2. In the long run, the key to identifying any categorical proposition as one of them is to categorize it as affirmative or negative and as universal or particular. Once that is done, you need to identify the proposition's subject and predicate. This being done, your understanding of any given categorical proposition should be satisfactory.

The property of being affirmative or negative we call the **Quality** of the proposition; the property of being universal or particular we call the **Quantity.** When you are speaking of all the members of a class, then the term used is said to be **Distributed;** when some members of the class are not being spoken of, the term is said to be **Undistributed.** Each of the four categorical proposition-forms has its own characteristic distribution pattern. If we were to add "d" to distributed classes and "u" to undistributed ones, and were to use "<" to represent the copula (the link between subject class and predicate class), then we wouldn't even need to indicate the quantity or quality. The pattern of distribution would tell us whether the proposition was affirmative or negative, universal or particular.

In propositions of the form "All S is P" your assertion says something about all S's but, at least possibly, only about some of the P's. For example, in the proposition "All Swans are Pretty," an assertion is made about ALL swans, but we have no reason to assume tht we know anything about ALL pretty things. Our information is only about those pretty things that are also swans. The distribution pattern for an A proposition will always be Sd < Pu.

In propositions of the form "No S is P" there is an assertion about all S's (that they are not P's) AND an assertion about all P's (that they are not S's). If no tasks asked of people are beyond the capability of humanity, then it is the case both that all tasks asked of people are excluded from the class of things beyond humanity's capability and that all things beyond humanity's capability are excluded from tasks which might be asked of humanity. The pattern of distribution in an E proposition will always be Sd < Pd.

In I propositions there is neither an assertion about all S's nor one about all P's. When some readers of this book are female, there is no universal knowledge either about the book's readership or about women. The pattern of distribution in a proposition asserting that some S is P is always Su < Pu.

An assertion that some S's are not P's tells us nothing about S's as a whole, but it does have information, albeit slight, about the whole of the class of P's. If some dogs are not friendly, then you know that if you had a complete list of things that are friendly there would be at least one dog that would not be on the list. O propositions' distribution patterns, then are always Su < Pd.

Note, then, the distribution patterns when they are inserted into the grids suggested above in 5.1.

	Universal	Particular
Affirmative	Sd < Pu	Su < Pu
Negative	Sd < Pd	Su < Pd

When you examine the grid, certain characteristics seem more obvious. You can look at these characteristics either from the point of view of the quantity or quality of the proposition:

1. Universal propositions have distributed subjects.
2. Particular propositions have undistributed subjects.
3. Affirmative propositions have undistributed predicates.
4. Negative propositions have distributed predicates.

or from the viewpoint of distribution:

1. Distributed subjects mean universal propositions.
2. Distributed predicates mean negative propositions.
3. Undistributed subjects mean particular propositions.
4. Undistributed predicates mean affirmative propositions.

or from the point of view of subject or predicate:

1. Subject distribution or the lack thereof determines number.
   a. Distribution means universality.
   b. Lack of distribution means particularity.
2. Predicate distribution or the lack thereof determines quality.
   a. Distribution means a negative proposition.
   b. Lack of distribution means affirmation.

If you use the information above or the diagram in Copi at the end of section 5.2, the exercises following 5.2 should present no great challenge for you. You may wish to confirm your answers both here and in Copi.

(2)   The assertion is afirmative (that they ARE dupes) and universal (that ALl of them are dupes). Here, as in any A proposition, the subject is distributed and the predicate undistributed.

(6)   Sub-classes and conditions notwithstanding, this
           too is affirmative (that they ARE such people) and
           universal (that ALL of them will be so remem-
           bered). Here, too, the subject is distributed,
           the predicate undistributed.

5.3   The Traditional Square of Opposition

     Professor Copi's very detailed discussion of the Square of
Opposition may leave you a bit awed by the complexity of inferences
that can be drawn from such a simple diagram. Perhaps a brief review
will serve to simplify the complexity.

(superaltern) A   (contraries)   E (superaltern)

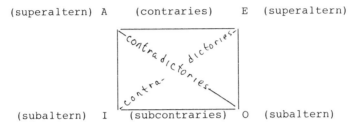

(subaltern) I   (subcontraries) O (subaltern)

The contradictoris (A and O, E and I) must have one of the pair true
and the other false. The contraries (A and E) can both be false, but
cannot both be true. The subcontraries (I and O) can both be true,
but cannot both be false. If a superaltern (A or E) is true, then
its subaltern (I or O, respectively) is true. And if a subaltern (I
or O) is false, then its superaltern (A or E, respectively) is false.

     From this review or from the list of immediate inferences at the
end of section 5.3 of Copi, you should be able to work the exercises
following 5.3. The answer to number 2 is below:

(2)   If a is true, then b is false (being a's contradictory)
            c is true (being a's subaltern) and d is false (being
      a's contrary).
      If a is false, then b is true, and c and d are both
      undetermined.

5.4   Further Immediate Inferences

     There are three forms of immediate inferences for categorical
propositions other than those found on the Square of Opposition. To
describe them esily, it is necessary to introduce the conception of a
class and its complement. If you have studied geometry, then comple-
mentarity should already be familiar to you. Geometrically, the
complement of an angle is another angle, the one which, when added to
the original angle, would total 180 . Obviously, if angle B is the
complement of angle A, then angle A is also the complement of angle B
(Since if A + B = 180 , then B + A = 180). In the case of comple-
mentary classes, they sum to totality (everything that is) instead of
180 . Thus, if class A is station wagons, then in class B will be
anything that does not qualify as a station wagon. Class B will be
non-station wagons.

     Most reliable of these added immediate inferences is the one
called OBVERSION. If you take a categorical statement and change its
quality, replace its predicate term with its complement, and leave
the quantity and subject as they are, then you have obverted the
original proposition. Explained in this form, the process sounds
horribly complicated, but that impression is wrong. If you use "S'
to represent the subject term of a categorical proposition and "P" to
represent the predicate term, then any categorical proposition has
the form:

quantifier S copula (qualifier) **P**

The qualifier is in parentheses because, in affirmative propositions, it is not stated.

You know that each class has a complement. Quality and quantity have similar related concepts, which might be called the quantifier-opposite and the qualifier-opposite. The quantifier-opposite of universality is particularity and vice versa. THe qualifier-opposite of affirmative is negation and vice versa.

Based upon the general categorical form above, then the obverse of a categorical proposition has the form:

quantifier S copula (qualifier-opposite) **P-complement**

The nice thing about obversion is that it is valid as a means of inference: any categorical proposition may be validly obverted.

The simplest immediate inference is called CONVERSION. Unfortunately it is not valid for all categorical forms. You arrive at the converse of a categorical proposition simply by exchanging the subject and predicate terms. Based upon the general categorical form above, the converse is

quantifier S copula (qualifier) **P.**

Conversion is entirely satisfactory for the contradictory pair E and I. Whenever no whales are fish or some horses are jumpers, we ought to feel perfectly confident that no fish are whales or some jumpers are horses. The other contradictory pair, A and O, do not fare so well in conversion. If we are sure that some scholars are not reliable, we remain utterly ignorant about the likelihood of finding any non-scholars among the reliable. Thus, nothing like conversion is possible, for an O proposition. The situation is not quite so dire for A propositions. When you know that all diamonds are crystals, you do have some knowledge about the membership of the class of crystals. What you do not have is universal knowledge. You know something about some crystals (that they are diamonds). From an A proposition, then, you may only validly convert by limitation, getting the form:

quantifier-opposite P copula (qualifier) **S.**

Of course, since you must have started with "all S is P" you must get "some P is S."

The third added form of immediate inference is called CONTRA-POSITION. In actuality it is just a combination of obversion and conversion. It is, however, easier to introduce contraposition as an immediate inference in its own right than it is to have to go through the process of obverting, then converting, then obverting again. Following the general categorical proposition-form, the contraposition is

quantifier P-complement copula (qualifier) **S-complement**

As you might infer, from the fact that contraposition involves an intermediate step of conversion, you are not free to contrapose any categorical proposition. If the pattern of obverting, converting, then obverting again is followed, you can see what can and what cannot be contraposed.

Original proposition validly obverts to 1st derived proposition:

A.	All S is P	-	-	-	- E. No S is non-P
E.	No S is P	-	-	-	- A. All S is non-P
I.	Some S is P	-	-	-	- O. Some S in not non-P
O.	Some S is not P-	-	-	-	- I. Some S in non-P

1st derived proposition converts to 2nd derived proposition

E.	No S is non-P -	-	- E. No non-P is S (valid)
A.	All S is non-P -	-	- I. Some non-P is S
			(valid by limitation)
O.	Some S is not non-P -		- Will not convert validly
I.	Some S is non-P-	-	- I. Some non-P is S (valid)

2nd derived proposition validly obverts to contrapositive:

E.	No non-P is S	-	-	-	A. All non-P is non-S
I.	Some non-P is S	-	-	-	O. Some non-P is not non-S
No valid conversion	-	-	-	Nothing to obvert
I.	Some non-P is S	-	-	-	O. Some non-P is not non-S

Note that this shows the contradictory pair A and O have full contra-positives, that the E has a limited contrapositive (which happens to be the contrapositive of its subaltren), and that the I has no contrapositive.

For review, it is probably best to put all of the immediate inferences in chart form:
Valid Immediate Inferences
(other than from the Square of Opposition)

Proposition	Obverse	Converse	Contrapositive
A. All S is P	No S is non-P	Some P is S (limited)	All non-P is non-S
(when true)	(true)	(true)	(true)
(when false)	(false)	(indeterminate)	(false)
E. No S is P	All S is non-P	No P is S (limited)	Some non-P is not non-S
(when true)	(true)	(true)	(true)
(when false)	(false)	(false)	(indeterminate)
I. Some S is P	Some S is not non-P	Some P is S	None valid
(when true)	(true)	(true)	-----
(when false)	(false)	(false)	-----
O. Some S is not P	Some S is non-P	none valid	Some non-P is not non-S
(when true)	(true)	-----	(true)
(when false)	(false)	-----	(false)

The answers to several of the problems following 5.4 are given below to be compared with your work.

I   (2)   The converse is "All commissioned officers in the U.S. Army are graduates of West Point." It is not equivalent to the original. The converse by limitation is "Some commissioned officers in the U.S. Army are graduates of West Point" which is implied by the original, but still is not equivalent to the original.

II   (2)   All organic compounds are non-metallic. Equivalent.

III (2)   Some non-officers are not non-soldiers. Equivalent.

IV   (2)   This is the obverse of the assumed proposition. Since the obverse of any categorical proposition is equivalent to that proposition, this, too, is true.

     (6)   This is the contrapositive of the original proposition. Since the contrapositive of any A or O proposition is equivalent to the original, this is true.

V   (2)   This is the contrapositive of the subaltern of the original. Since the subaltern of a true E is a true O and the contrapositive of a true O is also true, then this proposition is true.

     (6)   This is the converse of the contrary of the original proposition. Since the original is true, its contrary would have to be false. But the contrary of the original would be "All scientists are philosophers" and would be false. But, when an A proposition is false, even its limited converse is indeterminate. However, since the originally assumed true proposition is "No scientists are philosophers," its obverse "All scientists are non-philosophers" must also be true. But the contrapositive of that true statement, "All philosophers are non-scientists," must also be true. If all philosophers ARE non-scientists, then it seems unlikely that they could also be scientists (as exercise 6 suggests). The only way to conceivably make exercise 6 anything but false is a by-product of the considerations to be discussed in 5.5 on Existential Import.

VI   (2)   By obversion and conversion (both valid inferences) this statement may be transformed to "Some saints were nonmartyrs." Since it is quite possible (and happens to be true) that some saints could be martyrs while others were not, the truth of proposition 2 is indeterminate. Notice please that, although we may know on other grounds that the proposition is true, we are not permitted to claim to infer this from the original proposition.

     (6)   By obversion and conversion this statement yields "All martyrs were saints." You surely can't infer such a universal proposition from only particular information. The proposition is indeterminate.

   (11)   Essentially this claims that there were somee people who were neither saints nor martyrs. This is consistent with the original proposition (that is, does not contradict it), but its truth is undetermined.

   (16)   This is the obverse of exercise 11. Thus it, too, is indeterminate.

   (21)   The contrapositive of the original, "Some martyrs were saints," would be true. But it is also possible that some were not saints. We don't know from this evidence, so the given proposition is indeterminate.

(26)   The obverse of this would be "No saints were
            martyrs." This is the contradictory of the origi-
            nal proposition so must be false.

VII (2)   By conversion and obversion this would yield "All
            pirates are merchants." This does not contradict
            the original proposition nor does it follow from
            the original. Thus it is indeterminate.

(6)   This is the superaltern of the original proposi-
            tion, thus is consistent with it but does not
            follow from it. It is thus indeterminate.

(11)   By obversion and conversion this asserts the sub-
            contrary. Since the subcontrary of a true propo-
            sition may be either true or false, this is inde-
            terminate.

(16)   By obversion and conversion this is the same as
            exercise 6. Thus it, too, is indeterminate.

(21)   This asserts that some people are neither pirates
            nor merchants. This is consistent with the origi-
            nal but does not follow from it, thus is indeter-
            minate.

(26)   By obversion this becomes "All merchants are pi-
            rates" which is the contradictory of the original
            proposition. It is therefore false.

5.5   Existential Import

The question of existential import is, basically, which (if any)
categorical propositions imply the existence of the kind of things
referred to in their subject terms. It certainly seems obvious that,
if someone talked to you about some (or all) of his brothers being
wealthy, you would feel deceived were you to learn that he was an
only child. We usually think of a deception as the assertion of
something false. Thus, it seems reasonable to infer that we do assume
that assertion of a categorical proposition is also the assertion or
the existence of the things to which its subject term refers.

There is a problem with this view. It seems unquestionable that
the proposition "All unicorns have one horn" is true. But most
people who would be certain that that is a true proposition would be
equally certain that unicorns do not exist.

There are several possible solutions to this dilemma, none
entirely satisfactory. The one that seems closest to "fitting" with
the intuitions of most people is the one that Profesor Copi has
chosen to adopt. This interpretation, called the Boolean one, claims
that A and E propositions do not assert existence while I and O
propositions do. This means that the only immediate inference left
for us are obversion and conversion (for E & I only--contraposition
by limitation is also eliminated). The only relationship which still
holds from the traditional square of opposition is contradiction.

You should now work 5.5's exercises, then check your results.

II   (2)   This is the conversion of (1) and is acceptable.

     (3)   This is the obversion of (2) and is acceptable.

     (4)   This is the subaltern of (3) and is no longer an
            acceptable inference. It commits the Existential
            Fallacy.

(5)   This is the conversion of (4) which, in itself, is
      fine, but since it is based upon (4) which commit-
      ted the Existential Fallacy it also (at least
      indirectly) commits that fallacy relative to the
      original proposition (1).

5.6   Symbolism and Diagrams for Categorical Propositions

There are two means which Professor Copi offers for representing
categorical propositions.   One is in symbols, the other in diagrams.
The systems are derived from the works of two 19th century British
logicians: the symbolic from the work of George Boole, the diagram-
matic from the work of John Venn.

The Boolean system introduces zero (0) as a sign for an empty
class.   Thus, if a class equals zero, it is an empty class; if it is
unequal (=) to zero, it is a non-empty class.   By juxtaposing (writing together) two classes you symbolize the new class that is formed
out of those things that are in both of the juxtaposed classes.   And
you indicate the complement of a class by putting a bar (-) over the
symbol for the class of which it is a complement.   Given these new
symbols, you can express all of the categorical propositions in
Boolean form:

A.	All S is P	$S\bar{P} = 0$
E.	No S is P	$SP = 0$
I.	Some S is P	$SP \neq 0$
O.	Some S is not P	$S\bar{P} \neq 0$

From this, too, it is easy to see the contradictory relationships
between A and O and between E and I.

Venn diagrams are very straightforward ways of representing
class relationships.   They use circles to represent classes.   There
is, of course, no reason why other geometric figures could not have
been used except that the circle is easy to draw both singly and in
combination. The conventional reading of the areas within a Venn
diagram is that any shaded area is empty, any area with an "X" on it
is non-empty, and any unmarked area is indeterminate.   A convention
which Professor Copi does not introduce, but which seems useful, is
to enclose the circle or circles in a square or rectangle.   That puts
at least visual bounds upon the classes which complement those represented by the circles.   Circles occurring within the same box are
usually drawn with overlapping areas to represent possible common
membership in those classes.   Given these diagrams and conventions
for reading them, you can now express all of the categorical propositions in Venn diagrams:

A.   All S is P

E.   No S is P

I.   Some S is P

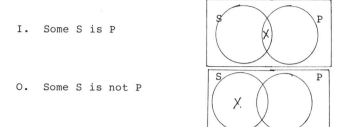

O.   Some S is not P

Now that you have the basis for representing categorical propositions as either Boolean equations or by Venn diagrams, you are ready to work the problems at the end of chapter 5. Given below are answers to some of the problems so that you can check your own results. Remember that it really is important to try the exercises before you look at the solutions either here or in Copi.

(2) PM =O

(6) PS ≠ O

(11) SM ≠ O

(16) PS̄ ≠ O

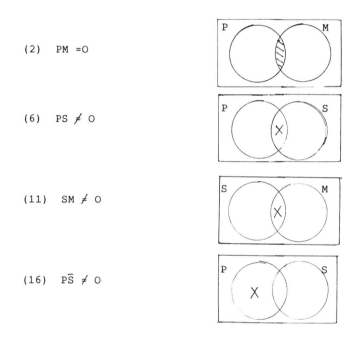

CHAPTER FIVE SUMMARY

I.   Categorical propositions assert a relationship between two cate-
     gories (or classes).

    A.   Universal affirmative (A) propositions assert that
          all of one class is included within another.

    B.   Particular affirmative (I) propositions assert that
          at least one member of one class is a member of
          another.

    C.   Universal negative (E) propositions assert that all
          of one class is excluded from another.

    D.   Particular negative (O) propositions assert that at
          least one member of one class is excluded from
          another.

II. Whether a proposition is affirmative or negative, universal or
     particular, may be determined by examining the distribution (or
     lack thereof) of the terms of the proposition.

    A.   Universal propositions have distributed subject
          terms.

    B.   Particular propositions have undistributed subject
          terms.

    C.   Negative propositions have distributed predicate
          terms.

    D.   Affirmative propositions have undistributed predi-
          cate terms.

III. The traditional square of opposition states relationships among
     the four propositional forms.

    A.   A & E are contraries: they can be false together,
          but not true at the same time.

    B.   I & O are subcontraries that can be true but not
          false together.

    C.   A & O, E & I are contradictories, one of which must
          be true and the other false.

    D.   A & E are the superimplicants of I & O, respective-
          ly. When the superimplicants are true, so must be
          the subimplicants.

    E.   I & O are subimplicants of A & E, respectively.
          When the subimplicants are false, so must be the
          superimplicants.

IV. Obversion occurs when the quality of a proposition is changed
     and the predicate term is replaced by its complement. It is a
     valid inference for all categorical propositional forms.

V.   Conversion occurs when the subject and predicate terms are ex-
     changed.

    A.   Conversion is valid for E and I propositions.

    B.   Conversion is invalid for A and O propositions.

    C.   Conversion by limitation allows valid inference from
       the A form "All S is P" to the I form "Some P is
       S."

VI. Contraposition occurs when the complements of predicate and
     subject replace subject and predicate, respectively.

    A.   Contraposition is valid for A and O propositions.

    B.   Contraposition is invalid for E and I propositions.

    C.   Contraposition by limitation allows valid inference
       from the E form "No S is P" to the O form "Some
       non-P are not non-S."

VII. Existential import is the assumption that a proposition implies
     that there exist members of the proposition's subject class. The
     most useful assumption of existential import is that I & O propo-
     sitions imply existence while A & E ones do not.

    A.   This eliminates all square of opposition relation-
       ships except contradiction.

    B.   This eliminates immediate inferences of conversion
       and contraposition by limitation.

VIII. Boolean equations state that classes do or do not equal the
      empty class (0).

    A.   The juxtaposition of two class terms represents the
       class formed of things common to both classes.

    B.   All four categorical propositions can be represen-
       ted in Boolean form.

        1.   All S is P (A) $S\overline{P} = 0$

        2.   Some S is P (I) $SP = 0$

        3.   No S is P (E) $SP \neq 0$

        4.   Some S is not P (O) $S\overline{P} \neq 0$

IX. Venn diagrams represent classes by circles, emptiness by shading
     and membership with an X. All four categorical propositions may
     be represented in Venn diagrams.

A. All S is P

B. Some S is P

C. No S is P

D. Some S is not P

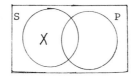

6

Categorical Syllogysms

6.1 Standard-Form Categorical Syllogisms

One of the most frequently-heard descriptions of a standard-form categorical syllogism is that it is an argument composed of three categorical statements (two premisses and a conclusion) which are in turn composed of a total of three categories each of which occurs twice. Unfortunately that description serves better as a reminder for people who are already familiar with syllogisms than as an introduction to the idea. It is useful, however, as a starting point for understanding the structure.

The conclusion of a standard-form categorical syllogism is always a categorical proposition. The term which serves as subject for that proposition is said to be the subject term (or sometimes the minor term) of the argument in which it occurs. That subject (or minor) term will also occur in the second premiss (which is often called the minor premiss). Similarly the predicate term of the conclusion of the standard-form categorical syllogism is considered to be the predicate term (or major term) of the argument. That predicate (or major) term will also occur in the first (or major) premiss. The third term used in the syllogism, then, must be the term which **mediates** or comes in the middle of, the other two. It is called the middle term and will occur once in each premiss, but not in the conclusion. Thus, the standard-form categorical syllogism is composed of a major premiss containing the major (predicate) and middle terms, a minor premiss containing the minor (subject) and middle terms, and a conclusion whose subject is the minor term and whose predicate is the major term. Now you understand the original description: three categorical propositions, three terms each occurring twice.

Since what are considered to be the subject and predicate terms of the argument are identified relative to their function in the conclusion of such an argument, the conclusion always has its terms ordered as S-P. The premisses are not so limited. The middle term could be the subject or the predicate term in either of the premisses, **relative to that premiss.** That means that one can identify four different combinations of locations for the middle term in the premisses. [Of course, one could almost as easily refer to the locations of the major and minor terms in the premisses, but the fact that the middle term is found in both premisses makes the pattern easier to see when looking for the location of the middle term.] The relative locations of the middle term in a syllogism is called the figure of the syllogism and is easily displayed on a grid like the ones used in earlier chapters:

	Major Subject Term	Major Predicate Term
Minor Subject Term	M-P M-S	P-M M-S
Minor Predicate Term	M-P S-M	P-M S-M

When read with the conclusion form, these four possibilities constitute the four figures of the standard-form categorical syllogism:

I	II	III	IV
M – P	P – M	M – P	P – M
S – M	S – M	M – S	M – S
------	------	------	-------
S – P	S – P	S – P	S – P

Within a given syllogism there are still many possible variations which result from differences in the forms of categorical
propositions which occur as premises and conclusion. The major
premiss may be an A, an E, an I or an O proposition, and so may both
the minor premiss and the conclusion. Thus, with both the premisses's forms being, say, A, the conclusion's form could be any of the
four forms, yielding four possible arguments: AAA, AAI, AAE and AAO.
The first letter always tells the form of the major premiss, the
second the minor and the third the conclusion and the three together
are called the mood of the syllogism.

To see how many possible syllogisms could be generated all you
need to do is multiply out the combinations:

4 (major forms) x 4 (minor forms) x 4 (conclusion forms)

=   64 (moods).

But you must recall that there are also four possible figures. That
means that each of the 64 possible syllogistic moods could appear in
each of the four moods, yielding 256 possible standard-form syllogisms.

The idea of having to deal with 256 different forms of argument
may seem a bit overwhelming when you first encounter it, but there is
hope. In the first place, in studying logic you want to learn to
sort good from bad arguments. Since syllogisms are deductive arguments, the good/bad distinction for them will be a valid/invalid
distinction. If the possible syllogisms were divided evenly between
valid and invalid, then you'd only have to learn one of the halves --
anything that wasn't in the half you'd learned would have to be in
the other. And if they are unevenly divided, then the prudent thing
to do would be to learn the small "half." And it ought not take you
much reflection to recognize that there are offered in the world many
more bad arguments than good ones. That pattern is followed with
syllogisms: most possible syllogistic forms are invalid.

You are now prepared to work the exercises following 6.1 and
will probably want to check your results here and in Copi.

> (2)   Some objects of worship are fir trees.
>   All fir trees are evergreens.
>   Thus some evergreens are objects of worship.
>
>   IAI-4
>
> (6)   No expensive and delicate mechanisms are suitable
>   toys for children.
>   All hi-fi sets are expensive and delicate mecha-
>   nisms.
>   Thus no hi-fi sets are suitable toys for children.
>
>   EAE-1

6.2   The Formal Nature of Syllogistic Argument

You have now learned to look at syllogistic arguments in terms
of the location of their major, minor and middle terms. You have
also learned to look at the mood of a syllogism without concerning

yourself with the specific content of the argument. Perhaps without realizing it, you have taken your first steps toward doing logic formally. (By "formally" I mean "according ot its form.") In fact, the rest of the discussion of validity and invalidity both here and in Copi will be in terms of formal relationships.

The use of forms rather than the actual arguments has several benefits. Most obvious is the fact that looking at forms alone protects you from being swayed by the sort of emotional byplay that you studied in Part I. A second value of stydying arguments formally is that you do not find yourself diverted from the analysis of the argument into the factual questions of the truth or falsity of the premises and conclusion. The greatest benefit, however, is likely to be the sharpening of your ability to argue from logical analogy. Two arguments are said to be logically analogous if their formal elements "line up" in the same way. In the case of two categorical syllogisms, they are logically analogous if their figures and moods are the same. As Professor Copi suggests, it is quite useful to be able to show an argument to be bad by being able to demonstrate its formal identity with another argument which is obviously bad.

There is a problem, however, with the use of logical analogy as a tool for proving arguments unsatisfactory. Clearly, if you can show that argument A is logically analogous to argument B, and you can prove that argument B is invalid, then argument A must also be invalid. But, if you cannot think of an invalid argument with a form matching the one you hope to refute, you do not have a proof that no such argument exists. That is, of course, a possibility, but it is also possible that such an analogy exists but that you are (or have been so far) unable to think of it. THe fact that, no matter how hard we train, neither you not I can run a sub-four-minute mile (or swim the English Channel, or lift a 200 kilo barbell, or whatever) certainly is no proof that that action cannot be performed by anyone. It is simply a biographical note about each of us as an individual.

The fact that disproof by logical analogy has limitations, however, ought not be taken as sufficient reason to ignore it as a reasoning technique. It is, as Profesor Copi says, very useful in that way. You should now put it to use working the exercises following 6.2.

(2)   This is a valid argument with an EIO-1 form.

(6)   This is a valid argument with an AII-3 form.

6.3   Venn Diagram Technique for Testing Syllogisms

In the same way that a two-circle Venn diagram was used in chapter 5 to represent all the possible interrelations between two classes, a three-circle one can picture such relationships for three classes. The bare Venn Diagram for three classes looks like:

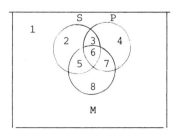

The areas in this diagram are numbered 1-8 and identify the eight possible combinations of occurrence and non-occurrence among three classes and their complements. If you find the diagram a bit confusing, the list below may help to clarify those relationships.

1. $\overline{SMP}$ 5. $SM\overline{P}$

2. $S\overline{MP}$ 6. SMP

3. $S\overline{M}P$ 7. $\overline{S}MP$

4. $\overline{SM}P$ 8. $\overline{SM}\,\overline{P}$

In examing syllogisms you will not be given immediate relationships among three classes. The major premiss tells you about the relationship between the predicate and the middle term; the minor about the subject and the middle term. The conclusion CLAIMS to follow from the premisses and to show the relationship between the subject and the predicate term. The problem, then, in applying a Venn Diagram to a standard-form categorical syllogism is to determine whether the information provided by the premisses is a satisfactory warrant for the conclusion.

Professor Copi directs you to focus your attention on only two of the circles in the three-circle diagram at a time. That is easier for some people than for others, and is easier at some times than at others. An added suggestion, which some students find helpful, is to begin by representing each of the premisses and the conclusion separately on two-circle diagrams. Once that is done, it is rather easier to transfer the information about the premisses from the two-circle diagrams to the three-circle one. When the premiss-transfer is completed, you check the argument to see whether the conclusion's two-circle version can be read from the three-circle diagram.

As an example, look at exercise 2 from the last set of exercises. It was described there as an EIO-1 argument. It's form, then is:

No M is P

Some S is M

_____

Some S is not P

Its three propositions represented on two-circle Venn Diagrams are:

No M is P

Some S is M

Some S is not P

One rule of thumb in transferring information to three-or-more-circle Venn Diagrams is always to handle universal information first. That is, do your shading before you insert X's. In this case you will need to first transfer the shading of the major premiss to the diagram

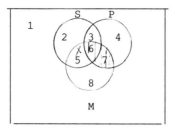

You should note that this shades both areas 6 and 7 (SMP and S̄MP) since to deny that any M's are P's will include the denial for either S's or non-S's. You need next insert an X in the area shared by S and M (as shown above). But area 6, which is one of the two areas in which you have both S and M, is already shaded (shown to be empty). That means that you must put the X in the only remaining common area between S and M, that is, area 5. This results in the three-circle diagram

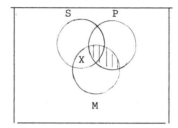

The third two-circle diagram required that there be an X inside the area of S but outside the area of P. When you look at teh three-circle version above you see that there is an X in it and that that X is within S and outside P. That indicates that the conclusion of this particular argument-form CAN be read from the information provided by the premisses and that, therefore, the argument is valid. Incidentally, the fact that there is an additional area (area 2) that is also inside S and outside P is no problem. The minimal condition for the truth of the conclusion--that there be something in S and not in P--was met in one way, thus it need not be met in any other.

It is interesting to note that an EIO argument is going to be valid regardless of its figure. (Both E and I propositions are validly convertible, so neither the two-circle nor the three-circle representations above will change if the figure were to be changed). In contrast, the sixth exercise in that set, an AII, was valid in figure 3 (and will also be so in figure 1), but is invalid in figures 2 and 4. That is shown by the same technique as before:

All P is M

Some S is M
[or Some M is S]

Some S is P

Transfer the universal major

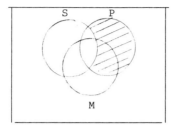

Then you need to transfer the particular minor, but there is a difficulty with doing this. Note that in the diagram representing the
minor premiss you have an X in the area shared by S and M. In the
three circle diagram, however, there are two areas so shared. One
(area 5) is not shared with P; one (area 6) is. Professor Copi's
technique for representing such an ambiguous case (ambiguous because
you don't have any knowledge whether the thing that is S and M is
also P or not) is to place the X on the line between the two possible
areas. So long as you are very careful in the placement of this X
this will work quite satisfactorily. If you are, as many of us are,
a little prone to inaccuracy when writing things down, there is a
slight modification of Professor Copi's method which you may find
helpful. If you place an X in EACH of the possible areas and join
the two X's with a heavy line, you achieve the same result (showing
the ambiguity of information) without such a need for precision in
the placement of the X. In the AII-2 or -4 argument whose diagram
was begun above, the diagram of both premisses on the three-circle
form can be done by the "line" or "bridge" method:

          Line   Bridge

To read the conclusion from either of these, you'd have to KNOW that
the things that were both S and M were also P. Since you don't know
that, the conclusion doesn't follow and the argument-form is an
invalid one.

Being familiar with the techniques for testing the validity of categorical syllogisms as explained both here and in Copi, you should find the exercises following 6.3 quite straightforward.

I   (2)

There is an X inside S but outside P; thus it's valid.

(6)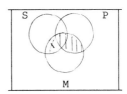

There is an X inside S but outside P; thus it's valid.

(11)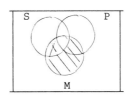

There is an X inside S but outside P; thus it's valid.

II   (2)   Some philosophers are mathematicians.
            All scientists are mmathematicians.
            Some scientists are philosophers.

                IAI-2

Since the "bridge" between philosopher-mathematicians who are and who are not scientists does not specifically assert that there are philosopher-mathematician-scientists, the argument is invalid.

(6)   No pioneers were unsavory persons.
       All criminals are unsavory persons.
       No criminals were pioneers.

            EAE-2

Since all of the area shared by S and P is shaded, and that is what the the conclusion claims, this is valid.

6.4 Rules and Fallacies

If you preferred evaluating categorical arguments without the aid of Venn Diagrams (or had you lived prior to Venn's work in the mid-19th century) you would have to approach the syllogism from the point of view of rules for its proper use. The way they are expressed here will be slightly different than their form in Copi, but the principle each is intended to state will remain the same.

RULE   1: Valid standard-form categorical syllogisms contain a
          major term, a minor term and a middle term. Each is used
          twice with no alteration in meaning in the argument.

The original definition of a standard-form categorical syllogism (in 6.1) required that it have three and only three terms and that each be used twice and in specific locations. Thus, any argument with more (or fewer) terms than three will not be a standard-form categorical syllogism and lies outside the scope of what is discussed in chapter 6. Tradition says that arguments with four or more terms commit the Fallacy of Four Terms. There seems to be no traditional analysis of arguments with fewer than three terms, probably because they would be so obviously faulty they would almost never occur.

The area in which you have to guard most carefully against committing this error is in the case of an equivocation. An argument may include two occurrences of the same word or phrase (giving the impression of having the required two uses of a term) but in actuality be a four-term argument. If you look back at argument 12 on p. 134 of Copi, you should see that it can be rewritten as an apparent standard-form categorical syllogism:

> All departures from law should be punished.
> All chance happenings are departures from law.
> All chance happenings should be punished.

This looks as if it were an AAA-1 syllogism, which is a valid form. The problem, as you surely saw when studying chapter 3, is that the phrase "departures from law" which is used as if it were the middle term is actually two different terms. In the major premiss the phrase referred to violations of rules set down by legislative agencies; in the minor premiss it referred to occurrences not in line with previously observed physical (or biological, social, etc.) regularities. If the argument were stated in terms of what the phrase means in each case, its four-term nature would be evident:

> All violations of social regulations ought to be punished.
> All chance happenings are scientifically unexpected
>   occurrences.
> All chance happenings ought to be punished.1

RULE 2: Valid standard-form categorical syllogisms include at least one distributed occurrence on the middle term.

Traditionally any argument which violates this rule is said to have committed the Fallacy of the Undistributed Middle. Such a rule is necessary to insure that the interrelation of the two premisses, through the mediation of the middle term, does not accidentally identify different individuals. If you recall the Venn Diagram analysis of the invalid AII-2 (and AII-4) argument form, (above) you will also recall that it involved the difficulty with diagramming "some S is M" when the class SM was divided in the diagram into SMP and SMP. That argument-form was invalid because you had no guarantee of the location of the known SM, in or out of P. In the case of the undistributed middle there is a similar lack of sufficient knowledge. If both occurrences of the middle term are undistributed, then in each premiss you do not know whether your knowledge applies to all or only some of the individuals in the class named by the term. If both premisses actually refer only to part of that class, then it is possible that the individuals referred to in one premiss are wholly distinct from those to which the other premiss refers. But, if the middle term-possessing individuals in the two premisses are wholly separate, you have lost the point of interrelation between the premisses. Consider the argument

> All Messy people are Pests.
> All Slobs are Messy people.
> All Slobs are Pests

You know that any individual who qualifies as a Slob will also be found within the class of Messy people. You do not know in which particular sub-class or sub-classes they will be, but you know that they're there somewhere. Similarly, you know that each andn every Messy person, no matter which sub-class or sub-classes he or she is in, will be found somewhere within the group identified as Pests. In particular, you can be assured that the Slobs, wherever they were in the class of Messy people, will also be Pests, since no matter in what sub-class of Messy people they resided that sub-class (like all sub-classes of Messy people) is to be found within the class of Pests.

On the other hand, consider the argument:

> All **P**arts for a car are **M**anufactured.
> Some **M**anufactured things are not **S**eats of cars.
> Some **S**eats of cars are not **P**arts for cars.

Here you do not know anything about all manufactured things. What you do know is that there are four distinct sub-classes within that class: SMP, SMP, SMP and SMP. You do know that somewhere in the first two classes there is at least one thing. What this argument does not tell you, but you surely know independently, is that there are no individuals inside the class of Seats of cars that are outside the class Parts of cars. The first premiss provided you with information about some of the individuals in the classes SMP and SMP, namely that if there are any P's they are in one of these two classes. The second premiss provided you with information about the classes SMP and SMP, namely that there is at least one individual in at least one of them. The conclusion, however, wants to assert something about classes SMP and SMP, namely that there is at least one individual in at least one of them. Had you ever had information about all of the class M, you would hope that you might have made some inference about individuals in SMP, but you had such knowledge so you could draw no such conclusion. The knowledge about Manufactured things, being only partial, didn't do anything to connect your knowledge about P's with that about S's.

> RULE 3: Valid standard-form categorical syllogisms require that any term distributed in the conclusion must also have been distributed in the premiss in which it occurred.

Profesor Copi and tradition subdivide the difficulties arising from ignoring this rule according to premiss-location of the term that "gets distributed" in the conclusion. Whether the "illicitness" was in the major or in the minor, however, the problem is the same. In effect both the Illicit Major and the Illicit Minor are guilty of fallacies of hasty generalization: in the premiss you have information about some of a class, but in the conclusion you make an assertion about all that class.

> RULE 4: Valid standard-form categorical syllogisms have no more than one negative premiss.

The sort of difficulty that this rule is intended to avoid is most easily seen by using Venn Diagrams. There are only four possible premiss combinations involving two negative Premisses: EE, EO, OE, and OO. Typical Venn Diagrams of them are:

EE

EO

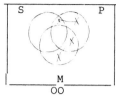

OE   OO

Of course, additional variations would come from varying the figure, but you should see a constant characteristic of all four diagrams: nowhere is there unambiguous information about the relationship between individuals with respect to their being included in or excluded from S and P.

> RULE 5: Valid standard-form categorical syllogisms with a negative premiss (and there can be at most one--see Rule 4) must also have a negative conclusion.

Negative premisses deny, in part or in whole, that one class is within another. This results in your knowing where something ISN'T but not where it IS. For the purpose of these arguments, thenc, you can't slide from isn't-information to is-information. If you were told (truly) tht syzygy isn't a very common occurrence, you would probably feel quite reluctant to say that it IS an astronomical arrangement, a part of the body, a technical term from stamp-collecting, or anything else. You do know that either "occurrences of syzygy" or "common occurrences" is the middle term of any standard-form categorical syllogism in which the denial that syzygy is common was a premiss (since each such premiss must contain an instance of the middle term). But that leaves you in the dark about the inclusion relationships of the non-middle term in the statement.

> RULE 6: Valid standard-form categorical syllogisms do not draw particular conclusions without a particular premiss.

The need for such a rule was basically outlined in chapter 5, in the discussion of existential import. Essentially, the problem is with drawing a particular conclusion, which thereby asserts something's existence. Deductive arguments which have information in their conclusions which was not, even in disguised form, in their premisses are suspect. With the exception of inferences like the rule of Addition (which will be discussed in chapter 9), new material in the conclusion of a deductive argument is a reliable sign of invalidity.

You ought now to feel prepared to work the exercises following 6.4.

I   (2) EAA-1 This violates Rule 5, thus commits the Fallacy of Drawing an Affirmative Conclusion from a Negative Premiss. Note that you can discover the fallacy here merely by looking at the argument's mood.

(6) IAI-2 This does not obviously violate a rule, so you must examine the argument's internal structure. Since you know that the subject terms of universal categorical propositions are distributed, but that the subject terms of particular ones and the predicate terms of affirmative ones are undistributed, you can "map out" the distribution pattern of this argument:

> Pu-Mu
> Sd-Mu
> -----
> Su-Pu.

Since the middle term is undistributed in both premisses, the argument violates Rule 2, committing the Fallacy of the Undistributed Middle.

(11) EAO-1 As in exercise 2 the fallacy can be seen from the mood of the argument. Rule 6 forbids inferring a particular conclusion from universal premisses. Any EAO argument will commit the Existential Fallacy.

II (2) This is an AAA-1 argument and all such arguments are valid.

(6) This is an OAA-3 argument. Since the major premiss is negative, Rule 5 requires that the conclusion also be negative. This argument, then, commits the Fallacy of Drawing an Affirmative Conclusion from a Negative Premiss.

III (2) In standard categorical form this argument is

All eccentrics are people who see new patterns in familiar things.
All inventors are people who see new patterns in familiar things.
Thus, all inventors are eccentrics.

This is an AAA-2 argument. Since the middle term occurs as the predicate term of both premisses and both premisses, being affirmative, have undistributed predicate terms, this argument commits the Fallacy of the Undistributed Middle, violating Rule 2.

(6) In standard categorical form this argument is

No writers of lewd and sensational articles are honest and decent citizens.
Some journalists are not writers of lewd and sensational articles.
Therefore, some journalists are honest and decent citizens.

This is an EOI-1 argument. This argument commits two fallacies--Exclusive Premisses and Drawing an Affirmative Conclusion from a Negative Premiss--violating both Rule 4 and Rule 5.

IV   (2)   The problem is how best to arrive at the valid moods in the first figure that have a particular conclusion. Although there may be several equally acceptable approaches, one might ought by now to seem natural to you is the one applied in chapter one to the brain teasers: arrive at the satisfactory by eliminating the unsatisfactory.

1. Keep in mind the distribution patterns of categorical propositions:

    a. Affirmative propositions have undistributed predicate terms.
    b. Negative propositions have distributed predicate terms.
    c. Universal propositions have distributed subject terms.
    d. Particular propositions have undistributed subject terms.

2. Recall the first figure

$$M - P$$
$$S - M$$
$$-----$$
$$S - P$$

3. Generate the 16 possible patterns for premisses. AA, AI, AE, AO, IA, II, IE, IO, EA, EI, EE, EO, OA, OI, OE, OO

4. Eliminate the unsatisfactory.

    a. IA, II, OA and OI all have a particular major and an affirmative minor. This means that both occurrences of the middle term are undistributed and that Rule 5 is violated. Thus these forms cannot occur in valid 1st figure syllogisms.

    b. AE, AO, IE and IO all have a negative premiss, so must have a negative conclusion. But all have affirmative major premisses, so the predi- cate term in those premisses must be undistrib- uted. This would mean that any negative conclusion would violate Rule 3. Thus these forms cannot occur in valid first-figure syllogisms.

    c. EE, EO, OE and OO would all commit the Fallacy of Exclusive Premisses, violating Rule 4. Thus these forms cannot occur in valid first-figure syllogisms.

    d. AA and EA arguments could not have a particular conclusion without violating Rule 6, thus they could not occur in a valid first-figure.

    e. An AII argument would be valid, but AIA would violate Rule 6 and AIE and AIO would both violate Rule 5.

    f. An EIO argument would be valid, but EIE would violate Rule 6 and EIA and EII would violate Rule 5.

Thus the only forms of syllogism which have a particular conclusion, are in the first figure, and are valid are AII and EIO.

(6)   Since Rule 2 requires that the middle term be distributed at least once, the middle term would have to be one of the twice-distributed terms. If the predicate term is distributed, then the subject term cannot be distributed. This means that the conclusion must be an O form. Since both the middle and the predicate terms are distributed, the major premiss must be an E. To avoid violating Rule 6, the minor premiss must be particular; to avoid violating rule 4, the minor premiss must be affirmative. But if the minor premiss is an I, then neither its subject nor its predicate term will be distributed, and that violates the original requirement that the middle term be distributed in both premisses. If the subject term were the other twice-distributed one, then both S and M would be distributed in the minor premiss. That means that the minor would be negative and Rule 5 would demand that the conclusion be negative. However, that would require the predicate term of the conclusion be distributed and that violates the assumption of only two terms being distributed. Therefore it is not possible to have a valid argument in which two and only two terms are each distributed twice.

CHAPTER SIX SUMMARY

I. Standard-form categorical arguments are composed of three propo-
    sitions: a major premiss, a minor premiss and a conclusion.

    A.   The major premiss contains the major term (predicate term of
         the conclusion) and the middle term.

    B.   The minor premiss contains the minor term (subject term of
         the conclusion) and the middle term.

    C.   The subject and predicate terms of the conclusion are defined
         as the minor and major terms, respectively, of the argument.

II. The mood of a standard-form categorical argument is the three
    letter sequence naming the major premiss, the minor premiss and
    the conclusion of the argument in that order.

III.The figure of a standard-form categorical syllogism is determined
    by the location of the middle term in the premisses.

    A.   First Figure: M–P
                               S–M
                               –––
                               S–P

    B.   Second Figure: P–M
                               S–M
                               –––
                               S–P

    C.   Third Figure: M–P
                               M–S
                               –––
                               S–P

    D.   Fourth Figure: P–M
                               M–S
                               –––
                               S–P

IV. Syllogistic forms are strictly analogous, that is, if one occur-
    rence of a form is valid (or invalid) then so will all other
    occurrences be valid (or invalid).

V. When the two-circle Venn Diagrams of the premisses of an argu-
    ment are transferred onto a three-circle Venn Diagram, the
    validity or invalidity of the argument can be seen by whether
    the two-circle diagram of the conclusion can be read from the
    three-circle one.

VI. There are six rules (or conditions) which valid standard-form
categorical syllogisms must meet.   They must:

   A. contain exactly three terms, each of which must be used
twice in exactly the same sense.

   B. have at least one distributed occurrence of the middle
term.

   C. have distributed occurrences in the premisses of all terms
distributed in the conclusion.

   D.   not have two negative premisses.
   E. have a negative conclusion when and only when there is a
negative premiss.

   F. have a particular premiss when and only when there is a
particular conclusion.

7

Arguments in Ordinary Language

7.1 Reducing the Number of Terms in a Syllogistic Argument

For the most part you have been working with arguments that were stated either in standard categorical form or something very close to it. The difficulty you will encounter in applying the knowledge you have gained about standard-form categorical syllogisms is that most "real-life" arguments do not appear in standard form. If you want to use the tools for evaluating standard-form categorical syllogisms, then you have to be able to translate the non-standard into the standard.

You have already been doing the simplest sort of translation, for example, in the exercises in part III of 6.4 of Copi. In those exercises, the propositions were in standard categorical form, but they were not in the "correct" order. The only thing required, then, to translate such arguments into standard form is to follow three simple steps:

1.   Identify the conclusion, its subject and predi-
        cate. Place it last.

2.   Identify the major premiss (with the conclusion's
        predicate term) and place it first.

3.   Check to see that the remaining proposition is the
        minor (with the conclusion's subject term) and
        place it second.

The second form of translation is little more complex than the re-ordering required in the first. In the attempt to avoid a child-ish or boring writing and speaking style, we all learn to use synonyms. But, strictly speaking, in a standard-form argument you couldn't use synonyms without being guilty of having a Four Term Fallacy, a violation of Rule 1. When synonymous terms occur in an argument, all that is required to translate it into standard form is to change one of each pair of synonymous terms to the other. It would thus be possible to translate what looks at first to be a Fallacy of Four Terms (with what seems to be as many as SIX terms) into a standard-form categorical syllogism. Professor Copi's example in section 7.1 involves three sets of synonymous terms: wealthy people and rich people, vagrants and tramps, lawyers and attorneys. By replacing the second term of each pair by the first, he obtains a standard-form categorical syllogism.

The third way in which you may have to translate elements of an argument to get to standard form seems more complex, but really is pretty straightforward. What you need to do is keep well in mind the valid immediate inferences which you learned in chapter 5. (If you want a quick refresher on them, you might look back at the summary of chapter 5.) The use of these inference forms is particularly desir-able when you encounter arguments which contain terms representing both a class and its complement.

While translating arguments into the standard form by these methods may not appear terribly complicated, you have to realize that it becomes more complex when you have to apply more than one of them at a time. It would be possible that you might have to translate an argument in all three ways in order to get it into standard form. For example, the argument

All canines are animals. Therefore all beagles are animals since no beagles are non-dogs.

requires three translations:

1.   The position of the clauses of the second sentence
        must be reversed in order to have the minor
        premiss and the conclusion in the correct order.

2.   One of the synonymous terms "dog" and "canine"
        must be replaced by the other.

3.   The minor premiss must be obverted to replace the
        term "non-dogs" by its complement "dogs."

Performing all three translations changes the original non-standard-
form argument into the standard-form one:

                    All dogs are animals.
                    All beagles are dogs.

                    All beagles are animals.

Of course, the particular translations that were made are not the
only ones that could have been used to change the original to a
standard form.   One alternative set of translations would have
yielded:

                    All non-animals are non-dogs.
                    No beagles are non-dogs.

                    No beagles are non-animals.

The first standard-form argument is an AAA-1, the second is an AEE-2,
but both are "correct" translations of the original argument and all
three are valid arguments.

    It is important that you realize that neither of the transla-
tions (nor any other legitimate one) is any more correct than any
other. What is important is for you to be able to select the methods
of translation that work most easily for you. That does mean, however, that the answers given here and by Professor Copi to the exercises following 7.1 may not be quite the same as the ones you work
out yourself. What you should be able to do, however, is to transform the FORM of your translation into the FORM given here or in
above Copi. For example, the two translations offered were AAA-1 and
AEE-2 forms, respectively. Their structures, (using S, M and P as
determined from the AAA-1 argument) then, are

        All M's are P's.   All non-P's are non-M's
        All S's are M's   No S's are non-M's.
        ----------------   -----------------------
        All S's are P's.   No S's are non-P's.

In either of the forms if you contrapose the major premiss and obvert
both the minor premiss and the conclusion, then will obtain the
other.

        (2) Some metals are rare and costly substances.
             All welder's materials are metals.

             Thus, some welder's materials are rare and costly
               materials.

    This "standardization" involved only obverting the minor pre-
miss. In translated form it is now an IAI-1 argument. By the rules
of chapter 6 it is an invalid form because its middle term never is
distributed: neither term is distributed in the I major and only the
minor term is distributed in the A minor.

Had you checked the argument by Venn Diagram, you would have had

Since the right-hand diagram allows the possibility that the individual that is both M and R might not be W also, the argument can be
seen to be invalid.

 (6) All material things are changeable things.
   All worldly goods are material things.

   Thus, all worldly goods are changeable things.

 Translating the original into this standard form necessitated
changing the order of the propositions and obverting both of the
premisses. It resulted in an AAA-1 form. AAA-1 arguments have the
middle term distributed in the first premiss and the minor term
distributed in both the second premiss and the conclusion. They
violate none of chapter 6's rules and are thus valid. Their Venn
Diagram check is

Since the only area left within S (in the three-circle diagram) is
also within P, the argument-form is valid.

7.2 Translating Categorical Propositions into Standard Form

 It would be too much to hope that the fairly simple and direct
translations discussed in section 7.1 would be the only ways in which
propositions would need to be altered. The many thousands of years
in which language has shifted to meet the changing demands of human
life have resulted in our natural languages being very complex and
subtle structures. Profesor Copi offers general ways in which more
subtle translations may be made. These, however, ought not be taken
so much as rules as they ought be considered rules of thumb. The

guiding principle in the more complex transformations that you need to learn to use will be your own common sense applied to the particular context of the argument.

First you need to understand singular propositions. They combine resemblances of both universal and particular propositions. If you say "Charles (son of Elizabeth II and Phillip Mountbatten) is the Prince of Wales," then you are asserting that all individuals who are in the (admittedly very small) class of Charleses who also have the appropriate parents are also in the class of Princes of Wales. But you are also asserting that such an individual does exist. Traditionally singular propositions have been handled as if they were universal propositions which happened to have extremely small, that is, one member, subject classes.

Professor Copi points out, however, that there is some risk in slavishly following this traditional approach. In the case of an argument which is composed of two singular premisses with the same individual as their subjects, you would be led to evaluate the argument to the conclusion that something shared the predicate properties of the premisses as being invalid. It would, in such a case, actually be valid. He shows that a similar difficulty occurs if you try to treat singular propositions as if they were particular, too.

His solution is quite simple: treat singular propositions as universal propositions with existential import. That approach works quite well when you use Venn Diagrams, but may cause you to feel a bit shakey about the six rules for standard-form categorical syllogisms. Since those rules were not stated for universals with existential import, you may be concerned about difficulties that might arise from the application of these rules to singular propositions. In practice they ought to give you no problems. Arguments which depend upon their resemblance to universals will check out satisfactorily. For example,

> No wrestler is a litterbug.
> Mark is a wrestler.
> ----------------------------
> Mark is not a litterbug.

when the singular minor premiss and conclusion are treated as universal propositions, becomes an EAE-1 argument. It has three unequivocated terms, a distributed middle term, terms distributed in the premisses which were distributed in the conclusion, only one negative premiss but a negative conclusion following from it, and (as an EAE) no particularity with which to be concerned. Violating none of the rules, it is valid.

Similarly, had the singular propositions in this argument been treated as if they were particular, the argument would have been seen to have been an EIO-1 form. This, too, would check against the rules as being valid.

The challenging cases result from the simultaneous use of two singular propositions as the premisses of an argument. Perhaps a closer look at a problematic argument will suggest a simple solution. Begin with an argument having two singular premisses:

> Morna is a straight-A student.
> Morna is a soccer player.
> ----------------------------
> Some soccer players are straight-A students.

Treating the premisses as universal propositions results in an AAI-3 form which is invalid by violating rule 6 (committing the Existential Fallacy); treating them as particular propostions results in an III-3 argument violates rule 2 and commits the Fallacy of the Undistributed

Middle. If you follow Professor Copi's advice to "...construe singular propositions as conjunctions of standard-form categorical propositions," then the argument becomes:

```
All M is S and some M is S.
All M is B and some M is B.
--------------------------
Some B's are S's.
```

But this, of ocurse, is NOT a standard-form categorical syllogism.
It turns out that what you need to do in such cases to arrive at a
standard-form categorical syllogism is to treat one of the premisses
as a universal proposition and the other as a particular one. Which
you select for each role makes no difference. You will obtain either
of the following arguments, both of which are valid:

```
All M is A.              Some M is S.
Some M is B.            All M is B.
-------------           -------------
Some B's are S's.       Some B's are S's.
```

   A second form of translation which is a bit simpler to handle
occurs when part of the argument is not actually in categorical form.
Specifically, statements are frequently made which amount to the same
thing as a categorical statement, but which have adjectives describing the subject in place of the categorical predicate. Translation in such cases usually involves nothing more than adding the noun
"things" to the predicate. Thus the proposition "no snakes are
slimey" translates into the standard-form categorical proposition "no
snakes are slimey things."

   Similarly, you will sometimes encounter statements which do not
use a form of the verb "to be" (which usually functions as the copula
of a categorical proposition). In such cases the best technique is
to move the concept expressed by the verb into the predicate term.
Thus, "some people study hard" would translate into "some people are
hard studiers" or "some people are individuals who study hard."

   To avoid the sort of subject-verb-object monotony of expression
that we frequently associate with first-grade reading texts, a writer
sometimes varies the order of the elements within his sentences.
This means that the standard-form categorical proposition "all men
are mortal" might be expressed as "men are all mortal," as "mortal
are all men," as "mortality is a property of all men," or several
other ways. When such a non-standardly-formed statement is made, its
translation is just the re-arrangement of its elements until you have
a standard-form proposition.

   Verbal variety also results in synonyms being used for the
standard quantity and quality indicators. "Every," "any," "each,"
and the like are clearly replacements for "all" and return to it
serves as translation. On some occasions, however, there is no
quantity indicator or at least nothing which obviously serves as one.
In such cases many people find it helpful to think up a situation in
which the quantity-lacking statement might have been used. Once that
is done, it usually is a fairly simple matter to decide whether the
intention would have been to speak universally or particularly. For
example, "the catcher is the most skilled position on a baseball
team" and "the catcher was voted Most Valuable Player in the game"
are such quantity-less statements. The first statement would likely
be said in an argument about the relative merits of the different
positions or about the greatest all-time baseball player. It clearly
does not mean to address the particular abilities of any one person
(who might have been atypical among his peers anyway). It seems
evident that it is meant to be an abstract general description of the
demands of that position. The scond statement would probably be used
in describing the performance of a particular individual on a parti-

cular occasion. Thus, putting statements into possible contexts seems a useful method of sorting out unstated quantities.

A commonly encountered variant of the universal quantity indicators is the exclusive indicator. "Only" and "none but" are the usually occurring forms. These exclusive usages are universal, but they reverse the order of the terms from the standard universal forms. Thus "all subjects are predicated" would be "only predicates are subjects." One of the most effective ways of insuring that you have the terms in the right order when translating from an exclusive to a categorical form is to test your translation using terms referring to classes the relationship between which is perfectly clear. A good example (unless there is a radical alteration of the Pope's position) might be "only women are nuns." Most people raised in a Western culture know that there are large numbers of women who are not nuns, but there are no male nuns. This checks against the translation of the known truth that only women are nuns into "all nuns are women."

Some statements are not categorically formed at all. In some cases they amount to the denial of categorically formed statements. When this occurs, you need to return to the square of opposition and reformulate them as the contradictory of that which they denied. Others require that you figure out what is meant, then express it as categorically as you can. In any event, the primary requirement is that you think carefully and try always to keep in mind what is MEANT by the original statement.

In Professor Copi's discussion of numerical or quasi-numerical quantity-indicators, he focuses upon the translation of so-called exceptive propositions. He explains how it is that such propositions actually express two propositions. In the case of the exceptive propositions what you find is a combination of assertion and denial. Thus the exceptive proposition "all students except those on probation are eligible to hold student office" contains the assertion "all non-probationary students ARE ELIGIBLE to hold student office" and the denial "NO probationary students ARE ELIGIBLE to hold student office." Similarly the exceptive proposition "nearly all philosophers enjoy a good joke" contains the assertion "some philosophers ENJOY a good joke" and the denial "some philosophers DO NOT ENJOY a good joke." Of course, in this latter case you actually have the additional information that the number who do enjoy a good joke is substantially larger than the number of those who don't, but there is no immediately useful way to express this categorically.

Since standard-form categorical syllogism arguments must have three and only three propositions, arguments in which the two propositions expressed by an exceptive proposition are stated will not be in standard form. To apply the standard-form tests, what you must do is write the argument multiple times, allowing all combinations of the elements of the exceptive propositions in the original premises to appear. If the conclusion of the original argument is an exceptive, then the argument is surely invalid for it would require a violation of the rules for valid syllogisms to allow both elements of the exceptive conclusion to be provable.

You ought now to be fully prepared to work the exercises following 7.2. Your answers should match or be translatable into the answers in Copi and here.

(2)   No orchids are fragrant things.

(6)   No non-Havana cigars are Ropo cigars, or, perhaps
      better, all Ropo cigars are real Havana cigars.

(11)   This one has several possibilities:
       All times when she sings are times of inspiration.
       All persons who hear her sing are people who are
           inspired by her singing.
       No person who hears her sing is a person who can
           remain uninspired.

(16)   All party regulars are supporters of any candidate of
       the Old Guard.

(21)   Some things which glitter are not things made of gold.

7.3   Uniform Translation

In trying to translate from statements which are quite different
from standard-form categorical statements, you may find it useful to
introduce some additional symbols to ease the translation.   In a
sense you have already done some of this sort of thing when you did
things like add "activities" to "all sports are dangerous" to get the
standard form "all sports are dangerous activities."   Professor Copi
wants to caution you that the introduction of such an auxiliary
symbol may require that you modify the remainder of the argument to
insure that you do not commit a Four Term Fallacy.   Thus if you
introduce time or place, for example, as clarifying parameters in one
part of an argument, you may be compelled to make a similar introduction in the other parts.   Consider this argument:

He never had been able to ask a girl of whom he was truly fond
for a date, so he never had sought her company for he adored her.

As it appears here it seems a plausible argument, but surely not a
categorical syllogism.   The occurrence of "never" does suggest a
universality of time, so the introduction of the parameter "times"
seems reasonable.   Doing that yields:

No times at which he had been truly fond of a specific girl
    were times at which he was able to ask her for a date.
All times at which he had known this specific girl were
    times at which he had been truly fond of her.

Therefore no times at which he had known this specific girl
    were times at which he was able to ask her for a date.

This is an EAE-1 argument whose form you can easily show to be valid.

Your answers to the exercises following 7.3 should resemble the
ones here and in Copi in meaning, if not in specific detail.

(2)   No times at which she goes to work are times at which
      she drives.

      Of course, being a E proposition this could have appeared
      in either obverted or converted form:

      No times at which she drives are times at which she
      goes to work, or

      All times at which she goes to work are times at which
      she does not drive.

(6)   All places at which she is are places at which she
      tries to sell life insurance.

II   (2) All predicables are things that come in contradictory
          pairs.
          No names are things that come in contradictory pairs.

          Therefore no names are predicables.

          This is an AEE-2 argument.   Its Venn Diagram check
          shows it to be valid.

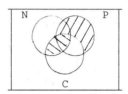

     (6) All acts of fanaticism are acts of vice.
          All acts of extremism are acts of fantaticism.

          Therefore all acts of extremism are acts of vice.

          This is an AAA-1 argument, which is a valid form.

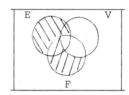

     (11)   No inebriated person is a dependable person.
               All alcoholicss are inebriated persons.

               Therefore no alcoholic is a dependable person.

               This is an EAE-1 argument and, although Alcoholics
               Anonymous would surely dispute the truth of its
               premises and conclusion, it is valid.

(16) All people are thinkers.
      All bridge players are people.

      Therefore all bridge players are thinkers.

      This is an AAA-1 argument. Its Venn Diagram will look
        just likethe one for exercise 2 above, proving it
        valid.

(21) All acts of medical practice are uses of medical theory
      All performances of surgery are acts of medical
        practice

      Therefore all performances of surgery are uses of
        medical theory.

      This, like exercises 2 and 16, is an AAA-1 argument and
        has been shown to be valid.

(26) All conference title games are good games.
      All tomorrow's game is a conference title game.

      Therefore all tomorrow's game is a good game.

      This, too, is an AAA-1 valid argument. Note that
      it required a fairly substantial translation to
      get it into standard form: the major premiss
      required use of synyony and obversion; the minor
      and conclusion are singular propositions, used
      here in their quasi- universal form.

(31) All cases of disease are occurrences to which the
        methods of epidemiology can usefully be applied.
      All cases of drug abuse are cases of disease.

      Therefore all cases of drug abuse are occurrences to
        which the methods of epidemiology can usefully be
        applied.

      This, too, is an AAA-1 valid argument.

(36)   All express trains are trains that do not stop at
       this station.
       All trains which, relative to the current time, were
       the last one to pass this station are trains that
       do not stop at this station.

       Therefore all trains which, relative to the current
       time, were the last ones to pass this station are
       express trains.

       Note the very awkward circumlocution used to
       change the singular minor premiss and conclusion
       into a universal-appearing form.   Note also the
       occurrence of "not" in the middle term; it indi-
       cates that the class being used is the complement
       of the class of trains stopping at the station,
       but it does not make the premisses negative.
       This argument is an AAA-2 form and the following
       Venn Diagrams show that it is invalid.

(41)   All times at which a great deal of money is at stake
       are times at which the competition is stiff.
       The current time is one at which there is a great deal
       of money at stake.

       Therefore the current time is a time at which competi-
       tion is stiff.

       This is another AAA-1 valid argument.

(46)   No sane witness is a person who incriminates himself.
       Some witnesses are persons who incriminate themselves.

       Therefore some witnesses are not sane witnesses.

       This is an EIO-2 argument.   The VennDiagram below
       proves it is valid.

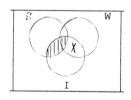

7.4   Enthymemes

If you think back to chapter one, section two (in which the concepts of premiss and conclusion were introduced), you will recall that some arguments were shown to have premisses or a conclusion that were not stated. When the context is clear or when the missing proposition seems obvious, this absence of a part of an argument can occur with categorical syllogisms, too. Such categorical arguments with "understood" elements are called enthymemes. Tradition divided enthymematic categorical syllogisms according to which proposition is unstated: first-order enthymemes are missing their major premiss, second-order ones are missing their minor premiss, and third-order enthymemes have their conclusion unstated.

Of course, if you are trying to evaluate a categorical syllogism which is offered in enthymeenatic form, you will have to add to what is given what you take to have been assumed. There is a hazard, however, in making such an addition to what an arguer has offered: he may accept no rsponsibility for what you add to his argument. And, if you can show that the proposition that you have added is necessary in order to make his argumenet valid, he must accept it or reject his own argument as invalid. Most crushing, obviously, would be showing that NO ADDED PROPOSITION would result in a valid argument. That, however, would require a fairly complex proof, eliminating quite a number of possibilities.

Ultimately, when treating an argument as an enthuymene, you ought to provide the proposition which best serves the purpose of making the argument plausible and valid. In general, deciding what the missing element ought to be is quite simple. Since you already have two of the propositions in the argument, you can determine which proposition is missing: If you have a first-order enthymene, then you can look to the conclusion to determine the predicate term and the minor premiss to identify the middle term. Once they are identi-fied, there are only eight possible candidates for the missing major premiss: the order M-P as an A, E, I, or O proposition or the order P-M as one of those four-forms. If one of those is not obviously the needed major premiss, you can always resort to an exhaustive check of each of them inserted into the argument. Similarly you can work out one of the third order. An arguer who uses enthymematic arguments must accept the risk of having a proposition other than the one he intended to the argument, but he ought not have to contend with additions which seek to invalidate his argument.

In the exercises following 7.4, you should indicate clearly the proposition which you add to the argument as you present the argument in standard form.

(2)   All things which are ever [always] in motion are
            immortal things.
        [All souls are things which are ever in motion.]

        Therefore all souls are immortal things.

        The added minor premiss is stated in brackets,
        indicating that it is not a stated part of the
        original argument. Since the minor premiss is the
        one assumed, the argument is a second-order enthy-
        meme. The added premiss is consistent with Pla-
        tonic philosophy and completes the argument as an
        AAA-1 valid form argument.

(6)   All successful people are well-groomed.
        Leslie Cole is well-groomed.

        [Therefore Leslie Cole is a successful person.]

This is an invalid AAA-2 argument. (See the
Venn Diagram below for proof.) You may ask why,
when I just argued for why you should make an
argument valid if possible, I allowed the added
conclusion not to do so. The answer is that there
is no standard-form categorical proposition that
can be inferred from the union of the two given
premises. And how did I know they were premises?
The argument as given said "...and we know what
that implies..." That is a clear sign that it is
the conclusion that is omitted. And none of the
eight propositions that could have ben formed from
the people would follow validly from the given
premisses. This seems most likely the one intended, violates the second rule for syllogisms and
commits the Fallacy of the Undistributed Middle.

(11)   All physicians are college graduates.
       [All members of the AMA are physicians.]

       Therefore all memmbers of the AMA are college graduates

The added minor converts this second-order enthymene into a valid AAA-1 argument. Although one
would have to check the AMA's membership records
to determine the truth of the added minor premiss,
it does at least seem plausible.

(16)   [All families with a telephone are families with their
           name listed in the telephone book.]
       The Adamsons are a family with their name not listed in
           in the telephone book.

       Therefore the Adamsons are a family without a
           telephone.

Treating the given singular minor premiss of this
first-order enthumene as a universal proposition
suggests the major premiss which has been added.
The form resulting in an AEE-2 which the following
Venn Diagram shows is valid.

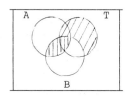

(21)   No sense knowledge is immaterial knowledge.
       Some knowledge that we possess is immaterial
         knowledge.

       [Therefore some knowledge that we possess is not
         sense knowledge.]

       The "...therefore, etc." in the quotation from
       Scotus is a clear indicator that the missing pro-
       position is the conclusion, making this a third-
       order enthymene. The EIO argument form is the
       only one valid in all four figures (due to the
       convertability of both premisses). You might note
       that an alternate conclusion, some things that
       are not sense knowledge are knowledge that we
       possess, would also have resulted in a valid ar-
       gument. It, however, would have required transla-
       tion of the first premiss by obversion to avoid
       violating rules 1 and 5. This argument, an EIO-
       2, is shown to be valid by the following Venn
       Diagram.

(26)   [All species which tend to increase at a greater rate
         than their means of subsistence are occasionally
         subject to a severe struggle for their existence.]
       HOMO SAPIENS is a species which tends to increase at
         a greater rate than its means of subsistence.

       Therefore HOMO SAPIENS is occasionally subject to a
         severe struggle for its existence.

       The needed major premiss for this first-order
       enthymene seems both consistent with Darwinian

theory and unobjectionable. The resulting AAA-1
argument is, as usual, valid.

(31)   All times at which the Democrats were successful
        in politics were times in which they could use
        the issues of high employment, high interest
        rates and high inflation against their oppo-
        nents.
    No current time is one in which they can use those
        issues against their opponents.

    [Therefore no current time is one in which the
        Democrats are successful.]

This third-order enthymeme requires the stated
conclusion to form an AEE-2 valid syllogism.
Since the context was Fraser's summation of Carter's problems, the addition of such a conclusion
seems quite reasonable. The Venn Diagram demonstrates the validity of the argument.

7.5   Sorites

You have seen that arguments may occur with parts missing, with
apparently multiple terms, with sentence forms which diverge widely
from standard categorical forms, and with more information than is
actually used in reaching their conclusions. It ought not, therefore, seem too strange to encounter arguments which appear to be
basically syllogistic, but which have too many premises. In the
case of enthymematic arguments it was your responsibility to provide
the missing proposition. In a chain argument or sorites, (the term
[like "deer"] is both singular and plural), it will not be required
that you eliminate excess premisses. If there were spare premisses,
ones which were unneeded in the inference, you could, of coursee,
discard them, but a sorites does not have more premisses than strict
categorical form allows simply by the addition of irrelevancies. A
sorites is, in a sense, an abbreviation for a string of categorical
syllogisms. From two premisses you draw a conclusion. That conclusion is then used as a premiss either with another of the given
premisses or with another conclusion-used-as-premiss derived from
different premisses. This using-conclusions-as-premisses continues
until you arrive at the overall conclusion of the argument.

If you looked at the subject and predicate terms of the conclusion of a sorites as the minor and major terms of the sorites, then
all of the other terms in it would be middle terms. Expressed in a
skeletal way a sorites might look like:

```
All M' is P.
All M'' is M'.
All M''' is M''.
All S is M'''.
--------------
All S is P.
```

Evaluation of a sorites is straightforward: you break the chain into
its component standard-form categorical syllogisms and evaluate each
of them. If all the component syllogisms of a sorites are valid,
then it is valid; if there is at least one of these syllogisms that
is invalid, then the sorites is invalid. (Valdity and invalidity are
in a way like being dead or pregnant: there is no such thing as "a
little bit.") When the sorites above is broken into its constitutent
syllogisms you have

```
All M' is P.
All M'' is M'.
------------
All M'' is P.

All M'' is P.
All M''' is M''.
-------------
All M''' is P.

All M''' is P.
All S is M'''.
------------
All S is P.
```

In this case, since all the arguments are instances of the valid
AAA-1 form, this sorites is valid.

     In terms of evaluation of arguments, then, sorites add no new
difficulties. Since the intermediate conclusions are not stated,
sorites constitute a kind of third-order enthymeme. Since they can
be broken down into standard-form categorical syllogisms, they need
no new evaluation techniques. All they are likely to do is require a
bit more patience. You ought now to try your patience in working the
exercises following 7.5. The annswers here and in Copi should serve
as a check on your approach.

I   (2)   (1') All experienced persons are competent persons.
           (3') No competent person is always blundering.
           (2') Jenkins is always blundering.

                 Jenkins is not an experienced person.

     This breaks down into two syllogisms:

(a) No competent person is   >(b) No experienced persons are
     always blundering.   always blundering
     All experienced persons   Jenkins is always
     are competent persons.   blundering.
     ----------------------   ----------------------
     No experienced persons are   Jenkins is not an
     always blundering.   experienced person.

     The first is an EAE-1 form and the second is an EAE-2. The Venn
Diagrams below show that both are valid forms.

(a)

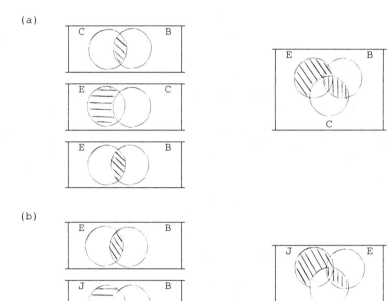

(b)

II   (2)   The standard-form sorites based upon these premisses
            is

            (3') No nice things are wholesome things.
            (1') All puddings are nice things.
            (2') This dish is a pudding.

                 [This dish is not a wholesome thing.]

            Its component syllogisms are

(a)   No nice things are   (b) No puddings are
        wholesome things.   wholesome things.
      All puddings are   This dish is a pudding
        nice things.   ----------------------
      -------------------   This dish is not a
      No puddings are   wholesome thing.
        wholesome things.

            They are both EAE-1 argument-forms and the Venn
            Diagram on the next page shows that they are both
            valid.

(a/b)

7.6   Disjunctive and Hypothetical Syllogisms

The next level of complexity beyond the categorical syllogism in the study of arguments will be arguments whose component parts are not categories but propositions.   More extensive consideration of such arguments will take place in chapter 8, but Professor Copi chooses to introduce two of the simplest propositional arguments (for so they are called) in this section and a third in 7.7.

One common way you have encountered for compounding propositions is by alternating them, that is, by joining them with the word "or." Such a compound proposition is called a disjunction or an alternation.   A very simple form of argument based upon elimination uses such a disjunction.   Traditionally an argument with the form called a disjunctive syllogism is

        Proposition 1 or Proposition 2.
        It is not the case that Proposition 1.

        Therefore Proposition 2.

It is a syllogism because it contains exactly two premises and one conclusion; it is disjunctive because its first premise is a disjunction.   This is the form of argument that Sherlock Holmes usually used when he told Watson he had deduced something.   In fact, on numerous occasions Holmes told Watson that if you eliminate all of the possible alternatives except one then that one, no matter how unlikely it seems, is the answer.

It is important to take care to follow the pattern shown above quite faithfully.   As Professor Copi points out, there do exist arguments which resemble this form but which are invalid.   Most common of these is one that argues:

        Proposition 1 or Proposition 2.
        It is the case that Proposition 1.

        Therefore it is not the case that Proposition 2.

Such an argument would only be satisfactory if we had the additional information that the truths expressed by Propositions 1 and 2 were somehow exclusive: that the truth of the one entailed the falsity of the other.   Since we do not have such information for disjunctions in general or this one in particular, this second argument-form is not valid.

The second type of propositional argument which Professor Copi introduces in this section may actually be broken down into three propositional argument-forms.   All three are based upon the compound proposition involving the conditional or hypothetical relationship: if Proposition 1 then Proposition 2. The form, which traditionally is called a hypothetiical sylllogism, Professor Copi calls a pure hypothetical syllogism. It is pure because all three compound propositions in it (two premisses and a conclusion) assert a conditional relation between their respective elements. If you are familiar with the mathematical concept of transitivity, then you will see that the pure hypothetical syllogism is merely the assertion of the transitive nature of the if-then relationship:

> If Proposition 1 then Proposition 2.
> If Proposition 2 then Proposition 3.
> ------------------------------------
> If Proposition 1 then Proposition 3.

On some occasions this sort of argument has been called the "logical domino theory." Just as, with properly aligned dominos, pushing over the first sets off a chain reaction that does not stop until the last has fallen, evidence for the first proposition in a pure hypothetical carries the inference on until the last is also supported.

Professor Copi identifies mixed hypothetical syllogisms as mixed because they assert a hypothetical relationship only in one premiss. Their other premiss either asserts the proposition in the if-part of the conditional or denies the proposition in the then-part of it. The mixed hypothetical syllogism, then, has two possible forms:

> If Proposition 1 then   If Proposition 1 then
>   Proposition 2.   Proposition 2.
> Proposition 1 is true.   Proposition 2 is false.
> ----------------------   -----------------------
> Proposition 2 is true.   Proposition 1 is false.

The left-hand version traditionally has been called MODUS PONENS; the right-hand one MODUS TOLLENS.

Each of these is often confused with an invalid argument-form which resembles it. These confusions are traditionally identified as the Fallacies of the Denial of the Antecedent and of the Affirmation of the Consequent. Those names make little sense if you do not recall that the if-part of a conditional statement is called the antecedent and the then-part is called the consequent. If you exchange the words "true" and "false" in the MODUS PONENS and MODUS TOLLENS argument-forms, then you have these fallacies:

> If Proposition 1 then   If Proposition 1 then
>   Proposition 2.   Proposition 2.
> Proposition 1 is false.   Proposition 2 is true.
> ----------------------   -----------------------
> Proposition 2 is false.   Proposition 1 is true.

One of the easiest ways to see that these fallacies really are unsatisfactory is to look at actual arguments following their form:

> If you are the result of   If you killed him then
>   an Immaculate Conception,   Abraham Lincoln is dead.
>   then you were born.   Abraham Lincoln is
> You were not the result of   dead.
>   an Immaculate Conception.   ------------------------
> --------------------------   Thus you killed him.
> Thus you were not born.

The premisses of both arguments seem unquestionably satisfactory, but the left-hand conclusion would surely come as a surprise to your mother and the right-hand one as a shock to a lot of American historians.

In working the exercises following 7.6 all you need to do to determine validity is to remember that disjunctive and hypothetical syllogisms that EXACTLY match the stipulated forms are valid, ones that do not are likely invalid.

(2)   This is a mixed hypothetical syllogism of the MODUS TOLLENS type. Re-written in standard form it is

If I have any more to do with that operation, then I'd have to lie to the Ambassador.
I can't lie to the Ambassador.

Thus I can't have any more to do with that operataion.

Since it is an exact match for the MODUS TOLLENS form, this is a valid argument.

(6)   This is a disjunctive syllogism in standard form. Since it exactly matches the stipulated form, it is valid.

(11)   This is an exact match for the mixed hypothetical syllogism MODUS TOLLENS pattern. THerefore it is valid.

(16)   This is a mixed hypothetical syllogism, but does not match either of the valid patterns. Instead it follows the form of the Fallacy of the Affirmation of the Consequent and is thus invalid.

(21)   This, too, is a mixed hypothetical syllogism of the MODUS TOLLENS form. Re-written in standard for it is

If mankind had understood him, then they would surelyhave built noble temples andaltars, and offered solemn sacrifices in his honor.
Mankind has not done such building and offering.

Thus mankind did not understand him.

Following a valid pattern, this is a valid argument.

(26)   This strictly follows the valid disjunctive syllogism form, thus is itself valid.

(31)   Once you have removed the explanatory material about astronomy and why it is not psychology, you are left with the argument:

If number were an idea, then arithmetic would be psychology.
Arithmetic is not psychology.

Therefore number is not an idea.

Since this matches the mixed hypothetical syllogism MODUS TOLLENS pattern, it is a valid argument.

(36)   This requires somewhat more sophisticated re-writing than any of the other arguments discussed this far.   A helpful technique for figuring out how the propo- sitions in the hypothetical clause ("you cannot have a general economic recovery without housing doing reasonably well....") is to substitute propositions of whose

relationship you are certain. In this case a
useful pair are "you can make an omelet" and "you
break eggs." We know that if you make an omelet
then you must have broken eggs (or had someone
break them for you) and we also know that it is
not the case that if you break eggs you will make
an omelet (for you may be baking a cake). Look
at the two compound propositions obtained by substituting these for the original propositions:

You cannot make an omelet without breaking an egg.
You cannot break an egg without an omelet being
  made.

Clearly the former is plausible while the latter
is ridiculous. That suggests that the correct
form for the argument given in this exercise is

If there is a general economic recovery, then
    housing will do reasonably well.
Housing will not do reasonably well.

Thus there will not be a general economic recovery.

This is another mixed hypothetical syllogism of
the MODUS TOLLENS form, thus is valid.

7.7   The Dilemma

Professor Copi's explanation of the dilemma is both detailed and
clear. You probably feel little need for any additional discussion
of how a dilemma operates or of how you might grapple with a dilemma
whose conclusion you wished to reject. There are, however, a few
details that may be of some interest.

The name "dilemma" derives from the Greek prefix "di-" meaning
"two" and the Greek word "lemma" which meant in its logical usage
"premiss." The "two-premiss-ness" refers not to the two premisses of
the argument but to the two conditional "premisses" which are conjoined in this form of argument.

A defining characteristic of categorical syllogisms was that
they contained exactly three terms. Analogously, a defining characteristic of full-blown dilemmas is that they contain four propositions. For the sake of brevity, I will indicate them as P-1, P-2, P-
3, and P-4 in this discussion. The basic, or root, form of the
dilemma. Structurally it looks like a sort of alternative MODUS
PONENS argument:

If P-1 then P-2, and if P-3 then P-4.
Either P-1 or P-3.

Therefore either P-2 or P-4.

The form is obviously satisfactory because of the MODUS PONENS buried
within it. Both the conditional statements are asserted, so if P-1
is true then P-2 would follow and if P-3 is true then P-4 would
follow. But you also know that either P-1 or P-3 is the case, so P-2
or P-4 (and perhaps both) must be the case.

Since the complex constructive dilemma is analogous, loosely, to
MODUS PONENS, you might suspect that there should be a dilemma form
that bears a similar loose analogy to MODUS TOLLENS. Your suspicions
are well-grounded. The argument is called a COMPLEX DESTRUCTIVE
DILEMMA and has the form:

```
If P-1 then P-2, and if P-3 then P-4.
Either P-2 is false or P-4 is false.
---------------------------------
Thus either P-1 is false or P-3 is false.
```

For reasons similar to those given in support of the complex constructive dilemma, this, too, is a valid argument-form.

Usually when there is a complex form of something there is also a simple form of it. This is the case with both of these dilemma forms. The simple (or degenerate) dilemma forms involve only three propositions, both conditionals sharing the same consequent in the constructive form or antecedent in the destructive one. The simple constructive dilemma is

```
If P-1 then P-2, and if P-3 then P-2.
Either P-1 or P-3.
-----------------------------------
Therefore P-2.
```

The simple destructive dilemma is

```
If P-1 then P-2, and if P-1 then P-3.
Either P-2 is false or P-3 is false.
-----------------------------------
Therefore P-1 is false.
```

The one thing that a good debater loves to find in a dilemma is that the disjuctive premiss is the alternation of a proposition and its denial. That insures that someone trying to counter his argument has no chance of "slipping between the horns of the dilemma," for there is no third option.

One classic use of a dilemma was offered at the peak of the war in Vietnam by Republican Senator George Aiken of Vermont. He had been a early opponent of that conflict, was convinced that the United states needed to withdraw from it quickly, and argued:

> If we win the conflict in Vietnam then we will lose face because we will appear to be such bullies-- "First-rate industrial power smashes tenth-rate agrarian power"), but if we lose the conflict in Vietnam then we will lose face (because we will appear ineffectual--"First-rate industrial power smashed by tenth-rate agrarian one"). We must win or lose the conflict in Vietnam. Thus we are doomed to a loss of face.

Of course, he wanted to take the conclusion as a premiss and go one step further: if we are doomed to a loss of face anyway, then we might as well just get out without paying any attention to what anyone else says. His whole argument is subject to the sorts of criticisms and oppositions that Professor Copi suggests. You might want to try your hand at arguing against Aiken's dilemma.

Whether you chose to try to refute Aiken or not, you should work the exercises following 7.7, checking your efforts here and in Copi AFTER you do the exercises.

(2)   You could probably mount an effective argument for slipping between the horns of this dilemma. It certainly would be plausible to claim that Circuit Courts can be more or less effective both in general and in specific cases. Being useful is subject to a broad spectrum of values, from indispensable to scarcely worth the trouble.
       The horns of this dilemma are vulnerable, too. It could prove quite useful to a State to deny

all the rights guaranteed in the Bill of Rights. That utility would almost surely not justify abolition of the Bill of Rights. And something's not being useful is surely not justification for its abolition. It would be very difficult to show much practical function in newborn infants, but the human race would find itself in a rather awkward position if newborn infants were banned for a century or so. (That awkward situation is frequently called extinction.)

Lincoln's dilemma, then, certainly is open to refutation, although a conter-dilemma either from the elements of this one or from other sources seems not to be a terribly fruitful approach.

(6)   Convincing arguments could be offered for why you could slip between the horns (starting with the arguments offered by Profesor Copi against exercise 5). It is also possible to grapple with either horn. An argument can be offered as deductive which turns out to be invalid but which, had it been considered as an INDUCTIVE argument, might have had significant value.   The second horn may be rejected because there may be, for example, psychological value in bringing into focus relationships which were already basically known. Refuting counter-dilemmas in this case (having a single-proposition conclusion) might also prove valuable.

(11) There seems to be rather a significant gap between living extravagantly and living modestly, so these horns ought to be fairly easy to slip between. Each horn has an obvious refuting argument. If you live extravagantly you may well have nothing left to contri- bute; if you live modestly you may well have had nothing with which to have lived more expansively. Counter-dilemmas would probably result in a conclusion which only appeared to refute this conclusion, actually being compatible with it.

(16) A good case can be made for claiming that this is not a dilemma in any of the sense of the term that have been discussed either in this Study Guide or in Copi. This argument's form actually is

        If P-1, then either P-2 or P-3.
        Both P-2 and P-3 are false.

        Thus P-1 must be false.

As an argument, this is valid, but calling it a dilemma is certainly questionable. There are, however, several plausible refutations that one might offer for it. First, it is reasonable to suggest that there is another motion-option: from one place to another. Second, depending upon how broadly you read being "...in the place where it is..." it surely is possible to move there, as when you rock in a rocking chair. And third, given a broad view of interactions (perhaps a sort of radical realtivism) there may be no place which really counts as a place "...where it [the moving object] is not..." Since it is doubtful that this ought to be considered a dilemma at all, seeking a counter-dilemma seems pointless.

(21)   Only a devout Muslim would see the alternatives as
        exhaustive and exclusive.   To the rest of the
        world slipping between the horns by claiming that
        there are many things which are not in the Koran
        but which also do not disagree with it (addres-
        sing, for example, issues and topics which it does
        not discuss). But the horns are vulnerable too.
        Since Islam does not sanction any translation of
        the Koran from Arabic, there may be necessity of
        repeating what is in it for all of us who do not
        read Arabic and who have little facility with
        languages.   To a non- Muslim there probably is
        nothing at all pernicious about differing with the
        Koran.   A counter-dilemma constructed from the
        elements of this argument would as in so many of
        the other exercises, not refute the conclusion of
        the stated dilemma.

CHAPTER SEVEN SUMMARY

I. Application of testing techniques for standard-form categorical syllogisms requires translation of non-standard arguments into standard forms.

    A. Translation may be by re-ordering propositions.

    B. Translation may be by using one term for synonyms.

    C. Translation may be by valid immediate categorical inference.

II. Some translations into standard form require sophisticated understanding of the meaning of the stated propositions.

    A. Singular propositions combine characteristics of both universal and particular propositions.

        1. They are universal when the individual is treated as a unit-class (class with one member).

        2. They are particular in that they have existential import.

    B. Properties delineated by adjectives need to be associated with neutral nouns (like "things") when translating to standard form.

    C. Verbs other than forms of "to be" need to be absorbed into the predicate when translating to standard form.

    D. Internal verbal order may have to be rearranged.

    E. Non-standard quantity-indicators (like "every") must be replaced by standard ones.

    F. Exclusive propositions (indicated by words like "only" and "none but") are translatted with their terms in the opposite order from the way they are given.

    G. Common sense should rule translation of radically non-categorically-formed propositions.

    H. Exceptive propositions should be treated as the conjunction of their assertations.

III. Time and place parameters may be introduced to maintain a uniformity of categorical expression.

IV. Arguments with unstated premisses or conclusion are called enthymemes.

    A. An enthymeme is first-, second-, or third-order depending upon whether the major premiss, the minor premiss or the conclusion is assumed.

    B. If at all possible, the unstated proposition which is added to the argument as given ought to serve to make the argument valid.

V.   A chain argument of categorical propositions is called a sorites.

   A.   Sorites are evaluated by being broken down into a series of categorical syllogisms.

   B.   Sorites are valid if and only if every categorical syllogism in their separate form is valid.

VI.   Syllogisms occur in non-categorical forms.

   A.   A disjunctive syllogism argues for one of a pair of alternatives based upon the denial of the other.

   B.   A hypothetical syllogism is based upon one or two conditional (if-then) propositions.

      1.   A pure hypothetical syllogism asserts two conditional premisses linked to show transitivity.
      2.   A mixed hypothetical syllogism relates a conditional proposition with a simple one.

         a.   MODUS PONENS derives the consequent of the conditional by asserting the conditional and its antecedent.

         b.   MODUS TOLLENS derives denying the antecedent of a conditional by asserting the conditional and the denial of its consequent.

VII.   The dilemma mixes conditional and disjunctive propositions to derive a disjunctive (usually) conclusion.

   A.   Dilemmas occur in constructive and destructive forms, both simply and complexly.

   B.   There are multiple ways of attacking a dilemma.

      1.   The alternative premiss may be shown not to be exhaustive. (Slipping between the horns.)

      2.   The conditional propositions may be shown not to be the case. (Grappling with the horn.)

      3.   A counter-dilemma may be offered, supporting the opposite of the conclusion.

8

Symbolic Logic

8.1   The Value of Special Symbols

Most of us have seen the advertisement in magazines that reads:
"F U Cn Rd Ths, U Cn B Mkng Bg Mny!" (In case you find it doesn't
make sense to you, it reads: "If you can read this, you can be
making big money." In general it involves dropping vowels and un-
sounded letters.) It is, of course, intended to persuade you to
enroll in the advertiser's course in rapid writing. This method, or
the more famous Gregg and Pitman methods of shorthand, are simply
sets of conventional abbreviations. Lots of people find that, in
areas where they have to record the same thing frequently, it is very
helpful to employ such "shorthand" techniques. Common examples include Rd., Ave., Feb., etc. (Note that even the last is also an
abbreviation.) Some abbreviations are ambiguous, such as St., which
means "street" in some contexts and "saint" in others. In any event,
we all recognize the value of such notations. If it were possible,
we would appreciate being able to abbreviate much of what we write.
The use of symbolic logic can provide some of that effect.

There is an additional problem that natural languages, that is,
ones which men developed through use, seem to share: they all tend
to be ambiguous, awkward and inconsistenet. English, perhaps as a
result of the checkered political history of the British Isles, seems
to be particularly blessed (or cursed) with such problems. This is
not to say that that is always a problem; in some areas each of the
natural languages is quite precise, and sometimes imprecision is
desirable. It is, of course, the "mushiness" of the language that
allows for its poetry, as was discussed in chapter 2. It has been
the drive to "clean up" languages that has led men to the development
of such artificial languages as Interlingua and Esperanto. In them
the attempt is made to remove the ambiguities, to eliminate the
inconsistencies, in short to generate a "logically" appropriate language. Such languages have precise grammars and vocabularies, so
that there are no irregular verbs, no homonyms, and no exceptions to
the rules. The problem that they encounter, beside the natural
resistence of humanity to trade in their old ways for new ones, is
that by eliminating the ability of the language to stretch and twist,
you also limit the breadth and depth of communication that is possible. When everything is drawn up into compartments, you find that
the things that seem to rest on the lines are very discomforting.

The adaptation of a logical set of symbols to be used to represent any major segment of our verbal arguments will have to encounter
the same problem, for it all really boils down to one thing--we have
to reach some balance between the detailed acccuracy of our artificial language (its ability to mirror our natural language) and the
usefulness of having it be artificial (its saving our efforts in
using it). If the artificial language does a really good job of
handling everything that we can handle in English, then it is likely
very nearly as complex as the natural language with which we started.
If that is the case then we will probably waste more time shifting
back and forth between the artificial language and the natural one
than if we used to--the natural one. If on the other hand, the
artificial one is sufficiently removed from the natural one that we
can really operate efficiently in it, it will likely be very difficult to make the translations from one to the other. If we have to
spend all of our time figuring out whether or not the artificial
language is really expressing meaning enough like the natural one to
make the effort worth our while, then the time lost again makes it
likely that we are better off with the natural language.

It may be, however, that IF we go into the use of a very efficient artificial language with our eyes wide open--knowing what its
shortcomings are--then we will be willing to accept the discrepancies
between the two. If we find that we save more time using the symbols
than we spend worrying about how accurately our symbols represent the
natural arguments, then we have a net saving. The more efficient the
symbolic system is, while still approximating the natural one, the
more useful it becomes. It is such a highly useful system that
Profesor Copi presents in Chapter 8.

8.2   The Symbols for Conjunction, Negation, and Disjunction

The logic which is introduced in Chapter 8 is called by several
names--propositional logic, the propositional calculus, sentential
logic, the logic of statements, and several others. Those names are
a result of the several ways logicians refer to the elements which
serve as the building blocks of the logic. No matter what you call
those component elements, they are representative of the sort of
thing that we express in simple declarative sentences like "it is
raining." The reason for the multitude of names is that logicians
cannot quite agree about those things "are," if indeed they are
anything. "It is raining" and "the rain is falling" are clearly
different sentences, but do seem to "say the same thing." It is that
property of "saying the same thing" that some logicians refer to as
"expressing the same proposition." That also allows the sentence (in
English) "it is raining" and the sentence (in German) "es regnet" to
be treated identically. The normal clue--whether you opt for calling
them sentences, statements or propositions--is that they are the sort
of thing that can be said to be true or false.

It is that property of being true of false that makes this sort
of statement useful in a system of logic. There are relationships in
which statements can occur, be compounded, or be analyzed largely in
terms of the relationships between the truth or falsity of the component statements. When the truth or falsity (called the TRUTH VALUE)
of a component statement can be discovered solely as a product of the
truth values of its component statements, that compound is said to be
a TRUTH-FUNCTIONAL compound. The logic of statements (or propositional calculus, etc.), then, is the study of statements, truth-
functional connectives, and how to work with them.

The most obvious of the truth-functional connectives really
isn't a connective at all, it's an operator. It doesn't hook two
statements together; it changes the value of one statement. Most
frequently it is called NEGATION. Its simplest occurrence in English
is the insertion into a statement of the word "not." Thus "it is
raining" becomes "it is not raining." The nice thing about negation
is its simplicity: a negation precisely denies what it negates.
Thus, if any statement is true, its negation is false; if a statement
is false, its negation is true. To represent this relationship, two
things are necessary: a symbolic representation of the statement and
a symbol for negation. In general logicians have agreed to use the
lower case letters "p," "q," "r," "s," and so on to serve as
VARIABLES standing for some statement or other. Copi uses upper case
letters which have some sort of connection to what is said as symbols
representing actual statements. The symbol used to represent the
operation of negating is the tilde or curl (~). It has been
suggested that you arrive at it if you try to write a capital N as a
single stroke while trying to do it with ever-increasing speed. Such
a series might look like this:

(Other systems of logical notation [and there are several] will represent negation as an apostrophe [p's], a dash [-p], a bar [p], or a prefixed capital N [Np].) One of the nicest things about the use of such symbols is that they can be fitted into a table that makes all of the relationships quite clear and easy to work with. The table (called a TRUTH TABLE) for negation is

P	~ P
T	F
F	T

You read across the table. Thus, when p is T (true), ~ p is F (false); when p is F, ~ p is T. Copi says that this table may be regarded as a definition of the negation operation; actually it MUST be regarded as such, at least for logic as it is normally done. (This defining characteristic of the truth tables doesn't seem too important for the curl, but will be quite important later.)

In addition to "not," the curl may be used to stand for any of the many words and phrases that indicate the operation of negation: "It is false that ...," "...is false," "...is not the case," and any of the compounding prefixes such as "il-," "un-," or "dis-." These prefixes are particularly difficult because you have to be very careful to insure that they are really functioning as a "not" would; that is, that they are denying what would be asserted if they were dropped. Thus, the statement "John is immoral" is not the same as "John is not moral" (and cannot be represented as ~ J) because there is a third option--John may be amoral, which is neither moral nor immoral. On the other hand "handcuffs were unnecessary," can be read as being the same as "handcuffs were not necessary," and both could be represented as ~ H. The key test for the occurrence of negation is to see whether or not the dropping of what you think is a negation causes the truth value of the statement to reverse.

The first connective that Professor Copi introduces is CONJUNCTION. Its most common form is the occurrence of "and." He uses a raised, heavy dot to symbolize this connective, and it is a connective that joins two statements. He symbolizes p and q as p · q. (Other systems of logical notation use an inverted wedge [p∧q], a capital K [Kpq], the ampersand [p&q] or, when it is unambiguous, the statements are juxtaposed or written together [pq]. The truth table for conjunction is

p	q	p·q
T	T	T
T	F	F
F	T	F
F	F	F

Again you read across the table. This means that when p and q are both true, then p·q is true, but when either (or both) component(s) is (are) false, the compound statement is also false. This corresponds well with our treatment of "and" statements in English, that the compound assertion "statement 1 and statement 2" is taken to be true if and only if both components are true. In talking of a truth table we frequently read it vertically, top to bottom, as a shorthand way of referring to it. That would make such reference to this standard table for conjunction be TFFF (Tee-Ef-Ef-Ef). If you were to memorize the table, the easiest way would be that when p and q are both true, p·q is true; otherwise it is false.

In addition to "and" Professor Copi gives you a good list of other words that you could represent by "·". You might, however, find it useful to make a small card on which you record all of the information you collect about each of the connectives. Such a card for conjunction might look like the example on the next page.

```
p · q              p   q  |  p · q
                   T   T  |   T
                   T   F  |   F
                   F   T  |   F
                   F   F  |   F
```

and	nevertheless
but	although
yet	moreover
still	however
also	in addition to

Notice that this sample leaves lots of room for you to add additional words as you encounter them. If you make one such card for each of the symbols, you will find that it is much faster to refer to them as you work problems than it is to look back into the text and the Study Guide.

As Professor Cooi points out, the most problematic thing about conjuction is identifying the cases that look like conjunctions of statements but are not, Thus "John and Jane are married" could appear to be a compact way of writing "John is married and Jane is married" but probably isn't. The former statement seems also to tell us that they are married TO EACH OTHER while that does not seem implicit in the latter at all. In fact it seems most likely that we would use the two different statements precisely to distinguish between the cases of persons who are marrried to each other and persons who each happen to be married. The key point to look for is whether the dropping of one of the supposed conjuncts loses information about the other conjunct too.

The third connective introduced is DISJUNCTION (or ALTERNATION). As Profesor Copi indicates, the English "or" is ambiguous. In Latin, for example, the ambiguity is removed by having two words "vel" and "aut" for the inclusive and exclusive meanings of "or," respectively. It is the "v" from "vel" that is the source of the wedge that is commonly used as the symbolization of alternation. In the absence of solid indication that an "or" is being used exclusively, logicians have accepted the convention of treating "or" inclusively. Thus any use of "v" in the logic means "and/or." This causes no problems, for if one wanted to symbolize "p or q, but not both" it could be done by symbolizing exactly what is there--(p v q) · ~ (p · q).

The truth table for disjunction is

```
        p     q   |  p  v  q
      --------    |  ---------
        T     T   |    T
        T     F   |    T
        F     T   |    T
        F     F   |    F
```

Note that, if you were memorizing it, the easiest way would be to notice that the only way to falsify a disjunction is to have BOTH disjuncts be false; all other cases are true.

The only common expressions symbolized by "v" are "Either ... or ..." "... or ...," and "... unless ...." The occurrence of the "either" has no real effect on the connective; it serves primarily as a sort of punctuation for the sentence. "Either," like "both," however, must be watched with particular care when they are used together with "not." The expression "not either p or q" is equivalent to saying "neither p nor q," while the expression "either not p or q is simply the disjunction; the former pair are symbolized

~ (p v q) and the latter expression is ~p v q. At first glance these might seem to be the same, but another logical convention applies: the curl applies to as little as it possibly can. This means that the former case has it applying to the QUANTITY (p v q) while the latter to the "p" alone. Using a few extra symbols, the former is ~ [(p) v (q)] and the latter is [~ (p)) v (q)]. One way to indicate "what belongs to what" in a symbolic expression until you get used to operating with these symbols is by the use of underlining. If you start with the simplest elements and progressively underline larger and larger compounds, then you can see at a glance what each operator is doing, then below it is the same expression with the appropriate underlining.

$$\sim ([p \text{ v } (q \cdot r)] \text{ v } \sim [\sim (\sim p \cdot s) \text{ v } t])$$

$$\sim ([\underline{p} \text{ v } (\underline{q} \cdot \underline{r})] \text{ v } \sim [\sim (\sim \underline{p} \cdot \underline{s}) \text{ v } \underline{t}])$$

In this case you can trace, for example, the location of the line which first occurs under the third "~ " (that line is the fourth one down on the right side) and note that it is under exactly the same expression as the previous line EXCEPT for the extension under the curl. That tells you that the third curl negates the quantity (~ p · s). If you should try this method and do not get a solid line under the entire expression, then either you have made a mistake in your underlining or the formula is not properly made.

At the end of section 8.2 Profesor Copi has 100 exercises. The starred ones, of course, are answered at the back of his book. A few of the others will be discussed below.

To work the problems in part I, you must know a bit of political geography:

> London is the capital of England.
> Rome is the capital of Italy.
> Stockholm is the capital of Sweden.
> Paris is the capital of France.

In general, when you know the truth values of the simple statements in a compound one, it is easiest to go through the complex one, substituting T for the true simple statements and F for the false ones. After that you just work inside out until you arrive at a single value for the complex statement. In the first example below you will see each step done separately. In the second you will see that some of them can be done simultaneously.

I   (2) a.   ~ (London is the capital of England · Stockholm is the capital of Norway)

        b.   (T · F)   [Replacing the true statement by T and the false one by F]

        c.   F   [Replacing (T·F) by F]

        d.   T   [Replacing ~ F by T]

   (6) a.   London is the capital of England v ~ London is the capital of England.

        b.   T v ~ T   [Replacing the true statement by T]

        c.   T v F   [Replacing ~ T by F]

        d.   T   [Replacing (T v F) by T]

Note that in this problem it really did not matter whether London is the capital of England. If it had not been, then step b. would have been F v ~ F. This also would have reduced to T.

(11) a.   Rome is the capital of Italy ˙ ~ (Paris is the capital of France v Rome is the capital of Spain)
    b.   T ˙ ~ (T v F)   [With T and F for true and false propositions, respectively.]
    c.   T ˙ ~ (T)   [T v F replaced by T]
    d.   T ˙ F   [~ T replaced by F]
    e.   F   [T ˙ F replaced by F]

(16) a.   Rome is the capital of Spain v (~ London is the capital of England v London is the capital of England)
    b.   F v (~ T v T)   [With F and T for false and true respectively]
    c.   F v (F v T)   [With F for ~ T]
    d.   F v T   [With T for F v T]
    e.   T   [With T for F v T]

(21) a.   ~ [~ (Rome is the capital of Spain ˙ Stockholm is the capital of Norway) v ~ (~ Paris is the capital of France v ~ Rome is the capital of Spain)]
    b.   ~ [~ (F ˙ F) v ~ (~ T v ~ F)]   [With F and T for the appropriate propositions]
    c.   ~ [~ F v ~ (F v T)]   [With F for F ˙ F, F for ~ T and T for ~ F]
    d.   ~ [T v ~ T]   [With T for ~ F and T for F v F]
    e.   ~ [T]   [Because (T v (anything) is T]
    f.   F   [With F for ~ T]

Note that in steps c and d there are two reductions performed at the same time. Since they are separate at this point in the argument, that is, neither depends upon the other, this is acceptable (and space-saving). Of course the " ~ T" in step d could have been reduced to "F," but, since the only way a disjunction can be false is to have both of its disjuncts false and since you can see that the first disjunct is "T", it is more efficient to reduce d to e directly.

II   In these solutions, the first step shown will be the substitution of T and F as directed in the instructions. The explanations of what has been done in each step will be abbreviated a bit from the problems in part I. For example, the explanation of step d in exercise 21 (above) would be:

$$[\sim F ==> T // F \ v \ F ==> F]$$

(2) a.   ~ T v F
    b.   F v F   [~ T ==> F]
    c.   F   [F v F ==> F]

(6) a.   (T ˙ T) v (F ˙ F)
    b.   T v F   [T ˙ T ==> T // F ˙ F ==> F]
    c.   T   [T v F ==> T]

(11) a.   (T v F) ˙ (F v T)
    b.   T v T   [T v F ==> T // F v T ==> T]
    c.   T   [T v T ==> T]

```
(16)   a.    ~ (T v T) v ~ (F · ~ F)
       b.    ~ T v ~ (F)         [T v T==>T//F · (anything)==>F]
       c.    F v T               [ ~ T==>F// ~ F==>T]
       d.    T                   [T v F==>T]


(21)   a.    [T v (T v T)] · ~ [T v T)  v T]
       b.    [T v T] · ~ [T v T]   [T v T==>T]
       c.    T · ~ T              [T v T==>T]
       d.    T · F                [ ~ T==>F]
       e.    F                    [T · F==>F]
```

In part III of the exercises, generally, if you arrive at a
fixed truth value, the statements symbolized by P and Q were not
really critical to the compound statement; if you are left with P's
and/or Q's, then the compound statement's value is indeterminate
until you discover values for P and Q.

```
III  (2)     a.   Q · F
             b.   F             [(anything) · F==>F]


     (6)     a.   ~ P v (Q v P)
             b.   T             [ ~ P v P==>T]
```

Although there are no determinate truth values in this problem,
this form can never be false. In chapter 9 you will learn formal
reasons for reordering things joined by a wedge; the rules are
called Association and Communication. The point is that because
either P or ~ P will be true (by the definition of " ~ ") and
because the only way for a disjunction to be false, any expression of the form P v ~ P is a tautology, that is, can never be
false.

```
     (11)    a.   (P v Q) · ~ (Q v P)
             b.   (P v Q) · ~ (P v Q)   [(Q v P)==>(P v Q)]
             c.   F                     [P · ~ P==>F]
```

This resembles exercise 6 (immediately above) in that it, too,
has no determinate truth values in it. The transformation in b
is called Commutation and will be introduced as a valid rule in
chapter 9. Since the two conjuncts in b are contradictory, that
is, since ~ (P v Q) is the negation of (P v Q), the definition of
" ~ " requires that they have opposite values. That means that,
as a conjunction, one of the conjuncts must always be false. But
the only way a conjunction can be true is to have both conjuncts
be true. Since that can't happen, any time you encounter such a
case you will know that you have seen a contradiction and that
all contradictions are false at all times.

```
     (16)    a.   ~ (P · Q) v (Q · P)
             b.   ~ (P · Q) v (P · Q)   [Q · P==>P · Q]
             c.   T                     [P v ~ P==>T]
```

Essentially this is the same sort of problem as exercise 6
(above). The only addition is that the disjuncts (which contradict each other) are more complex expressions in this exercise.

```
     (21)    a.   [P v (Q · T] · ~ [(P v Q) · (P v T]
             b.   [P v Q] · ~ [(P v Q) · T]  [Q · T==>Q//P v T==>T]
             c.   [P v Q] · ~ [P v Q]        [P · T==>P]
             d.   F                          [P · ~ P==>F]
```

The transition from c to d is exactly the same as in exercise 11.
The inferences in b and c are based upon the truth table definition of "v" and " · ". Since a conjunction is only true when
both conjuncts are true, knowledge that one of them is true
leaves the truth or falsity of the whole dependent upon the other
conjunct; however, since the only way that a disjunction can be

false is to have both disjuncts false, knowledge that one disjunct is true means that the whole expression is true regardless
of the truth or falsity of the other. Falsity effects expressions with " · " and "v" in just the opposite manner: if one
conjunct is known to be false, then the conjunction as a whole is
false; but if one disjunct is known to be false, then the truth
value of the whole is dependent upon the other disjunct.

The problems in part IV provide you with your first opportunity to "translate" from your natural (and probably native)
language of English into your new (and artificial) language of
logic. As with most things, such translation is best undertaken
slowly and with short steps. If you do not attempt to deal both
with statements and with connectives at the same time, you will
find that neither is likely to give you any difficulty; if you do
try them together, you are probably going to think that all this
is too hard. So, go slow to make it easy. It is often wise to
lay out the entire sentence before shifting to symbols.

IV   (2)   a. Either Iran raises the price of oil or Libya
                 raises the price of oil.
             b. Either I or L.
             c. I v L

Note that a is an expansion of the original. It is done to insure
that the "or" really is the truth-functional one and to identify
clearly the parts of the statement.

     (6)   a. Iran raises the price of oil or Libya raises the
                price of oil, but it is not the case both that
                Iran and Libya raises the price of oil.
            b. I or L, but not both I and L.
            c. (I v L) but not (I · L)
            d. (I v L) but ~ (I · L)
            e. (I v L) · ~ (I · L)

As you become more skilled (practice does it) at symbolizing, you
probably will not need to take so many steps as you sumbolize.
As you learn, however, you will find that it usually is wiser to
take more time, to use more steps, to insure that you are correct.

     (11)   a. Either it is not the case that E or J.
            b. Either ~ E or J
            c. ~ E v J

Please notice here that the original exercise did not have to be
expanded. It showed the formal detail satisfactorily as given.

     (16)   a. Unless both Iran raises the price of oil and Libya
                raises the price of oil neither Iran raises the
                price of oil nor Libya raises the price of oil.
            b. Unles both I and L neither I nor L.
            c. Unless (I · L) ~ (I v L)
            d. (I L) v ~ (I v L)

There are two equivalent symbolizations for the expression
"neither p nor q": ~ (p v q) and (~ p · ~ q). Sometimes you
will find one more useful, sometimes the other. In general you
should let your own preferences and intuitions choose which one
you use.

     (21)   a. Either E and S or either J or L.
            b. Either (E · S) or (J v L)
            c. (E · S) v (J v L)

This exercise, like number 11, was stated in satisfactory
fashion, so did not need expansion. You should notice that one

of the primary values of the "either" part of "either.. or..."
is helping identify what the disjuncts were intended to be.

8.3   Conditional Statements and Material Implication

The two remaining connectives are related to each other.   They
are sometimes called the conditional and the bi-conditional.   The
conditional relationship, usually expressed by "if... then ...," is
discussed at length by Professor Copi.   The result is the conventional acceptance of the relationship called MATERIAL IMPLICATION as
a useful approximation of at least one important feature of most "if-
then" statements.   That characteristic that they seem to have in
common is the fact that they all seem to be false in the event that
the antecedent (the statement that goes between the "if" and the
"then") is true and the consequent (the statement that follows the
"then") is false.   Using the horseshoe as the symbol for this relationship, the truth table is

p	q	p − q
T	T	T
T	F	F
F	T	T
F	F	T

Note that if you were memorizing it, the key element is that it is
false when the antecedent is true and the consequent false (its
defining characteristics) and it is true otherwise.   (Other systems
of notation use a single or double arrow [p --> q] or [p ==> q], a
claw [p —< q] or [p—⊰ q], or a capital C [Cpq] for implication).
Given the widespread use of the idea of conditionality, there are
probably more English expressions that ought to be symbolized by
horseshoe than there are for all of the other connectives put together.   A few of them (with p and q placed approximately so that
they all ought to be represented as p ⊃ q) are given below:

   If p then q   q is entailed by p
+ p only if q   If p. q
   p is a sufficient condition for q   p results in q
+ q is a necessary condition for p   + q if p
   q follows from p   p implies q
   p entails q   q is implied by p

This dozen is by no means exhaustive, but it does list the commoner
expressions.   The ones marked with a "+" are the ones that experience
shows tend to be mis-symbolized most frequently, usually by having
the p and the q exchanged.

Related to the conditional is the biconditional.   Essentially it
is just the conjunction of the conditionals p⊃q and q⊃p.   It means
that the two statements (or statement-forms) are said to be equivalent, or have the same truth value.   It is normally symbolized as a
triple bar and its truth table is

p	q	p ≡ q
T	T	T
T	F	F
F	T	F
F	F	T

Note that if you were memorizing this table you could key on either
the fact that the ' ≡ ' is true when both equivalents have the same
truth value or that it is false when their values are different.
(Other systems of logical notation use a single or double double-
headed arrow [p ⟷ q] or [p <==> q], a double-headed claw [p>—<q]

or [p Ξ q], or a capital E [Epq] for equivalence.) There are only
three expressions commonly used that are symbolized with a triple
bar: "...if and only if...," "...is a necessary and a sufficient
condition for...," and "...is equivalent to...." Do not be concerned
that you have not seen this symbol yet in Copi. It is formally
introduced by Professor Copi in section 8.5. I have included it
here, with the conditional, to emphasize to you the fact that the "Ξ"
is simply a BICONDITIONAL, that is, a " ⊃ " going in both directions.

Keeping in mind the truth table for the conditional, you should
find the exercises following 8.3 straightforward and fairly simple.
Remember, if you arrive at your own solution before looking at the
answers here and in Copi, you will gain far more from working the
exercises. (In the solutions to selected exercises here, the format
of the earlier exercises will be followed.)

I   (2)   a. T ⊃ F
              b. F   [T ⊃ F==>F]

The fact that the assertion that a true statement implies a
false one is itself false is something that you should keep well
in mind. Perhaps the commonest error made in using the " _ " is
getting confused about ORDER of truth and falsity that yields a
false conditional statement.

     (6)   a. (F ⊃ F) ⊃ F
              b. T ⊃ F   [F ⊃ F==>T]
              c. F   [T ⊃ F==>F]

     (11)   a. [(T ⊃ T) ⊃ T] ⊃ F
              b. [T ⊃ T] ⊃ F   [T ⊃ T==>T]
              c. T ⊃ F   [T ⊃ T==>T]
              d. F   [T ⊃ F==>F]

     (16)   a. [(F ⊃ T) ⊃ F] ⊃ F
              b. [T ⊃ F] ⊃ F   [F ⊃ T==>T]
              c. F ⊃ F   [T ⊃ F==>F]
              d. T   [F ⊃ F==>F]

     (21)   a. [(T · F)v(~ T · ~ F)] ⊃ [(T ⊃ F) · (F ⊃ T)]
              b. [F v (F · T)] ⊃ [F · T]   [T · F==>F// ~ T==>F
                                              ~ F==>T//T ⊃ F==>F
                                              F ⊃ T==>T]
              c. [F v F] ⊃ F   [F · T=/=>F (twice)]
              d. F ⊃ F   [F v F==>F]
              e. T   [F ⊃ F==>T]

You should notice that, although the reduction from step a to
step b is quite complicated **looking**, it's just a working out of
five quite simple reductions simultaneously.

II   (2)   a. F ⊃ Q
              b. T   [F ⊃ anything==>T]

The justification here may seem a bit strange to you. However,
if you look at the truth table for the " ⊃ ," you can easily see
the rationale.

	p	q	p ⊃ q
(1)	T	T	T
(2)	T	F	F
(3)	F	T	T
(4)	F	F	T

Notice the third and fourth rows. In both the antecedent (p) is
F and, despite the differences in the consequent (q), the value

of the entire expression remains T. For that reason, "F ⊃ anything" is a form that will always be T.

(6)   a. (F ⊃ Q) ⊃ F
         b. T ⊃ F   [F ⊃ anything==>T (see 2)]
         c. F   [T ⊃ F==>F]

(11)   a. (P ⊃ F) ⊃ (F ⊃ P)
         b. ~ P ⊃ T   [P ⊃ F==> ~ P//F ⊃ P==>T]
         c. T   [anything ⊃ T==>T]

This justification series contains two inferences that you may
find confusing. The transition from step b to step c is the
other side of the coin to at the discussion in exercise 2. If
you look at the table in that problem's analysis, then you will
see that in the first and third rows the consequent and the
expresion as a whole are T despite the fact that the antecedent
is T in the first row and F in the third. The stranger inference
lies between the antecedents a and b. If, however, you return to
the truth table of the " ⊃ " you will see why the inference
"works." In rows 2 and 4 the consequent is F. In row 2 the
antecedent is T but the "p ⊃ q" as a whole is F; in row 4 the
antecedent is F but "p ⊃ q" is T. Since, in those rows, "p ⊃ q"
has the opposite value of the antecedent, it must (when the
consequent is F) be in some sense the contradiction or negation
of the antecedent.

(16)   a. (P ⊃ F) ⊃ (~ F ⊃ ~ P)
         b. ~ P ⊃ (T ⊃ ~ P)   [P ⊃ F==> ~ P// ~ F==>T]
         c. ~ P ⊃ ~ P   [T ⊃ P==>P]
         d. T   [P ⊃ P==>T]

The transition from "T ⊃ P" to "P" follows a pattern similar to
the ones discussed earlier. In this case, however, you must
examine the first two rows of the " ⊃ 's" truth table. In those
cases, where the antecedent is T, "p ⊃ q" has the same value as
q, thus the reduction from b to c. The inferennce from c to d
simply recognizes that, if the same term is both antecedent and
consequent, then you can never get different values (in particular T then F) for the antecedent and consequent of a statement.
That being the case, anything implying itself must always be T.

(21)   a. ~ (T · P) ⊃ (~ T v ~ P)
         b. ~ P ⊃ (F v ~ P)   [T · anything==>anything//
                              ~ T==>F]
         c. ~ P ⊃ ~ P   [F v anything==>anything]
         d. T   [P ⊃ P==>T]

Since both conjuncts must be true, the truth of one means the
truth of the whole is dependent upon the other. Similarly,
since both must be false for the disjunction to be false, knowing
one disjunct is false means that the truth of the whole expression is dependent upon the other.

III (2)   a. If A then either B or C.
          b. If A then (B v C)
          c. A ⊃ (B v C)

    (6)   a. If either A or B, then C.
          b. If (A v B), then C.
          c. (A v B) ⊃ C

   (11)   a. If it is not the case that A then not B, and C.
          b. If ~ A then ~ B, and C
          c. (~ A ⊃ ~ B) and C
          d. (~ A ⊃ ~ B) C

(16)   a. If either B or C,A
          b. If (B v C), A
          c. (B v C) ⊃ A

Notice that in a, the word order was reversed to transform a "q if p" structure into an "if p then q" one.

(21)   a. If Argentina mobilizes, then Brazil protests to the U.N.
          b. A ⊃ B

This exercise is intended to remind you that "p is a sufficient condition for q" means the same thing as "if p then q."

One thing that you must always keep in mind is that each of these logical connectives is DEFINED by its truth table. That means that, for example, the ' · ' function is always commutative, that is, the two things conjoined by it can always be exchanged. That is NOT true for the English words it is used to symbolize. It is easy to see that the sentences "She became pregnant and got married" and "She got married and became pregnant" convey rather different images of "her" behavior; p · q and q · p are logically interchangeable. There are similar problems for each of the connectives--p ⊃ q and ~ q ⊃ ~ p are equivalent, but "If you want a piece of cake, it's on the table" and "If there isn't any cake on the table, you don't want any" surely aren't. The questions "Are you coming tomorrow?" and "Aren't you coming tomorrow?" differ by the presence of the contraction "n't" (meaning "not") but one responds as if they were identical, while p and ~ p are contradictory. There is no obvious way to tell if a natural language is being used in an unusual way; the artificial language of logic cannot be used except according to its definitions. The reason we have settled upon the connectives that are used here is largely one of accommodation to the natural language of English. "And," "or," "if...then," "not," and "if and only if" are commonly used to join or modify statements in English, so we search for the formal connectives that most closely resemble those natural connec- tives. That search can be seen on the charts below. The first shows all possible one-place operators (using only T and F as possible values); the second shows all possible two-place operators.

P	(1)	(2)	(3)	(4)
T	T	T	F	F
F	T	F	T	F

p	q	a	b	c	d	e	f	g	h	i	j	k	l	m	n	o	p
T	T	T	T	T	T	T	T	T	T	F	F	F	F	F	F	F	F
T	F	T	T	T	T	F	F	F	F	T	T	T	T	F	F	F	F
F	T	T	T	F	F	T	T	F	F	T	T	F	F	T	T	F	F
F	F	T	F	T	F	T	F	T	F	T	F	T	F	T	F	T	F

Of the one-place operators, three of the four are of no real use to us: (1) and (4) do not really concern themsellves with the truth value of the variable upon which they operate; they treat truth and falsity alike; (2) corresponds to an English phrase ("It is true that..."), but it is basically a valueless phrase, one which is usually better omitted. The fourth operator does what we usually want negation to do, that is, it precisely denies that upon which it operates. Thus we adopt it as the nearest symbolic operation to negation in English.

Weeding out the sixteen possible two-place operators is a some- what more complex task. It may, however, be made much simpler by noting that the second half of the table is the mirror-image of the first half. We can get operator i by negating operator h, j is ~ g, k is ~ f, and so on until p is ~ a. Operators d and f can be

eliminated as being complicated versions of p and q, respectively.
Dropping all of these leaves a considerably shortened table:

p	q	b	c	e	g	h
T	T	T	T	T	T	T
T	F	T	T	F	F	F
F	T	T	F	T	F	F
F	F	F	T	T	T	F

There is little difficulty recognizing h as a reasonable facsimile of
"and," and b as a fair match for an inclusive "or" (the exclusive one
was operator j). The problem is with "if... then ...". It seems
clear that "if p then q" is true when both p and q are true, and is
false when p is true and q is false. It is not so clear what ought
to be done when p is false. Most of us would prefer responding to
the false antecedent by saying "tilt" or "no decision" or the like,
but we are bound by the true/false range of the logic and must make a
decision. There are only four possible operators which begin T-F, so
perhaps it is best to begin by looking at them:

p	q	A	B	C	D
T	T	T	T	T	T
T	F	F	F	F	F
F	T	T	T	F	F
F	F	T	F	T	F

Notice that each of these proposed operators is true when both p and
q are true and false when p is true and q is false--that is the part
of the conditional that seemed obvious. The cases when p is false
cover all possible combinations of values. To decide which symbolic
definition is most acceptable (or perhaps least unacceptable) it is
helpful to look at a conditional statement which could be symbolized
p — q and whose components are quite clear: If you fail all of the
tests in this course, then you will fail the course. In this statement "you fail all of the tests in this course" is the simple statement located in the "p-position" and "you fail this course" is the
simple statement located in the "q-position." The compound statement
p ⊃ q is a true statement. You can easily see that proposed definition B is just the reassertion of q. That would mean that to assert
the compound statement p ⊃ q would be to assert that you will fail
the course. That is probably the assertion you would prefer not be
made, and you can pretty well se why that definition is unacceptable.
Definition D is the one already chosen for conjunction, and it too
would entail the truth of q following immediately from the truth of
the compound. It, obviously, is also unsatisfactory. Proposed definition C will result in the conditional being a commutative function,
like conjunction and disjunction. (It is easy to identify commutative operators, because they all have the same values for p = T/q = F
and p = F/q = T.) Implication cannot, however, be allowed to be
commutative, for, if it were, the following two statements would both
be true (when in fact the first is true, but the second is false):

1. If you fed Abraham Lincoln 3 lbs. of arsenic, then he is
    dead.
2. If Abraham Lincoln is dead, then you fed him 3 lbs. of
    arsenic.

The non-commutativity of implication eliminates D as an option. (D
is, in fact, equivalence.) The only definition left for the conditional, then, is A. The other column that was left (column c) can be
identified in short order--it is false when q is true and p is false
and true otherwise. That is a conditional sort of definition, but in
reverse order--it is q ⊃ p.

8.4   Argument Forms and Arguments

A truth table may be constructed for any statement or argument that is given or translated into propositional symbolic form. It is the sort of thing that a computer does very efficiently because it is essentially a purely mechanical task. But first you have to be able to figure out how big the table you will generate will be. Professor Copi shows guide (or initial or referennce) columns of differieng lengths. You may wonder what their rationale or their method of generation is. Both are quite simple. The guide columns are intended to be a well-organized listing of all possible combinations of values that the variables involved in the statement (or argument) might have. If they are not well-organized, then it is difficult either to be sure you have listed all combinations or to scan quickly a column to compare tables, If you do not have all possible combinations of values, then you might later find that the one that you omitted was THE crucial one. Below you will find what appear to be three methods for generating guide columns. If you examine them closely you will see that they are actually three alternate ways of describing the same method.

I.   Identify all the distinct variables that occur in the statement or argument you wish to check. A distinct variable is one that is counted on its first occurrence, but not at any later appearance. Thus p v (p $\equiv$ ~ p) contains only one distinct variable--p.

II.   Alphabetize them.

III. Calculate how many rows (horizontal lines--count them vertically).

Row 1	C	C C
Row 2	o	o . . . . o
.	l	l l
.	u	u . . . . u
.	m	m . . . . m
.	n	n . . . . n
Row n	1	2 . . . . n

The calculation is based upon raising 2 (the number of truth values we have--T and F) to the power of the number of distinct variables we will be considering. That is, if n = the number of distinct variables, then 2^n = the number of rows to put in the table. (Raising any number to a power simply means multiplying that number times itself as many times as the "power" says. Thus 2^5 = 2x2x2x2x2.)

IV.   Distribute the T's and F's

A. (1st method) Under the first variable (alphabetically) put T's in the first half of the rows and F's in the second half. Go on to the second variable and do the same thing, EXCEPT T's go in the first and third quarters and F's go in the second and fourth ones. Continue, shortening the T/F strings, with odd fractions being T and even ones being F. If you have not made a mistake, the last variable will alternate T and F. (If you begin alternating before you get to the last variable, then you have too short a table; if you get to that variable and still are not alternating, then there were more rows than you really needed. If you have to err, the latter is better because it can't omit a critical case.)

B. (2nd method) Under the LAST variable (alphabetically) alternate T's and F's. Go to the next-to-last and alternate pairs of T's and F's. Continue, doubling the length of the T/F strings each time you move back a variable. If you have not made a mistake, when you get to the first variable it will have the first half of the rows T and the second half F. (If it is all T, then you do not have enough rows; if it shifts from T to F and back again, then your table is longer than it needed to be.)

C. (3rd method) Number the alphabetized variables. For any specific variable you will need to alternate groups of $2^{(n-k)}$ T's and F's (where "k" is the number of the variable, "n" is the number of distinct variables, and 2 the number of truth values) until you have reached a string of rows that is 2^n long.

By using any of these methods, you will generate what could be called a set of standard guide columns. Using it as a basis, you are now in a position to generate a truth table for any statement-form.

All of this working with statement-form is fine, but it is not at the heart of logic. Logic is primarily concerned with arguments; its dealing with statements is only a preliminary to dealing with arguments. The real value of the truth tables will be found in their use to determine whether an argument is valid or invalid.

There are three ways commonly offered to define validity:

A. An argument is valid if and only if whenever all of its premisses are true its conclusion is also true.

B. An argument is valid if and only if whenever its conclusion is false at least one of its premisses is false.

C. An argument is valid if and only if it is never the case that all of its premisses are true but its conclusion is false.

If you look closely at the three you will see that they are actually just three alternative ways of saying the same thing.

The format that Professor Copi uses to check an argument-form to see if it is a valid one is to write a large truth table on which you simultaneously lay out the truth tables for each of the premisses and the one for the conclusion. Then, using one of the definitions given above, you scan across the table, looking for a case where all of the premisses are true, but the conclusion is false. If there is such a case the argument is invalid; if there is not such a case the argument is valid. The problem with this approach, for some people, is that it is too easy to overlook (or misread) values as you scan.

There is, however, a related method that some find does a good job of avoiding those problems. It is the use of the ASSOCIATED STATEMENT FORM (ASF). The use of the ASF is based upon a similarity between the validity relationship in an argument and the conditional relationship in a statement: the only case where an argument can be proven invalid is when all of its premisses are true and its conclusion is false; the only case where a conditional statement can be shown to be false is when its antecedent is true and its consequent is false. When you add to that the fact that the only way to make a conjunction true is to have all of its conjuncts true, you have the material for the generation of the ASF. First let's look at a "typical" argument, named "A." A has three premisses (P_1, P_2, and P_3) and a conclusion (C). There are two ways which logicians use to write A, depending upon their preferred way of handling arguments. The two ways correspond roughly to the two ways mathematical problems get written. If you wanted to add 7 and 5, you could write the problem/answer either vertically (V) or horizontally (H).

$$
\begin{array}{cc}
(V) & \begin{array}{r} 7 \\ +\ 5 \\ \hline 12 \end{array} \qquad (H)\quad (7+5)=12
\end{array}
$$

Similarly an argument can be written vertically or horizontally. To
read them, however, you need to know how to read two symbols with
which you may not be familiar. The first is "∴"; the second is "|-
". They are both said to be signs of illation, or conclusion-draw-
ing. The former is usually read "therefore" or "thus" and the latter
"yields." The argument from the premises p — q and q — r to the
conclusion p — r, then can be written

$$\text{(V)} \quad \begin{array}{c} p - q \\ q - r \\ \hline \end{array} \qquad \text{(H)} \quad p - q, \ q - r \ |- \quad p - r$$
$$\therefore \quad p - r$$

Many find that the vertical format is most useful when setting up
formal proofs of validity (as you will do in chapter 9) and the
horizontal most useful when doing truth tables. Our argument A,
then, can be written as

$$\begin{array}{c} P_1 \\ P_2 \\ P_3 \\ \hline \end{array}$$
$$\therefore \quad C$$

or as P_1, P_2, P_3 |- C. We can generate the ASF of A simply by
joining all of its premises together by conjunction, then using that
conjunction as an antecedent and C as a consequent in the statement-
form S. S has the form $\{[P_1 \cdot (P_2 \cdot P_3)] \supset C\}$. The only way for A
to be invalid is for there to be a case where P_1, P_2, and P_3, are all
true and C is false. If that is the case, then S will be false at
that same set of values. Similarly, the only way for S to be false
is for $[P_1 \cdot (P_2 \cdot P_3)]$ to be true and C to be false. But if $[P_1 \cdot$
$(P_2 \cdot P_3)]$ is true, then each element, P_1, P_2, and P_3 must be true,
and in that case A would be invalid. This could be summed up by
realizing that there is a strict relationship between any argument
and its ASF.

An argument is valid if and only if its ASF is a tautology. (A
tautology is a statement-form that is always true.) The ASF of the
argument p ⊃ q, q ⊃ r |- p ⊃ r is the conditional statement-form
$\{[(p \supset q) \cdot (q \supset r)] \supset (p \supset r)\}$.

The reason it is of some use to learn about the ASF is that you
can check the validity of an argument by setting up a truth table for
the ASF. If the truth table shows that the ASF is a tautology, then
the argument is valid; if there is any case where the ASF can be
false, then the associated argument is invalid. The use of the ASF
has the advantage of boiling the argument down to the values under a
single column--there is no need to scan across a table; you just look
at the last column. Using the argument shown just above, the table
below shows a validity check through the checking of its ASF.

p q r	p⊃q	q⊃r	(p⊃q)·(q⊃r)	p⊃r	[(p⊃q)·(q⊃r)] ⊃ (p ⊃ r)
T T T	T	T	T	T	T
T T F	T	F	F	F	T
T F T	F	T	F	T	T
T F F	F	T	F	F	T
F T T	T	T	T	T	T
F T F	T	F	F	T	T
F F T	T	T	T	T	T
F F F	T	T	T	T	T

Quickly scanning the last column you can see that the ASF is a tautology and that, therefore, the argument is valid.

A couple of examples from the exercises after 8.4 will help to solidify the means for checking for validity with truth tables.

11.13   p⊃(q⊃r),p⊃q |- p⊃r   [ASF:{ [p⊃(q⊃r] ·(p⊃q) } ⊃(p⊃r)

p q r	q⊃r	p⊃(q⊃r)	p⊃q	[p⊃(q⊃r)]·(p⊃q)	p⊃r	ASF
T T T	T	T	T	T	T	T
T T F	F	F	T	F	F	T
T F T	T	T	F	F	T	T
T F F	T	T	F	F	F	T
F T T	T	T	T	T	T	T
F T F	F	T	T	T	T	T
F F T	T	T	T	T	T	T
F F F	T	T	T	T	T	T

You can see that the ASF is a tautology, so the argument is valid.

III.6   K v L, K |- L   [ASF: { [(K v L) · K] ⊃ L}]

K L	K v L	K	(K v L) · K	~ L	ASF
T T	T	T	T	F	F
T F	T	T	T	T	T
F T	T	F	F	F	T
F F	F	F	F	T	T

This ASF is not a tautology, since it is false in the first row. That means that the associated argument is invalid. You might also note that, had you been working the problem row-by-row and had you noticed as you finished the first row that the ASF was false there, you could have stopped. You would have known at that point that the argument was invalid. Once you know that, further investigation is pointless, except for practice in making truth tables.

Technically the way in which the above problem was worked may not be quite correct. Since "K" and "L" represent actual propositions, they would each have some specific truth value. That means that only one of the four rows in the table actually represents these propositions as they are. The difficulty that you must encounter is that, because you do not even know what "K" and "L" represent, there is no way for you to know which of the rows does represent the actual state of affairs. The basis for claiming that an argument is invalid, as Profesor Copi says, is that the specific form of that argument is an invalid argument-form. Thus, what you probably should do (to be technically correct in trying to determine the validity or invalidity of an argument) is to check the argument-form that is the specific form of the argument in question. In the case of exercise III.6, that specific form would have been p v q, p |- q. The table which you would have generated to check that argument-form would have looked exactly like the one shown except that it would have had a "p" everywhere the given one has a "K" and a "q" everywhere that one has an "L." It really is pointless to translate the argument to its specific form (where the table beneath them would be unchanged) merely to satisfy a logical technicality. For that reason (and to avoid the simple copying errors that could creep in as you shift from argument to argument-form) in the solutions to exercises as done in this Study Guide I will use truth tables with both arguments and argument-forms as if there were no difference.

One more example shows an unusual characteristic of some arguments that might give you a bit of trouble. Below is the truth table for exercise III.9.

III.9 (R v S) ⊃ T, T ⊃ (R · S) |- (R · S) ⊃ (R v S)
    [ASF: ({[R v S) ⊃ T] · [T ⊃ (R · S)]} ⊃ [(R · S) ⊃ (R v S)])]

R	S	T	RvS	(RvS)⊃T	R·S	T⊃(R·S)	[(RvS)⊃T]·[T⊃(R·S)]	(R·S)⊃(RvS)	ASF
T	T	T	T	T	T	T	T	T	T
T	T	F	T	F	T	T	F	T	T
T	F	T	T	T	F	F	F	T	T
T	F	F	T	F	F	T	F	T	T
F	T	T	T	T	F	F	F	T	T
F	T	F	T	F	F	T	F	T	T
F	F	T	F	T	F	F	F	T	T
F	F	F	F	T	F	T	T	T	T

Here again the ASF is a tautology, so the argument is valid, but there is a strange feature about the argument. If you look you will see that the conclusion itself is a tautology. Of course, if the conclusion of an argument cannot be false then there will be no way for the premisses to be true **and** the conclusion false. There just doesn't seem to be any need for the premisses; the conclusion stands on its own. Nevertheless it is a valid argument.

Having followed through the several examples here and in Copi, you ought to find you have little difficulty with the exercises following 8.4. Remember, an exercise does the most good when you work it **before** looking at anyone else's solution.

I. (b) 6 is the specific form of b, so b is, of course, a substitution instance of 6.

(f) 16 is the specific form of f, so f is a substitution instance of 16.

(k) No exercise in part II is the specific form of k, but k is a substitution instance of 4:

$$p \qquad\qquad\qquad p \lor q$$

$$A \supset B \qquad\qquad (A \supset B) \lor C$$

As you can see, if you substitute (A ⊃ B) for p and c for q in exercise II.4, you get exercise I.k.

II. (2)

p	q	p ⊃ q	~ p	~ q	~ p ⊃ ~ q	(p ⊃ q)⊃(~p ⊃ ~q)
T	T	T	F	F	T	T
T	F	F	F	T	T	T
F	T	T	T	F	F	F
F	F	T	T	T	T	T

Since the third row shows that the ASF is false in the event that p is false and q true, the argument is invalid.

(6)

p	q	p ⊃ q	p · q	p ⊃ (p · q)	(p ⊃ q) ⊃ [p ⊃ (p · q)]
T	T	T	T	T	T
T	F	F	F	F	T
F	T	T	F	T	T
F	F	T	F	T	T

Since the ASF of the argument is a tautology, the argument is valid.

(11)

p q r	p ⊃ q	p ⊃ r	q v r	(p ⊃ q) · (p ⊃ r)	ASF
T T T	T	T	T	T	T
T T F	T	F	T	F	T
T F T	F	T	T	F	T
T F F	F	F	F	F	T
F T T	T	T	T	T	T
F T F	T	T	T	T	T
F F T	T	T	T	T	T
F F F	T	T	F	T	F

(16) One of the difficulties in writing out truth tables is that, when they include lots of premisses and/or variables, they can become very complicated (and long). A shortened approach to validity checks will be introduced in the next chapter, but some relief is available even in working problems in this format. Notice that in the truth table for this exercise some of the early columns are "named" (with Roman numerals) and later columns use the names instead of using the actual formulae. For example, the first premiss is "(p ⊃ q) · (r ⊃ s)." To get the column for that you first had to get columns for "p ⊃ q" and "r ⊃ s." The columns for those expressions are named "I" and "II." The name, then, of the first premiss is "I.II." Subsequent columns can also be given such names, shortening the headings of later columns greatly. The following is the validity check for exercise 16, using the naming device explained above.

	I	II	III	IV	V	VI	
p q r s	p ⊃ q	r ⊃ s	I · II	p v r	III · IV	q v s	V ⊃ VI
T T T T	T	T	T	T	T	T	T
T T T F	T	F	F	T	F	T	T
T T F T	T	T	T	T	T	T	T
T T F F	T	T	T	T	T	T	T
T F T T	F	T	F	T	F	T	T
T F T F	F	F	F	T	F	F	T
T F F T	F	T	F	T	F	T	T
T F F F	F	T	F	T	F	F	T
F T T T	T	T	T	T	T	T	T
F T T F	T	F	F	T	F	T	T
F T F T	T	T	T	F	F	T	T
F T F F	T	T	T	F	F	T	T
F F T T	T	T	T	T	T	T	T
F F T F	T	F	F	T	F	F	T
F F F T	T	T	T	F	F	T	T
F F F F	T	T	T	F	F	T	T

Since the ASF is a tautology, the argument-form is a valid one. This table, being 16 rows long, is a hard one to read. It is for that reason that the lines were added crossing the table: the varying density of the lines that separate the rows of the table make it easier to see which values come from which earlier values. Of course, if you were working on regular lines (or even better graph) paper lining up your table will be much simpler.

(21)   Notice that the table for exercise 21 uses the same sort of technique that 16 used, but that some columns can be used more than once.

		I	II	III	IV	V	VI	
p	q	p v q	p · q	I ⊃ II	~ I	III · IV	~ II	V ⊃ VI
T	T	T	T	T	F	F	F	T
T	F	T	F	F	F	F	T	T
F	T	T	F	F	F	F	T	T
F	F	F	F	T	T	T	T	T

Since this, too, has a tautologous ASF, it is a valid form.

III   (2)

		I	II	III	IV	V	VI	
C	D	C v D	C · D	I ⊃ II	~ I	III · IV	~ II	V ⊃ VI
T	T	T	T	T	T	F	F	T
T	F	T	F	F	F	F	T	T
F	T	T	F	F	F	F	T	T
F	F	F	F	T	T	T	T	T

It takes little effort to see that the table under III.2 and the one under II.21 are identical. That happens because III.2 has II.21 as its specific form. Since the specific form of III.2, then, is valid, so is III.2.

(6)

K	L	K v L	K	(K v L) · K	~ L	[(K v L) · K] ⊃ ~ L
T	T	T	T	T	F	F
T	F	T	T	T	T	T
F	T	T	F	F	F	T
F	F	F	F	F	T	T

Had you been working your way across the table, doing one row at a time, you should have seen that you could stop after the first row. Since the ASF is false in that row, it is not a tautology. And, when the ASF is not a tautology, the argument is invalid.

IV   (2)   Despite the apparent obviousness of the appropriate symbols to represent the propositions in this exercise (and the others of this set), it is always wise to specify exactly what you intend each propositional symbol to represent. The symbol "=df" which I used in the beginning of this analysis stand for "equals by definition" with "definition" being used in the stipulative sense (as explained in chapter 4).
Thus, exercise IV.2 should have this form:

D = df Denmark drifts further to the left.
E = df Estonia continues to b a puppet of Soviet Russia.
F = df Finland becomes increasingly subservient to Soviet Russia.

If D then if E then F.	[D ⊃ (E ⊃ F)]
E	E
--------------------	------------
So if D then F.	∴ (D ⊃ F)

| | | I | | | II | III | |
D E F	E ⊃ F	D ⊃ (E ⊃ F)	E	I · E	D ⊃ F	II ⊃ III
T T T	T	T	T	T	T	T
T T F	F	F	T	F	F	T
T F T	T	T	F	F	T	T
T F F	T	T	F	F	T	T
F T T	T	T	T	T	T	T
F T F	F	T	T	T	T	T
F F T	T	T	F	F	T	T
F F F	T	T	F	F	T	T

Since the ASF is true in all cases (tautologous), the argument is valid.

(6) E = df Equality of opportunity is to be achieved.
     S = df People previously disadvantaged should now be given special opportunities.
     P = df Some people receive preferential treatment.

If E then S.	E ⊃ S
If S then P.	S ⊃ P
If P then not E.	P ⊃ ~ E
----------------	---------
Therefore not E.	∴ E

| | I | II | III | IV | | V | | |
E P S	E ⊃ S	S ⊃ P	~ E	P ⊃ ~ E	I · II	III · IV	V ⊃ E
T T T	T	T	F	F	T	F	T
T T F	F	T	F	F	F	F	T
T F T	T	F	F	T	F	F	T
T F F	F	T	F	T	F	F	T
F T T	T	T	T	T	T	T	T
F T F	T	T	T	T	T	T	T
F F T	T	F	T	T	F	F	T
F F F	T	T	T	T	F	F	T

Since the ASF is a tautology, the argument is valid. Of course, on any of these problems you could have stopped once you have the table for all of the premisses and the conclusion. That would have required you to have figured out whether the argument was valid or not by comparing the values for the premisses and conclusion in each row. That seems, to me, to be an approach that is far more likely to produce errors than is the ASF technique. You may, to be sure, use whichever method seems easier to you (unless you have a teacher who specifies method).

8.5 Statement Forms and Statements

The relationship between arguments and argument forms which Professor Copi explained in 8.4 is essentially the same one as exists between statements and statement forms. In the same way that the substitution of propositions for the propositional variables in an argument form converted the form to an argument, a similar substitution within a statement form yields a statement.

Statement forms themselves can be identified by the sort of logical connectives that they involve: p ⊃ q is a conditional statement form, p v q is a disjunctive one, etc. Just as the specific form of an argument could be easily identified, the specific form of a statement is that form that would yield the desired statement by the consistent substitution of the appropriate simple propositions for the variables in the statement form.

In discussing the truth table generated relative to some given statement, there is another term which you may find makes it easier to identify what is being done. If you recall the complex statement forms that were created when the ASF of an argument was laid out, then you remember how the table consisted of a series of columns headed by ever-increasingly complex expressions. The final column was headed by the ASF. It is convenient to refer to the column of T's and F's that was under the ASF as the CHARACTERISTIC COLUMN or the SIGNIFICANT COLUMN of that particular expression. Using these terms allows us, for example, to describe two statement forms which in some sense "mean the same thing" as having the same characteristic column. In the case of the basic connectives you would say that the has a characteristic column of T-F-T-T, the v of T-T-T-F, and so on.

Statements and statement forms may, then, be classified by the sort of characteristic column which they have. Since there are only two truth values in the logic we are currently using, there are only three sorts of characteristic columns possible: ones that are all T's, ones that are all F's and ones that have a mix of T's and F's. Statements and statement forms whose characteristic columns are all T's are called TAUTOLOGIES; ones whose characteristic columns are all F's are called CONTRADICTIONS or SELF-CONTRADICTIONS; ones whose characteristics are a mixture of T's and F's are said to be CONTINGENT. If you look back to the introduction of the ASF IN 8.4, you will see that the use of "tautology" in that context was the same as introduced here.

Any two statements or statement forms which have the same characteristic column are said to be materially equivalent. Although "equivalence" may involve other aspects of similarity when used in everyday language, insofar as the logic we are using is concerned the term simply means that the two expressions that are siad to be equivalent have the same characteristic columns is an important reason for standardizing the guide columns that are the reference point for any truth table. If there were variability allowed in the guide column, then equivalence could not be recognized at a glance. For example, look at the two "truth tables" below; the left one has standard guide columns, the left non-standard ones;

p q	p ⊃ q		q p	q ⊃ p
T T	T		T T	T
T F	F		T F	F
F T	T		F T	T
F F	T		F F	T

If you looked casually at both of these tables you might be inclined to think that the two statement forms were materially equivalent. A bit of careful inspection; however, makes it clear that they are not: the left-hand one is false when p is T and q is F while the right-hand is false when o is F and q is T. Had the right-hand table had standard guide columns, the characteristic shown would have been T-T-F-T.

You should now be prepared to work the exercises following 8.5. Remember that you ought to do the problems yourself before you look at the solutions here or in Copi.

I   (2)   Both a and d could yield 2 with appropriate substitutions: use C for p and - D for q in a; use C for p and D for q in d. The specific form of 2 is d.

(6)   6 would result from b by replacing p with (O v P) and q
with (P · Q). There is no specific form of 6 stated.

II (2)   There are two distinct variables here: p and q. That
means that there will be 2^2 or 4 rows in the table. Using
any of the three methods of generating the guide columns
you will get:

p	q
T	T
T	F
F	T
F	F

The elements of the more complex structure are constructed one at
a time, always using the standard (or defining) tables for each
connective.   The table below shows the entire sequence of con-
structing the truth table.

| 1 | | 2 | 3 | 4 |
p	q	$p \supset q$	$(p \supset q) \supset q$	$p \supset [(p \supset q) \supset q]$
T	T	T	T	T
T	F	F	T	T
F	T	T	T	T
F	F	T	F	T

Since the characteristic of this statement form (the column
headed "4") is all T's, the statement is a tautology.

(6)   There are two distinct variables--p and q--so there will be
2^2 rows in the table. Using any of the three methods, the
guide columns will be

p	q
T	T
T	F
F	T
F	F

The elements of the more complex structure are constructed one at
a time, always using the defining tables for the various connectives as the reference when figuring out the column for any
particular expression.   The table below shows the sequence in
which the entire table is generated.

| 1 | | 2 | 3 | 4 | 5 |
p	q	$p \supset p$	~ q	q · ~ q	$(p \supset p) \supset (q · \sim q)$
T	T	T	F	F	F
T	F	T	T	F	F
F	T	T	F	F	F
F	F	T	T	F	F

First you generate the guide columns.
Second you calculate the values of $p \supset p$ given the value in thet
  guide columns and using the definitions of the connectives.
Third you figure that ~ q must be the mirror image of q.
Fourth, using the columns of q and ~ q, figure the values in the
  columns under (q · ~q).
Fifth you connect antecedent and consequent, again according to
  the basic definitions of the connectives.
From the table you can see this is a contradiction.

III   (2)

p q	p ⊃ q	~ p	~ q	~ p ⊃ ~ q	(p ⊃ q) ≡ (~ p ⊃ ~ q)
T T	T	F	F	T	T
T F	F	F	T	T	F
F T	T	T	F	F	F
F F	T	T	T	T	T

The characteristic column shows this is contingent, thus is not tautologous.

(6)

p q	p · q	p v (p · q)	p ≡ [p v (p · q)]
T T	T	T	T
T F	F	T	T
F T	F	F	T
F F	F	F	T

The characteristic column is all T's; the statement form is a tautology.

(11)

p q	~ q	q · ~ q	p v (q · ~ q)	p ≡ [p v (q · ~ q)]
T T	F	F	T	T
T F	T	F	T	T
F T	F	F	F	T
F F	T	F	F	T

The statement form, of course, is a tautology, but there is a more interesting aspect to the solution. Notice that the conjunction (q · ~ q) is a self-contradiction. When it is disjoined with p the resulting column is exactly the same as the original column for p. Obviously, then, when two expressions have the same characteristic column, a truth table of the expression having them connected by the ≡ (which is the sign of material implication) will always be a tautology.

(16)   This statement form has three distinct variables, so it must have a table with 2^3 (or 8) rows. The procedure for generating the table, however, is the same as for the earlier exercises.

		I	II	III	IV		
p q r	q v r	p · (q v r)	p · q	p · r	II v III	I ≡ IV
T T T	T	T	T	T	T	T
T T F	T	T	T	F	T	T
T F T	T	T	F	T	T	T
T F F	F	F	F	F	F	T
F T F	T	F	F	F	F	T
F T F	T	F	F	F	F	T
F F T	T	F	F	F	F	T
F F F	F	F	F	F	F	T

The greater number of variables makes the truth table longer, but the key thing to check is still the characteristic column for the statement form. For this statement form the characteristic column is a tautology.

8.6   The Paradoxes of Material Implication

The term "paradox" has several accepted meanings: a statement that appears self-contradictory but is acutally true, a statement that appears true but is actually self-contradictory, an unacceptable conclusion that is derivable from seemingly acceptable premisses, or a systematically ambiguous situation any resolution of which results in a self-contradiction. The closest of these to what is meant when logicians speak of the paradoxes of material implication is the first. In these particular cases a truth table clearly shows certain expressions to be tautologies but the "plain English" statements based upon these expressions seem at least counter-intuitive.

The logical statement forms which express the paradoxical nature of the " ⊃ " (or material conditional) are "p ⊃ (q ⊃ p)" and "~ p ⊃ (p ⊃ q)." Simply stated the first asserts that a statement which we KNOW TO BE TRUE is implied by any statement we might happen to select. That assertion is logically justified by recourse to the truth table for " ⊃ " which, you recall, is a DEFINITION of that connective. In that defining table it is clear that no statement or statement form whose consequent is true can itself be false. Thus, when the consequent "p" of any conditional "q ⊃ p" is KNOWN TO BE TRUE, the conditional itself is true.

Similarly, when both "p" and "~ p" are asserted as part of the antecedent of a conditional statement form, whatever you may wish can be claimed to "follow from" the "p" and "~ p," and do so truly. By the definition of the " ~ " we know that one of the pair "p" and "~ p" must be true and the other false. Both of them, then, cannot reasonably serve as anntecedent statements (or forms) within a conditional. The two of them asserted simultaneously would constitute a self-contradiction; that self-contradiction (according to the defining table for " ~ ") would yield anything whatsoever when it occurred as the antecedent of a conditional statement or form.

All of this paradoxical difficulty is a function of the original definitions relating to the " ⊃ ." If you recall the discussion of why the particular table for the " ⊃ " that we use HAD to be selected (after the exercises to 8.3, above), then you will see that to mirror ordinary English usage with "if...then...." statements we must also accept these paradoxical qualities. Fortunately, such acceptance rarely causes difficulties.

8.7   The Three "Laws of Thought"

Interestingly, George Boole (a bit of whose work you touched in the Boolean equations of the categorical proposition) titled his most significant work**An Investigation of the Laws of Thought.** It was originally published in 1849 and tried to give a basis for correct reasoning. In fact, he wrote in his opening remarks:

> The design of the following treatise is to investigate the fundamental laws of those operations of the mind by which reasoning is performed; to give expression to them in the symbolical language of a Calculus, and upon this foundation to establish the science of Logic and construct its method....

Professor Copi explains, however, that there are three so-called Laws of Thought that have traditionally been treated as if they were the foundation for logic to which Boole refers. There are fairly traditional ways of expressing these Laws of Thought:

Any true statement must be true. (Principle of Identity)

No statement is both true and false. (Principle of Contradiction--sometimes called the Principle of Non-contradiction).

Any statement is either true or false. (Principle of the Excluded Middle)

There probably is no good reason to single out these three tautologies as more fundamental than any others. It is the case, however, that there is a sense in which these principles are "built into" the structure of the truth table (which in many ways is funda-mental--at least to logic's efficient operation):

(1)   once a variable is found to be true (or false for that matter) it will have the same truth value throughout the table.

(2)   only one value, T or F, can occur at any single loca-tion within a problem.

(3)   each location within a truth table must have either a T or an F in it.

These can reasonably be taken as the statements of the Principle of Identity, of Contradiction and of the excluded Middle, respectively.

As Professor Copi suggests, however, detailed analysis either of the Laws of Thought or of the paradoxes of material implication would require vastly more work and understanding than it is reasonable to demand.

CHAPTER EIGHT SUMMARY

I.   The use of special symbols can be an important aid to reasoning.

    A.   Symbols can significantly decrease the volume of material you are trying to handle.

    B.   Symbols can remove you from emotional material.

    C.   Symbols can increase precision.

II.   Logic can be based upon the proposition as the smallest unit of information. Propositions have two truth values: true and false.

III. There are several connectives which can be defined as ways of combining propositions. The connectives which are important for us are ones which are defined in terms of the truth value they derive from set combinations of truth values of the propositions they combine. (Thus these are called truth-functional connectives.)

    A.   Specific propositions are represented by capital letters, usually derived from the proposition. (For example, "B" would seem a reasonable symbol for "Betty Brown burnt her banana bread.")

    B.   Lower case letters p, q, r, etc. are used as propositional variables. They represent forms which would become propositions if propositions were substituted for the variables within the forms.

    C.   Negation is represented by a " ~ " preceding the propositional variable or propositional symbol.

    D.   Although more connectives are identifiable, Professor Copi uses five:

        1.   " ~ " represents "not" in the sense of contradiction.

        2.   " · " represents "and" in the sense of joint assertion.

        3.   " v " represents "or" in the sense of inclusive alternatives (p or q or both).

        4.   " ⊃ " represents "if...then..." in the sense of material implication (you can't have p but not q).

        5.   " ≡ " represents "if and only if" in the sense of either joint occurrence or joint non-occurrence.

IV.   The truth-functional relationships can be defined by tables
      which show how derived values are obtained from all possible
      combinations of values of the simple propositions (or proposi-
      tional variables) in the relationship.

   A.   The one useful one-place "connective," the " ~ " is de-
        fined:

$$
\begin{array}{c|c}
p & \sim p \\
\hline
T & F \\
F & T \\
\end{array}
$$

   B.   Professor Copi uses four two-place connectives that are
        defined:

p	q	p · q	p v q	p ⊃ q	p ≡ q
T	T	T	T	T	T
T	F	F	T	F	F
F	T	F	T	T	F
F	F	F	F	T	T

V.   By using the definitions as stated in the tables for each of
      the connectives, you can derive a truthtable for any statement
      or statement form.

VI.   By using a truth table based upon all of the variables in an
      argument form, you can determine whether or not that form (or
      any argument derived from it by substituting statements [or
      propositions] for the variables) is valid.

VII. Statements (propositions) and statement forms can be classified
      by the sort of truth table that is associated with them.

   A.   If their characteristic column is always true, they are
        called tautologies.

   B.   If their characteristic column is always false, they are
        called contradictions of self-contradictories.

   C.   If their characteristic column is a mixture of trues and
        falses, they are called contingencies.

VIII. The " ⊃ " has characteristics which do not strictly coincide
      with our ordinary language uses of "if...then..."

   A.   A false statement "truly" implies any statement: any
        statement with a self-contradictory antecedent is a tauto-
        logy.

   B.   A true statement is "truly" implied by any statement: any
        statement with a tautologous consequent is a tautology.

IX.   The three traditional "laws of Thought" are built into truth table structures.

   A.   "Any true statement must be true" is conveyed by "p ⊃ p" being a tautology. (The Principle of Identity)

   B.   "No statement is both true and false" is conveyed by "p · ~p" being self-contradictory. (The Principle of Contradiction.)

   C.   "Any statement must be either true or false" is conveyed by "p v ~ p" being a tautology. (The Principle of the Excluded Middle)

9

The Method of Deduction

9.1   Formal Proof of Validity

If a friend was arguing some emotionally loaded issue with you, like abortion, nuclear power, or the sexual revolution, you might, in your own mind, draw upon what you learned in the last lesson in order to make sure that your own arguments were valid. If, however, you tried to "prove" to this friend (whom we shall assume has not had the good fortune to have taken a course in logic) that your argument was valid by the use of a full truth table, you might find this friend less than receptive. As a matter of fact, before you finished laying out your array of variables, connectives and T's and F's, your friend may well have departed to call the little men with the nets to carry you off to an upholstered room. This is because you have to be among the "initiated" for the truth tables to make a great deal of sense to you.

If the problem had been a linguistic one, that is, if your friend had failed to understand you because your vocabulary was too advanced or too specialized, you would have restated your point, so to speak, in "words of one syllable." The problem, then, is to find some way to break a complicated argument into simple components. That is essentially what the use of the propositional rules does. Those rules are a set of relatively simple arguments and equivalences, ones to which, for the most part, no one would object. They are strung together forming what can be called a **Formal Proof of Validity.** Such a proof is a sequence of steps which start with the premises of a valid argument, proceed by using the simple, unobjectionable rules of the propositional calculus, and terminate in the conclusion of the argument.

Several of those "simple, unobjectionable rules" are argument forms with which you are already familiar. If you recall the non-categorical argument forms from chapter 7, you already have over half the rules of inference from this section in mind.

One thing which might make the forms of these rules a bit easier for you to use would be a slight change in notation. Since the rules are intended to be patterns of argument, rather than specific argument, or even specific argument forms, you might find the use of "p," "q," and other variables a little confusing. Think for a minute about the relationship between an argument form and an argument. Any argument which could result from the substitution of specific propositions (not necessarily simple ones) for the propositional variables in an argument form is said to be an **instance** of that form. Thus it is easy for you to see that "A ⊃ B, A |- B" is an instance of "p ⊃ q, p |- q." It is also pretty simple to see that "(A v B) ⊃ (C ≡ D), (A v B) |-(C ≡ D)" is also an instance of that same form. The ambiguity which you may feel involves the question of whether "(pvq) ⊃ (r≡s), (p v q) |- (r ≡ s)" is an instance too.

A logical expression is sometimes called a well-formed formula, meaning that its components are joined together in a logically appropriate manner. This is usually abbreviated Wff. If numbers are associated with the term Wff (for example: Wff 1, Wff 2, etc.), there is then an easy way to rewrite the rules so that their generality is more evident. If MODUS PONENS were so rewritten it would appear as

$$(\text{Wff } 1) \supset (\text{Wff } 2)$$
$$\text{Wff } 1$$
$$\overline{}$$
$$\therefore \quad \text{Wff } 2$$

This seems to make it clear that, so long as they appear consistent-
ly, any well-formed expression at all may occur in the locations
designated as Wff 1 and and any other (or the same) expression may
occur at those locations marked Wff 2.   If you think of modus ponens
as a board with a set of windows at the locations marked Wff 1 and
Wff 2 and a set of mirrors behind (so that whatever appears at any
one Wff 1 or Wff 2 spot automatically appears at all other corresponding locations), you may have some grasp of how these rules-as-
patterns work.

A more graphic mechanism which would have the same purpose would
be to represent the Wffs of the argument by consistent geometric
forms.   That would have modus ponens, for example, having this form:

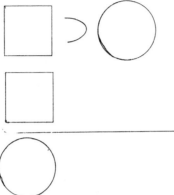

The explanation of use of the rule modus ponens, then, is that you
can put ANY Wff at all on the circle or the square (or the triangle
or rectangle in the case of a dilemma) so long as you put the same
thing of EVERY INSTANCE of that shape.   Some students have gone as
far as to make a card with such geometric representations of the
rules and to cut out a supply of circles, squares, etc.   When they
want to see if an inference fits a form, they fill out the appropriate shapes, lay them on the original card and look to see if the
form matches what they wanted to do.

The card for MODUS TOLLENS would have this form:

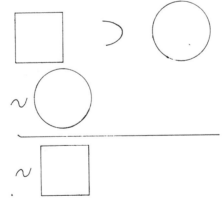

Possible expressions to be written on circles and squares would be
"(X v Y)" and "~ (Z · ~ A)." Writing them on the shapes as suggested
and laying them on the original modus tollens card would yield

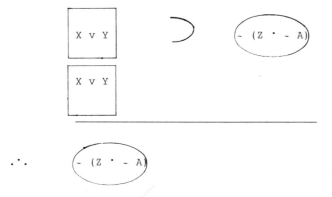

(Incidentally, this particular instance of modus tollens is exercise 6 in part I of the exercises discussed below.)

Although this approach may seem awfully elementary to you, I would recommend that, if you feel at all uncertain about the use of any of the rules introduced in this chapter, you try this sort of technique. All but one of the following argument-forms is an instance of modus ponens. Can you recognize which one is not?

A. $p \supset (q \supset r)$ B. $s \supset (r \vee t)$ C. $(p \supset q) \supset {\sim} q$ D. $p \vee (q \cdot s)$
  p s $p \supset q$ p
 -----------   ----------- ------------- ---------
$\therefore r$ $\therefore r \vee t$ $\therefore {\sim} q$ $\therefore q \cdot s$

In these examples, all but D are legitimate instances of modus ponens. The D problem cannot be (in fact it is invalid) because the major connective of the first premiss is a "v" instead of a " $\supset$ ". This is a common sort of error, but one which is easy to avoid. The internal structure of the expressions filling the locations of Wff 1 and Wff 2 (and Wff 3 and Wff 4 in the cases of Hypothetical Syllogism and Constructive Dilemma) can be anything at all so long as it is well formed, BUT anything else in the argument-form must remain exactly as it is for the rule-form to apply.

  The first two rules of inference are **modus ponens** and **modus ponens**. If you look at their forms, on the inside covers of Copi, you will see how very similar they are. They share a first premiss form: $p \supset q$. That constitutes an assertion that p cannot occur without q also occurring. The second premiss of **modus ponens** asserts that p DOES occur. Given the claim of the first premiss, you see that q must also occur. **Modus tollens**'s second premiss, ~ q, denies q's occurrence. Given the claim of the first premiss, you surely see that p, then could not occur. You might look at these argument forms as showing alternative outcomes of an initial assertion:

$$p \supset q$$

$$p \qquad\qquad {\sim} q$$
$$\text{---} \qquad\qquad \text{---}$$

$$\therefore q \qquad \therefore {\sim} p$$

$$\text{(M.P.)} \qquad \text{(M.T.)}$$

  If you look at problems 11 and 6 in part I of the exercises following this section you will see instances of each of these rules. In exercise 6 the argument given results from the substitution of "X v Y" for "p" and "~ (Z · ~ A)" for "q" in the basic modus tollens form. If you look at the example at the top of this page you will

see graphically how that substitution was made.   Exercise 11 is a
case of substituting "(A ⊃ B)" for "p" and "(C v D)" for "q" in the
basic modus ponens form.   If you used the graphic representation of
modus ponens you would have this form:

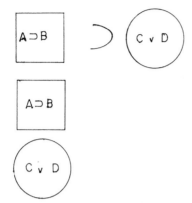

The third and fourth rules of inference are also ones which you
encountered in chapter 7:   the hypothetical syllogism (there called
the PURE hypothetical syllogism) and the disjunctive syllogism.
Exercise 10, which you could see is an instance of the hypothetical
syllogism in Copi, is significant for another reason.   The form of
this rule is

$$p \supset q$$
$$q \supset r$$
$$-----$$
$$\therefore \quad p \supset r$$

If you look at (I ≡ H) as the "p-term, "~ (H · ~ I) as the "q-term"
and (H ⊃ I) as the "r-term" of the argument in exercise 10, then it
has this form:

$$q \supset r$$
$$p \supset q$$
$$-----$$
$$\therefore \quad p \supset r$$

That resembles, but is not an exact match for the form given for the
hypothetical syllogism: the premises are in reversed order.   For
the purposes of the propositional logic proofs, however, that difference is considered to be no difference.

It is also the case that, in longer proofs like those of parts
II, III and IV, it is not even necessary that the two premises of
the rule forms appear next to each other.   For example, in exericse 2
of part II you obtain step 6 from steps 3 and 5 by the use of the
disjunctive syllogism.   In this case there is an intervening step AND
the steps are reversed.   For all practical purposes, once you have a
step accepted in a formal proof of validity (either as a premiss or
as a step proven) you may treat it as if it were next to any other
step in the proof.

If you find yourself feeling insecure about any of the four
rules of inference discussed so far, or the rule of constructive
dilemma, you should look back at the more extended discussion of them
in chapter 7.   Incidentally, note that in the exercise just mentioned, number 2 in part II, the fifth step results from the second
and fourth by use of the constructive dilemma form (called the complex constructive dilemma in chapter 7).

The sixth rule in Professor Copi's list is called absorption. It looks more complicated than it is. Consider the case of a conditional statement. There are three ways in which it can be true: a true antecedent and a true consequent, a false antecedent and a false consequent, and a false antecedent and a true consequent. If the antecedent term is false, then the consequent of the "absorbed" form will have at least one false conjunct which means that the consequent and the antecedent are false and the conditional true. If the antecedent is true, then the "absorbed" consequent will be true when the original consequent was true and false when it was false. An alternative way of looking at the relationship expressed in this rule is to consider how the form "p ⊃ (p.q)" could be false. Given the definition of the " ⊃ ," the antecedent (p) would have to be true and the consequent (p.q) would have to be false. But, for p ⊃ q to be false when p is true (as the assumption above shows) q would have to be false. However, when p is true and q is false, p ⊃ q is false, not true. Thus absorption cannot lead you astray. You may, by the way, wish to file away in your memory the fact that this rule is often used together with the rule of exportation which will be explained in the next section.

The rules of simplification and conjunction are really just two sides of the same coin. Simplification occurs as in exercise 2, part I in Copi. It is simply the assertion that, when you know that a conjunction is the case, you may infer that its first conjunct is also true. This ought to seem reasonable since the truth table definition of the is that it is true only when both conjuncts are true. You will need to be very careful using this rule. It is, of course, valid to infer the SECOND conjunct rather than the first, but it cannot be done directly. If you examined exercise 2, part II, carefully, you surely noticed that step 5, (G v H), which I asserted came from steps 2 and 4 by D.C., also appears to come from step 1 by simplification. It does not, however, follow so directly. Since it occurs as the SECOND conjunct, the rule of simplification will not justify its inference. Do not fear, however, for the means to infer second conjuncts will be offered in the next set of rules.

It is in relation to the rule of simplification that one of the commonest errors is made in generating formal proofs of validity. In the application of the rules of inference, you may only use them upon whole steps that match the forms of the rules. For example, when you encounter an expression like p ⊃ (q · r), it seems quite natural in infer p ⊃ q by Simplification. As a matter of fact the inference to p ⊃ q from p ⊃ (q · r) is valid, but the inference is not a direct one. The reason for forbidding such an inference is that there are cases where what looks like the same sort of move is not a valid argument.   Most obvious is the attempted inference of p ⊃ r from (p · q) ⊃ r. The easiest way to see what is wrong here is to replace the variables with three statements: p =df I throw this lighted newspaper into that tank, q =df The tank is filled with 90-octane gasoline, and r =df There is an explosion. The premiss statement, then, becomes:

> If I throw this lighted newspaper into that tank and that tank is filled with 90-octane gasoline, then there is (or will be) an explosion.

That seems a reasonable supposition. If simplification were (incorrectly) applied to the antecedent, the resulting statement would be:

> If I throw this lighted newspaper into that tank, then there if (or will be) an explosion.

That is clearly false. The lesson to be learned from the example is that the logic cannot accept as a rule anything that will not work ALL OF THE TIME. Thus, even though there are some contexts in which a simplification upon an interior part of a statement-form would seem useful, the rules of inference must be confined to whole steps.

The rule of conjunction follows an analogous path of reasoning: If two propositions are true apart from each other, then they will remain true as a conjunction.

The final rule of inference is called addition. It is a simple, straightforward rule which, at least in my teaching experience, is misunderstood more often than any other. If you know something to be the case, then either that thing or something else (as yet unspecified) is the case. This has to be the case since all that a disjunction needs to be true is to have one of its disjuncts true and you KNOW that one of them is true.

The error that frequently is made in applying the rule of addition is the attempt to use it backward. This means that you are trying to infer p from p v q. That, of course, is not addition, but is an invalid inference which, I guess, you might call subtraction or simplification of the wedge. With the rules of inference it is critical that you be use to use them only in the direction that they are given.

The three basic guidelines, then, for using the rules of inference are (1) apply the rules only when you have an exact match of connectives, (2) apply the rules to whole steps only, and (3) apply the rules only in the direction in which they are given.

Professor Copi shows you many examples of the correct format for formal proofs of validity. You may not be certain about what they are intended to do. The format is set up in such a way that anyone who reads it can re-trace the pattern of reasoning that took place in it. Each step must be justified, in two ways:

(1) You must be able to identify HOW the person working the problem arrived at that particular step.

(2) You must be able to identify FROM WHERE that particular step came.

In the case of a premiss, saying that it is a premiss is an indication that it came FROM and BY assumption. In the case of all other steps it is necessary that the justification for a step contain both a number (or numbers) and a rule name (or abbreviation of a name), the number(s) telling you FROM WHERE the step came and the name telling you HOW it came. If you double-check to insure that no rule has been used erroneously, then the formal proof is its own verification--when you are done with it you know that it is right.

It would be wise for you, now, to work a few of the problems in sections I and II following 9.1. Section 1 problems go from premiss to conclusion in one step; that is, they are really just examples of the rules where the expressions taking the places referred to as Wff 1, etc., are of varying complexities. Professor Copi has the solutions to 1/5 of the problems in the back of the book. Below you will find several more solutions to problems which should be helpful to you. Since several problems have been used as examples in this section, the problems whose solutions appear below may not be the ones you might have expected from previous chapters. The exercises "solved" below are ones which I judge to be particularly useful in learning tricky techniques. WORK THE PROBLEMS BEFORE YOU LOOK AT THE ANSWERS. Since the answers are a retracing of the reasoning applied to the problem, people who read the answers first tend to think that they understand how to work the problems better than they actually do. It's like the Exercises in Reasoning in the first lesson; once you know the answer it's easy.

1.   (3)   1, Add. WFF 1 is (H ⊃ I); Wff 2 is (H ⊃ ~ I). Note
                  that you were NOT required to have had Wff 2 anywhere
                  else in the problem.
            (6)   1, 2, M.T. Wff 1 is (X v Y); Wff 2 is (~ (Z · ~ A)).
                  Note that, since Wff 2 begins with ~ , its negation
                  (in the second premiss) must begin with ~ ~. Students
                  frequently ask why premiss 2 could not have been
                  (Z · ~ A). There are are two basic reasons: (1) there
                  are logic systems in which p and ~ ~ p are not inter-
                  changeable, so it's a bad habit treating the dropping
                  (or adding) of a double negation as if it were accept-
                  able, because it's "obvious". Doing so is an intuitive
                  move, and one of the primary motivations for having a
                  formal system was to avoid operation on the intuitive
                  level. The need for avoiding intuition as a justifi-
                  cation for reasoning was stated, perhaps most bitterly
                  but eloquently, in 1877 by C.S. Peirce: "Few persons
                  care to study logic, because everybody conceives him-
                  self to be proficient enough in the art of reasoning
                  already. But I observe that this satisfaction is
                  limited to one's own ratiocination [reasoning], and
                  does not extend to that of other men."
                  ["Illustrations of the Logic of Science--First Paper,
                  The Fixation of Belief," THE POPULAR SCIENCE MONTHLY,
                  V. 12 (1877-78), p. 1.]

            (12) 1, 2, DS. Wff 1 is [E ⊃ (F ≡ ~ G)]; Wff 2 is (C v D).
                  Note that in this case Wff 1 is quite complex, but can
                  still be handled as if it were simple: you just treat
                  it as a unit.

            (16) 1, 2, Conj.   Wff 2 is   [N ⊃ (O v P)], Wff 1 is
                  [Q ⊃ (O v R)]. Note that the premisses occurred in
                  reverse order. That is fine, the order of the premis-
                  ses is not significant.

            (19) 1, 2, C.D. Wff 1 is (H · ~ I), Wff 2 is (C), Wff 3
                  is (I · ~ H), and Wff 4 is (D). This is the sort of
                  really simple problem that tends to cause problems
                  because it "looks" so hard.

II.   (3)   1. Premiss
                  2. Premiss
                  3. Premiss
                  4. Premiss   Note that the conclusion is stated after
                                 the /∴ . Be VERY careful not to try to
                                 USE the conclusion as if it too were a
                                 premiss.
                  5. 1, 2, H.S. Wff 1 is I, 2 is J, 3 is K.
                  6. 3, 5, Conj. Wff 1 is (I ⊃ K), Wff 2 is (L ⊃ M).
                  7. 4, 6, C.D. Wff 1 is I, 2 is K, 3 is L, 4 is M

            (7)   1. Premiss
                  2. Premiss
                  3. Premiss
                  4. 3, Simpl. Wff 1 is A, Wff 2 is D.
                  5. 4, Add.   Wff 1 is A, Wff 2 is B.
                  6. 1, 5, M.P. Wff 1 is (A v B), Wff 2 is C.
                  7. 6, Add.   Wff 1 is C, Wff 2 is B.
                  8. 2, 7, M.P. Wff 1 is (C v B), Wff 2 is
                                     [A ⊃ (D ≡ E)].
                  9. 4, 8, M.P. Wff 1 is A, Wff 2 is (D ≡ E).
                                 Note that this step uses step 4 for a
                                 second time (step 5 had also used it).
                                 That is perfectly permissible. Once a
                                 step is established, it may be used as
                                 often as you like.

The problems in part III are a bit harder, and the ones in parts IV, V and VI a bit harder yet. They are all intended to provide you with a graduated introduction into doing this sort of problem. The difficulty is that the sort in III and IV involve what is sometimes called the "ingenuity" problem. In some subject areas there are absolutely right and wrong answers and/or ways of doing things; in the area of generating formal proofs of validity that is not the case. This does not mean that you cannot make errors--anyone who has tried to learn logic has made a bookful of them--it means that there is seldom one RIGHT way of doing a problem. The situation may be well compared to the following: Suppose you were told on a Thursday that you were to go from, say, Chicago (where you happened to be) to St. Louis and be there by noon on Tuesday. It is obvious to almost anyone that you could, in that span of time, drive, take a plane, bus, or train, ride a horse, or run (if you were in very good condition). But, if you were particularly perverse (or adventurous) you might catch the Icelandic flight to Luxembourg, take the train from there to Amsterdam, catch the shuttle cruiser (boat) to England, rent a car and drive to London, fly on the polar circle flight to Seattle, catch the coastal commuter flight to San Francisco and finish out with a non-stop flight to St. Louis. [As of January of 1986 that particular route could get you from Chicago to St. Louis--and would cost you just under $4,200.] That surely would not be an efficient route, but it would get you there. The same is true of some logical proofs--they are roundabout, but they get you there.

It is that very flexibility in doing such problems that makes it difficult to "teach" you how to do them. This is compounded by the fact that different people seldom find that the same sets of rules are comfortable. Professor Copi's selection of the rules to use in this text is based upon what he finds most useful and upon what he infers, through his years of teaching logic, will be easiest for the greatest number of students to use. But the selection is just one of many possible. What you will have to accept is that **this is the set** of rules that you have. It is no more arbitrary than most sets of rules for anything. In baseball, for example, a left-handed batter has a distinct advantage: he stands about six feet closer to first base and, after a swing, his momentum is toward the base to which he has to run while a right-handed batter's is away from it. This could be rectified by letting right-handed hitters run the bases clock-wise (third-second-first-home) while southpaws ran counter-clockwise (first-second-third-home). This would be "fairer" to them, but horrible for the umpires. In any event, there has been no major move for such a system; the rules are just accepted as they are. In logic, too, the rules are the rules. In general, the best that can be done is for you to work enough problems for you to begin to feel comfortable with generating formal proofs of validity. The most helpful thing that anyone teaching this material can do is to warn you about the sorts of errors you are likely to make and to suggest rules of thumb for attacking problems. A rule of thumb is a guiding principle which experience has shown to be generally helpful although not universally reliable. (One rule of thumb, for example, is that, when wagering at a dog race always bet the dog with the pole (inside) position. Without jockeys to intelligently guide the dogs, the number one dog will win about 22% of the time. This is, of course, a by-product of the position in which it starts).

III	(2)	1.	$D \supset E$	Premiss	
		2.	$D \cdot F$	Premiss	$/\therefore$ E
		3.	D	2, Simp	
		4.	E	1, 3, MP	

Note that here premisses 1 and 3 are in the same order as their corresponding forms in the MP rule, but that premiss 2 lies between them. Remember that so long as the internal structure matches the form of the rule, the order of proximity of the premisses is irrelevent.

(6)   1.   P · Q   Premiss
      2.   R   Premiss   /∴. P · R
      3.   P   1, Simp
      4.   P · R   2, 3, Conj

If you want to be particularly clear about your understanding of the rule forms you might have written the justification of step 4 as 3, 2, Conj. That would indicate that
you saw that the elements that you wanted to conjoin
appeared in this argument in an order reversed from the
conjunction rule form.   Although that might be a nice
touch, it surely is not necessary.

(11) 1.   D ⊃ E   Premiss
      2.   (E ⊃ F) · (F ⊃ D)   Premiss   /∴. D ⊃ F
      3.   E ⊃ F   2, Simp
      4.   D ⊃ F   1, 3 HS

This is another of those problems that looks hard but
really is quite simple.

(16) 1.   (T ⊃ U) · (T ⊃ V)   Premiss
      2.   T   Premiss   /∴. U v V
      3.   T ⊃ U   1, Simp
      4.   U   2, 3, MP
      5.   U v V   4, Add

The instructions for this section say that you can complete the proof with two added steps. I have included it
because I believe that it is the most "natural" way to
prove this problem. The two-additional-step proof involves a bit more "cleverness" in its solution:

      1.   (T ⊃ U) · (T ⊃ V)   Premiss
      2.   T   Premiss   /∴. U v V
      3.   T v T   2, Add
      4.   U v V   1, 3 CD

This is instructive because it shows you a little more of
the freedom you have to choose that second disjunct when
using addition. In practice, however, few people would
quibble about the one additional step in the first proof.
If you got the second form on your own, give yourself a
gold star.

(21) 1.   (K ⊃ L) ⊃ M   Premiss
      2.   ~ M · ~ (L ⊃ K)   Premiss /∴. ~ (K ⊃ L)
      3.   ~ M   2, Simp
      4.   ~ (K ⊃ L)   1, 3 MT

It is very easy in this exercise to be distracted by the
~ (L − K) in the second premiss. It looks as if you
ought to be able to get it out then swap the antecedent
and consequent terms. You should see, however, that the
simplification rule won't let you get the second conjunct
and that you don't yet have (and don't want) a rule
allowing the antecedent and the consequent of a conditional to be exchanged.

(27) 1.   (E · F) v (G ⊃ H)   Premiss
      2.   I ⊃ G   Premiss
      3.   ~ (E · F)   Premiss   /∴. I ⊃ H
      4.   G ⊃ H   1, 3, DS
      5.   I ⊃ H   2, 4, HS

This may well be the most difficult problem in this set
of exercises. It involves treating complex expressions as
units (in step 4) and seeing them as separated elements
(in step 5). Even with those difficulties, you probably
found it a fairly simple exercise.

In working the more complex problems of parts IV-VI, you may
find another rule of thumb helpful. The most useful rule of thumb I
know (at least for working out formal proofs of validity) is that you
should work many problems backward. That sounds strange, but really
isn't. Consider this argument:

$$D \supset E, \sim (D \cdot E) \mid - \sim D$$

First instinct says to use simplification of the second premiss, but
that is "illicit." (You can't apply an inferential rule within a
step.) If you look back over the rules, you will notice that there
is only one of the first nine that has a negation in its conclusion--
modus tollens. If ~ D were taken as the „~ Wff 2" of the conclusion
of a modus tollens argument, you would know that there would have had
to have been two previous steps of the form:

$$D \supset \text{Wff 2}, \sim (\text{Wff 2}) \mid - \sim D$$

In this problem you are given a premiss with a negation, the second.
If this is taken to be ~ (Wff 2), then the modus tollens argument to
~ D would have to be

$$D \supset (D \cdot E), \sim (D \cdot E) \mid - \sim D$$

The only difference of this from the original argument is in the
first premiss. The problem now is to find an acceptable way to go
from D — E to D — (D · E). Scanning the list of rules, you will find
that there are only two rules with " — " as their major connec-
tive--H.S. and Abs. In the case of the H.S., another premiss
contain-ing a " — " would be needed--that only leaves Abs. It is, of
course, the correct answer. You are now in a position to rewrite the
formal proof according to the correct format.

1. D ⊃ E   Premiss
2. ~ (D · E)   Premiss
3. D ⊃ (D · E)   1, Abs.
4. ~ D   2, 3, M.T.

As a working arrangement, you can even write a proof backward, beginning with step n (the conclusion.) Consider the argument:

$$E \text{ v} \sim F, F \supset \sim G, \sim E \mid - (F \supset \sim G) \cdot \sim F$$

n. (F ⊃ ~ G) · ~ F   m, k, Conjunction (this is rule
                            thus far that results in a · .)

m. F ⊃ ~ G   Premiss (this is actually premiss
                            2.)

k. ~ F   {j, i, modus tollens (This looks
                            like the right approach, pat-
                            terning after problem 2. As it
                            happens it is not, for you have
                            no way to get ~ ~ G. If you
                            look, however, you will see
                            another choice.)}

                           j, i, Disjunctive Syllogism (This
                           takes advantage of looking at
                           premiss 1 and 3.)

The reordered proof, then, is

```
1.   E v ~ F            Premiss
2.   F ⊃ ~ G            Premiss
3.   ~ E               Premiss    /∴ (F ⊃ ~ G) · ~ F
4.   ~ F               1, 3, D.S.
5.   (F ⊃ ~ G) · ~ F   2, 4, Conj.
```

As this problem notes (step k), working in reverse order is not always the best approach. A second technique, one that best applies to somewhat more complex problems, is to begin by trying to find where the variables or statements that occur in the conclusion were located in the premisses. Part V, exercise 4 is one in which this approach works well.

```
Premiss 1    (A)      (K v L) ⊃ (M v N)
Premiss 2    (B)      (M v N) ⊃ (O · P)
Premiss 3    (C)      K
                      ----------------------
Conclusion   (D)      ∴  O
```

The conclusion (D) is the statement O. The only occurrence of O in the premisses is in the consequent of (B). Of the rules you now have, the only one that isolates the consequent of an implication, is M.P. To use M.P. you would have to have had the antecedent of (B), that is, (M v N). That occurs also as the consequent of (A). Again you would need an antecedent to isolate that consequent by M.P. There the needed antecedent is (K v L). Among the rules of inference there are but two that result in a disjunctive statement: C.D. and Add. Since the latter is so much simpler, it is probably best to see if it could be used before going on to check the more complicated rule. And, in this case, addition is the correct route. You wanted to obtain the antecedent of (A), which is (K v L); to apply addition you would have to see it as (Wff 1 v Wff 2) with K = Wff 1 and L = Wff 2. To arrive at this disjunction by addition you would have to have had its Wff 1 component, i.e., K, previously, and, of course, you did have it as (C). Using the reasoning that has developed here the problem can be rather straightforwardly written:

```
1.   (K v L) ⊃ (M v N)    Premiss
2.   (M v N) ⊃ (O · P)    Premiss
3.   K                    Premiss    /∴  O
4.   K v L                3, Add.
5.   M v N                1, 4, M.P.
6.   O · P                2, 5, M.P.
7.   O                    6, Simpl.
```

Please notice that there was at least a slight variance of route that would probably occur if the problem had been worked "forward":

```
1.   Same
2.   Same
3.   Same
4.   (K v L) ⊃ (O · P)    1,2 H.S. [with Wff 1 = (K v L),
                          2 = (M v N) and 3 = (O · P)]
5.   K v L                3, Add.
6.   O · P                4, 5 M.P.
7.   O                    6, Simpl.
```

Perhaps one more example of this approach might be useful. It will, however, be offered in a bit briefer terms. In the same set, look at problem 10. Again, you ought to try the problem on your own before looking at the solution.

EXPRESSION SOUGHT	FOUND IN	GET BY	ALSO NEED
Conclusion (R)	Conseq. of P-2	M.P.	P v Q
P v Q	Antec. of P-2	Add.	P
P	Conseq. of P-1	M.P.	N v O
N v O	Antec. of P-1	Add.	N
N	Second disj., P-3	D.S.	~ Q
~ Q	P-4	Premiss	--

This gives you sufficient information to get the proof:

```
1.  (N v O) ⊃ P        Premiss
2.  (P v Q) ⊃ R        Premiss
3.  Q v N              Premiss
4.  ~ Q                Premiss    /∴ R
5.  N                  3, 4, D.S.
6.  N v O              5, Add.
7.  P                  1, 6, M.P.
8.  P v Q              7, Add.
9.  R                  2, 8, M.P.
```

You should now find yourself at the point at which you intellectually understand how to generate formal proofs of validity. However, your situation is much like that of the person who has read all of the how-to books available on tennis: unless that person has "gone onto the court" and practiced, John McEnroe, Martina Navratilova and all of the other leading players have nothing to fear. You should now work as many of the exercises in parts IV, V, and VI as you can find time to attempt. The more "hands-on" time you have with the rules, the easier proofs are to generate. If you choose not to try all of the exercises, be sure to attempt ones from the ends of the sections. The problems sometimes get more difficult, so you do not want to mislead yourself about your preparation by doing only the easier ones. Again, work the exercise on your own before looking at the answers here or in Copi: most proofs are easier to follow once done than they are to generate.

```
IV  (3)     1.  (H ⊃ I) · (H ⊃ J)   Premiss
            2.  H · (I v J)         Premiss    /∴ I v J
            3.  H                   2, Simp
            4.  H v H               3, Add
            5.  I v J               1, 4, CD
```

This exercise ought to remind you of exercise 16 in section III. It too relies upon the "clever" use of addition. And the problem itself also has an alternate proof involving just one more step:

```
            1.  (H ⊃ I) · (H ⊃ J)   Premiss
            2.  H · (I v J)         Premiss    /∴ I v J
            3.  H ⊃ I               1, Simp
            4.  H                   2, Simp
            5.  I                   3, 4, MP
            6.  I v J               5, Add
```

It's also the case that, if you had had a means to infer the second conjunct in premiss 2, you could have arrived at the conclusion directly from that premiss, without any reference to the first premiss at all.

```
    (8)     1.  ~ X ⊃ Y             Premiss
            2.  Z ⊃ X               Premiss
            3.  ~ X                 Premiss    /∴ Y · ~ Z
            4.  ~ Z                 2, 3, MT
            5.  Y                   1, 3, MP
            6.  Y · ~ Z             4, 5, Conj
```

Since, among the rules you presently have, only conjunction results in an expression whose primary connective is a " · ", chances are very good that you
will have had to have used that rule. That being the
case, your goal was to have found the most obvious
method of arriving at each of the conclusion's conjuncts. Since "Y" is the consequent of premiss 1 and
"~ Z" is the negation of the antecedent of premiss 2,
it should have followed fairly obviously that you were
going to use MP and MT. A quick check of premiss 3
showed that ~ X is the missing element for both of
those inferences, and the proof was complete. Again,
the use of premiss 3 twice should have emphasized to
you the fact that multiple uses of any step, once
assumed or proven, is not only permissible, but sometimes absolutely necessary.

(15)   1. (Z · A) ⊃ B   Premiss
              2. B ⊃ A   Premiss
              3. (B · A) ⊃ (A · B) Premiss   /∴. (Z · A) ⊃ (A · B)
              4. B ⊃ (B · A)   2, Abs
              5. B ⊃ (A · B)   3, 4, HS
              6. (Z · A) ⊃ (A · B) 1, 5, HS

It is very likely that you saw quickly that the antecedent of premiss 1 and the consequent of premiss 3
served the same roles in the conclusion. All you
needed was to find some sort of HS "Bridge" between
the two. Absorption did nicely.

The exercises in section V are of the same sort as those of the
earlier sections, just a bit longer. Problems 4 and 10 were solved
earlier (pp. 159 & 160), but one more, problem 7, may prove helpful.
First, you can see that the conclusion is a disjunction. You have
availablee to you only two rules that result in a disjunction: CD
and addition. Since addition is the "simpler" it makes sense to try
it first. Addition infers the form "p v q" from "p." In the case of
exercise 7's conclusion, A · B would have to be the p-term and C · D
the q-term. THe only rule that results in a conjunction is conjunction, so to get the A · B that you need for the premiss of the
addition step you must have had A and B previously. But there is the
difficulty, for to get B you must use MP (the only rule that gets the
consequent of a conditional out by itself) and that would require
that you have had an A. The only occurrence of A other than in the
first premiss, however, is as the first disjunct of the third premiss. At this point you have no rule that allows you to obtain the
first of two disjuncts. Thus, the use of addition is apparently a
dead-end.

The other rule that you might have used was CD. It has the
form:

$$(p ⊃ q) · (r ⊃ s)$$
$$p v r$$
$$\text{------------------}$$
$$∴ \quad q v s$$

In this problem you know that the q-term must be A · B and that the
s-term must be C · D, since the conclusion sought is (A · B) v (C · D).
You can see that you have A v D as the third premiss, so it seems
reasonable to assume that the p-term is A and the r-term is C.
Knowing what the p-, q-, r-, and s-terms are, you also know that the
needed first premiss for a CD is [A ⊃ (A · B)] · [C ⊃ (C · D)]. As a
conjunction it is almost certain that this expression was a result of
conjoining its two conjuncts. Seeing the match-up of propositional
constants, you surely see that you need to find out how you could
have inferred A ⊃ (A · B) from A ⊃ B and C ⊃ (C · D) from C ⊃ D. Of

the rules you have available only HS and absorption result in conditionals. Since you don't have premiss expressions with A — B and
C — D in them, absorption looks like the better choice. In fact the
inferences you need are exact instances of that rule.

Tracing back through this mass of discussion, then, you should
find buried the elements of the formal proof of ex. 7.

V   (7)   1. A ⊃ B   Premiss
                2. C ⊃ D   Premiss
                3. A v C   Premiss /∴ (A · B) v (C · D)
                4. A ⊃ (A · B)   1, Abs
                5. C ⊃ (C · D)   2, Abs
                6. [A⊃ (A·B)]·[C⊃ (C·D)]   4, 5, Conj
                7. (A · B) v (C · D)   3, 6, CD

The problems in part VI are simply a combination of the symbolization that you did in Chapter 7 with the formal proofs of validity
that you are working now; there is nothing of nay added importance in
them, except that if you missymbolize, the problem may become unwork-
able. Most logic teachers have, at one time or another agreed to
work in class a problem that the students confidently claim is valid,
then have found to the teacher's great embarassment that the problem
should have been double-checked, since it was in fact invalid. Sometimes it has taken as many as 50 or 60 steps before the teacher was
willing to recheck validity. Should you hit even the thirty-step
level, it would probably be wise to recheck for validity.

VI   (2) If A, then S; and if B, then F.   (A ⊃ S) · (B ⊃ F)
          Either A or B.   A v B
          If S, then B; and if F, then W.   (S ⊃ B) · (F ⊃ W)
          ------------------------------   ------------------
          Therefore either B or W.   ∴ B v W

          Notice that the symbolization was as close a match for the
          original English grammatical structure as was possible.
          The only point that teachers of logic might quibble about
          was whether or not the semicolon should have been treated
          as an "and" or as a break between propositions. Had it
          been split into two premisses each, each with a simple
          conditional statement in it. Generally, however, you will
          find it more useful to treat whole sentences as units,
          leaving them a single proposition (however complex).

          1. (A ⊃ S) · (B ⊃ F)   Premiss
          2.   A v B   Premiss
          3. (S ⊃ B) · (F ⊃ W)   Premiss /∴ B v W
          4. S v F   1, 2, CD
          5. B v W   3, 4, CD

          If you are keeping a list of suggested rules of thumb, you
          might want to include the idea that any time you have a
          mixture of "⊃'s" and "v's" there is a good chance that you
          will be using the CD rule.

     (6) If J, then R; but if not J, then E.
          If R, then I.
          If J implies R and R implies I,
             then either J and I or not J and not I.
          If J and I, then T.
          But if not J and not I, then D.

          Therefore either T or D.

```
(J ⊃ R) · (~ J ⊃ E)
R — I
[(J ⊃ R) · (R ⊃ I)] ⊃ [J · I) v ( ~ J · ~ I)]
(J · I) ⊃ T
(~ J · ~ I) ⊃ D
--------------------------------
∴ T v D
```

The hardest part of symbolizing (and proving) this problem
is psychological: when you have 5 premisses most of which
look complex, it is natural to assume that the complexity
is a sign of conceptual difficulty. That is not the case.

In this exercise the mixture of — 's and v's should
suggest to you that you will, eventually, want to use CD.
When you look at the last two premisses you see that their
conjunction, with an appropriate disjunction, would yield
the conclusion by CD. If you scan the earlier premisses
you see that the consequent of the third premiss is that
appropriate disjunction. To get the consequent of any
conditional, you recall that you must use MP. That means
that you also need the antecedent of premiss three. Since
it's a conjunction, you probably also need each of its
elements separately. You have the second of them in the
second premiss and the first as a conjunct in the first
premiss. Backtracking this information, you should discover this proof:

```
1.   (J ⊃ R) · (~ J ⊃ E)                              Premiss
2.   R ⊃ I                                            Premiss
3.   [(J ⊃ R) · (R ⊃ I)] ⊃ [(J · I) v (~ J · ~ I)]   Premiss
4.   (J · I) ⊃ T                                      Premiss
5.   ( ~ J · ~ I) — D                                 Premiss/∴ T v D
6.   J ⊃ R                                            1, Simp
7.   (J ⊃ R) · (R ⊃ I)                                2, 6, Conj
8.   (J · I) v ( ~ J · ~ I)                           3, 7, MP
9.   [(J · I) ⊃ T] · [( ~ J · ~ I) ⊃ D]              4, 5, Conj
10.  T v D                                            8, 9, CD
```

9.2   The Rule of Replacement

You may find Profesor Copi's reference to **THE rule** of Replacement a little confusing. In a sense what he is doing is treating the
material as if there were but one replacement rule. In practice he
will treat replacement as a general category in which there are 16
subrules. The rule is actually a set of different rules, all of
which share the characteristic of allowing intersubstitution of any
one member of a pair for the other. It is probably esier to think of
replacement as a set of allied rules. In any event, the substitution
of one of the given forms for another **anywhere** is acceptable.

From a practical point of view, the reason that you can make
such substitutions is that the expressions on both sides of the
triple bar witll be found to have the same characteristic column when
checked on a truth table. If, for example, you worked out a truth
table for the first of the DeMorgan's Theorerms given you would have
the following table:

		I			II		
p q	p·q	~ (p·q)	~ p	~q	~p v ~q	~ (p · q) ≡ (~ p v ~ q)
T T	T	F	F	F	F	T
T F	F	T	F	T	T	T
F T	F	T	T	F	T	T
F F	F	T	T	T	T	T

When you compare the significant columns below the I and the II you see that they are identical. That means that, if you were generating a truth table in which one of the expressions occurred, you could replace the expression with the other without any change in the column and, thus, without any change in the ultimate column generated.

The DeMorgan's Theorems were so named for the English logician Augustus DeMorgan who was one of the pioneers of modern formal logic. They make explicit the relationship between " v " and " · " as logical connectives. Essentially they state that negated conjunctions become disjunctions and vice versa. The second form involves the two alternate ways that you could symbolize "neither...nor...." With either of the Theorems you see that denying the truth of one of these connectives is roughly the same (practically) as asserting that the other relation holds between the negations of the elements of the first.

If you look at exercise 6 in part I after 9.2 of Copi then you will see DeMorgan's Theorems in action. The expression "~ (R v S)" is replaced by "(~ R · ~ S)." This follows the second form exactly, so it must be a valid inference. Notice, please, that the consequent of both expressions could be modified by this rule, too. That expression "~ R v ~ S," matches the RIGHTHAND side of DeM, form 1. Thus you could have replaced it with "~ R · S)" which is the left-hand side. It is important to recognize this possibility because, all too frequently, students forget that the rules of replacement differ from the rules of inference in allowing the inference to run either direction.

The second form of replacement rule is the sort that should seem very familiar to you. Commutation, or exchanging the order of the expressions, is done all the time in arithmetic. (1 + 2) = (2 + 1), (2 x 3) = (3 x 2), and, generally, any additions or multiplications may be commuted. As it happens, equivalences, too, could have been included in the commutation rule, but they were not. The inference from step 1 to step 3 in exercise 2 of part II is made by commutation. Within the antecedent of (D · E) ⊃ F the D and E are exchanged to yield (E · D) ⊃ F. This inference should also remind you that the rule of replacement, unlike the rules of inference, can be made INSIDE a step.

Association, like commutation, ought to seem familiar: it shows that among three expressions all connected by either conjunction or disjunction you are free to group them left or right. There is a strong temptation to write a compound statement like "Gene or Hubie or Dick was elected" without internal differentiation: G v H v D. According to the agreed-upon conventions of our logic, however, that expression is not well-formed. The wedge connects two well-formed formulae, so the elements must be grouped in pairs: (G v H) v D or G v (H v D). The association rule allows you to transfer back and forth between these two expressions, so, since there is no clear reason for preferring one over the other, you are free to use the one that seems to you more appropriate. The inference of step 7 from step 1 in problem 5 in part II is this sort of reasoning

Association, like commutation also, could have been admitted for equivalence, since p ≡ (q ≡ r) does generate the same truth table as (p ≡ q) ≡ r. Arguments involving the " ≡ " are so rare that it really isn't worth the effort required to learn added rules involving that connective. There is, however, one thing that you need to be very careful to avoid: you must never try to apply either the rule of commutation or that of association to the " ⊃ ." In fact, you can always check to see if a connective is commutative and associative by checking the second and third rows of its truth table. If it has the same value when you have p = T/q = F and when you have p = F/q = T, then it is a commutative/associative function; if its values are different in those cases (as is the case with the " ⊃ ") then you can't commute or associate it.

Distribution looks a lot more complicated, but really is pretty simple. Essentially it confirms that you can carry a conjunction through a disjunction or vice versa. Thus if, for example, you knew that someone had had orange juice and toast or cereal for breakfast, then you would feel sure that she had had either orange juice and toast or orange juice and cereal. The inference "in that direction" seems clear, but many of us tend to forget that you could also have taken the second information ([O · T] v [O · C]) and inferred the former (O · [T v C]). The inference done this way is particularly useful because it results in a form upon which you can use simplification (from the last set of rules).

The other form of distribution, with which you distribute alternation through conjunction, is particularlly valuable also for its "setting up" simplifications. If you look again at problem 5 in part II you will see that the inference from step 2 to step 4 is a distribution of this sort. Note that the following step (6) is a simplification of the distributed form.

Inference form 14 will probably look too simple to dignify with a rule of its own. We have all been taught since early childhood about double negations. One of the important values of a formal logic is that it takes us away from relying upon our intuitions. Since there is little we can do to discuss differences in intuition when they occur, except to state the differences, such disagreements tend to become hostile quickly. Thus, it is necessary to include double negation as a rule. You should be careful to note that it allows you to insert two negations as well as delete them. One of the common cases in which inserting a double negation is needed is together with DeMorgan's theorems. If you have "A v B" and want to uses DeM, you will see that there is no match for the form you have. There are, however, two ways in which you can use DN to get a form upon which you can apply DeM:

1.	A v B	Given		1.	A v B	Given
2.	~ ~ (A v B)	1, DN		2.	~ ~ A v ~ ~ B	1, DN
3.	~ (~ A · ~ B)	2, DeM		3.	~ (~ A · ~ B)	2, DeM

In the left-hand case you applied the second DeM form within the outer negation; in the right-hand case you applied the first form (going right to left) treating A and B as the p- and q-terms, respectively. Incidentally, you may wonder at the use of "Given" instead of "Premiss." In this case I am not meaning to assert the given expression, as a premiss would do, I am just demonstrating how one relationship could be derived IF YOU WERE GIVEN another.

The equivalence called transposition is one with which you should feel comfortable because of your work with the categorical propositions. Roughly, it asserts that if q results from p then q's non-occurrence means that p also must not have occurred and vice versa. The inference in exercise 12 on part I of 9.2 is a transposition run right to left.

One of the best ways to understand the rule of material implication is by looking at the truth table for implication:

p q	p ⊃ q
T T	T
T F	F
F T	T
F F	T

When you check for rows in which the implication itself is true, you
see that, regardless of the value of the q-term, whenever the p-term
is false the implication is true. You should also see that whenever
the q-term is true, regardless of the value of the p-term, the implication is true. Written together that means that asserting "if p
then q" is the same as asserting that "either p is false or q is
true." Since so many of our real-life inferences involve conditional
relationships, it is very important that you feel at ease with the
rule of material implication. Note that exercise 11 of part of I 9.2
is an instance of material implication going from right to left.

It is interesting to observe that another way that you could
have asserted the conditional relationship, given the truth table for
the horseshoe, would be to deny the occurrence of the second row:
∼(p · ∼ q). If it were important for you to derive that expression
from p ⊃ q, you wuld have to use not only material implication, but
also DeM and DN:

1.	p ⊃ q	Given
2.	∼ p v q	1, Impl
3.	∼ p v ∼ ∼ q	2, DN
4.	∼ (p · ∼ q)	3, DeM

As you can see, the whole trick to mastering formal proofs of validity while in figuring out just which combination of inferences will
carry you from the premises of an argument to its conclusion.

Material equivalence takes two forms. One you should recall:
the " $\equiv$ " which is called a **biconditional** is simply the " ⊃ " read as
going in both directions. Its occurrence can be seen in Copi in
exercise 5 of part I; the other form of material equivalence is seen
in exercise 17 on that same page. That form is easily read from the
truth table for " $\equiv$ ":

p q	p $\equiv$ q
T T	T
T F	F
F T	F
F F	T

There are two cases where the expression is true: p and q are both
true and p and q are both false. Expressed symbolocally that would
be (p · q) v (∼ p · ∼ q). The "or" used in the expression is, of
course, the inclusive one, but you need have no worry about the
joint-occurrence case happening, for it would demand p and ∼ p to
occcur simultaneously.

The rule of exportation will prove a quite useful tool for
arrangement of conditions within conditional statements. Take, for
example, the statement "if you have a combustible material, an oxidizing element, and the heat of combustion of that material, then you
will have a fire of some sort." Although it may be valuable to have
the three fire-conditions lumped together, it may also be important
to "string them out" in such a way as to be able to handle each of
them separately. If that were done to this statement you would get
the statement: "if you have a combustible material, then if you have
an oxidizing element, then if you have the heat of combustion of that
material, THEN you will have sort of fire." Essentially that sort of
transformation is what exportation is all about: you either string
out or bunch up the conditions in a conditional. Note that in exercise 3 of part I you use exportation to move from the right to the
left in the rules form.

The last rule of replacement (or instance of the rule of replacement) is called "tautology." Since there was an earlier discussion of tautologies, that name may be unfortunate. However, the

other likely name would be "identity" which may result in greater
confusion in more advanced logic. All of the equivalences under the
heading of "The Rule of Replacement" are, of course, tautologies.
This rule, however, identifies two quite simple relationships. If
you were offered two alternatives and were to discover that they were
actually the same thing, you would not hesitate to claim that you
have really been offered only one choice. Similarly, if you were told
that you were to meet, say, the author of TARZAN and the author of
the John Carter of Mars series, you would expect to meet two individuals only as long as you did not realize that Edgar Rice Burroughs
wrote both (among many other works). The conjunctive form of this
rule is used in Copi in exercise 16 of part I; the disjunctive one is
used between steps 5 and 6 of exercise 5 of part II.

You should notice that there are some constant principles among
the replacements, just as there were among the rules of inference.
Your inference may follow the pattern of any of these equivalences,
going left to right or right to left. Again the connective pattern
must match exactly. (If the matching is not clear, you might want to
consider using the graphic method suggested above.) You might also
note that since the replacements are based upon equivalences, if you
had a proof in which ONLY rules of replacement were used, then you
could reverse the order of the steps and prove the premiss from the
conclusion. (Note that I said "premiss" not "premisses"--there are
no cases of the rule of replacement that use more than one premiss.)

As you did after 9.1, you should work a substantial number of
the exercises following 9.2. Recall that Professor Copi has about
1/5 of the solutuions in the back of his book, that a number of the
answers were mentioned above in the explanation of the rules and that
several more will be given below. Also recall that it is wise to
WORK THE PROBLEMS YOURSELF BEFORE YOU LOOK AT THE SOLUTIONS.

I   (3)   1, Exp. This takes place solely within the left-hand
                 conjunct. In it Wff 1 = 1, 2 = J and 3 = K. Note
                 that, relative to the way the form is given in Copi,
                 you are are moving right-to-left.

     (8)   1, Distr. Wff 1 = (X v Y), 2 = X, 3 = Y. One of the
                 hardest things for beginning students of logic to
                 recognize is the use of a compound expression like
                 (X v Y) where Copi's rule-form had had p.

     (12)   1, Trans. This takes place solely within the conse-
                 quent. Wff 1 = J, 2 = I. As in problem 3, this
                 inference takes place right-to-left relative to
                 Professor Copi's form of the rule.

     (17)   1, Equiv.   Wff 1 = (~ A · B), 2 = (C v D). The
                 only rule that goes from or arrives at a " ≡ " is
                 this rule.

II   (3)   1. Premiss
                 2. Premiss
                 3. 2, Add
                 4. 3, Com.
                 5. 1,4, M.P.
                 6. 5, Assoc.
                 7. 6, Simp.

                 There are, of course, other routes from these pre-
                 misses to that conclusion. The these premisses to
                 that conclusion. The proof marked 3A below is an
                 alternative proof that is less direct, but never-
                 theless quite acceptable. Note how few similarities
                 the two proofs have, except premisses and conclu-
                 sion.

(3A)
```
1.  (H v I) ⊃ [J · (K · L)]              Premiss
2.  I                                    Premiss /∴ J · K
3.  ~ (H v I) v [J · (K · L)]            1, Impl
4.  [J · (K · L)] v ~ (H v I)            3, Com
5.  [J · (K · L)] v (~ H · ~ I)          4, DeM
6.  {[J · (K · L)] v ~ H} · {[J · (K · L)] v ~ I}
                                         5, Dist
7.  {[J · (K · L)] v ~ I} · {[J · (K · L)] v ~ H}
                                         6, Com
8.  [J · (K · L)] v ~ I                  7, Simp
9.  ~ I v [J · (K · L)]                  8, Com
10. ~ ~ I                                2, DN
11. J · (K · L)                          9, 10, D S
12. J                                    11, Simp
13. (K · L) · J                          11, Com
14. K · L                                13, Simp
15. K                                    14, Simp
16. J · K                                12, 15, Conj
```

Note that this alternate proof avoids the use of both modus ponens and addition, but at the cost of nine extra steps.

(7)
```
1.  Premiss
2.  Premiss
3.  Premiss
4.  Premiss
5.  3, Equiv
6.  4, 5, DS
7.  6, DeM
8.  1, 2, HS
9.  8, Exp
10. 9, Taut
11. 7, 10, MT
```

III (3)
```
1.  E                                    Premiss /∴ (E v F) · (E v G)
2.  E v F                                1, Add
3.  E v G                                1, Add
4.  (E v F) · (E v G)                    2, 3, Conj
```

It is important here to remember that once a step is justified in a proof it may be used as many times and in as many contexts as you find desirable.

(7)
```
1.  Q ⊃ [R ⊃ (S ⊃ T)]                    Premiss
2.  Q ⊃ (Q · R)                          Premiss /∴ Q ⊃ (S ⊃ T)
3.  (Q · R) ⊃ (S ⊃ T)                    1, Exp
4.  Q ⊃ (S ⊃ T)                          2, 3, HS
```

The pairing of the use of exportation and absorption (for, in a longer proof, step 2 might well have been the result of absorption upon a simpler premiss "Q ⊃ R") is one that merits remembering.

(12)
```
1.  F ≡ G                                Premiss
2.  ~ (F · G)                            Premiss /∴ ~ F · ~ G
3.  (F · G) v (~ F · ~ G)                1, Equiv
4.  ~ F · ~ G                            2, 3, DS
```

Since there are only two forms of single rule which involve the " ≡ ," figuring out what to do with a step containing a " ≡ " is seldom difficult.

(17)
```
1.  (W · X) ⊃ Y                          Premiss
2.  (X ⊃ Y) ⊃ Z                          Premiss /∴ W ⊃ Z
3.  W ⊃ (X ⊃ Y)                          1, Exp
4.  W ⊃ Z                                2, 3, HS
```

The greatest difficulty here is treating X — Y as a
unit rather than as a relationship.

(23)   1.   ~ [(U ⊃ V) · (V ⊃ U)]   Premiss
          2.   (W ≡ X) ⊃ (U ≡ V)   Premiss /∴ ~ (W ≡ X)
          3.   ~ (U ≡ V)   1, Equiv
          4.   ~ (W ≡ X)   2, 3, MT

Here the key is not to get excited or overwhelmed
quickly. Since the conclusion has occurred between
the same proposition-place-holders as it did in the
premiss, it is unlikely that you will tamper with that
part of the expression. On the other hand, since the
first premiss and the second one each contain the same
statement symbols, but one has a " ≡ " and the other
does not, you must surely use equivalence rule to
transform one into the other. That could, however,
have taken place in the second rather than the first
step. That would have yielded a different, but equally correct, proof:

          1.   ~ [(U ⊃ V) · (V ⊃ U)]   Premiss
          2.   (W ≡ X) ⊃ (U ≡ V)   Premiss /∴ ~ (W ≡ X)
          3.   (W ≡ X) ⊃ [(U ⊃ V) · (V ⊃ U)]   2, Equiv
          4.   ~ (W ≡ X)   2, 3, MT

(27)   1.   (J · K) ⊃ [(L · M) v (N · O)] Premiss
          2.   ~ (L · M) · ~ (N · O)   Premiss /∴ ~ (J · K)
          3.   ~ [(L · M) v (N · O)]   2, DeM
          4.   ~ (J · K)   1, 3, MT

The DeM step is the hardest one to see here. If you
look at (L · M) as Wff 1 and (N · O) as Wff 2, then
the inference from step 2 to step 3 is an instance of
the second form of DeM, reasoning right to left. Once
that is done all you have to do is is stand far enough
back to see that step 3 is the negation of the consequent of step 1. That should suggest the use of MT.

     The exercises in part IV are one more step more difficult. The
greatest value in your working such progressively harder problems is
in the recognition you have come to have of your own skill in con-
structing formal proofs of validity.

IV   (2)   1.   ~ B v (C · D)   Premiss /∴ B ⊃ C
              2.   (~ B v C) · (~ B v D) 1, Dist
              3.   ~ B v C   2, Simp
              4.   B ⊃ C   3, Impl

This sort of inference is one that you will encounter
with a fair degree of regularity. Note please that
the premiss could have been the result of a use of
implication (from B ⊃ (C · D)). Any time you feel the
urge to simplify the consequent of conditional statement, change it to a disjunction and follow this
pattern.

     (6)   1.   O ⊃ P   Premiss
              2.   P ⊃ ~ P   Premiss /∴ ~ O
              3.   ~ P v ~ P   2, Impl
              4.   ~ P   3, Taut
              5.   ~ O   1, 4, MT

This second premiss is a very curious-looking one.
Many people are inclined to think that, somehow, it is
a self-contradiction, but it is not. Any time that

you encounter the assertion tht some statement implies
its own negation, you can use the inference pattern in
steps 2, 3, and 4 to show that the statement in question is merely false. Similarly, be aware of the
pattern derived from statements like "~ P ⊃ P." Their
reduction can be shown in an inference like this one:

```
        1.  ~ P ⊃ P              Given
        2.  ~ ~ P v P            1, Impl
        3.  P v P                2, DN
        4.  P                    3, Taut
```

(14)   1. (N · O) ⊃ P   Premiss
        2. (~ P ⊃ ~ O) ⊃ Q   Premiss /.·. N — Q
        3. N ⊃ (O ⊃ P)   1, Exp
        4. (O ⊃ P) ⊃ Q   2, Trans
        5. N ⊃ Q   3, 4, HS

If you have been working exercises faithfully, then
this proof should have almost leapt from the page at
you: such is the reward of practice. The uses of
transposition and HS should also have seemed straightforward, since there are only 4 rules which begin and
end with conditional statements.

The problems in part V are of particular importance. As Professor Copi indicates, these patterns are recurrent ones in formal
proofs. In at least half the problems you work either one of these
inference patterns or something quite like one of them will occur.
It is worth your while, therefore, to work all of them. In addition
to the two answers in Copi, three more are given below::

V   (4)   1. H ⊃ (I · J)   Premiss /.·. H ⊃ I
             2. ~ H v (I · J)   1, Impl
             3. (~ H v I) · (~ H v J) 2, Dist
             4. ~ H v I   3, Simp
             5. H ⊃ I   4, Impl

Notice that this gives you a way to arrive at that
"simplification" of the consequent that you couldn't
get by the rule of simplification.

      (7)   1. (Q v R) ⊃ S   Premiss
             2. ~ (Q v R) v S   1, Impl
             3. (~ Q · ~ R) v S   2, DeM
             4. S v (~ Q · ~ R)   3, Com
             5. (S v ~ Q) · (S v ~ R) 4, Dist
             6. S v ~ Q   5, Simp
             7. ~ Q v S   6, Com
             8. Q ⊃ S   7, Impl

If you were given the problem (A v B) ⊃ (C · D) |— A ⊃ C you could,
for example, follow the patterns of 4 and 7; then you'd have the
solution.

      (10)   1. Z ⊃ A   Premiss
             2. Z v A   Premiss /.·. A
             3. A v Z   2, Com
             4. ~ ~ A v Z   3, D N
             5. ~ A ⊃ Z   4, Impl
             6. ~ A ⊃ A   1,5,HS [Remember the proof
             7. ~ ~ A v A   6, Impl   at the top of the
             8. A v A   7, DN   page.]
             9. A   8, Taut

The problems from part VI are picked NOT to utilize the proofs
that you worked out in part V. That should show you a few more

approaches to formal proofs. And doing them is a lot like any other
skill area--the more you do it the better you get at it.

VI.   (2)   1. (D · ~ E) ⊃ F   Premiss
            2. ~ (E v F)   Premiss   /∴ ~ D
            3. D ⊃ (~ E ⊃ F)   1, Exp
            4. D ⊃ (~ ~ E v F)   3, Impl
            5. D ⊃ (E v F)   4, DN
            6. ~ D   2, 5, MT

The approach used here is to recognize that, because E
and F are together in the second premiss, it is necessary to get them together from the first premiss,
too. Once that is done, the conclusion follows quickly.

(8)   Look at this one backward. You want to get "A v C" and
      there are only nine of the rules that wind up with a
      "v." You have no other statements involving "A v C," so
      you probably didn't use Com, Dist, or Assoc, at least
      directly. There were no " ≡ " or " ⊃ " signs invol-
      ving them either, so Impl and Equiv are out. The two
      disjuncts are different, so it isn't a tautology.
      There are no denied conjunctions, so DeM is an unlike-
      ly candidate. All that leaves are Add and CD. To get
      (A v C) as a result of a CD you had to have had as
      premisses (or prior references) (Wff 1 v Wff 2) and
      [Wff 1 ⊃ A] · [Wff 2 ⊃ C]. If Wff 1 = (Y · Z) and
      Wff 2 = (Y · B), then premiss 1 fits. You then need
      (Y · Z) v (Y · B).   That would come if you had
      [Y · (Z v B)], which you can see will tease out of
      premiss 2. The proof, then is

            1. [(Y · Z) ⊃ A] · [(Y · B) ⊃ C]   Premiss
            2. (B v Z) · Y   Premiss /∴ A v C
            3. Y · (B v Z)   2, Com
            4. (Y · B) v (Y · Z)   3, Dist
            5. (Y · Z) v (Y · B)   4, Com
            6. A v C   1, 5, CD

The sort of elimination of options that was done above is frequently
a worthwhile approach to solving such a problem. It can be, however,
very time-consuming to try to keep going back through all of the
rules to see which ones involve the connective that you happen to be
seeking at the time. To try to simplify that task, the following
chart has been developed. On it you can look up the connective you
have in a premiss (or inferred step)--you do this by looking across
the top. And, by reading the headings on the left side as you go
down the column under that connective, you will see what other connectives (if any) you can get to. Thus, for example, when you start
with a " ⊃ ," you see that you can arrive at a simple statement from
the " ⊃ " by MP, a negated one by MT, a " v " by Impl, and another
" ⊃ " by HS, Exp, Abs, or Trans. Or, you can begin on the left,
selecting the connective at which you wish to arrive, and read across
to see from what you could have obtained it. For example, if you
have "~ (-- · --)" you can see that the only rule that results in a
denied conjunction is DeM. The chart is, of course, not foolproof:
you could, for example, have arrived at that "~ (-- · --)" by MT if
you had had "(-- · --) ⊃ ___" and "~ (___)." You could also have arrived
at it by Simp if you had had "~ (-- · --) · ___" as a previous step.
The point is, the chart is only intended as a reference tool, suggesting at least reasonable things for which to look.

Premiss \\ Conclusion	--	~ --	- · -	- v -	- _ -	- ≡ -	~(- · -)	~(- v -)
--	MP	DS DN	Simp Taut	DS Taut	MP	--	--	--
~ --	DN	MT	--	--	MT	--	--	--
-- · --	Conj Taut	--	Com Assoc	Dist	--	Equiv	--	DeM
-- v --	Add Taut	--	Dist CD	Assoc Com CD	Impl	Equiv	DeM	--
-- _ --	--	--	--	Impl	HS Exp Abs Trans	--	--	--
-- ≡ --	--	--	Equiv	Equiv				
~(- · -)	--	--	--	DeM	--	--	--	--
~(- v -)	--	--	DeM	--	--	--	--	--

IV (17) This problem looks far more difficult than it is because its premisses are so long. A sketchy run backward looks like:

n. F ⊃ (F · I)   m, Abs
m. F ⊃ I   k, j, HS
k. ? ⊃ I
j. F ⊃ ?   Now there is a " ⊃ I" in the second premiss and a "~ F v " which can yield a "F ⊃ " by Impl.) in the first, so that's the way to approach this one. This problem then becomes:

1. ~ F v ~ [~ (G · H) · (G v H)]   Premiss
2. (G ⊃ H) ⊃ [H ⊃ G) ⊃ I]   Premiss
                                     /∴ F ⊃ (F · I)
At least the stuff in the second half of the first premiss and in the first half of the second premiss—supposedly the material from which the "?" of steps k and j above will come—is all made up of G's and H's.

3. F ⊃ ~ [~ (G · H) · (G v H)]   1, Impl
4. F ⊃ [~ ~ (G · H) v ~ (G v H)]   3, DeM (a reasonable move, since the chart says that this is the only thing you can do with a denied conjunction.)

```
 5.  F ⊃ [(G · H) v ~ (GvH)]          4, DN
 6.  F ⊃ [(G · H) v (~ G · ~ H)]      5,DeM (same move
                                      as step # 4)
 7.  F ⊃ (G ≡ H)                      6, Equiv (because
                                      this a sufficiently
                                      odd formula, you will
                                      come to see it quick-
                                      ly.)  Since you now
                                      have G ≡ H as a can-
                                      didate for the role
                                      of ? in j, try to get
                                      it as the same for k
                                      from step 2.

 8.  [(G ⊃ H) · (H ⊃ G)] ⊃ I          2, Exp
 9.  (G ≡ H) ⊃ I                      8, Equiv
10.  F ⊃ I                            7, 9, H S
11.  F ⊃ (F · I)                      10, Abs
```

(19)   Backward you'll get

```
n.  Q                                3, m, MP
m.  ~ (M · O)                        k, DeM  (the only route
                                     the other chart suggests)
k.  ~ M v ~ O                        Several options are avail-
                                     able.  One of  the most
                                     promising  would appear to
                                     be  CD, since the first
                                     two premisses look  so
                                     much like a dilemma.  As
                                     a  matter of fact the
                                     inference from them to k
                                     is  sometimes called  a
                                     DESTRUCTIVE DILEMMA.  But
                                     you don't have it as a
                                     rule; you have its cousin
                                     the constructive dilemma.
                                     What is needed is a way to
                                     convert  one  into the
                                     other.   That way is to
                                     use transportation on the
                                     conditional  statements in
                                     the first premiss.  The
                                     proof then is:

 1.  (M ⊃ N) · (O ⊃ P)               Premiss
 2.  ~ N v ~ P                        Premiss
 3.  ~ (M · O) ⊃ Q                   Premiss /∴ Q
 4.  (~ N ⊃ ~ M) · (~ P ⊃ ~ O)       1, Trans (Since you
                                     are doing the same thing
                                     to both conjuncts, there
                                     is no good reason not to
                                     do them together.)
 5.  ~ M v ~ O                       2, 4, CD (Notice
                                     that by transposing, what
                                     had been the disjunction
                                     of the negations of the
                                     consequents has become the
                                     disjunction of the antece-
                                     dents.)
 6.  ~ (M · O)                       5, DeM
 7.  Q                               3, 6, MP
```

Here you see that what had appeared to be a very complex proof is actually rather simple.

Some people find that, since, as the chart shows, the greatest number of rules going from a connective to itself is found with the " ⊃ ," it is sometimes helpful to convert anything that you can into " ⊃ 's" and then proceed. If that is coupled with another rule of thumb--whenever you can, break things down as far as possible--the proof of this same problem could become:

1.	(M ⊃ N) · (O ⊃ P)	Premiss
2.	~ N v ~ P	Premiss
3.	~ (M · O) ⊃ Q	Premiss /∴ Q
4.	M ⊃ N	1, Simp
5.	(O ⊃ P) · (M ⊃ N)	1, Com
6.	O ⊃ P	5, Simp
7.	N ⊃ ~ P	2, Impl
8.	M ⊃ ~ P	4, 7, H S
9.	~ P ⊃ ~ O	6, Trans
10.	M ⊃ ~ O	9, 8, H S
11.	~ M v ~ O	10, Impl
12.	~ (M · O)	11, DeM
13.	Q	12, 13, M P

The exercises in part VII are just a combination of the symbolization techniques you learned in chapter 8 and the proof techniques you have been working on in this chapter. One thing that should seem quite noticeable in these exercises is the frequency with which conditional statements are made. You should see that there are more conditional statements than all other sorts combined. One possible explanation of this phenomenon is that human fondness for identifying causal patterns leads us to see as many things as possible in such terms. Since the closest thing that our logic has to expressing causality is the material conditional, that means that we will often find ourselves compelled to symbolize conditional and causal statements in the same way.

VII   (3)   A =df A political leader who sees her former opinions
                  to be wrong alters her course.
            D =df She is guilty of deceit.
            I =df She is open to a charge of inconsistency.

If not A, D; and if A, I   (~ A ⊃ D) · (A ⊃ I)
A or not A   A v ~ A
--------------------------   ------------------
Therefore either D or else I   ∴ D v I

1.	(~ A ⊃ D) · (A ⊃ I)	Premiss
2.	A v ~ A	Premiss /∴ D v I
3.	~ A v A	2, Com
4.	D v I	1, 3, CD

There is a real temptation here to overlook the Com step, but without it the proof does not EXACTLY follow the rule forms and would then be incorrect.

   (9)   C =df We extend credit on the Wilkins account.
            M =df They will have a moral obligation to accept our
                  bid on their next project.
            P =df We can figure a more generous margin of profit
                  in preparing our estimates.
            I =df Our general financial condition will improve
                  considerably.

If C, M.   C ⊃ M
P if M.   M ⊃ P
P causes I.   P ⊃ I
_____   _____
Hence I follows from C   ∴ C ⊃ I

```
1.  C ⊃ M              Premiss
2.  M ⊃ P              Premiss
3.  P ⊃ I              Premiss  /∴ C ⊃ I
4.  C ⊃ P              1, 2, HS
5.  C ⊃ I              3, 4, HS
```

There is surely no problem in generating the proof of this problem. The only thing that might have caused you difficulties is thet symbolization. Be sure you know which is antecedent and which is consequent when you symbolize a conditional. In this argument, for example, the first and third premisses have their symbols occur in the formal structure, while the second premiss and the conclusion have them occur in opposite orders.

(13)   C =df The new courthouse is conveniently located.
        H =df It is located in the heart of the city.
        A =df It is to be adequate to its function.
        L =df It will have to be built large enough to house
                 all the city offices.
        O =df Its cost will run to over a million dollars.

```
If C, H; and if A, L.              (C ⊃ H) · (A ⊃ L)
If H and L, then O.                (H · L) ⊃ O
Not O.                             ~ O
----------------------             ----------------
Therefore either not C or not A    ∴ ~ C v ~ A
```

```
1.  (C ⊃ H) · (A ⊃ L)         Premiss
2.  (H · L) ⊃ O               Premiss
3.  ~ O                       Premiss  /∴ ~ C v ~ A
4.  ~ (H · L)                 2, 3, MT
5.  ~ H v ~ L                 4, DeM
6.  (~ H ⊃ ~ C) · (~ L ⊃ ~ A) 1, Trans (twice)
7.  ~ C v ~ A                 5, 6, CD
```

Note that this uses the destructive dilemma form that was identified in the solution of problem 19 on page 173 (above).

(18)   W =df World population is increasing.
        A =df Agricultural production is declining.
        M =df Manufacturing remains constant.
        N =df New food sources will become available.
        R =df There will be a radical redistribution of food
                 resources in the world.
        H =df Human nutritional requirements diminish.
        P =df Family planning will be encouraged.

```
Although W, A and M.            W · (A · M)
If A and W then either N or R
unless H.                      (A · W) ⊃ [(N v R) v H]
Not N, yet neither P nor H.    ~ N · ~ (P v H)
------------------------------ ----------------------
Therefore R                    ∴ R
```

Important here are the various ways in which you can express the " · ." You should be cautious when symbolizing, lest you accidentally misrepresent knowledge that you have.

```
1.  W · (A · M)                  Premiss
2.  (A · W) ⊃ [(N v R) v H]      Premiss
3.  ~ N · ~ (P v H)             Premiss /∴ R
4.  ~ N                          3, Simp
5.  (W · A) · M                  1, Assoc
6.  W · A                        5, Simp
7.  A · W                        6, Com
8.  (N v R) v H                  2,7, MP
9.  N v (R v H)                  8, Assoc
10. R v H                        9,4, DS
11. H v R                        10, Com
12. ~ (P v H) · ~ N             3, Com
13. ~ (P v H)                   12, Simp
14. ~ P · ~ H                   13, DeM
15. ~ H · ~ P                   14, Com
16. ~ H                          15, Simp
17. R                            11,16, DS
```

(25)   G =df   Socrates was a great philosopher.
            H =df   Socrates was happily married.

If either H or not H, then G   (H v ~ H) ⊃ G
-----------------------------   -------------
Therefore G   ∴ G

```
1.  (H v ~ H) ⊃ G                Premiss
2.  ~ (H v ~ H) v G              1, Impl
3.  (~ H · ~ ~ H) v G            2, DeM
4.  G v (~ H · ~ ~ H)           3, Com
5.  (G v ~ H) · (G v ~ ~ H)     4, Dist
6.  (G v ~ H)                    5, Simp
7.  ~ H v G                      6, Com
8.  H ⊃ G                        7, Impl
9.  (G v ~ ~ H) · (G v ~ H)     5, Com
10. G v ~ ~ H                    9, Simp
11. ~ ~ H v G                    10, Com
12. ~ H ⊃ G                      11, Impl
13. ~ G ⊃ ~ H                    8, Trans
14. ~ G ⊃ G                      12, 13, H S
15. ~ ~ G v G                    14, Impl
16. G v G                        15, D N
17. G                            16, Taut
```

It is interesting to notice that an argument that is
so obviously valid takes so many steps to prove.
Since the antecedent of the premiss is a tautology, it
would have been nice if there had been a rule that
allowed us just to add it to the proof. Had such a
move been allowable, the proof would have been

```
1.  (H v ~ H) ⊃ G                Premiss
2.  H v ~ H                      Added Tautology
3.  G                            1,2, MP
```

There is, however, no rule in the system that allows
the addition of selected tautologies to any premisses,
so you have to settle for the earlier proof.

9.3   Proof of Invalidity
9.4   Inconsistency

When you were doing truth tables, you may have thought that they
were fine for arguments with two or three variables but wondered what
happened when the arguments became more complex. That is a wise

concern, because the length of a truth table doubles every time a new
and distinct variable (or constant) is added. That means that while
an argument with three distinct variables has an eight-row table, one
with four has a sixteen-row one, one with five has a thirty-two row
table and an argument with six distinct variables requires a sixty-
four row table. An argument that involves the interrelationships
among ten distinct statements (complex but certainly not uncommon in
real life) would require that to check it for validity you use a
table with one-thousand-and-twenty-four rows!

  You may have also thought that there ought to be some way of
sorting out the rows of the table that can easily be seen to be
unproductive for proving invalidity. For example, you can see that
only two of the eight rows of the truth table for problem II.13 (the
table is in chapter 8 above) are even potentially useful for proving
invalidity. They are the second and fourth rows. The reason for
this assertion is that they are the only rows of the table in which
the conclusion, "p ⊃ r," is false. The other six rows, although interesting, are ones where the conclusion is true as a result of the
assumed values for the variables, and an argument cannot be shown to
be invalid by a case where the conclusion is true. The only demonstration of invalidity is when the PREMISES ARE ALL TRUE and the
CONCLUSION IS FALSE. Thus, about three-fourths of the work done on
the truth table for III.13 was pointless. Argument III.6 is an
invalid one; it required a table with four rows to demonstrate it,
but you got lucky and could have stopped at the end of the first row.
You would not always be so fortunate. The argument "[~ p ⊃ ~ q, q
v ~ r, s ⊃ r, s ≡ t, ~ (~ t · u) |- ~ p ⊃ u]"is also an invalid
one, but it requires a table with sixty-four rows and (unfortunately)
you will not find that it is invalid until the sixty-fourth row.
Fortunately, however, there does exist a method by which you can
considerably reduce your efforts at checking for validity. Professor
Copi discusses it in section 9.3 and calls it the METHOD OF ASSIGNING
TRUTH VALUES. Essentially it involves a recognition that finding ANY
case where all of the premises of an argument are true and its
conclusion is false is sufficient to prove that that argument is
invalid. The fact that there may be several cases which would do the
same is of no consequence. (A truth table would find them all, but
why would you want to know them all? Doesn't that seem like some of
the "consecutive executions"--where a really foul criminal would be
hanged, then beheaded, then drawn and quartered, then boiled in oil,
then burned at the stake--where, after the first capital punishmentt,
the criminal very likely didn't care about any of the later ones?)
Using the 6-variable argument suggested above, the initial assignments of values would look like this:

[~ p ⊃ ~ q, q v ~ r, s ⊃ r, s ≡ t, ~ (~ t · u) |-- ~ p ⊃ u]
      | | | | | |
      T   T   T   T   T   F

This amounts to the assumption that the argument is invalid, since
the ONLY way it could be shown to be invalid would be precisely this
case--where each of the premises is true but the conclusion is
false. These values "force" some other values--if ~ (~ t · u) is
true, then (by the definition of " ~ ") (~ t · u) is false. Also if
~ p ⊃ u is false, then (by the definition of " ⊃ ") p must be T and u
must be F. The initial assumption of invalidity does not force
values immediately for the first four premises, since there are
three ways for the " ⊃ " and " v " to be T and two ways for the " ≡ "
to be T. A second stage of assigning values, then might look like
the following (note that each new set of assigned values is located
directly under the element haveing the assignment and that the order
of assignment can be recognized by the distance down from the argument-form):

[~ p ⊃ ~ q,   q v ~ r,   s ⊃ r,   s ≡ t,   ~ (~ t · u)   ⊢—   ~ p ⊃ u]
   | | | | | | | | |
   T   T   T   T   T   F   T   F F

If ~ p is T, then p is F, and if p is T and u is F in the conclusion,
then those same elements must have the same values wherever they
occur in the argument--in this case in the first and last premisses
respectively.   Such assignments become:

[~ p ⊃ ~ q,   q v ~ r,   s ⊃ r,   s ≡ t,   ~ (~ t · u)   ⊢—   ~ p ⊃ u]

If ~ p (as the antecedent of the first premiss) is T, then ~ q (as
the consequent) must also be T (or the premiss would be F--and to
check for invalidity it has to be T).

[~ p ⊃ ~ q,   q v ~ r,   s ⊃ r,   s ≡ t,   ~ (~ t · u)   ⊢—   ~ p ⊃ u]

If ~ q is T, then q must be F in both the first and second premiss.

[~ p ⊃ ~ q,   q v ~ r,   s ⊃ r,   s ≡ t,   ~ (~ t · u)   ⊢—   ~ p ⊃ u]

If q is F in the second premiss, the ~ r must be T (or the alternation q v ~ r would be F v F and the second premiss would be false--
and, of course, to check validity it must be T).

[~ p ⊃ ~ q,   q v ~ r,   s ⊃ r,   s ≡ t,   ~ (~ t · u)   ⊢—   ~ p ⊃ u]

If ~ r in the second premiss is T, then r must be F in both the
second and third premisses.

If r is false in the third premiss, then s must also be F (or that
premiss--which has to be T--would be F).

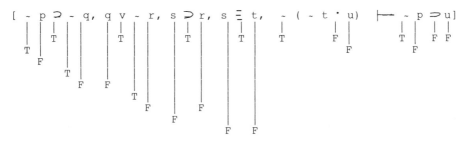

If s is F in premiss three, then it must also be so in the fourth
premiss. And if s is F then t must also be F for s ≡ t to be true,
as it must be.

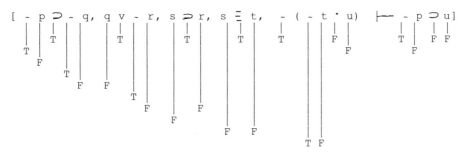

If t is F in the fourth premiss, it must also be F in the last one,
and ~ t there must be T.

The problem thus far, is that all of the T's and F's are so strung
out that it is a bit hard to read. You might find that using 1/8 to
1/4 inch graph paper would line everything up nicely. If, however,
all of the T's and F's are pushed upward so that all of the values
for each statement form are close, it looks like this:

[~ p ⊃ ~ q, q v ~ r, s ⊃ r, s ≡ t, ~ (~ t · u) ⊢ ~ p ⊃ u]

Notice that the order in which values were determined in each premiss
is shown, but not the order in which values were forced from premiss
to premiss (which you saw in the sequence preceeding this last version). You can see that, in the last premiss, when ~ t is T and u is
F, then (~ t · u) is F, which was what the original assignment was.
This means that you now have a set of assignments of truth values for
all of the variables in the argument and that those values make each
of the premisses true and the conclusion false. It might all be
summarized by saying that this shows that, when p, q, r, s, t, and u
are all F, this argument is shown to be invalid.

Such an extended discussion looks far more complicated than it really is. The problems following 9.3 provide good practice in assigning values to show invalidity. The example below (number 6) is done, with a notation in the margin showing forcings of values.

```
                      A ≡ (B v C)    B ≡ (C v A)    C ≡ (A v B)    ~ A ⊦ B v C
Assume Inv.           T              T              T              T         F
" v " = F                                                                  F   F
From concl.                 F F F    F     F            F              F
" ~ " = F                                                                F
From last pr.      F                          F                F

Summary of values  F    F    F  F      F  F   F       F   F         F    F   F
Summary of " ~ "                                                       T
Summary of " v "        F              F              F                     F
Summary of " ≡ "      T              T              T
```

You can see that, when all of the elements (A, B, and C) are false, all of the premisses are true and the conclusion is false. The consistent assignment of values shows the argument to be invalid. You may wonder how this method proves something valid. That proof is based upon a time-honored method that is called an indirect proof of a REDUCIO AD ABSURDUM (reduction to absurdity). The basic operation of this sort of proof is to assume one thing, to show how that assumption forces you to hold an absurd position. In a formal logic, like the sort that you are now studying, an absurdity is a contradiction. If you find that there is a contradiction (the assertion of something and its negation, or the assertion that something is true and false at the same time), then the assumption with which the method of assigning truth values began, that is, that the argument is invalid, must be wrong. This means that getting a contradiction while using the method of assigning truth values is the way in which you find that an argument form is valid.

A return to the problems following 8.4, in fact to problem II.13 which was earlier shown to be valid by a full truth table, yields an example which shows the use of the method of assigning truth values to prove validity. Notice that there is really nothing to be gained by using the ASF when applying this method.

```
                                    p ⊃ (q ⊃ r),  p ⊃ q  ⊦  p ⊃ r
[Assume argument invalid]              | T |  | |     | T |    | F |
[Forced by definition of ⊃ ]                                   T  F
[Forced by assignment above]         T |      | F |  T |
[Forced by definition of ⊃ ]              | T |            T
[Forced by assignment above]            T |
[Forced by definition of ⊃ ]            F
```

The two values beneath the second horseshoe of the first premiss, of course, contradict each other -- if p is true, then for "p ⊃ (q ⊃ r)" to be true, "q ⊃ r" must be true, but q and r are forced elsewhere to be T and F respectively, so "q ⊃ r" must also be false. Since it cannot be the case that any expression is simultaneously true and false, the original assumption of invalidity must have been wrong -- the argument is valid.

The following problem I.6 from the sets after 9.4, is a bit longer, but is worked on in a similar fashion:

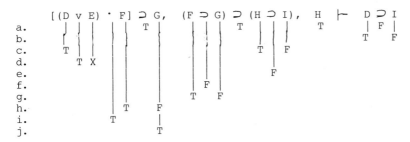

Here you can see that, since G cannot be both T and F, the argument is valid. The steps a-j, in case you did not follow all of them, are for the following reasons:

a. Assumption that the argument in invalid.
b. Forced in order to have the conclusion F.
c. D and I values carried from the conclusion, H from last premiss.
d. If one (or more) disjunct is true, the disjunction is T.
e. When the antecedent is T and the consequent is F, the ⊃ is F.
f. When the ⊃ is T and the consequent is F, the antecedent is F.
g. Forced in order to have the ⊃ be F.
h. Values carried from the second premiss.
i. When both conjuncts are T, the conjunction is T.
j. When the ⊃ is T and the antecedent is T, the consequent is T.

It would be nice if problems always worked themselves out as neatly as these have. Unfortunately they don't. Sometimes, when assigning values, you will encounter a case where you become stalled, because there are values yet to be asssigned, but none of them are forced by whatever you already have. A simple example is p ≡ q, q ≡ r, p ≡ r. Intuitively you probably have no doubt that it is valid, but intuitions are not adequate proof, so you might begin to assign values:

$$p \equiv q, \qquad q \equiv r \qquad \vdash \qquad p \equiv r$$
$$\quad T \qquad\qquad\quad T \qquad\qquad\qquad\qquad\quad F$$

At this point you will find yourself stopped because there are no more forced values--there are two ways for " ≡ " to be true and two ways for it to be false, and there is no way to tell which ones to use. With such a short problem you might decide to generate a full truth table, but that is evading the difficulty. What if it occurs in a problem with a dozen variables? The answer is to make a secondary assumption, that is, to assume something more than the original assumption of invalidity. In this case a helpful assumption would be that p = T. The problem then goes quickly.

[asspt.]
[forced]
[carried]
[forced]

The second premiss is now forced to be both T and F. That contradiction proves the argument valid, right? **Wrong!** At this point you have no way to tell whether the contradiction was a result of the initial assumption (that the argument is invalid) or the secondary assumption (that p = T). To eliminate the possibility that the contradiciton is due to the secondary assumption, you must go back and recheck USING THE OPPOSITE SECONDARY ASSUMPTION.

Even with the opposite secondary assumption there is a contradiction
in the second premiss. Since the value of the secondary assumption
did not affect the occurrence of a later contradiction--the contradiction occurred no matter what value the secondary assumption had--
the contradiction must have been due to the original assumption, that
the argument was invalid. Thus the argument is valid. When you make
a secondary assumption it is ALWAYS necessary, if you find a contradiction, to go back and check the opposite assumption. The need for
this can be seen in following problem.

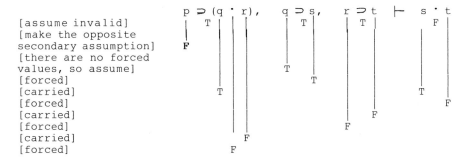

The unwary might infer that the contradiction means the argument is
valid, but you should remember to check the opposite secondary assumption.

	p ⊃ (q · r),	q ⊃ s,	r ⊃ t	⊢ s · t
[assume invalid]	T	T	T	F
[make the opposite	F			
secondary assumption]				
[there are no forced		T		
values, so assume]			T	
[forced]	T			T
[carried]				
[forced]			F	
[carried]				F
[forced]		F		
[carried]				
[forced]	F			

Here all variables have a value, each of the premisses is true, and
the conclusion is false--there are no contradictions--so the argument
is shown to be invalid. Had there been a contradiction, you still
would not have known that the argument was valid because there was a
tertiary assumption (that q = T) made. If there had been a contradiction, you would have had to go back to the point that q was
assumed to be true and check it when q was false. Cases requiring
secondary assumptions occur less frequently than ones that have all
forced values; ones needing tertiary assumptions are rare; ones
requiring four or more could occur, but are so scarce that you need
not worry about them.

    Once you understand how the method of assigning truth values can
show an argument to be valid or invalid, the exercises following 9.3
and 9.4 should be pretty simple. These problems, like the formal
proofs of validity, should be worked before you look at the answers.
Start after 9.3.

(3)

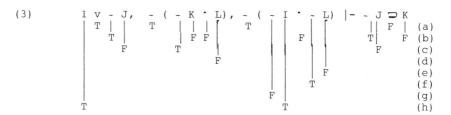

(a)   Begin by assuming the argument is invalid. That
      means assume each of the premises is true and
      that the conclusion is false. Then work out
      values that are forced by this assumption.
(b)   The only way that a negation can be false is for
      what it negates to be true. This means that
      (~ K · L) and (~ I · ~ L) must both be false.
      Also the only way for a conditional statement
      to be false is for its antecedent to be true
      and its consequent false. This means that ~ J
      must be   true and K false wherever in the
      exercise they   occur.
(c)   These follow by the definition of negation.
(d)   Since (~ K · L) must be false (from b) and ~ K
      must be true (from c) the other conjunct, L,
      must be false.
(e)   The value is carried from d.
(f)   This follows the definition of negation.
(g)   This uses the same reasoning as d.
(h)   This follows the definition of negation. You
      should now see that all of the premises of the
      argument can be true while the conclusion is
      false. That means that the argument is shown to
      be   invalid.

(6)   Worked earlier

     The problems after 9.4 of Copi should give you more realistic
challenges: you don't know in advance which are valid and which are
invalid.

I.   (4)   Always begin by checking the argument to see if it is
              valid. If it is not, of course, you cannot construct
              a formal proof of validity.

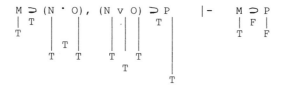

              As always begin by assuming the argument to be
              invalid, that is, that all the premises are true and
              the conclusion is false. Given the single way for the
              conditional conclusion to be false, you know that, for
              the argument to be invalid, M must be true and P false
              throughout this argument. For the first premise to be
              true when M is true, you should see that both of the
              conclusion's conjuncts will also have to be true. But
              if N and O are both true, then N v O will be true and
              P will have to be true to make the second premiss
              true.   That, however, forces you to claim that the P
              in the second premiss is true but that the P in the
              conclusion is false. That, obviously, cannot be the
              case. The only thing that could have led you to argue

that a statement was both true and false would have
been a bad assumption. But the only assumption that
you made was that the exercise was invalid. Thus that
asssumption must be bad, or, what amounts to the same
thing, the argument is valid.

Since it is valid, you need to construct a formal
proof of validity. This one is a snap IF you did as I
suggested and worked all of the problems in Part V in
9.3 of Copi. If you look at exercises 4 and 7, then
you should see that this exercise is little more than
the combination of those two exercises.

To show you how you can use problems which you have
already proven to make new ones easier, I will prove
first exercise 4 then exercise 7 from that group, then
I will suggest a proof of exercise 4 of this set to
show the two earlier proofs blended.

9.3 V.4

1. H ⊃ (I · J)   Premiss /∴ H ⊃ I
2. ~ H v (I · J)   1, Impl
3. (~ H v I) · (~ H v J)   2, Dist
4. ~ H v I   3, Simp
5. H ⊃ I   4, Impl

V.7

1. (Q v R) ⊃ S   Premiss /∴ Q ⊃ S
2. ~ (Q v R) v S   1, Impl
3. S v ~ (Q v R)   2, Com
4. S v (~ Q · ~ R)   3, DeM
5. (S v ~ Q) · (S v ~ R)   4, Dist
6. S v ~ Q   5, Simp
7. ~ Q v S   6, Com
8. Q ⊃ S   7, Impl

9.4 I.4

1. M ⊃ (N · O)   Premiss
2. (N v O) ⊃ P   Premiss /∴ M ⊃ P
3. ~ M v (N · O)   1, Impl
4. (~ M v N) · (~ M v O)   3, Dist
5. ~ M v N   4, Simp
6. M ⊃ N   5, Impl
7. ~ (N v O) v P   2, Impl
8. P v ~ (N v O)   7, Com
9. P v (~ N · ~ O)   8, DeM
10. (P v ~ N) · (P v ~ O)   9, Dist
11. P v ~ N   10, Simp
12. ~ N v P   11, Com
13. N ⊃ P   12, Impl
14. M ⊃ P   6, 13, HS

If you look at steps 1 and 3 through 6 you will see
that they are formal duplicates of the proof of V.4;
if you look at steps 2 and 7 through 13, then you will
see that formally they match the proof of V.7. All
you added was the hypothetical syllogism at the end.

(7)

(a) Assume the argument is invalid, that is, that all
     the premisses are true and the conclusion false.
(b) Work out forced values based upon negation.

(c) Work out forced values from denied conditionals.
(d) Work out forced values based upon negation and carry determined values to all instances.
(e) The conjunction of true statements is true; the consequent of true when the antecedent is true.
(f) Work out forced values based upon negation or true conditionals with true antecedents.
(g) Work out values as in e and f; note that the argument is valid because, for the premisses to be true while the conclusion is false. M would have to be both true and false. That, obviously, cannot be the case.

Since you know that the argument is valid, you need to generate a formal proof of validity.

1.	(J · K) ⊃ (L ⊃ M)	Premiss
2.	N ⊃ ~ M	Premiss
3.	~ (K ⊃ ~ N)	Premiss
4.	~ (J ⊃ ~ L)	Premiss /∴ ~ J
5.	~ (~ J v ~ L)	4, Impl
6.	~ ~ (J · L)	5, DeM
7.	J · L	6, DN
8.	J	7, Simp
9.	L · J	7, Com
10.	L	9, Simp
11.	~ (~ K v ~ N)	3, Impl
12.	~ ~ K · ~ ~ N	11, DeM
13.	K · N	12, DN (twice)
14.	K	13, Simp
15.	N · K	13, Com
16.	N	15, Simp
17.	~ M	16, 2, MP
18.	J · K	8, 14, Conj
19.	L ⊃ M	1, 18, MP
20.	M	10, 19, MP
21.	M v ~ J	20, Add
22.	~ J	21, 17, DS

As you surely noticed, steps 17 and 20 contradict each other. That means that the premisses are self-contradictory and that any conclusion at all could be derived from them. When you encounter such a contradiction, you can follow the pattern shown by steps 17, 20, 21, and 22 to derive any conclusion at all.

You may have felt a little insecure because the comments about the truth value assignments and about the proofs have not followed a set pattern. That is deliberate. It seems to me that it is important that you see that there are are multiple acceptable approaches. In the above exercise, for example, steps 5 and 11 have the same specific form, but the DeM steps from them (6 and 12) used different approaches.

The exercises in Part II are really no more difficult than the ones done earlier; there are just more operations to be performed. Like anything else, working problems is subject to the rule of thumb that the more times you handle something, the more likely you are to drop it. In these, since you have to symbolize, then check for validity, then (if valid) construct a formal proof of validity, you must be particularly careful not to make careless errors.

```
II       (3)        W =df God is willing to prevent evil.
                    A =df God is able to prevent evil.
                    I =df God is impotent.
                    M =df God is malevolent.
                    E =df Evil exists.
                    G =df God exists.

                    If W, but not A; if A, but not W, M.
                    E only if either not W or not A
                    E
                    If G, neither I nor M.
                    -----------------------------------
                    Therefore not G

                    [W · ~ A) ⊃ I] · [(A · ~ W) ⊃ M]
                    E ⊃ (~ W v ~ A)
                    E
                    G ⊃ ~ (I v M)
                    -----------------------------------
                    ∴ ~ G
```

(a)   Assume the argument invalid, i.e., all premisses to be true and
      the conclusion false.
(b)   Work out the values forced by the definitions of conjunction
      and negation and carry all determined values to all the
      instances where they apply.
(c)   When the antecedent of a true conditional is true, the conse-
      quent must also be true.
(d)   If a negation is true, what it negates must be false.
(e)   Work out the values of a false disjunction and carry them to
      other instances.
(f)   When the consequent of a true conditional is false, the antece-
      dent must also be false.

But this leaves no more forced values and as-yet-unvalued statements.
You have only two choices available: go back and work a full truth
table (in this case one 64 rows long) or make an added assumption.
The former seems so undesirable that the latter should be tried.

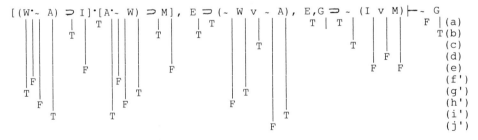

(f') This is the place where the earlier sequence ended.
(g') Assume W is T and carry that to all instances of W.
(h') Work out negations, and note that ~ A must be F to make W · ~ A
      be F when W is T.
(i') Work out from the definition of negation and carry value to
      other instances.
(j') Work out from the definition of negation. Since an in consis-
      tency occurs in thee consequent of the second premiss, you

might think that you have now proven the argument to be
valid, but, unfortunately, that is not the cases. To this
point you have made two assumptions: the argument is invalid
and W is T. One of those assumptions led to the inconsistency in the values for premiss two, but you don't know which
is the bad assumption. For that reason, you must go back to
step g' and assume the opposite value for W.

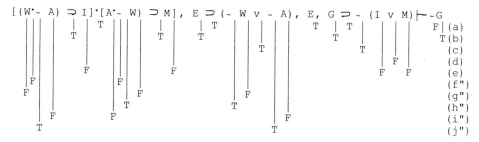

(f") This, like (f') is where the original sequence stopped.
(g") Assume W is F and carry out values (opposite of g').
(h") Work out the values from the definition of negation.
(i") If A · ~ W is F and ~ W is T then A is F and will be so in all
      its instances.
(j") Work out from the definition of negation. Since no inconsis-
      tency occurs and since you have arrived at values for each
      statement symbol, the argument must be invalid. This shows
      you why it is necessary to check both sides of the assump-
      tion, not having done so would have led you to believe an
      invalid argument was valid.

(7)   P =df The butler was present.
           S =df The butler was seen.
           Q =df The butler was questioned.
           R =df The butler replied.
           H =df The butler was heard.
           D =df The butler was on duty.

If P, S; and if S, Q. $(P \supset S)$ · $(S \supset Q)$
If Q, R; and if R, H. $(Q \supset R)$ · $(R \supset H)$
Not H.   ~ H
If neither S nor H, D; and   [~ (S v H) $\supset$ D] · $(D \supset P)$
   if D, P.
--------------------------------   --------------------
Therefore Q   ∴ Q

$(P \supset S)$·$(S \supset Q)$, $(Q \supset R)$·$(R \supset H)$, ~H, [~(S v H) $\supset$ D]·$(D \supset P)$ |- Q

(a) Assume the argument invalid.
(b) Work out forced values from the definitions of conjunction
     and negation, and carry values to other instances.
(c) When the consequent of a true conditional is false, so is
     the antecedent; so infer the values and carry them to
     other instances.
(d) Work out the same inference as in c, infer that the dis-
     junction of two false statements is alsos false, and
     carry inferred values.
(e) Infer as in c.
You can see here that in the first conjunct of the last premiss
the antecedent is true and the consequent is false. However,
earlier inference had shown that that conditional had to be
true. That inconsistency proves the argument is valid.

1.	(P ⊃ S) · (S ⊃ Q)	Premiss
2.	(Q ⊃ R) · (R ⊃ H)	Premiss
3.	~ H	Premiss
4.	[~ (S v H) ⊃ D] · (D ⊃ P)	Premiss /∴ Q
5.	P ⊃ S	1, Simp
6.	(S ⊃ Q) · (P ⊃ S)	1, Com
7.	S ⊃ Q	6, Simp
8.	Q ⊃ R	2, Simp
9.	(R ⊃ H) · (Q ⊃ R)	2, Com
10.	R ⊃ H	9, Simp
11.	~ (S v H) ⊃ D	4, Simp
12.	(D ⊃ P) · [~ (S v H) ⊃ D]	4, Com
13.	D ⊃ P	12, Simp
14.	P ⊃ Q	5, 7, HS
15.	P ⊃ R	14, 8, HS
16.	P ⊃ H	15, 10, HS
17.	D ⊃ H	16, 13, HS
18.	~ D	3, 17, MT
19.	~ ~ (S v H)	18, 11, MT
20.	S v H	19, DN
21.	H v S	20, Com
22.	S	3, 21, DS
23.	Q	7, 22, MP

But notice that two additional steps would yield an interesting result:

24.	R	22, 8, MP
25.	H	10, 24, MP

The third premiss was ~ H. What these results tell you is that the premisses of this argument are self-contradictory. Nevertheless, having self-contradictory premisses does mean that you have a valid argument and the conclusion IS provable from such premisses.

(19)   W =df Weather predicting is an exact science.
       R =df It will rain tomorrow.

W.	W
-----------------------	-----------
Therefore R or not R.	∴ R v ~ R

```
W |-   R v ~ R
  T        | F |        (a)
         F   F  |        (b)
                 T       (c)
```

(a)   Assume the argument invalid.
(b)   Work out the values for a false disjunction.
(c)   Work out the value for a false negation. Since the forced values would require that R be T and F at the same time, there is an inconsistency and the argument is valid.

1.	W	Premiss /∴ R v ~ R
2.	W v ~ R	1, Add
3.	~ R v W	2, Com
4.	R ⊃ W	3, Impl
5.	R ⊃ (R · W)	4, Abs
6.	~ R v (R · W)	5, Impl
7.	(~ R v R) · (~ R v W)	6, Dist
8.	~ R v R	7, Simp
9.	R v ~ R	8, Com

Since R doesn't appear in the premiss, the rule of

thumb suggested for using addition ought to tell you to add something to W. In the proof above ~ R was added, but R could just as well have been the addition (but would have required a couple of DN steps). Ultimately, however, this is a sort of gimmick proof. The conclusion is a tautology, and it follows validly from any premiss or premiss-set. As a matter of fact, no matter what premiss you had had, you could follow this pattern to prove R v ~ R.

CHAPTER NINE SUMMARY

I.   Validity can be proven not only by truth tables but also by identifying a sequence of inferences, each of which is taken to be obviously acceptable.

II. One group of acceptable inferences is identified as the rules of inference.

   A.   They are listed in 9.1 of Copi.

   B.   Their application is restricted.

      1.   The beginning (premiss) and ending (conclusion) forms must match the structure of the rules EXACTLY.

      2.   The inference must be made in the same direction (premiss to conclusion) as the one in which the rule is stated.

      3.   The inference must be made using whole steps only--it cannot be made within a step.

III. The other group of acceptable inferences is identified as the rule (or rules) of replacement.

   A.   They are listed in 9.2 of Copi.

   B.   Their application is less restricted than that of the rules in inference.

      1.   The beginning and ending forms must match the struc-ture of the rule EXACTLY.

      2.   The inference may be drawn left-to-right or right-to-left relative to the original statement of the rule.

      3.   The inference may be drawn upon whole steps or within a single step.

IV. Validity or invalidity can be proven by assigning truth values to the elements of an argument.

    A. You begin by assuming the argument is invalid, i.e., that all the premisses are true and the conclusion is false.

    B. You work out forced values for increasingly smaller elements of the argument.

        1. If all elements have consistently assigned values, then the argument is invalid.

        2. If some inconsistency is discovered in trying to assign values, then the argument is valid.

        3. If there are elements left without values being forced for them, then you must assume some added value.

            a. If all elements then have consistently assigned values, then the argument is invalid.

            b. If some inconsistency is discovered, go back and assume the opposite of the added value.

                (1) If all elements then have consistently assigned values, then the argument is invalid.

                (2) If some inconsistency is discovered in trying to assign values, then the argument is valid.

                (3) If there are elements left without values being forced, proceed as in 3.

            c. If there are elements without forced values left, make another assumption and proceed as in 3.

10

Quantification Theory

10.1 Singular Propositions

You may recall that in chapter 7 there was an extended discussion of how to handle statements which resemble categorical propositions but refer only to one individual. Singular propositions, as they are called, assert that some individual has some property. In the categorical logic part of his book, Professor Copi treated the individual as it it were a class with a single member. You read of some of the difficulties with that approach both in Copi and in this Study Guide. It would be nice to use the techniques of symbolic logic that you have learned in the last two chapters to handle the singular propositions. You can't, however, because the **internal structure** is important in such a proposition but is ignored by propositional logic. What is needed, then, is some means of symbolizing the individual/property relationship.

If, for example, you were to encounter the singular proposition "Abraham Lincoln wore a beard," one possibility would be to represent Lincoln by the lower case letter "a" and the property of wearing a beard by the upper case letter "B." That means that the proposition "Abraham Lincoln wore a beard" could be represented as "Ba." (Notice that--unless there is some special reason for paying attention to time in a statement--past, present and future are all treated as if they were the same. It is also important to notice that the techniques for "translating" statements into a categorical [or category-like] form that were detailed in chapter 7 will be used here, too.)

The conventions, then, to be used in this refinement of the symbolic logic of the last two chapters are three:

(1)   Capital letters symbolize attributes or properties; they are called predicate variables.
(2)   Lower case letters from **a** through **w** designate specific individuals; they are called individual constants.
(3)   Lower case letters **w**, **y**, and **z** serve as place holders for individual constants; they are called individual variables.

The use of these conventions means that, for example, "Fa" is a representation of some specific singular proposition and is either true or false. "Fx" in contrast does not designate any specific proposition, but would if you were to replace the "x" by some individual constant.

10.2 Quantification
10.3 Traditional Subject-Predicate Propositions

You may wonder why all this emphasis is put on a new way of dealing with concepts and is being introduced when you already knew how to use categorical logic. One reason, obviously, is to avoid the difficulties mentioned in 10.1. Another is the need to have a logical tool that is more sensitive to the internal structure of propositions than is the categorical approach.

An easy way to see the sort of superiority that quantificational logic has over categorical logic is to look at a statement that is sort-of-categorical-but-not-quite: Everyone who smokes runs the risk of cancer or heart disease. It is universal and afirrmative, but to claim that it is an orthodox   **A** proposition is to put it on a Procrustean bed. (This refers to the mythological giant Procrustus who measured his guests according to his bed and altered them to

fit--lopped off their legs if they were too long for it, stretched
them to fit if they were too short.) If this statement were treated
as an **A** proposition, then the subject term would be "people who
smoke" and that is unobjectionable, but the predicate would have to
be "people who run a great risk of lung cancer or heart disease."
But what really seems called for is the use of two predicates--
"People who run a great risk of lung cancer" and "People who run a
great risk of heart disease"--joined together by our old friend the
wedge, v. Its inclusive character allows the risks to be separate or
shared. A start, then, would be to rewrite the statement in a way
that emphasizes connectives like the wedge rather than in a way that
resembles a standard categorical form. For this statement it might
bee: "Pick anyone you choose; if that individual is a person who
smokes, then either that individual runs a great risk of lung cancer
or that individual runs a great risk of heart disease." That is
certainly a longer, less comfortable sentence, but it does make the
connectives more apparent. However, more can be done. If you follow
the lead of mathematics you could replace the phrase "that individual" with x and lose little (if any) clarity. That would yield:
"No matter which x you choose, if x is a person who smokes, then x
either runs a great risk of lung cancer or x runs a great risk of
heart disease."

But further reduction is possible, for each of the three properties mentioned in the statement couldd be replaced by symbols defined
to mean exactly what those property-references mean. In this case we
could define as follows:

>Sx =df   x is a smoker.
>Lx =df   x runs a great risk of lung cancer.
>Hx =df   x runs a great risk of heart disease.

The statement would then be written:

>"No matter which x you choose, if Sx, then either Lx or Hx."

That clearly is a vast improvement, but more is possible--the connectives can be replaced by their symbols yielding:

>"No matter which x you choose, [Sx $\supset$ (Lx v Hx)]."

All that seems wanting is a symbol for the phrase "No matter which x
you choose" to convert the entire statement. SInce it might be
replaced by (and more traditionally was stated as) "for all x," the
choice seems to be Ax for a symbol. That, however, will not work,
for how could we distinguish between "for all x" written as "Ax" and "x
is an artichoke" written as "Ax?" Historically the decision was to
invert the A, yielding "($\forall$a)". For a lot of reasons (which need not be
detailed here), it was decided to simplify that symbol further so
that "(x)" as opposed to "($\forall$x)" was to be used for "all." The variable
can, of course, vary, but the meaning is constant. THis symbol, "(x),"
is called the UNIVERSAL QUANTIFIER because it indicates that the
number (or quantity) of individuals to which it applies is univer-
sal--it refers to all of them. By introducing the universal quantifier into the statement-form above, you complete the symbolization of
the original statement:

>(x) [Sx $\supset$ (Lx v Hx)]

If the additional property--Fx =df x is foolish--is introduced, then
the statement "all smokers are foolish," which is a clear-cut instance of an A proposition, could be cycled into quantificational
symbolism analogously:

All smokers are foolish.

No matter whom you choose, if they smoke then they are foolish.
No matter which x you choose, if x smokes then x is foolish.
No matter which x you choose, (Sx ⊃ Fx).
(x)(Sx ⊃ Fx)

Here the basic structure of the categorical A statement is made clear, and the relationship between the earlier, more complex example and the basic form for an A proposition becomes more evident.

If an additional property is introduced--Tx =df x is thoughtful --then the other universal statement-form (that is, the E -form) can be examined. Consider the proposition "No smokers are thoughtful." Its symbolization might go:

No smokers are thoughtful.

Nomatter whom you choose, if they are smokers,then it is not the case that they are thoughtful.

No matter which x you choose,if x is a smoker,then it is notthe case that x is thoughtful.

No matter which x you choose,if Sx then it is not the case that Tx.

No matter which x you choose, (Sx ⊃ ~ Tx).

(x)(Sx ⊃ ~ Tx)

This shows that, symbolically, the A and the E propositions are in reality quite close to each other.

All that is left to complete symbolization is a way to handle particular propositions. Perhaps the easiest way to approach them is through the universal propositions and the use of the relationships shown on the square of opposition. Since the A and the O are contradictory, the A and the negation of the O (~ O) must mean the same thing. Consider the following proof:

1.	~ (x)(Fx ⊃ Gx)	Premiss
2.	~ (x)(~ Fx v Gx)	1, Impl
3.	~ (x)(~ Fx v ~ ~ Gx)	2, DN
4.	~ (x) ~ (Fx · ~ Gx)	3, DeM

But also look at the O statement that would amount to the denial of the A statement "all smokers are thoughtful": "Some smokers are not thoughtful." Try that as a reduction similar to those done upon the universal affirmative statements:

Some smokers are not thoughtful.

There is at least one individual such that he or she is both a smoker and a thoughtless person.

There is at least one x such that both Sx and ~ Tx.

There is at least one x such that (Sx · ~ Tx).

If the model of the universal is followed, a new symbol needs to be introduced--(∃x) =df: "There is at least one x such that," and the statement becomes
(∃x)(Sx · ~ Tx).

Now, if the last symbolization is compared with the last line of the proof (above), an interesting correspondence can be noted.

$$\sim (x)(Fx \supset \sim Gx)$$
$$(\exists x)(Sx \cdot \sim Tx)$$

This shows graphically how the universal and particular quantifiers are related to one another. That relationship is detailed more fully in 10.2 of Copi.

The symbolizations of the categorical forms can be of great help when trying to translate statements from English into the quantificational format. The list below gives them all:

A.	All S are P	$(x)(Sx \supset Px)$
I.	Some S are P	$(\exists x)(Sx \cdot Px)$
E.	No S are P	$(x)(Sx \supset \sim Px)$
O.	Some S are not P	$(\exists x)(Sx \cdot \sim Px)$

Notice that the universal almost **always uses the** " $\supset$ " **as the major connective** and that **the particular** almost **always uses the** " $\cdot$."

There is a very practical reason for insisting upon the use of the " $\supset$ " for universal propositions and the " $\cdot$ " for existential ones: if you exchange their uses, you wind up with trivialities.

If you didn't have the quantifiers and wanted to represent universal and existential propositions, you would find it difficult but not impossible. If you think about what it takes to prove a universal proposition false or true, you get a clue about how you can represent universality without a quantifier. If you find any one exception to the universal statement, then the universal is false; for the universal statement to be true, it must be true of each and every individual in the universe (or at least in the universe about which you are conversing). When you think about it, those characteristics are roughly the same as the ones that were identified as belonging to the propositional function of conjunction. That means that, if the individuals in the universe were listed as **a, b, c,....** and **n**, then the universal proposition "$(x)(Fx \supset Gx)$" could be represented as "$(Fa \supset Ga) \cdot (Fb \supset Gb) \cdot (Fc \supset Gc) \cdot ... \cdot (Fn \supset Gn)$." [Please notice that this "symbolization" is not strictly correct, for the conjunctions are not grouped in pairs. However, since you know that conjunction is both associative and commutative, there is little likelihood that the shorthand form used here, and in the next paragraph for the particular and alternation, will confuse you.]

Similarly, if you consider what is required to prove or disprove an existential proposition, you see how to handle particularity without quantifiers. All tht is needed for a particular to be true is one individual for which it is true; to prove a particular false, you'd have to show that it held for no individual. Using individuals as above, the existential proposition "$(\exists x)(Fx \cdot Gx)$" could be represented as "$(Fa \cdot Ga) \lor (Fb \cdot Gb) \lor (Fc \cdot Gc) \lor ... \lor (Fn \cdot Gn)$."

An added benefit of seeing these non-quantified representations of quantificiational relationships is that it makes the equivalences that Professor Copi introduces at the end of section 10.2 more clearly resemble the DeMorgan Theorem relationships with which you are already familiar. Now, if you look at the short proof on the previous page of this book, you see how, if you replace the " $\sim (x)$" in step 4 with "$(\exists x)$" in accordance with the second "DeMorgan-like" equivalence in Copi, the denied **A** proposition becomes the asserted **O** proposition. If you carry that sort of inference a little further using the non-quantificational representations, then you see how the DeMorgan's theorems allow you to make the same transformation (using the DeM rules a bit loosely):

```
1. ~ [(Fa ⊃ Ga) · (Fb ⊃ Gb) ·...· (Fn ⊃ Gn)]                    Given
2.~ (Fa ⊃ Ga) v ~ (Fb ⊃ Gb) v...v ~ (Fn ⊃ Gn)                  1, DeM
3.~ (~ Fa v Ga) v ~ (~ Fb v Gb) v...v ~ (~ Fn v Gn)            2, Impl
4.(~ ~ Fa · ~ Ga) v (~ ~ Fb · ~ Gb) v...v (~ ~ Fn · ~ Gn)      3, DeM
5.(Fa· ~ Ga) v (Fb · ~ Gb) v...v (Fn · ~ Gn)                   4, DN
```

You now have most of the tools necessary for symbolizing quantificational statements (and arguments). You will find tht making the
transition from English to symbols in the manner that has been shown
here (by successively replacing elements by their symbolic counter-
parts) may take slightly longer than trying to leap from full English
to full symbol. However, you will almost surely find that the greater the leap you make the more likely you are to make a mistake. By
making the "translation" gradually, you avoid the sort of confusion
that usually results when you are trying to do more than one new
thing at once. To check out the symbolization technique, look at a
few of the problems from 10.3.

I.   (3)   This is affirmative, but does not assert that all
               reporters are present, thus is particular affirmative
               (I).
               Some reporters are present.
               There are some individuals that are reeporters and are
                 present.
               There are some x such that x are reporters and x are
                 present.
               There are some x that (Rx and Px).
               There are some x such that (Rx · Px).
               (∃x)(Rx · Px)

      (7)   No boy scout ever cheats.
               No matter whom you choose, if that individual is a boy
                 scout, then that individual does not cheat.
               No matter which x you choose, if x is a boy scout,
                 then x does not cheat.
               No matter which x, if Bx then not Cx.
               No matter which x, (Bx ⊃ ~ Cx).
               (x)(Bx ⊃ ~ Cx)

      (12)   Not all children pointed their fingers at the emperor.
               (You can attack this statement in two alternative
               ways.)

               a. It is not the case that you can pick anyone you
                   choose such that, if that individual is a
                   child, then that individual pointed a finger at
                   the emperor.
                   It is not the case that you can pick any x such
                   that, if x is a child, then x pointed a finger
                   at the emperor.
                   It is not the case that you can pick any x such
                   that if Cx then Px.
                   ~ [you can pick any x such that (Cx ⊃ Px)].
                   ~ (x)(Cx ⊃ Px)

               b. There is someone who is a child but did not point
                   a finger at the emperor.
                   There is an x such that x is a child and x did not
                   point a finger at the emperor.
                   There is an x such that Cx and not Px.
                   There is an x such that (Cx · ~ Px).
                   (∃x)(Cx · ~ Px)

               (Notice that the a-case is the denial of an A proposi-
               tion, while the b-case is the assertion of the contra-
               dictory O proposition.)

(14)   None but the brave deserves the fair.

This particular phrase "none but," like "only," tends
to be confusing. Probably the best way to clarify
them is by using them with classes the relations of
which are certain to you. The statement is clearly
true, at least for the present, that all nuns are
women. Its converse that all women are nuns is clearly false. If you consider the statement "none but
women are nuns" and "none but nuns are women" (or the
same expressions with "only" replacing "none but"),
the first statement is the true one, the second false.
All that is necessary is to recongize that the two
true statements must be roughly equivalent. Thus "All
nuns are women" and "Only women are nuns" can be
treated as if they were the same. This technique (of
clarifying awkward cases through the use of known
class-relationships) may prove helpful to you anytime
you encounter a new expression.

No matter whom you choose, if that individual deserves
    the fair, then that individual is brave.
No matter which x you choose, if x deserves the fair,
    then x is brave.
No matter which x you choose, if Dx then Bx.
No matter which x you choose, (Dx ⊃ Bx).
(x)(Dx ⊃ Bx)

II   (2)   (∃x)(Cx · Dx)

One of the easiest ways to find the appropriate normal
form formula (one where negations apply to simple
predicates only) is to use the relationships on the
traditional square of opposition. In this case the
original expression was ∼ (x)(Cx ⊃ ∼ Dx) which is the
denial of the universal negative (E) proposition "No
C's are D." Since, on the square of opposition, the
contradictory of an E is an I with the same subject
and predicate terms, you could infer that the desired
expression would be the symbolization of the I proposition "Some C's are D's." This, you should see,
ought to be symbolized as (∃x)(Cx · Dx), which is the
answer above. A proof-like tracing of the inferential
sequence from the original in Copi to the answer might
look like this:

1.   ∼ (x)(Cx ⊃ ∼ Dx)   Given
2.   It is false that no   1, symbolic definition
     C's are D's   (df) of E proposition
                                 and of negation
3.   Some C's are D's   2, square of opposition
4.   (∃x)(Cx · Dx)   3, symbolic df of I
                                 proposition.

(8)   (x)(Px ⊃ Ox)   or (x)(Ox v ∼ Px)

This is an expression that looks far more complex than
it really is. As you can see, the normal form formulas
are rather simple and easy to understand. You could
arrive at them by a relatively straightforward proof
if you use the equivalences in 10.2 of Copi as if they
were rules of replacement. (Given their resemblance
to DeMorgan's Theorems, perhaps they should be called
the DeMorgan's Quantificational Theorems [DeMQ].)

```
1. ~ (∃x)[~ (Ox v ~ Px)]     Given
2. (x) ~ [ ~ (Ox v ~ Px)     1, DeMQ
3. (x)(Ox v ~ Px)            2, DN
4. (x)( ~ Px v Ox)           3, Com
5. (x)(Px ⊃ Ox)              4, Impl
```

As you can see, the proof works just like the ones you did in propositional logic, with the addition of the DeMQ step as if it were a replacement rule. You can tell that the DN step (from 2 to 3) is one that follows the form, despite the brackets that appear to intervene between the negations, because there is NOTHING ELSE BUT THE BRACKETS BETWEEN THE TWO NEGATIONS.

10.4 Proving Validity

Once you have mastered the transformations called DeMQ above, you will have no difficulty positioning your quantifiers so that they are initially placed and apply to the whole following formula. The only other thing you will then need to generate quantificational proofs is a set of rules that account for the removal and addition of quantifiers. If you begin with the simplest of valid arguments, you will find that the needed rules quickly make themselves evident. The argument that Professor Copi introduces to discuss the UI rule in 10.4 with Greeks, Humans, and Mortals, is fine for our purposes. A proof of the argument, indicating the rules that "cry out to be introduced" might look like:

```
1. (x)(Hx ⊃ Mx)      Premiss
2. (x)(Gx ⊃ Hx)      Premiss /∴ (x)(Gx ⊃ Mx)
3. Hy ⊃ My           1, a needed (x)-take-off rule
4. Gy ⊃ Hy           2, the same rule
5. Gy ⊃ My           3, 4, HS (the same old rule)
6. (x)(Gx ⊃ Mx)      5, a needed (x)-put-on rule
```

Similarly, the argument with the same first premiss, but "Some vegetarians are human" (∃x)(Vx · Hx) as a second premiss and "Some vegetarians are mortal" (∃x)(Vx · Mx) as the conclusion suggests more needed rules:

```
1.  (x)(Hx ⊃ Mx)      Premiss
2.  (∃x)(Vx · Hx)     Premiss /∴ (∃x)(Vx · Mx)
3.  Vy · Hy           2, a needed (∃x)-take-off rule
4.  Hy ⊃ My           3, the needed (x)-take-off rule
5.  Vy                3, Simp
6.  Hy · Vy           3, Com
7.  Hy                6, Simp
8.  My                4, 7, MP
9.  Vy · My           5, 8, Conj
10. (∃x)(Vx · Mx)     9, a needed (∃x)-put-on rule
```

There would appear, then, to be four rules that need to be added so that quantified logic can be worked: two universal rules and two existential ones--one of each that takes off the quantifier (called INSTANTIATION because it is taking an instance of the quantified statement), and one of each that put quantifiers on (called generalizing).

There is a problem, however, with these rules: not all of them are valid as they stand. This is most easily seen in cases where using the rules in the fashion suggested above would lead you into trouble. Simplest would be to exchange the following tenth step for the one that occurs in the second example above:

```
10. (x)(Vx · Mx)      9, the (x)-put-on rule
```

There seems to be little doubt that you would not want to be able to reason from the fact that all humans are mortal and some humans are vegetarians to the conclusion that EVERYTHING, no matter what else it might be, is both a vegetarian and mortal. That would have you asserting such nonsense as that your immortal soul (if you believe you have one) is mortal since everything is, or that man-eating tigers are vegetarians (which might lead you to rather foolish actions in the presence of one).

A second problematic inference might be generated from the premisses "Some animals are dogs" and "Some animals are cats." It could go:

1.	(∃x)(Ax · Cx)	Premiss
2.	(∃x)(Ax · Dx)	Premiss
3.	Ay · Cy	1, the (∃x)-take-off rule
4.	Ay · Dy	2, the (∃x)-take-off rule
5.	(Ay · Cy) · (Ay · Dy)	3, 4, Conj
6.	[(Ay · Cy) · Ay] · Dy	5, Assoc
7.	[Ay · (Ay · Cy)] · Dy	6, Com
8.	[(Ay · Ay) · Cy] · Dy	7, Assoc
9.	(Ay · Cy) · Dy	8, Taut
10.	Ay · (Cy · Dy)	9, Assoc
11.	(∃x)[Ax · (Cx · Dx)]	10, the (∃x)-put-on rule

But this has you asserting that some animals are both cats and dogs.

Informally it is not hard to see that the first problem is due to taking particular information (in the form of an existential premiss) and arriving at a universal conclusion. The second problem results from having information about two, at least potentially, different individuals and treating it as if it were definitely about a single individual. (Had the properties A, C, and D in the above example stood for actors, charming persons, and debonair, the inference would not have seemed so ridiculous, for that conclusion is at least reasonable.) There are a number of ways that these problems can be resolved, but it must be done in such a way that the rules are still reasonable. The best approach is to apply restrictions to the use of the rules in such a way as to prevent them from leading an inference astray.

If you know that some statement is true of all individuals, then there ought to be no problem with choosing to apply it to any specific individual. That is what the rule of UNIVERSAL INSTANTIATION does: it permits the removal of the universal quantifier and, if desired, the replacement of every occurrence in the expression of the variable contained in that quantifier by any individual symbol. This rule, called UI for brevity, is essentially unrestricted insofar as it will be used in this book. Similarly, if you have a property (or properties) asserted of some individual symbol (no matter what that symbol might be), then you ought to feel free to assert that that property (or those properties) is true of something. That is what the rule of EXISTENTIAL GENERALIZATION does: it permits that addition of the existential quantifier and, if desired, the replacement of every occurrence in the expression of any individual symbol which is not affected by an already positioned quantifier by the variable found in that existential quantifier. This rule, called EG for brevity, is essentially unrestricted, too, insofar as it will be used in this book.

The other two rules are the ones that require restriction. The only time you want to have to avoid the use of the rule of UG (UNIVERSAL GENERALIZATION) is when the information upon which you are generalizing is about specific individuals. Thus Professor Copi adds the restrictiton that this rule can be used only upon "arbitrarily selected variables," meaning that you can't use it in most problems that, in their premisses, contain either individual symbols that are not governed by a quantifier or that in their proofs contain uses of EI (the fourth rule). Given this restriction, the rule is fine. So long as you do not inadvertently identify distinct individuals, there is no problem with EXISTENTIAL INSTANTIATION. The simplest of the possible restrictions that might be applied to ensure that is not to ever use EI in such a way that the individual constant at which it arrives had appeared earlier in the proof. If you look back at the dog-and-cat example, you will see that the use of EI would have been no problem had the steps involved instantiated to different individual constants instead of to the "arbitrarily selelcted individual "y."

The best way to get the rules firmly seated in your mind is to use them in the generating of some proofs. You will notice that all of the problems in part I after 10.4 are basically variations upon two proofs, the one with all universal premisses and the one with a universal and an existential one. Problems 3 and 7 can be taken as representing the two types.

I. (3)
1. (x)(Gx ⊃ Hx)   Premiss
2. (x)(Ix ⊃ ~ Hx)   Premiss /∴ (x)(Ix ⊃ ~ Gx)
3. Gy ⊃ Hy   1, UI
4. Iy ⊃ ~ Hy   2, UI
5. ~ Hy ⊃ ~ Gy   3, Trans
6. Iy ⊃ ~ Gy   4, 5, HS
7. (x)(Ix ⊃ ~ Gx)   6, UG [Acceptable because y is an arbitrarily chosen variable.]

(7)
1. (x)(Sx ⊃ ~ Tx)   Premiss
2. (∃x)(Sx · Ux)   Premiss /∴ (∃x)(Ux · ~ Tx)
3. Sa · Ua   2, EI [Acceptable since a is an individual constant that has not appeared previously in the proof. If you always do your EI steps first, this restriction should never bother you.]
4. Sa ⊃ ~ Ta   1, UI [which can go to ANY individual symbol]
5. Sa   3, Simp
6. Ua · Sa   3, Com
7. Ua   6, Simp
8. ~ Ta   4, 5, MP
9. Ua · ~ Ta   7, 8, Conj
10. (∃x)(Ux · ~ Tx) 9, EG

If you look closely at the remaining eight problems in part I and at the nine problems (after the first) in part II, you will see that, with the use of an occasional commutation or MT-for-MP-substitution, all of the proofs are variants of these two.

II. (3)
Dx =df x is a dancer.
Ex =df x is exuberant.
Fx =df x is a fencer.

There are two approaches to the sort of step-wise transition from natural language to complete symbolism. You can try to make the language sound as categorical as possible or you can try to approximate the quantificational structure. Take, for example, the first premiss of this exercise. The English version is "all dancers are exuberant." The categorical one is "all D's are E." The quantificational on is "for all x's, if x is a D, then x is an E." So long as the statement is fairly simple, you are probably better off approaching symbolism form the categorical form. Since you know how to translate each of the categorical forms into quantificational form, symbolizing by means of a categorical step probably requires less effort than any other way. For exercise 3, then the transition to symbols is straightforward.

<pre>
      All D are E.   (x)(Dx ⊃ Ex)
      Some F are not E.   (∃x)(Fx · ~ Ex)
      -----------------   --------------
Therefore some F are not D.   ∴ (∃x)(Fx · ~ Dx)
</pre>

<pre>
 1.   (x)(Dx ⊃ Ex)   Premiss
 2.   (∃x)(Fx · ~ Ex)   Premiss /∴ (∃x)(Fx · ~ Dx)
 3.   Fa · ~ Ea   2, EI
 4.   Fa   3, Simp
 5.   ~ Ea · Fa   3, Com
 6.   ~ Ea   5, Simp
 7.   Da ⊃ Ea   1, UI
 8.   ~ Da   6, 7, MT
 9.   Fa · ~ Da   4, 8, Conj
10.   (∃x)(Fx · ~ Dx)   9, EG
</pre>

When you compare this proof with that of exercise of 7 from Part I you can see that there is very little difference in the two proofs. As was suggested there, as long as the argument is categorical, the proof must be one of those two proofs discussed earlier.

(7)   Sx =df x is a swindler.
       Tx =df x is a thief.
       Ux =df x is underprivileged.

<pre>
      All S's are T's.   (x)(Sx ⊃ Tx)
      All T's are U's.   (x)(Tx ⊃ Ux)
      -----------------   ------------
   Therefore all S's are U's.   ∴ (x)(Sx ⊃ Ux)
</pre>

<pre>
 1.   (x)(Sx ⊃ Tx)   Premiss
 2.   (x)(Tx ⊃ Ux)   Premiss /∴ (x)(Sx ⊃ Ux)
 3.   Sy ⊃ Ty   1, UI
 4.   Ty ⊃ Uy   2, UI
 5.   Sy ⊃ Uy   3, 4, HS
 6.   (x)(Sx ⊃ Ux)   5, UG
</pre>

The most difficult thing in working this exercise is translating it from English to symbols. If you do not already have notes to yourself indicating some of the unusual wordings possible and how to symbolize them, you might want to start one. One way to identify how to symbolize is to decide what was meant by using analogous statements in which the relationships are clear, For example, in the case of the first premiss you might offer this analogy:

To make an omelet you must break eggs.

There is little doubt that the statement means that if you want to make an omelet then you must break eggs. It seems equally clear that the converse, if you break eggs then you must make an omelet, is false. The order of the elements of premiss one is therefore as indicated. The approach to symbolizing statements like premiss two was explained in some detail in the solution of problem 14 of section 10.3 of this STUDY GUIDE. Symbolizing the conclusion is uncomplicated.

This exercise requires the "other" categorical proof.
The point is that a categorical argument (at least a
valid one) either has two universal premises--in
which case you will have to combine them by using a
hypothetical syllogism--or it has one universal and
one particular one--in which case you will use conjunction, simplification and either MP or MT. Given
the very few categorical forms, there can be little
variety in the corresponding quantificational proofs.

10.5   Proving Invalidity

In his description of how you prove a quantificational argument
invalid (or valid), Professor Copi introduces the rough equivalences
that the quantifiers are NOT truth functions like the connectives of
the propositional calculus, and you therefore need some way to convert from expressions with quantifiers to expressions with only truth
functions.

Obviously, one method which he suggests is easier than using
those equivalences. If you can come up with an argument which has
exactly the same form as the argument undere consideration, but your
"other" argument is clearly invalid, then the argument under consideration must be valid. The difficulty with this method of showing
invalidity is that it really has no negative force. That is, if you
are unable to think of such an invalidating analogy, you have no
guarantee that your argument is valid. The difficulty is that you
have no way to tell whether the inability to come up with the appropriate analogy is because no such analogy exists or because you are
just not a very talented analogy-maker. The issue resembles the
problem of determining whether or not a man can run a sub-four-minute
mile: the fact that I cannot even come close to doing this is merely
an autogiographical datum about me; it says nothing about general
human capacity for running speed.

The use of the equivalences to convert quantification to truth
functions is more reliable, but a good deal more complex. The key
difficulty that you will encounter in trying to apply it is the
determination of how many individuals you need to take into account
when setting up your truth table. Intuitively, the number of individuals to be considered should be sufficient to allow any references
to individuals in the argument to refer to separate individuals. For
example, consider this argument:

```
Some people reading this book are male.
Some people reading this book are female.
----------------------------------------
Therefore some females are males.
```

Symbolically this would be

$$(\exists x)(Rx \cdot Mx)$$
$$(\exists x)(Rx \cdot Fx)$$
$$\overline{}$$
$$\therefore \ (\exists x)(Fx \cdot Mx)$$

If you checked this argument for a single individual, you would have
this assigned truth value check:

```
(Ra · Ma),   (Ra · Fa) |—    (Fa · Ma)
  |  T  |      |  T  |         |  F  |      (a)
  T     T      T     T         |     |      (b)
                               T     T      (c)
```

(a) Assume the argument invalid.
(b) Work out the values forced by the definition of con-
    junction.

(c) Carry the forced values and recognize the contradiction in the conclusion. This means that, relative to a single individual, this argument is valid.

If, however, you were to expand your check to apply to TWO individuals, you would find this check:

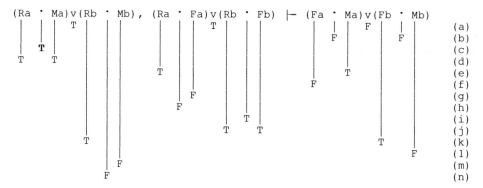

(a) Assume the argument invalid.
(b) Work out values based upon disjunction.
(c) Since there are no more forced values, make an assumption.
(d) Work out values based upon conjunctions.
(e) Carry over forced values.
(f) When a conjunction is false and one conjunct is true, the other one must be false.
(g) Carry over forced values.
(h) Work out values based upon conjunction.
(i) If one disjunct of a true disjunction is false, the other must be true.
(j) Work out values based upon conjunctions.
(k) Carry over forced values.
(l) If one conjunct of a false conjunction is true, then the other one must be false.
(m) Carry over forced value.
(n) Work out value based upon conjunction.

When you arrive at (n) with a value for each of the elements of the argument and have not encountered an inconsistency, then you know that the argument is invalid.

The fact that the argument was invalid when considered to apply to a pair of individuals but was valid when applied to a single one suggests that you must tread softly when claiming a quantificational argument is valid. The intuitive solution is that you will be safe if you use enough individuals to let all the particular information elements apply to separate individuals.

For the most part you would be secure in your selection of individuals for such validity checks if you were to count the number of existential quantifiers and add that to the number of distinct individual constants. That number of individuals (or 1 if that sum happened to be zero) would usually suffice for your validity check. Exceptions could occur, but they would be a result of kinds of expressions that you will not encounter in Copi or in this book.

Roughly, once an argument is proven valid for some set number of individuals, you know that it is also valid for any smaller number of individuals. In contrast, once an argument is proven invalid for some set number of individuals, you know that it is also invalid for any greater number of individuals.

You ought now to feel ready to work the exercises following 10.4. The often-repeated suggestion that you do your own work before looking at the solution still applies.

I. (2) Consider for one individual.

```
Da ⊃ ~ Ea,   Ea ⊃ Fa   |-   Fa ⊃ ~ Da
   T              T           F              (a)
                          T    F             (b)
                   F                T         (c)
 T                                           (d)
      T                                      (e)
         F                                   (f)
             F                               (g)
```

(a) Assume the argument invalid.
(b) Work out values based upon the conditional.
(c) Carry value and work out value based upon negation.
(d) Carrry the value.
(e) Work out value based upon the conditional.
(f) Work out value based upon negation.
(g) Carry the value and note the absence of contradiction. That proves the argument invalid.

(8) Consider for one individual.

```
Va • ~ Wa,   Wa • ~ Xa   |-   Xa • ~ Va
   T    T       T    T        F              (a)
 T    T       T    T            T            (b)
         F           F      F       T        (c)
                                       F     (d)
```

(a) Assume the argument invalid.
(b) Work out forced values based upon conjunction.
(c) Work out values based upon negation and carry earlier values.
(d) Work out values based upon negation.

Since there is no contradiction in the assignment of these values, you should see that this argument is invalid. You may wonder, when there were three potentially different individuals identified (two in the premisses, one in the conclusion), why the validity check was done for only a single individual. The reason is economy. Although you would have to have this argument check out at VALID for more individuals, you can feel secure in proving it invalid in the simplest case you can find. As an operating principle, it's not a bad idea to check out any quantificational argument in the single individual case before going on to consider more complex cases. The time lost in checking cases where the single individual case is indecisive is usually more than offset by the time saved in cases that will prove invalid in that single individual case.

The exercises in Part II are really pretty much the same as the ones following 10.3 and 10.4 with regard to symbolism and are like the ones in Part I in the way that you show them invalid.

II (2) Dx =df x is a diplomat.
Ex =df x is an extremist.
Fx =df x is a fanatic.

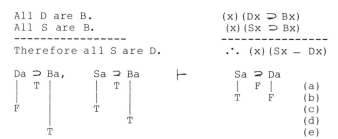

No D are E.   (x)(Dx ⊃ ~ Ex)
Some F are E.   (∃x)(Fx · Ex)
Therefore some D are not F.   (∃x)(Dx · ~ Fx)

```
Da — ~ Ea,   Fa · Ea  ⊢  Da · ~ Fa
|    T    |   |   T |        | F  |        (a)
|         |   |   T |  T     |    |        (b)
|         |   |  T  |        |    | T      (c)
|         F   |     |        | F  |        (d)
F            |              F               (e)
```

(a)   Assume the argument invalid.
(b)   Work out frced values based upon conjunction.
(c)   Carry those forced values.
(d)   Work out forced values based upon negation.
(e)   When the consequent of a true conditional is
        false, then the antecedent must also be false.
        When you carry that forced value to the con-
        clusion, you will see there are no contradic-
        tions and that the argument is invalid.

(8)   The trick here is to remember the discussion of problem
      14, discussed earlier in this chapter. Keeping the
      fact that "none but" and "only" statements are uni-
      versal and affirmative but that they state their
      subject and predicate in reversed order, neither the
      first premiss nor the conclusion will give you any
      difficulty.

All D are B.   (x)(Dx ⊃ Bx)
All S are B.   (x)(Sx ⊃ Bx)
-----------------   -----------------
Therefore all S are D.   ∴ (x)(Sx — Dx)

```
Da ⊃ Ba,   Sa ⊃ Ba   ⊢   Sa ⊃ Da
|  T  |   |  T  |        | F |      (a)
|     |   |     |        T   F      (b)
F         |  T  |                   (c)
|         |     | T                 (d)
|  T      |                         (e)
```

(a)   Assume the argument invalid.
(b)   Work out values based upon the conditional.
(c)   Carry forced values.
(d)   When the antecedent of a true conditional is
        true, then the antecedent must also be true.
(e)   Carry the forced value and note that there is no
        contradiction. Therefore the argument is
        invalid.

10.6   Asyllogistic Inference

All of the quantificational arguments that have been considered
thus far have been roughly syllogistic. It was, however, the claim
at the beginning of this chapter that the syllogism was not adequate
to handle the sort of arguments you will encounter in everyday discourse. Profesor Copi uses section 10.6 to introduce this kind of
argument, the kind that he calls ASYLLOGISTIC (meaning not-of-
syllogistic-form) arguments.

Many of the asyllogistic arguments depend upon propositions
which still resemble categorical forms but are somewhat more complex.
The argument which was introduced here (on pp. 193ff.) to show the
inadequacy of the categorical form is such a case. The statement
"everyone who smokes runs a grat risk of lung cancer or heart disease" could have been treated as an A proposition with the subject

class being "people who smoke" and the predicate being "people who run a great risk of lung cancer or heart disease." If these were represented, respectively, by "Sx" and "Rx," then that statement would be symbolized as "(x)(Sx — Rx)." But to assert "Rx" would really be to assert "either Lx (people who run a great risk of lung cancer) or Hx (people who run a great risk of heart disease)." Since you learned how to represent "either...or...." while working propositional exercises, the transformation of " (x)(Sx ⊃ Rx) " into (x)[Sx ⊃ (Lx v Hx)] should not seem particularly unusual.

In symbolizing asyllogistic arguments you must be careful not to allow the ambiguity of the language mislead you. Professor Copi particularly notes three forms that tend to be mis-symbolized.

A teacher might look up the files for a class and find out a fact which he could express as "all members of this class are either 18 or 19 years old." It would be important to realize that in saying this, he would not mean to assert the disjunction of the two categorical statements "all members of this class are 18 years old" and "all members of this class are 19 years old." With, for example, a lower-division college course, it would not be particularly unusual for the original statement to be true, but for either of the latter ones to be true would certainly seem surprising. Using the obvious symbols, then, the correct symbolization should be "(x)[Mx ⊃ (Ex v Nx)]."

A second misleading locution would be a form like "Oysters and clams are delicious." Professor Copi discusses it near the end of 10.6. His explanation makes it quite clear in terms of what is MEANT by the statement why it must be symbolized with a "v" where the English clearly has an "and." You may, however, still feel a bit insecure in making such a change in symbol from the English. The following proof may make the formal reason for the symbolization a little clearer:

1. (x)[(Ox v Cx) ⊃ Dx]	Given as Professor Copi's symbolization.
2. (x)[~ Dx ⊃ ~ (Ox v Cx)]	1,Trans
3. (x)[~ Dx ⊃ (~ Ox · ~ Cx)]	2,DeM
4. (x)[~ ~ Dx v (~ Ox · ~ Cx)]	3,Impl
5. (x)[(~ ~ Dx v ~ Ox) · (~ ~ Dx v ~ Cx)]	4,Dist
6. (x)[(~ Dx ⊃ ~ Ox) · (~ Dx ⊃ ~ Cx)]	5,Impl(on each conjunct)
7. (x)[(Ox ⊃ Dx) · (Cx ⊃ Dx)]	6,Trans(on each conjunct)

First, you should particularly notice that all of the steps were justified by rules of replacement. That means that you could write the proof in reverse order: step 6 could come from step 7 by transposition, step 5 from step 6 by implication, and so on. The proof shows you that, from a logical point of view, when you assert (x)[(Ox v Cx) ⊃ Dx] you are really asserting that, no matter what you happened to pick, if it is an oyster then it is delicious AND if it is a clam then it is delicious.

The third kind of expression that may cause some kind of difficulty is the exceptive. Professor Copi discusses the sort of exceptive that can be handled as a biconditional at the end of 10.6. There is a second kind of exceptive that occurs in a statement like "all members of the team except those who joined the team after the cut-off date are eligible to play in post-season competition." In this case there is a greater difficulty in figuring out exactly what is meant by the given statement. If the exceptive part of the sentence ("except those who joined the team after the cut-off date") had not been there, the remaining statement would have been "all members of the team are eligible to play in post-season competition." Using the natural symbolism, this would be (x)(Mx ⊃ Ex). If the "members of the team" part of the statement had not been there, you would have had an exceptive of the sort that Professor Copi discussed, one that would be symbolized as (x)(~ Jx ≡ Ex). The most reasonable way, it seems, to symbolize the statement in its entirety is by combining the two simpler forms to get (x)[Mx ⊃ (~ Jx ≡ Ex)].

In general it is easiest to approach asyllogistic statements by first relating them as best you can to one of the four categorical forms. Thus, among the problems in part I following 10.6 in Copi, you would approach number 3 in the following sort of way:

I.   (3)   No car is safe unless it has good brakes.

This is a "sort-of-E-Form"--had it been "no car is safe" it would have been an E. Fortunately "safe" is a word that can easily have a negtion attached direct- ly to it ("unsafe"), so the statement can be rewritten as

All cars are unsafe unless they have good brakes.

Following the symbolization-technique-model introduced for categorical statements the statement can be treated in a relatively straightforward manner:

No matter what you choose, if it is a car, then it is unsafe unless it has good brakes.
No matter what x you choose, if x is a car, then it is unsafe unless x has good brakes.
No matter what x you choose, if Cx, then not Sx unless Bx.
No matter what x you choose, [Cx ⊃ (~ Sx v Bx)].
(x)[Cx ⊃ (~ Sx v Bx)]

(7)   Not all people who are wealthy are both educated and cultured.

It is easiest to approach this sort of problem as if the initial "Not" were not there, then tack on a " ~ " at the beginning when you are otherwise done. Cate- gorically, the subject class is people-who-are-wealthy and the predicate class is they-who-are-both-educated- and-cultured. If you deal with these expressions first (sort of "pre-symbolize," so to speak), the overall problem becomes fairly simple. Using the property symbols that Professor Copi suggests, the subject becomes (Px · Wx), and the predicate becomes (Ex · Cx). With the initial negation set up outside, the original statement becomes:

~ [All (Px · Wx) are (Ex · Cx)]

This is just the negation of an A-form, which you can easily symbolize as

~ [(x)[(Px · Wx) ⊃ (Ex ⊃ Cx)]

Of course, you could have first restated the original so as to shift from the denied-A-form to the O-form:

Some people-who-are-wealthy are not educated-and- cultured.

This would have become:

(∃x)[Px · Wx) · ~ (Ex · Cx)]

Either symbolization is acceptable, but the first seems to require less thinking effort.

A couple of the problems from Part II show how the rules are uused with more complex formalisms.

II.   (3)   1. (x){[Ix ⊃ (Jx · ~ Kx)] · [Jx ⊃ (Ix ⊃ Kx)]}   Premiss
            2. (∃x)[(Ix · Jx) · ~ Lx)]   Premiss
                                                      /∴ (∃x)(Kx · Lx)
            3. (Ia · Ja) · ~ La   2, EI
            4. [Ia ⊃ (Ja ⊃ ~ Ka)] · [Ja ⊃ (Ia ⊃ La)]   1, UI
            5. [Ja ⊃ (Ia ⊃ Ka)] · [Ia ⊃ (Ja · ~ Ka)]   4, Com
            6. Ja ⊃ (Ia ⊃ Ka)   5, Simp
            7. (Ja · Ia) ⊃ Ka   6, Exp
            8. Ia · Ja   3, Simp
            9. Ja · Ia   8, Com
           10. Ka   7,9, MP
           11. Ia   8, Simp
           12. Ia ⊃ (Ja · ~ Ka)   4, Simp
           13. Ja · ~ Ka   11,12, MP
           14. ~ Ka · Ja   13, Com
           15. ~ Ka   14, Simp

[Notice that at this point steps 10 and 15 contradict each other. Once you find such a contradiction in a problem, any conclusion at all follows in the way shown by steps 16 and 17.]

           16. Ka v (∃x)(Kx · Lx)   10, Add
           17. (∃x)(Kx · Lx)   15,16, DS

      (8)   This appears to be a particularly complicated problem, but its quantificational elements are quite straight-forward--you remove each of its quantifiers by UI, work the heart of the problem, then add on the quanti-fier by UG. Thus the first eight steps and the last one are already determined by "premiss" and UI and UG.

            1. (x)(Hx ⊃ Ix)   Premiss
            2. (x)[(Hx · Ix) ⊃ Jx]   Premiss
            3. (x)[~ Kx ⊃ (Ix v Hx)]   Premiss
            4. (x)[(Jx v ~ Jx) ⊃ (Ix ⊃ Hx)]   Premiss
                                                      /∴ (x)(Jx v Kx)
            5. Hy ⊃ Iy   1, UI
            6. (Hy · Iy) ⊃ Jy   2, UI
            7. ~ Ky ⊃ (Iy v Hy)   3, UI
            8. (Jy v ~ Jy) ⊃ (Iy ⊃ Hy)   4, UI
            9. ~ (Iy v Hy) ⊃ ~ ~ Ky   7, Trans
           10. (~ Iy · ~ Hy) ⊃ ~ ~ Ky   8, DeM
           11. (~ Iy · ~ Hy) ⊃ Ky   10, DN

[Steps 9-11 are, in a sense, the key ones for the problem. The conclusion is an alterntion, in parti-cular the alternation of the consequents of steps 6 and 11. The alternation of the antecedents of those steps is one of the equivalence forms. In steps 5 and 8 you will have the seeds of the needed equivalence.]

           12. (~ Hy · ~ Iy) ⊃ Ky   11, Com
           13. [(Hy · Iy) ⊃ Jy] · [(~ Hy · ~ Iy) ⊃ Ky] 6,12,Conj

[The difficulty facing you now is that you need to get the Iy ⊃ Hy from the consequent of step 8. The ante-cedent Jy v ~ Jy is a tautology, so Iy ⊃ Hy must follow, but there is no rule allowing any tautology to be "stuck into" a proof. A little clever manipula-tion, however, will do the job.]

14. ~ (Jy v ~ Jy) v (Iy ⊃ Hy)   8, Impl
15. (Iy ⊃ Hy) v ~ (Jy v ~ Jy)   14, Com
16. (Iy ⊃ Hy) v (~ Jy • ~ ~ Jy)   15, DeM
17. [(Iy ⊃ Hy) v ~ Jy] • [(Iy ⊃ Hy) v ~ ~ Jy] 16, Dist
18. [~ Jy v (Iy ⊃ Hy)] • [~ ~ Jy v (Iy ⊃ Hy)] 17, Com
                                                                (twice)
19. [~ ~ Jy v (Iy ⊃ Hy)] • [~ Jy v (Iy ⊃ Hy)] 18, Com
20. ~ ~ Jy v (Iy ⊃ Hy)   19, Simp
21. ~ Jy v (Iy ⊃ Hy)   18, Simp
22. Jy ⊃ (Iy ⊃ Hy)   21, Impl
23. ~ ~ Jy ⊃ (Iy ⊃ Hy)   20, Impl

[To this point thte steps 14-23 ought to look a bit
familiar--it is essentially the same sort of problem
as 9.2, III,7, which was discussed earlier in this
Study Guide.]

24. ~ (Iy ⊃ Hy) ⊃ ~ Jy   22, Trans
25. ~ (Iy ⊃ Hy) ⊃ (Iy ⊃ Hy)   24,23, HS
26. ~ ~ (Iy ⊃ Hy) v (Iy ⊃ Hy)   25, HS
27. (Iy ⊃ Hy) v (Iy ⊃ Hy)   26, DN
28. Iy ⊃ Hy   27, Taut
29. (Hy ⊃ Iy) • (Iy ⊃ Hy)   5,28, Conj
30. Hy ≡ Iy   29, Equiv
31. (Hy • Iy) v (~ Hy • ~ Iy)   30, Equiv

[You now have the conjunction of conditionals [step
13] and the alternation of their antecedents [step 31]
to perform the CD implied by the discussion after step
11.]

32. Jy v Ky   13,31, CD
33. (x)(Jx v Kx)   32, UG

The important thing to see here is that the difficulties that are
encountered in this problem have nothing to do with the quantification; they are proof subleties of the sort studied in Chapter 9.

    The exercises in parts III and IV add the complication of sym-
bolization. Care in translating from English to symbols becomes even
more important when you do not know whether the argument in question
is valid or not. A misplaced parenthesis, an extra negation, exchanged quantifiers and the like can convert a valid argument into an
invalid one, or vice versa.

III.   (3)   Ax =df x is an argon compound.
                Sx =df x is a sodium compound.
                Ox =df x is oily.
                Vc =df x is volatile.

                A's and S's are either O or V.
                Not all S's are O.

                Therefore some A's are V.

                Before symbolizing the first premiss, you should think
                a moment about what it MEANS. Although it would not
                deny the possibility of a sodium-argon compound, the
                premiss surely does not mean to claim that such are
                the only sort that it asserts are oily or volatile.
                This statement, then, must be like the example of
                oysters and clams discussed in Copi and here in sec-
                tion 10.6. Thus the argument is symbolized as
                follows:

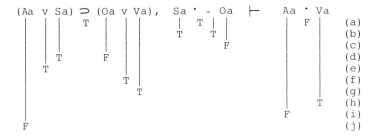

```
(x)[(Ax v Sx) ⊃ (Ox v Vx)]
~ (x)(Sx ⊃ Ox)   OR   (∃x)(Sx · ~ Ox)
---------------------------------------
.·. (∃x)(Ax · Vx)
```

```
(Aa v Sa) ⊃ (Oa v Va),   Sa · ~ Oa  |—   Aa · Va
 |  |  |           T              |  T |            F          (a)
 |  |  |                          |T |              (b)
 |  |  |                             T              (c)
 |  T  |          F                                 (d)
 |  T  |                                            (e)
 |                      T |                         (f)
 |                         T                        (g)
 |                                           T      (h)
 |                                         F        (i)
 F                                                  (j)
```

(a)   Assume the argument invalid.
(b)   Work out values based upon conjunction.
(c)   Work out value based upon negation.
(d)   Carry determined values.
(e)   If one disjunct is true, the disjunction is true.
(f)   If the antecedent of a true conditional is true,
      then the other disjunct must be true, too.
(g)   If one disjunct of a true disjunction is false,
      then the other disjunct must be true.
(h)   Carry the determined value.
(i)   If one conjunct of a false conjunction is true,
      then the other conjunct must be false.
(j)   Carry the determined value. Since there are no
      contradictions and all statements have values
      assigned to them, the argument is invalid.

(7)   Tx =df x is made of tin.
      Cx =df x is cheap.
      Rx =df x is a ring.
      Lx =df x is made of lead.

For all x not both T and not C   (x) ~ (Tx · ~ Cx)
No R are L.   (x)(Rx ⊃ ~ Lx)
Not all things are T or L.   ~ (x)(Tx v Lx)
-------------------------------   -------------------
Therefore not all R are C.   .·. ~ (x)(Rx ⊃ Cx)

When you assign values you will find that applying the
DeMQ equivalence to the last premiss and the conclusion will significantly simplify your work. Thus they
become (∃x) ~ (Tx v Lx) and (∃x) ~ (Rx ⊃ Cx).

```
~(Ta · ~ Ca),   Ra ⊃ ~ La,   ~(Ta v La)  |—   ~(Ra ⊃ Ca)
 T |  |                T |  |      T |  |         F |  |       (a)
   |  F                  |  |        |  F           |  T      (b)
   |                     |  |      F    F           |         (c)
   F                     |  |    F                  |         (d)
                         |  | F                     |         (e)
                            T                             T   (f)
```

(a)   Assume the argument invalid.
(b)   Work out values based upon negation.
(c)   Work out values based upon disjunction.
(d)   Carry determined values.
(e)   Work out value based upon negation.
(f)   Since no more values are forced, make an assumption.
      In this case, if you assume that "Ca" is true then
      no further values are needed to determine that each
      of the premisses is true and the conclusion false
      under the assignments already made. Thus the argu-
      ment is invalid.

Notice that the "~ Ca," which could have been worked out as F after the assumption was made, was unnecessary, as was any value at all for "Ra." The point is, once enough information is gathered to demonstrate that an argument is invalid, there is no value in further exploration of values for its elements.

IV   (3)   Lx =df x is a lawyer.
Px =df x is a politician.
Mx =df x is a member.
Cx =df x is a college graduate

Only L's and P's are M's.
Some M's are not C's.

Therefore some L's are not C's.

You should recall tht "only F's are G's" is properly understood as "all G's are F's." That would seem to mean that the first premiss should become "all M's are L's and P's." But, again, this is an expression that means to assert a disjunction despite the use of the word "and" as its connective. Surely there is no intention to claim that those who are not both lawyers and politicians are barred from membership. Thus, the following is the correct symbolization.

(x)[Mx ⊃ (Lx v Px)]
(∃x)(Mx · ~ Cx)

∴ (∃x)(Lx · ~ Cx)

(a)   Assume the argument invalid.
(b)   Work out values based upon conjunction.
(c)   Work out value based upon negation.
(d)   Carry determined values.
(e)   A true antecedent of a true conditional means a
       true consequent. A true conjunct of a false
       conjunction means the other conjunct is false.
(f)   Carry determined value.
(g)   A false disjunct to a true disjunction means the
       other disjunct is true. This also means that
       all elements have had values assigned to them
       without contradiction. Therefore the argument
       is invalid.

(8)   Predicates are given with the exercise.

All C who K are V if F.
All C are F except I or P.
All C   are K
No K is P.
Not all C are V.

Therefore there are I's

```
(x)[(Cx · Kx) ⊃ (Fx ⊃ Vx)]
(x)[Cx ⊃ (Fx ≡ ~ (Ix v Px))]
(x)(Cx ⊃ Kx)
(x)(Kx ⊃ ~ Px)
~ (x)(Cx ⊃ Vx)
----------------------
∴ (∃x)Ix
```

The complex-appearing first premiss is quite straight-forward. The second, with its exceptive, is not dif-ficult if you keep in mind the discussion of excep-tives both by Professor Copi and here. Otherwise the exercise is fairly simple.

If you try to prove this argument invalid, no matter for how many individuals you expanded the statements, you will find your check indicating validity. Since there were no individual constants in this argument and there were only two existential quantifiers (one, in effect, in the last premiss and one in the conclu-sion), a check that allows 2 or perhaps 3 distinct individuals should have been adequate to find a case where the argument was proveably invalid if there were such a case possible. The fact that invalidity wasn't so proven suggests that you ought to try to prove it.

```
1.   (x)[(Cx · Kx) ⊃ (Fx ⊃ Vx)]        Premiss
2.   (x)[(Cx ⊃ (Fx ≡ ~ (Ix v Px))]     Premiss
3.   (x)(Cx ⊃ Kx)                       Premiss
4.   (x)(Kx ⊃ ~ Px)                     Premiss
5.   ~ (x)(Cx ⊃ Vx)                     Premiss  /∴ (∃x)Ix
6.   (∃x)~ (Cx ⊃ Vx)                    5, DeMQ
7.   ~ (Ca · ~ Va)                      6, EI
8.   Ka ⊃ ~ Pa                          4, UI
9.   Ca ⊃ Ka                            3, UI
10.  Ca ⊃ (Fa ≡ ~ (Ia v Pa))           2, UI
11.  (Ca · Ka) ⊃ (Fa ⊃ Va)             1, UI
12.  ~ ( ~ Ca v Va)                     7, Impl
13.  ~ ~ Ca · ~ Va                      12, DeM
14.  ~ ~ Ca                             13, Simp
15.  ~ Va · ~ ~ Ca                      13, Com
16.  ~ Va                               15, Simp
17.  Ca                                 14, DN
18.  Ka                                 9, 17, MP
19.  ~ Pa                               8, 18, MP
20.  Fa ≡ ~ (Ia v Pa)                   17, 10, MP
21.  Ca · Ka                            20, Conj
22.  Fa ⊃ Va                            21, 11, MP
23.  ~ Fa                               16, 22, MP
24.  [Fa ⊃ ~ (Ia v Pa)] · [~ (Ia v Pa) ⊃ Fa]   20, EQ
25.  [~ (Ia v Pa) ⊃ Fa] · [Fa ⊃ ~ (Ia v Pa)    24, Com
26.  [~ (Ia v Pa) ⊃ Fa]                 25, Simp
27.  ~ ~ (Ia v Pa)                      23, 26, MT
28.  Ia v Pa                            27, DN
29.  Pa v Ia                            28, Com
30.  Ia                                 19, 29, DS
31.  (∃x)Ix                             30, EG
```

The fact that this proof is so long might discouurage you from trying to prove similar exercises. However, if you look closely at it, you will see that any complexities in it are not due to its being a quantified argument but to the number and complexity of its premis-ses. And, if you review the steps of this proof, you will see tht it is actually quite simple and straightforward. Of its thirty-one steps, five are premisses, five are quantifier-removal steps (1-EI, 4-UI), four are **modus ponens**, three each are simplification and commutation, two each are double negation and **modus tollens,** and the remainder are single uses of rules like conjunction, implication and the disjunctive syllogism. Probably the most difficult step in the entire proof is the transformation of the last premiss by the DeMorgan Quantification theorems. And the only reason that that might seem a bit obscure is that those equivalences are not explicitly described as rules by Professor Copi. It turns out that formal proofs of validity, like the longest journey mentioned in the proverb, begins with (and is made up of) the smallest step.

If there is any of these exercises that is likely to intimidate you out of trying it, it is exercise 10. Nine premisses would seem too much for a mere mortal to attempt. But, if that is your reaction to this argument, then you are almost surely underestimating your skill with quantificational arguments. The predicates are defined with the argument.

(10) Some C are R. $(\exists x)(Cx \cdot Rx)$
     Whoever is R is either S or B. $(x)[Rx \supset (Sx \lor Bx)]$
     To be B one must D or P. $(x)[Bx \supset (Dx \lor Px)]$
     Only L are P. $(x)(Px \supset Lx)$
     Had one been D one would be H. $(x)(Dx \supset Hx)$
     Nobody was H. $(x) \sim Hx$
     If C who R'ed was F, then A. $(x)\{[(Cx \cdot Rx) \cdot Fx] \supset Ax\}$
     No R unless F. $(x)(\sim Rx \lor Fx)$
     No C is both L and A. $(x)[Cx \supset \sim (Lx \cdot Ax)]$
     ------------------------------   ----------------------
     Therefore some C was S. $\therefore (\exists x)(Cx \cdot Sx)$

As was the case with exercise 8, there is no proof of invalidity for this argument. Thus it must be proven.

1.	$(\exists x)(Cx \cdot Rx)$	Premiss
2.	$(x)[Rx \supset (Sx \lor Bx)]$	Premiss
3.	$(x)[Bx \supset (Dx \lor Px)]$	Premiss
4.	$(x)(Px \supset Lx)$	Premiss
5.	$(x)(Dx \supset Hx)$	Premiss
6.	$(x) \sim Hx$	Premiss
7.	$(x)\{[(Cx \cdot Rx) \cdot Fx] \supset Ax\}$	Premiss
8.	$(x)(\sim Rx \lor Fx)$	Premiss
9.	$[Cx \supset \sim (Lx \cdot Ax)]$	Premiss/$\therefore (\exists x)(Cx Sx)$
10.	$Ca \cdot Ra$	1, EI
11.	$Ra \supset (Sa \lor Ba)$	2, UI
12.	$Ba \supset (Da \lor Pa)$	3, UI
13.	$Pa \supset La$	4, UI
14.	$Da \supset Ha$	5, UI
15.	$\sim Ha$	6, UI
16.	$[(Ca \cdot Ra) \cdot Fa] \supset Aa$	7, UI
17.	$\sim Ra \lor Fa$	8, UI
18.	$Ca \supset \sim (La \cdot Aa)$	9, UI

Notice here that the proof is already 18 steps long and all you have done is state the premisses and remove their quantifiers.

19.	Ca	10, Simp
20.	$Ra \cdot Ca$	10, Com
21.	Ra	20, Simp
22	$Sa \lor Ba$	21,11, MP
23.	$(Ca \cdot Ra) \supset (Fa \supset Aa)$	16, Exp
24.	$Fa \supset Aa$	10, 23, MP
25.	$\sim Da$	15, 14, MT
26.	$Ra \supset Fa$	17, Impl
27.	Fa	21, 26, MP
28.	Aa	24, 27, MP
29.	$\sim (La \cdot Aa)$	18, 19, MP
30.	$\sim La \lor \sim Aa$	29, DeM
31.	$\sim Aa \lor \sim La$	30, Com
32.	$Aa \supset \sim La$	31, Impl

33.	~ La	28, 32, MP
34.	~ Pa	33, 13, MT
35.	~ Da · ~ Pa	25, 34, Conj
36.	~ (Da v Pa)	35, DeM
37.	~ Ba	12, 36, MT
38.	Ba v Sa	22, Com
39.	Sa	37, 38, DS
40.	Ca · Sa	19, 39, Conj
41.	(∃x)(Cx · Sx)	40, EG

At first glance this exercise would have looked more difficult than the previous one because its proof is longer. However, that greater length was, in part, due to the fact that this one had four more premisses and, thus, four more required quantifier-removal steps. Add to that the fact that this argument used nine steps justified by either **modus ponens** or **modus tollens** and you will have seen just how simple its proof really is.

The only thing that is likely to give you any problem in such proofs is your own memory: with more than three dozen st eps it is easy to forget what you have already proven and what you w ere trying to do in proving any individual step. So long as you are careful in your symbolizations and can keep in mind the strategy that you map out for proving multi-premiss arguments, quantificational arguments should give you little dificulty.

CHAPTER TEN SUMMARY

I.   Arguments in which internal structure is as important asthe
      relationship between propositions cannot be satisfactorily
      represented in propositional logic.

II.   Arguments in which the internal structure is more complexthan
      the subject/predicate relationship cannot be satisctorily re-
      presented in categorical logic.

III. Quantificational logic allows the representation of both propo-
      sitional and categorical relationships with only slight modifi-
      cations to the propositional calculus.

      A.   Properties are symbolized by upper case letters together
            with an indication of some individual.
      B.   Specific individuals are symbolized by lower case letters
            "a" through "w."
      C.   A place for an individual may be marked by an individual
            variable: "x," "y," or "z."
      D.   The acceptability of any individual as a substitution for
            anindividual variable " x " is indicated by prefixing
            the universal quantifier "(x)" to an expression.
      E.   The acceptability of at least one specific substitution
            for an individual variable " x " is indicated by pre-
            fixing the existential quantifier, "($\exists$x)," to an ex-
            pression.

IV.   Quantified expressions can be approximated by truth-functional
      expressions based upon substitutions of individuals for vari-
      ables in the original expressions.

      A.   Universally quantified expressions are treated as con-
            junctions of the assertation for all individuals:
            (x)$\emptyset$x becomes [$\emptyset$a · $\emptyset$b · $\emptyset$c ·...· $\emptyset$n (where a-n are
            all the individuals that are)].
      B.   Existentially quantified expressions are treated as dis-
            junctions of the assertion for all individuals: ($\exists$x)$\emptyset$x
            becomes [$\emptyset$a v $\emptyset$b v $\emptyset$c v ... v $\emptyset$n (where a-n are all
            the individuals tht are)].

V.   The universal and existential quantifiers are related to each
      other by equivalences here called the DeMorgan Quantification
      Theorems.

VI.   Formal proofs of validity in quantificational logic are basical-
      ly the same as they were in propositional logic, with the
      addition of rules for the addition of and elimination of the
      quantifiers. Those rules are found in section 10.4.

VII. Invalidity is proven through the use of the method of assigning
      values, as in chapter 9.

      A.   Since the quantifiers are not truth functions, the pre-
            misses and conclusion must first be converted to
            truth-functional form as explained in IV (above).
      B.   In general, the conversion (mentioned in VII-A) must
            include enough individuals to allow one for each dis-
            tinct individual constant and for each existential
            quantifier in the argument to insure that a validity
            check that indicates "valid" is correct.

11

The Logic of Relations

11.1 Symbolizing Relations

In chapter 9 the logical unit that you studied was the proposition. Whole sentences were used to convey the idea of a proposition. In chapter 10 you added the concept of a predicate, a property of individuals. But if you encountered the predicate "x is married" symbolized as "Mx," then you might try to represent "John and Mary are married" as "Mj · Mm." Chances are, however, that that is a bad symbolization. Why? Usually that statement means to assert that they are married **to each other.** But while that symbolization is consistent with John and Mary being married to each other, it is also consistent with John being married to Jane and Mary being married to Mack. The problem with the symbolization is that, when treated as a predicate, being married is a property held by an individual, incapable of indicating that individuals are married **to each other.** The **relation,** however, might well be viewed as a property that is held jointly by 2, 3, or more individuals. Thus, John and Mary **together** hold, have, possess, or whatever, the relation "is married to."

The relation that John and Mary share is a two-place (that is, binary or dyadic) one. Normally we would symbolize a relation like "x is married to y," then as "Mxy." A similar, but three-place (triadic or ternary) relation in which John and Mary have a share is that of being married to each other according to the laws of Missouri. The relation "x is married to y according to the laws of z," then would be symbolized "Mxyz." It is important to note that there is no significant difference between "Mxy" and "Myx," (since our concepts allow no way for **a** to be married to **b** without **b** also being married to **a**). There are, however, very significant differences among "Mxyz," "Mxzy," "Myxz," "Myzx," "Mzxy," and "Mzyx." While "John is married to Mary according to the laws of Missouri" and "Mary is married to John according to the laws of Missouri" express roughly the same thing, neither of them bears any significant similarity to the admittedly strange assertion "Missouri is married to John according to the laws of Mary." If you recall the discussion here and in Copi of the commutivity of the " v " and " · " connectives, and the fact that the " ⊃ " connective is **not** commutative, then the order of co-holders of a relation will not seem alien to you: some relations are ordered, some are not.

As Professor Copi says, the use of the quantifiers that you studied in chapter 10, should seem quite familiar to you. There may, perhaps, be another way of looking at quantifiers that may make them a bit easier to understand, especially when applied to relations. The American philosopher/logician Charles S. Peirce used to analyse quantified expressions as if they were to be bet upon. The assumption was that the person asserting the statement "got to pick" the individuals indicated by the existential quantifiers while the other person (who presumably wanted to prove the "asserter" wrong) "got to pick" the individuals indicated by the universal quantifiers. Thus the expressions (∃x)(y)Lxy and (y)(∃x)Lxy, given the relation "x loves y" ("Lxy"), are shown to be different in their "gambling" versions: "I can so carefully pick an individual that, no matter whom you pick, the individual you pick will love the one that I pick" and "Once you pick an individual, I can pick an individual so that yours loves mine." The obvious difference between the two assertions suggests that great care must be taken when identifying order of quantifiers. It is this difference that Professor Copi is discussing when he compares statements 7 and 8, that is, "Everything repels something" and "Something is repelled by everything."

The point is that when all of the quantifiers are initially placed in a formula and when they are all the same quantity, there is little chance of misinterpretation: active and passive voice are, after all, equivalent modes of expression. The problems are most apt to occur when you have a mixture of quantifiers or a mixture of relational and predicate expressions.

The mixture of predicate and relational expressions usually occurs in the trying to state restricted generalizations. Quite frequently you will want to talk about properties and/or relations that always occur **but only to members of a specified group.** In chapter 10 you learned how to express conditional relationships among properties of objects. For example, no one would dream of claiming that fire always occurs. But, given the appropriate conditions, it **does** always (so far as we know) occur. In the now-simple format of quantification, the obvious symbolization would be "(x)(Cx ⊃ Fx)." What Professor Copi wants you to see is that this approach can be extended to apply to relational assertions too.

Looking at some sample expressions will probably make this material a bit clearer for you. Problem 2 in part II following this section says "A lawyer who pleads his own case has a fool for a client." That's a universal affirmative assertion. Rewritten in the "semi-categorical" form that I suggested in the last chapter this would become "All people who are both lawyers and plead their own cases are people who have a fool for a client." Following the step-wise symbolization procedure of the last chapter and using the symbols with the problem, this becomes

For all x, if (Lx and Pxx), then there is a y where (Fy and Cxy)

For all x, [(Lx · Pxx) ⊃ there is a y where (Fy · Cxy)]

For all x, [(Lx · Pxx) ⊃ (∃y)(Fy · Cxy)]

(x)[(Lx · Pxx) ⊃ (∃y)(Fy · Cxy)]

As a check to see if the symbolization does, in fact, represent what the original intended, try reading it in the "Peircean" manner:

Pick anyone **you** wish, if that person is both a lawyer and pleads his own case, then I can select at least one individual who is both a client of the person you picked and a fool.

Of course, the real claim in the original statement was that the client-fool is the lawyer him-/herself. If you follow the Peircean version of the statement, then all I'd have to do is wait for you to pick your self-defending lawyer and then I can pick the same individual as my client-fool. Clearly, then, the symbolization does capture the intent of the original.

As Professor Copi indicates, this sort of symbolization is amazingly flexible. Had you so desired, for example, you could have added the predicate "Hx" (representing "x is a person") to the symbolization that was just done. After all, how many lawyers do you know who are not people? Such an addition would yield

(x){[Hx · (Lx · Pxx)] ⊃ (∃y)[Hy · (Fy · Cxy)]}

[Actually, you might have used the more natural-seeming "Px" for "x is a person," since a careful reader should have little difficulty recognizing the difference between "Px" and "Pxy." However, while you are just starting to represent relations with symbols, it is probably wiser to avoid any symbolic representation that has a reasonable chance of being misread.]

Professor Copi showed you how to symbolize the remark "You can fool some of the people all of the time, and all of the people some of the time, but you cannot fool all of the people all of the time" [which is also sometimes attributed to P.T. Barnham]. Despite the obvious usefulness of such representations (for example, in "unpacking" what is "really meant" by such assertions), you may have noticed that it may seem funny seeing such a commonplace expression in the abstraction of symbolism.

Other well-known expressions, too, look strange when symbolized. For example, consider going to a jukebox and seeing a listing that said

$$Lxyt =df \quad x \text{ loves } y \text{ at time } t$$

$$(x)(\exists y)(\exists t)Lxyt.$$

To the poor soul who is uninitiated into the secret mysteries of the quantificational/relational representation such a listing would be wholly unintelligible. And, even to an initiate like you, it's going to take some serious thought to look at

Pick anyone you please. After you do, I can select both an individual and a time so that your individual will love my individual at the time that I picked.

and see the title of the old Dean Martin song "Everybody Loves Somebody Sometime." [If you were going to insist on the "personhood" property being included in this one, you should probably have had

$$Lxyt =df \quad x \text{ loves } y \text{ at time } t$$
$$Px =df \quad x \text{ is a person}$$

$$(x)\{Px \supset (\exists y)[Py \cdot (\exists t)Lxyt]\}$$

which says

Pick anyone you please. If you picked a person then, after your pick, I can select a person (perhaps the same, perhaps different) and I can also pick a time so that your person will love my person at the time that I picked.]

Probably, the best way for you to become more at ease with the symbolizations used by the logic of relations is to work the exercises following section 10.1.

I   (2)   Pick anything you please, if there is a person for whom that that you picked is fair, then, no matter whom you pick, that that you picked is fair for them.

or, more colloquially,

Everything that's fair for anyone is fair for everyone.

(6)   Pick anything you please, if it is a home then pick anything you please, and if that second thing is a place, then it is not the case that the second place is like the first one.

or

There's no place like home.

Please note here that there **is** a little difference between the colloquial and the strict versions. Since both quantifiers are universal, one possible selection of individuals would be for them both to be the same individual. That would result in asserting that, if something were both a home and a place, it would not be like itself. This sort of problem will be solved by the addition of the identity relation in section 11.3.

(11)   Pick anything you wish, if that thing is a place then, if there is at least one thing such that the thing is smoke and that smoke is at the chosen place then, there is at least one thing such that that is fire and it is at the same place as the smoke.

or

Where there's smoke there's fire.

Here the identity of the two places is conveyed by the "x" of "Px" which identifies the place is repeated in both the "Wyx" and "Wzx" relations. The common occurrence of the "x" shows that it is the same "x" that is a place, is where the smoke is located and is where the fire is located.

(16)   Pick anyone you wish, if you chose a person and you pick any action you want such that your person does not venture your action, then you may pick anything you wish and that last pick will not be gathered by the person you picked.

or

"Persons who venture nothing gather nothing" or maybe "Nothing ventured, nothing gathered."

My guess is that this was intended to be "Nothing ventured, nothing gained."

(21)   Pick anyone you wish, if you pick a person then if you pick anyone (possibly different) you wish, if your second choice is also a person, then no matter what you choose, your first person does not borrow your third choice from your second person.

or

No one borrows anything from anyone.

II   (2)   Done above on p. 218

(6)   Pick anyone you wish, if there is at least one psychiatrist such that the person you chose consults him/her, then the person you chose should have his/her head examined.

Pick any x you wish, if there is at least one y such that (Px and Sy and Cxy) then Ox

Pick any x you wish, {there is at least one y such that [Px $\cdot$ (Sy $\cdot$ Cxy)] $\supset$ Ox}

(x){($\exists$y)[Px $\cdot$ (Sy $\cdot$ Cxy)] $\supset$ Ox}

(11)   Pick any x you wish and pick any y you wish, if x is a person, y is a fish and x catches y, then there is a z such that z is bait and x has z.

Pick any x you wish and pick any y you wish, if [(Px and Fy) and Cxy] then there is at least one z such that (Bz and Hxz)

Pick any x you wish and pick any y you wish, {[(Px · Fy) · Cxy] ⊃ there is at least one z such that (Bz · Hxz)}

(x)(y){[(Px · Fy) · Cxy] ⊃ (∃z)(Bz · Hxz)}

(16) Pick any x you wish, if there is at least one y and there is at least one z such that x is a doctor, y is a patient, z is an ailment, x treats y, and y does not have z, then pick any v you wish, if v is a scruple, then x does not have v.

Pick any x you wish, if there is at least one y and there is at least one z such that [(Dx and Py) · Az] and (Txy and not Hyz) then pick any v you wish, if Sv then not Hxv

Pick any x you wish, [there is at least one y and at least one z such that {[(Dx · Py) · Az] · (Txy · ~ Hyz)] ⊃ pick any v you wish, (Sv ⊃ ~ Hxv)]

(x)[(∃y)(∃z){[(Dx · Py) · Az] · (Txy · ~ Hyz)}
⊃ (v)(Sv ⊃ ~ Hxv)]

(21) There is at least one x such that x is a person and no matter which y you pick, if y is a store and there is at least one z such that x buys z at y, then you may pick any v you wish and x will buy v at y.

There is at least one x such that [Px and pick any y you wish if (Sy and there is at least one z such that Bxzy) then pick any v you chose, Bxvy]

There is at least one x such that {Px · pick any y you want [(Sy · there is at least one z such that Bxzy) ⊃ pick any v you want, Bxvy]}

(∃x){Px · (y)[(Sy · (∃z)Bxzy) ⊃ (v)Bxvy]}

Notice that the strange addition of the conditional clause of "no matter which y you pick, if y is a store and there is at least one z such that x buys z at y, ..." is needed to formally insure that x does buy something somewhere.

(26) Pick any x you wish, if x is a person then there is at least one y such that if y is a charity, then it is not the case that there is at least one z such that x donates z to y.

Pick any x you wish {if Px then there is at least one y such that [if Cy then not there is at least one z such that Dxzy]}

Pick any x you wish {Px ⊃ (∃y)[Cy ⊃ ~ there is at least one z such that Dxzy]}

(x){Px ⊃ [Cy ⊃ (∃z)Dxzy]}

(31) This problem is tough because it really needs the concept of identity that will be introduced in section 11.3. Why? because what you want to express is something like the following:

Pick any person you choose, if that person
donates anything to any charity then there are
**at least two different charities and at least
two different donations** such that that person
makes both donations to both charities.

But what you have learned of the logic of relations,
to this point, has no mechanism to show "difference"
between individuals. Probably, then, the best approximation you can make for this statement with the logic
of relations as you now know it is

Pick any x you wish if x is a person then if there is
at least one y and at least one z such that y is a
charity and x donates z to y [showing x does make some
charitiable donations], then it is not the case that
when you pick any v and any u you wish, then if u is a
charity and x donates v to u then x donates z to y
[showing that any contribution in general made by x
cannot be assumed to be made to y].

This is still unsatisfactory, because it allows the
possibility that the contribution "z" which was
conditionally made to "y" also qualifies as a
contribution not made to "y." Nevertheless, it's
about as close as you can get without the identity
relation.

Pick any x you wish, if {Px then if [there is at least
one y and at least one z such that (Cy and Dxzy) then
~ pick any v and any u you choose, (if [Cv and
Dxuv] then Dxuy])]}

Pick any x you wish, {(Px $\supset$ [if there is at least one
y and at least one z such that (Cy $\cdot$ Dxzy) $\supset$ ~ pick
any v and any y you wish, ([Cv $\cdot$ Dxuv] $\supset$ Dxuy])]}

(x){Px $\supset$ [($\exists$y)($\exists$z)(Cy $\cdot$ Dxzy)
$\qquad\qquad$ $\supset$ ~ (v)(u)([Cv $\cdot$ Dxuv] $\supset$ Dxuy])]}

(36)   Pick any x you wish, if x is a charity then there is
at least one y and at least one z such that y is not
money and z donates y to x.

Note that this does not require that the donor be a
person--after all there is a substantial amount of
corporate giving in the world.

Pick any x you wish [if Cx then there is at least one
y and at least one z such that (not My and Dzyx)]

Pick any x you wish [Cx $\supset$ there is at least one y and
at least one z such that (~ M $\cdot$ Dzyx)]

(x)[Cx $\supset$ ($\exists$y)($\exists$z)(~ My $\cdot$ Dzyx)]

(41)   There is at least one x such that x is a charity and
pick any y you wish if y is a person then there is at
least one z such that Dyzx.

There is at least one x such that [Cx and pick any y
you wish (if Py then there is at least one z such that
Dyzx)]

There is at least one [Cx $\cdot$ pick any y you wish (Py $\supset$
there is at least one z such that Dyzx)]

($\exists$x)[Cx $\cdot$ (y)(Py $\supset$ ($\exists$z)Dyzx)]

III. (2)   There is at least one x such that x is a person and pick any y you wish if y is also a person then x's hand is against y and y's hand is against x.

Again, as in problem 26 (above), this statement cries out for the identity relation. Without it, the statement is forced to admit the possibility that x's hand is against himself. But, without identity, we have to make the best of things. In a case like this, where you were not given abbreviations, you must begin by defining the abbreviations you want to use:

Hxy =df x's hand is against y
Px =df x is a person

There is at least one x such that {Px and pick any y you wish [if Py then (Hxy and Hyx)]}

There is at least one x such that {Px · pick any y you wish [Py ⊃ (Hxy · Hyx)]}

(∃x){Px · (y)[Py ⊃ (Hxy · Hyx)]}

(6)   Notice that you can view the relations "x borrows from y" and "y lends to x" either as alternative versions of the same relation or as separate relations. In this solution, I will assume they are reeally the same.

Pick any x and any y you wish, if x borrows from y then x is the servant of y.

Bxy =df x borrows from y
Sxy =df x is the servant of y

Pick any x and any y you wish, (Bxy ⊃ Sxy)

(x)(y)(Bxy ⊃ Sxy)

11.2 Some Attributes of Relations

Relations can be seen as having many attributes (or properties). In the interest of staying within the appropriate scope of an introductory text, Professor Copi discusses only a few of these attributes, and then only as they apply to **binary** (or **dyadic** or **two-place** relations.

You should be sensitive to the fact that there are three related relations within each of the three groups he introduces. In each case the group has one relation that asserts a connection that occurs universally between the relation's two individuals, one that asserts that that universal connection never occurs and a third that claims that the connection occurs sometimes, but not always.

You may not realize it, but you are already familiar with this sort of three-member group. Think back to chapter 8 and the concepts of "tautology," "self-contradiction," and "contingency." These are properties of statements and are not usually viewed as binary relations, but they fit the pattern described in the last paragraph: a tautology is always true, a self-contradiction is always false, and a contingency is sometimes true and sometimes false. You may also be familiar with this sort of triad in moral discussions: some actions are claimed to be moral (in accord with social propriety), some are immoral (violations of social propriety), and some are amoral (not involved with propriety at all). For example, under normal conditions in most middle-class American society, sharing your banana with

a hungry five-year-old child would be moral, taking a banana from a
hungry five-year-old child would be immoral, and having a banana
instead of an orange would be amoral.

A binary relation is said to be **symmetrical** if it "goes both
ways." That is, if you know that a symmetrical relation exists
between two individuals, "a" and "b," then the assertion of the
relation "Rab" and the assertion of the relation "Rba" functionally
interchangeable. "Sibling" (meaning brother or sister), for example,
is a symmetrical relationship: if John is the sibling of Mary then
Mary is also the sibling of John. "Mother" is just as obviously an
asymmetrical relation: if "Jane is the mother of Mary" then there is
no way (barring some sort of science-fictional time travel paradox)
for it to be true that "Mary is the mother of Jane." "Sister" and
"brother" are neither symmetrical or asymmetrical relations, for,
although "John is the brother of Jim" is equivalent to "Jim is the
brother of John," "John is the brother of Mary" is clearly not equivalent to "Mary is the brother of John." The "brother" and "sister"
relations, then, are **non-symmetrical**.

Formally, a relation can be said to be symmetrical if and only
if

$$(x)(y)(Rxy \supset Ryx).$$

It can be said to be asymmetrical if and only if

$$(x)(y)(Rxy \supset \sim Ryx).$$

It can be said to be non-symmetrical if and only if it is neither
symmetrical nor asymmetrical, i.e.,

$$\sim [(x)(y)(Rxy \supset Ryx) \lor (x)(y)(Rxy \supset \sim Ryx)].$$

This is equivalent, by DeM and DeMQ to

$$(\exists x)(\exists y)(Rxy \cdot \sim Ryx) \cdot (\exists z)(\exists v)(Rzv \cdot Rvz).$$

Binary relations may also be **transitive**, that is establish a
sort of "chain of dominoes" relationship. The " $\supset$ " or horseshoe
truth function describes a transitive relation: it is explicitly
shown in the HS rule ot truth-functional logic. "Sibling" is a
relation that holds between pairs of individuals, but is also transitive: if John is the sibling of Mary and Mary is the sibling of Jack,
then John is the sibling of Jack, too. "Mother," just as it was
asymmetrical, is also **intransitive**: if Mary is the mother of Jane and
Jane is the mother of Jill, then there is no way for Mary to be the
mother of Jill (since Mary is Jill's grandmother). "Not the twin of"
qualifies as a **non-transitive** relation: "if Romulus is not the twin
of Julius Caesar and Julius Caesar is not the twin of Remus, then
Romulus is not the twin of Remus" does not hold. As anyone familiar
with Roman mythology knows Romulus and Remus may well be the most
famous twins (in their case, twins) in history. On the other hand,
if we relace Romulus with Pontius Pilate, the assertion "if Pontius
Pilate is not the twin of Julius Caesar and Julius Caesar is not the
twin of Remus, then Pontius Pilate is not the twin of Remus" is, so
far as history and mythology tell us, entriely satisfactory.

The formal statements of transitivity, intransitivity and non-
transitivity are

[transitive]
$$(x)(y)(z)[(Rxy \cdot Ryz) \supset Rxz]$$
[intransitive]
$$(x)(y)(z)[(Rxy \cdot Ryz) \supset \sim Rxz]$$
[non-transitive]
$$(\exists x)(\exists y)(\exists z)[(Rxy \cdot Ryz) \cdot Rxz] \cdot (\exists x)(\exists y)(\exists z)[(Rxy \cdot Ryz) \cdot \sim Rxz]$$

The third group of relations that Professor Copi introduces deals with individuals' relations with themselves. The most extreme version of such a relation is that of being **totally reflexive.** Such a relation must hold for any and all individuals. "Is identical to" is the most frequently encountered totally reflexive relation. Its formal presentation would be

$$(x) Rxx.$$

The simpler form of reflexivity, Professor Copi calls the **reflexive** relation. If the existence of anything else standing in a given relation to an individual entails that that relation holds with itself, too, then that relation is relexive. Virtually all "same as" relations--"is the same color as," "is the same price as," "is the same age as," "is the same height as," and so on--are in this sense reflexive. Totally reflexive relations are all, of course, reflexive. Its formal representation would be

$$(x) [(\exists y) (Rxy \lor Ryx) \supset Rxx].$$

An **irreflexive** relation, then, is one that can never occur between an individual and itself. Note, then, that, to maintain complete consistency, it should probably be called totally irreflexive. Ordered relations, that is, ones in which the order of the individuals is critical for meaning, are typical examples of irreflexive relations: no one is likely to be mother to herself, at least insofar as we normally understand "mother." The formal way of stating irreflexivity is

$$(x) \sim Rxx.$$

The other relation in the triad with reflexivity and irreflexivity is, not unexpectedly, nonreflexivity. Such relations may or may not exist between an individual and itself. Emotional attitudes are common instances of the nonreflexive relation. John may love himself or not, there's no abstract way of knowing which. Probably the most straightforward formal version of the nonreflexive relation is

$$(\exists x) (Rxx) \cdot (\exists y) (\sim Rxx).$$

These attributes of relations may occur in virtually any combination. "Is the sibling of" is, for example, both a symmetrical and a transitive relation, but it is also an irreflexive one. You may want either to think of relations and try to determine which attributes they have or to put together combinations of attributes and see if you can think of a relation that shares the particular combination you have specified. In any case it is worthwhile becoming a bit more aware of the attributes that relations have.

11.3   The Relation of Identity

Identity is a relation that we acknowledge frequently. Most often it will involve the attempt to make a point more specific than it had previously been. In virtually any identity assertion you will find either the use of one or more **proper names** or that of a **definite description.** A definite description takes the form "the whatever" and, like the proper name, usually serves to specify a particular individual. As Professor Copi says, it is most commonly indicated by the " = ." For those of us raised on a stiff diet of mathematics, there is a slight possibility of confusing this symbol with the ordinary mathematical "=." We might, therefore, choose to restrict the relational variable "I" for use only as identity, thus asserting the identity of **a** and **b** by "Iab" rather than by "a = b." There seems, however, to be no particular value in doing so, in trying to avoid confusing the "=" of "(a - b) = c" with the "=" of

"Px = Fx" we would bar natural symbolic representations like "Ixy"
for "x identified y (as the criminal)" or for "x insured y's success."

In the discussion of problem 31 in part II of 11.1 (pp. 221-2,
above), you will recall that I indicated that its symbolization cried
out for the identity relation. The version of that problem that I
wanted to use, but couldn't without identity, was

> Pick any person you choose, if that
> person donates anything to any charity
> then there are **at least two different
> charities and at least two different
> donations** such that that person
> makes both donations to both charities.

In "identity-form" this becomes

> Pick any x you choose, if x is a person then
> there is at least one u and at least one v and
> at least one y and at least one z such that v is
> a charity and z is a charity and x donates u to
> v and x donates y to z and u is not identical to
> y and v is not identical to z.

Reducing it as was done earlier, you get, successively,

> Pick any x you wish, {if Px then there is at least one
> u and at least one v and at least one y and at least
> one z such that {[(Cv and Cz) and (Dxuv and Dxyz)] and
> [not (u = y) and not (v = z)]}}

> Pick any x you wish, {Px ⊃ there is at least one u,
> v, y, and z such that {[(Cv · Cz) · (Dxuv · Dxyz)] ·
> [∼ (u = y) · ∼ (v = z)]}}

> (x){Px ⊃ (∃u)(∃v)(∃y)(∃z){[(Cv · Cz) · (Dxuv · Dxyz)]
>   · [(u ≠ y) · (v ≠ z)]}}

This could also have been symbolized as

> (x){Px ⊃ (∃u)(∃v)(∃y)(∃z){[(Cv · Cz) · (Dxuv · Dxyz)]
>   · [∼ (u = y) · ∼ (v = z)]}}

> The former, using " ≠ " for "not identical with," is a
> bit more commonly used (and is the form used by Pro-
> fessor Copi). Regardless of which symbolization you
> use, notice how clearly, and relatively simply, the
> statement can be represented when you have identity to
> use.

One of the most powerful uses of the identity principle is to
deal with exceptions to generalizations. If you were to dig into the
dim recesses of your local university library, you might come upon a
group of translations of logic books from the Middle Ages. Among
them you might find one by Peter of Spain (or Petrus Hispanius) and
one by William of Sherwood, titled **Tractatus Syncategorematum** and
Syncategoremata, respectively.[1] [Sherwood was Hispanius' teacher.]
Both books deal with words that are not "categorical," that is, that
don't fit as subject or predicate terms in traditional categorical
propositions. If you feel a little rusty in using these terms,

----
[1] Peter of Spain. Tractatus Syncategorematum, **Joseph P. Mullally,**
translator. **Marquette University Press: Milwaukee, WI, 1964. and**
    William of Sherwood. Syncategoremata, **J.R. O'Donnell, translator,**
Pontifical Institute of Medieval Studies: Toronto, 1941 and
    ----------. Introduction to Logic, **Norman Kretzman, translator,**
University of Minnesota Press: Minneapolis, 1966.

glance back at the summaries of chapters 5 and 6. The words "every,"
"some," "many," "all," "is," and "not" are common examples of the so-
called syncategorematic words. The really troublesome words, for
Sherwood and Hispanius, were the exceptives. Hispanius devoted many
pages[2] to discussion of how to treat inferences from propositions
like "Every man but Sortes is running." His starting point was that,
normally, it is legitimate to infer from a universal proposition a
lesser universal proposition, that is, one whose subject class is a
subclass of the original. I can, therefore, infer "Every American
Indian is running" from "Every man is running" with no problem. But
if I try to make a similar inference using Hispanius' excepted universal, I'll get "Every American Indian except Sortes is running."
If Sortes is not a American Indian, then my inferred proposition is,
at best, misleading or confusing and at worst, false, despite the
(supposed) truth of the original.

There is a similar problem with the attempted inference of a
universal proposition whose predicate class contains the predicate
class of the original as a subclass. I can infer from "Every woman
is running" to "Every woman is moving" with no fear of error. However, the transition from "Every woman but Margaret is running" to
"Every woman except Margaret is moving" clearly leads me astray in
the event that Margaret is not running but is walking, crawling, or
moving in any other manner. The attempts of Sherwood, Hispanius, and
great numbers of their colleagues to explain why there inferences are
problematic fill page after page of medieval writing on logic, with
only modest success and with little clarity.

Using the logic of relations, in particular the identity relation, makes short work of what the problems were. One possible
symbolization of the first pair would be

$$Mx =df \ x \text{ is a man}$$
$$Rx =df \ x \text{ is running}$$
$$Ax =df \ x \text{ is an American Indian}$$
$$s \ \ =df \ \text{Sortes}$$

(a.) $(Ms \cdot \sim Rs) \cdot (x)\{Mx \supset [(x \neq s) \supset Rx]\}$
(b.) $(As \cdot \sim Rs) \cdot (x)\{Ax \supset [(x \neq s) \supset Rx]\}$
(c.) $(x)(Ax \supset Mx)$
(d.) $(Ms \cdot \sim Rs) \cdot (x)\{Ax \supset [(x \neq s) \supset Rx]\}$

The relation between "A" and "M" (called by the medievals "descent
under the subject") is easily represented by (c.). A little simple
quantification manipulation would allow the inference from (a.) and
(c.) to (d.), but not to (b.). There's no way to alter "Ms" to "As"
with the information given without using the fallacy of the
affirmation of the consequent.

Similarly, the other problematic inference (called by the
medievals "ascent over the predicate") can be clarified by

$$Wx =df \ x \text{ is a woman}$$
$$Rx =df \ x \text{ is running}$$
$$Mx =df \ x \text{ is moving}$$
$$m \ \ =df \ \text{Margaret}$$

(a.) $(Wm \cdot \sim Rm) \cdot (x)\{Wx \supset [(x \neq m) \supset Rx]\}$
(b.) $(Wm \cdot \sim Mm) \cdot (x)\{Wx \supset [(x \neq m) \supset Mx]\}$
(c.) $(x)(Rx \supset Mx)$
(d.) $(Wm \cdot \sim Rm) \cdot (x)\{Wx \supset [(x \neq m) \supset Mx]\}$

In this case, again, the inference from (a.) and (c.) to (d.) is
legitimate, but the one to (b.) is not--it would require using the
fallacy of the denial of the antecedent.

----
2   Peter of Spain, _Op. cit._, pp. 33ff., q.v. both Sherwood volumes.

In quantificational logic, as you learned it in chapter 10, you had to symbolize every natural language expression from "There is at least one" to "All but one" by the same "(∃x)." The identity relation, however, allows some distinction, at least at the extremes. We can now separate "Exactly one" and "All but one" from the other particular expressions. "All but one" is represented in the manner shown above, as an exceptive. "Exactly one" has, in some systems, its own symbolic representation, "(∃x!)," which sometimes is called the "E-shriek." Adding another symbol, however, to handle a single case seems to violate the whole point of abbreviation by symbolization. Using the identity relation we can represent, for example, "Exactly one man is present" as "(∃x){(Mx · Px) · (y)[(My · Py) ⊃ (y = x)]}" without resorting to adding the E-shriek.

You do not, of course, need any special approach to represent "at least one," since that is the precise meaning of the "(∃x)" symbol. If, however, you wanted to express "at least two" or "at least three," then the identity relation would be the way to go. Assume that the property that you want two (or three) individuals to have is "F." "There are at least two F's" becomes

$$(∃x)(∃y)[(Fx · Fy) · (x ≠ y)]$$

and "There are at least three F's" becomes

$$(∃x)(∃y)(∃z){[(Fx · Fy) · Fz] · {[(x ≠ y) · (x ≠ z)] · (y ≠ z)}}.$$

The point is, you now can symbolize the occurrence of a property or relation for any specific number of individuals by merely generalizing the approach used above.

11.4   Frege on Sense and Reference

Professor Copi's discussion of Frege's distinction between sense and reference is one of the clearest you are likely to find in an introductory philosophy text. The distinction is a crucial part of an area of philosophy now knows as semiotics, or sign theory, and Frege was not alone among nineteenth-century logicians in his concern with the topic. The American Charles Peirce, who was also mentioned earlier also was interested in how it is that one thing--a sign, a symbol, or whatever--"stood for" something else. Unfortunately for us, the issue is not at all a settled one, even today.

At first glance it might appear that Frege's sense/reference distinction is roughly the same as chapter 4's denotation/connotation one (for which John Stuart Mill is actually due credit), but that is not the case. Mill's dichotomy was intended to analyze properties of general or class terms, while Frege's apply to individual terms (including proper names) as well. A proper name, for Mill, denotes an individual, but does not connote any attributes of that individual. In modern computerese, we would say that a proper name is an "atom head" that "points to" some specific individual, but that has no "property list" attached to it. In contrast, Frege's distinction would indicate that the proper name has a sense, that is that it "points to" an individual (in the manner of identifying what an individual **would be** if it happens to exist) from some perspective or other. This does not, he would say, constitute a claim for the actual existence of the individual. This means that, for a thorough-going Fregean, the name "Hamlet" has sense, in that virtually any adult in the English-speaking world understands the name and its appropriate uses (that is, we "see" its sense), but few of us would make claims about the **actual** individual whose name it is (that is, we would likely deny that it has a reference, except as a fiction).

The distinction, for Frege, extends to sentences, too. His arguments are clear, showing that the elements of the sentence that go to make it true or false, the "propositional element" that was discussed in chapters 7 and 8, must be the sense of the sentence. The actual truth value, then, of the sentence is its reference.

By similar inferences, we come to see that in saying, writing, or otherwise **using** a term we are involving its reference. If we want to talk, write, etc. about the term itself, or its sense, then the convention adopted by philosophers has been either to set the term off in quotation marks or to preface it with the phrase "the sense of." This convention is the source of one of an intriguing linguistic joke. If I were to claim that I could use the word "and" five times in immediate sequence in an easily understandable English sentence, I feel reasonably sure that you would be willing to bet me that I was wrong. I am not, but using it requires a little story-telling:

> Once upon a time there was an English pub called **The Pig and Whistle.** Over the years its sign became so weathered that it was scarcely readable, so the owner hired a man to repaint it. After the job was done the painter came to the owner and asked to be paid. He was told that there was no pay because the words on the sign were irregularly spaced. When the painter insisted on a specific case or mis-spacing, the owner said to him, "There should be the same space between "Pig" and "and" and "and" and "Whistle."

Go ahead and count. In the publican's statement there are three **uses** of the word "and" and two **mentions** of it, all in immediate sequence. If you feel at least modestly mislead by the "five-in-a-row" claim, you should, for you were. The point here is that the sense/reference distinction, if nowhere else in your ordinary usage, is worth making for this use/mention differentiation in language alone.

11.5   Russell on Denoting

Professor Copi's summary of Russell's theory of denoting is as straightforward as was his statement of Frege's theories. As he indicates, the crucial problem for Russell was the need to show how expressions that **seemed** to "point to" individuals could be meaningful even when the individuals themselves were found not to exist. In this case, Russell focused his attention upon a what he called "a denoting phrase" and what philosophers now usually call "a definite description." In an ordinary sentence this is likely to take the form "**the** whatever" (emphasis mine).

Russell showed that the use of such definite descriptions could frequently be clarified to show that they involved multiple assertions. For example, the proposition "The present editor of **Gee-Whiz Wonder Tales** is a confirmed optimist" can be seen to assert three different things:

(1)   There is a present editor of **Gee-Whiz Wonder Tales.**
(2)   There is only one present editor of **Gee-Whiz Wonder Tales.**
(3)   That individual is an optimist.

Using the obvious abbreviations, these wind up being symbolized:

(1) $(\exists x)(Ex)$
(2) $(y)[Ey \supset (y = x)]$
(3) Ox.

Putting them all together into the representation of the original proposition, we have

$$(\exists x)(\{Ex \cdot (y)[Ey \supset (y = x)]\} \cdot Ox).$$

Professor Copi goes on to explain to you how it is that the original puzzles set by Russell are solved by his theory of denoting. It is, of course, not surprising that this happens since they are, after all, Russell's puzzles and Russell's answers. Professor Copi also shows how it is that Frege's theory of sense and reference can deal with Russell's puzzles. That is somewhat more significant, for Russell posed the puzzles substantially after Frege developed his theory. It is, in any event, not likely that an introductory-level logic book will definitively decide a philosophic controversy that has disquieted the philosophic community for over three-quarters of a century.

CHAPTER ELEVEN SUMMARY

I. Relations are properties shared by two or more individuals.

    A. Relations shared by exactly two individuals are said to be dyadic (or binary).

    B. Relations shared by exactly three individuals are said to be triadic (or ternary).

.
.
.
.

    N. Relations shared by exactly **n** individuals are said to be polyadic.

    O. Dyadic, triadic, ..., and polyadic relations are symbolized by a capital letter followed by the appropriate number of individual symbols: Fxy, Gabc, ..., Habc...n.

II. Relations possess attributes (which might be looked upon as properties of the properties themselves).

    A. Some relations involve properties of symmetry.

        1. If a relation is symmetrical, then if it holds between **a** and **b** then it also holds between **b** and **a**.

        2. If a relation is asymmetrical, then if it holds between **a** and **b** then it does not hold between **b** and **a**.

        3. If a relation is non-symmetrical, then if it holds between **a** and **b** sometimes it holds between **b** and **a** and sometimes it does not hold between **b** and **a**.

    B. Some relations involve properties of transitivity.

        1. If a relation is transitive, then if it holds between **a** and **b** and it holds between **b** and **c**, then it also holds between **a** and **c**.

        2. If a relation is intransitive, then if it holds between **a** and **b** and it holds between **b** and **c**, then it does not holds between **a** and **c**.

        3. If a relation is non-transitive, then if it holds between **a** and **b** and it holds between **b** and **c**, then it sometimes it holds between **a** and **c** and sometimes it does not.

C. Some relations involve properties of reflexivity.

    1. If a relation is totally reflexive, then all individuals hold that relation with themselves.

    2. If a relation is reflexive, then if there are two individuals which have that relation with each other, then all individuals hold that relation with themselves.

    3. If a relation is irreflexive, then no individual holds that relation with itself.

    4. If a relation is non-reflexive, then some individuals hold it with themselves and others do not.

III. The identity relation states that what may appear to be two distinct individuals are, in fact, one and the same individual.

A. The identity of **a** and **b** is symbolized "(a = b)."

B. Identity is used to indicate exceptions to generalizations.

C. Identity is used to indicate a specific number of individuals.

IV. Frege distinguished between **sense** and **reference**.

A. "Sense" is the mode of presentation by which a sign refers to an object designated.

B. "Reference" is the object designated by a sign.

V. Russell described denoting in terms of definite descriptions.

A. Definite descriptions are, for all practical purposes, proper names.

B. Denoting phrases usually involve a three-part assertion:

    1. There is at least one individual with some property.

    2. There is at most one individual with that property.

    3. That individual has some other property.

PART THREE
INDUCTION

12

Analogy and Probable Inference

12.1   Argument by Analogy

If you were able to find a copy of the short story "Love is a Fallacy" that was mentioned in chapter 3, you will recall that it mentioned a fallacy called "False Analogy." In the story Dobie Gillis was accused by Polly Espey of committing this fallacy when he claimed that they were well-matched, based upon five dates and that their compatibility was proven by the fact that you didn't have to eat a whole cake to know that it was good. Her rejoiner was that, being a girl, she was too dissimilar to a cake for the reasoning to be useful. She was correctly inferring that he was using the analogy between their relationship and the cake as an argument. Whether the analogy was a bad one, however, will be a question for you to decide later in this chapter, after you have had a chance to see what makes a **good** analogy.

Although, as Professor Copi indicates, the analogical argument is among the commonest forms of nondeductive argument, not all analogies are intended to be argumentative. Drawing parallels between things that might otherwise seem quite different can serve to explain ideas or make them more vivid. Such vivacity was achieved by one observer of American foreign policy. He wished to point out how ill-trained he considered many of our high-ranking diplomats to be, especially concerning the beliefs and customs of the lands to which they are posted. He told of a state banquet in India, where our ambassador served roast prime rib of beef to his guests. He was unaware that Hinduism, the major religion of India, is vegetarian, believing that animals, especially cattle, possess the souls of people. His descriptive analogy was to suggest that the serving of a beef roast to Hindu dignitaries would have had about the same effect upon them that Americans would have felt had they been invited to dinner and been served broiled six-month-old human babies. This analogy does exactly what he wants it to do; no one who hears it is likely to forget about Hindu restrictions, ever.

By contrast, an analogy may be used to relate the unfamiliar with the familiar. Most people are not terribly well informed about the details of the biological theories of spontaneous generation of life and evolution to contemporary forms of life. In particular most of us cannot well evaluate the work by Miller, Urey, Nakashima, Ponnamperuma, and others in the synthesiis of pre-living organic compounds. Thus, when someone wants to explain what he takes to be the probabilistic assumptions involved in a theory of the spontaneous generation of life, he offers analogies like "the probability of life originating from accident is comparable to the probability of an unabridged dictionary resulting from an explosion in a print shop." We may not know what would go into creating life, but the type in a print shop and the ordered character of an unabridged dictionary are things to which we can relate.

The key in each use of analogy is to discern the intent of the writer/speaker. If the purpose of an analogy is to explain, describe or clarify, then any evaluation should be of its effectiveness in doing so. If, on the other hand, the analogy is used to lay out evidence and show how that evidence serves as support for some conclusion, then clearly it is argumentative and can be evaluated by how well the stated evidence supports the stated conclusion. A few examples of the exercises following 11.1 in Copi may help clarify how such distinctions are made.

(3)   Conclusion: Marriage as an institution is not dead as
                         it might seem.

           Evidence: The Church is accused of becoming de-
                         funct, so is marriage.
                         God has been pronounced dead, so has
                         marriage.
                         Preachers of the Church claim a revival
                         is coming, so do advocates of mar-
                         riage.
                         Churches **are** being revived.

(7)   Nonargumentative--This is an attempt to clarify what
                         goes on mentally by laying out a phys-
                         ical model that it is supposed to
                         mimic.

(12)   Conclusion: Having his tooth extracted without anaes-
                         thetic hurt him.

           Evidence: His physiology and nervous system are
                         roughly like the writer's.
                         The writer's tooth hurt when it was
                         worked upon.
                         (By the way, Ayer's reference to having a
                         tooth "stopped" is a British collo-
                         quialism meaning having a tooth fil-
                         led, that is, having a filling put in
                         a tooth.)

(17)   Conclusion: The particle-electron's motion is orbital
                         around the nucleus, to which it is
                         attracted.

           Evidence: The model of the atom is like the model
                         of solar system.
                         The laws governing the solar system are
                         roughly the same as those governing
                         the atom.
                         The planet, which is attracted by the
                         sun, moves in an orbital path around
                         the sun.

(22)   This passage as it stands would appear to be non-
           argumentative, serving to clarify how the intellect
           that is developed progresses from ignorance to know-
           ledge. It is in context, however, an argument. The
           argument is intended to be a refutation of the argu-
           ment that, since a tool which requires itself before
           it can be made cannot be made, the intellect (which is
           such a tool) would seem unable to extend knowledgee,
           In this context, the conclusion is:

           Conclusion: The intellect can "pull itself up by its
                         bootstraps."

           Evidence: The hammer, like the intellect, seems to
                         require itself before it can be made.
                         The hammer can be explained as to how it
                         comes into being in an evolutionary
                         fashion.

12.2   Appraising Analogical Arguments

Some nondeductive arguments are clearly better than others, but none of them can ever be valid. This means that we need some means other than a validity check, truth table, or formal proof of validity for determining the satisfactoriness of argements which are not deductive. Professor Copi offers half a dozen criteria for evaluating analogies which are used as arguments:

(1)   The greater the number of individuals (or the like) about which the evidence is known, the more sure the conclusion becomes. This is simply because, as we all know, things do happen in atypical ways sometimes. Recently the Social Security Administration found that they had issiued the same number to two women. Both women lived in the same state, had the same name, were born in the same year, and applied for their cards in the same month of the same year. Apparently their applications hit the computer at the same time, and it treated them as if they were one individual. That sort of thing happening is a fluke. If instead the SSA had found that everyone with the same name, or with the same birthdate, or something similar, had been assigned the same number, then it would be reasonable to infer that there was some sort of flaw in the program and that anyone else who shared that characteristic would wind up with that same number. The larger the group from which the analogy is drawn , the less likely that they will all be similarly atypical for the sort of thing they are. This group is sometimes called a reference class. The individual, or case pointed to in the conclusion is sometimes called the target individual and the characteristic claimed in the conclusion to be shared by the reference class and the target invividual is sometimes called the target characteristic.

(2)   The greater the number of characteristics that the members of the reference class share, the greater the chance that they will share other characteristics, too. Two people who come from the same socio-economic background might be claimed (weakly) to be more likely to behave in a certain manner than two persons of widely different antecedents. The greater the number of other things they have in common, like education, employment, religion, hobbies, family size and composition, ethnic backgrorund, the more reasonable it would seem to expect them to behave in a similar fashion when placed in similar surroundings. These characteristics that they share are sometimes called the reference characteristics.

(3)   The wider the range that the conclusion accepts as a "match" for the evidence, the more likely the conclusion is to be true. Recent Amtrak publicity has emphasized that the trains are running on schedule more frequently now than they did a year ago (90+% on time now as opposed to less than 60% a year ago). What they have not said is that they revised their definition of "on time" to become "within an hour" where it had been "within fifteen minutes." By accepting a wider range of times as "on time," they made it more likely that a train would be so.

(4)   If the case identified in the conclusion is too different from those used as evidence, then the argument is significantly weakened. If you were hiring someone to replace your best worker, you might initially be drawn to someone from a similar background and with similar education to that worker. The more things that you found out that they did not have in common, however, the less sure you would be that getting the new person really was like getting a younger version of the person whom you were replacing.

(5)   The fourth criterion spoke about the dissimilarlity of the case

in the conclusion from the reference class. The greater the disparity among the cases used as the reference class, however, the more secure the conclusion becomes. What happens in this situation is that great range among the cases in the reference class serves as a sort of insurance against the conclusion being dissimilar to all of them. That is, if the individuals in the reference class are sufficiently disanalogous, then criterion 4 ought not to be a problem.

(6)   Relevance is, of course, the most important of the criteria, for if the characteristics held in common by the reference class and the conclusion case are not characteristics relevant to the one about which the conclusion is drawn, then the argument is worth nothing. Caligula, Attila the Hun, Adolph Hitler, and Idi Amin have (or had) two arms, two legs, two eyes, weighed less than 20 pounds at birth, and were more than four feet tall at maturity. You (probably) share all of those characteristics. There is good evidence that all of them were/are mass-murderers. Thus, by analogy, you are probably a mass-murderer. Hopefully, this conclusion is false, despite the analogous "fit" shown in the reference class and you. The reason is that those properties are not relevant to the characteristic of being a mass murderer. Virtually every human being ever born shares those properties. Such a list doesn't sort out the mass murderers from the rest of humanity.

The problems in part I after 11.2 provide practice in applying the criteria in limited contexts. You can identify what sort of change each new piece of information brings about and, from that, identify which, if any, criterion is being evoked. Problem 4 seems typical:

a.   This shows disanalogy among the reference cases, and criterion 5 applies. It strengthens the argument.

b.   This adds another characteristic which the conclusion case has in common with the reference class and evokes criterion 2. It strengthens the conclusion.

c.   This shows the conclusion case to be disanalogous with the reference class. Criterion 4, which this suggests, says that the conclusion thereby becomes less certain.

d.   Here the conclusion is substantially less emphatic than the evidence, pointing to criterion 3 and strengthening the conclusion.

e.   Professor Copi suggests that this might fail criterion 6 and thereby have no impact, but he also indicates that, given some personal preference of Bill's for morning classes, it might be another case of additional characteristics in common, thereby recalling criterion 2, which asserts a strengthened conclusion.

f.   If you are willing to accpet the common ground of the social sciences, then, since these other courses are such, this evidence strengthens the conclusion.

In part II, Professor Copi has a substantial number of analogical arguments for analysis. If you look at this examples of the starred problems at the back of the book, you will see very extensive analysis. It may even be more detailed than necessary in most cases. A somewhat briefer approach to, say, problem 3, would be:

The argument concludes that children, like vines, need direction and support so that they can grow. Information is listed below according to the criteria:

1. Although there are only two groups--children and vines-- there are large numbers of each of them. Moderate plus.

2. That they are living organisms and that they seem to go off in all directions when left to themselves seem to be the only things they have in common. Moderate minus.

3. Since there are vast differences in positions which would all be seen as direction and support, the conclusion is not very specific with regard to the evidence. Strong plus.

4. The differences between children and plants are tremendous. The sort of direction and support meant for the vines is physical; for the children it is psychological, emotional, etc. You could probably list several dozen differences in a few mintues. Very strong minus.

5. There are undoubtedly great numbers of different types of vines all of which benefit by support, but what is really needed is a wider range of types of things that benefit from support. Essentially neutral.

6. That we even use the word "support" in the two cases is due to metaphor. It is very difficult to identify the connection between a vine's climbing up a pole and a child's accepting guidance from teachers. Neutral to negative.

All of these criteria, taken together, add up to an argument by analogy which is not terribly persuasive. It provides an interesting image, but little more.

II.   (7) The argument concludes that people, like mice, could be caused to have longer life spans if the same sorts of dietary and lifestyle alterations were made for people as had been made for the experimental mice.

1. The reference class of mice does include a fairly large number of mice, 23,000. Although that is no guarantee that the results are not the produce of some fluke set of circumstances, it seems unlikely that the records for any other large group of mice would vary significantly. Plus.

2. Sharing the common heritage of being mammals means that humans and mice share a great number of characteristics, including endothermy (warm-bloodedness), hair, a four-chambered heart, young that are born alive, mammary glands in the female and a dorsal spinal column. Plus.

3. Since the conclusion claims only that greater longevity could be induced in humans, not any specific increase, the conclusion is relatively modest in comparison to the evidence. Plus.

4. There are, of course, many disanalogies between mice and humans, the most obvious of which is size. Carrel mentions, indirectly, another: age span, where a long-lived mouse lives 42 months while a long-lived human may survive more than 100 years. Another disanalogy, which there is no good reason to expect you

to know, is the difference in some critical physio-
logical and dietary areas: humans who are deprived
of vitamin C develop scurvy while mice somehow manu-
facture it in their own bodies. This raises the
question of whether there is some other significant
metabolic difference between the two species. Strong
minus.

5. There is no mention of the similarity or dissimilarity
    of the mice in the Rockefellere Institute mousery.
    The argument seems to tacitly assume that size of the
    reference class has thorougly eliminated the possi-
    bility of some systematic longevity-mutation in the
    mouse population. Neutral.

6. It seems clear that the long-term position of medical
    researchers has been that there are sufficient simi-
    larities between humans and mice to warrant the use
    of mouse populations to mimic the human one, Barring
    some startling new discovery, then, it seems quite
    reasonable to claim the reference class is relevant.
    Moderate to strong plus.

Overall the analogical argument offered by Carrel is not
perfect but seems reasonable.

(14) One would certainly be inclined to think that this is an
argument. After all, the last line begins "the would,
therefore, I infer, is an animal...." If Hume is inferring
AND the conclusion-indicator "therefore" is there, then an
argument seems to be present. (One might, however, claim
that the argument-signs were incidental.) Assuming that
Hume is arguing here, the conclusion seems to be that the
universe is a soul-bearing animal.

1. The reference class of animals is quite large, but in
    many theological circles the question of whether or
    not all those animals bear sould is not rhetorical.
    (A rhetorical question is one to which you do not
    expect an answer, believing the answer is obvious.
    For example, a very angry parent might ask a child
    who has done something very foolish, "What kind of
    idiot are you?" In such a case the parent expects no
    reply because what looked like a question was really
    a statement, or at least an expression of anger.)
    Thus, the large reference class may be a plus for the
    argument IF the analogs are held to be related in any
    significant way.

2. Hume states four ways in which he claims the universe
    is like an animal: circulation of matter without
    disorder, self-repair, internal "sympathy" (which,
    historically, was a medical term meaning physiologi-
    cal interdependence), and the "fitting" of each part
    into its proper place in the whole. This is not an
    extensive list of similarities and, in all probabil-
    ity, many observers would question the truth of the
    list, too Probable minus.

3. The conclusion is actually rather strong, in the sense
    of being rather specific in the role of the Deity as
    analogous to that of the soul. Additionally, there
    had been no mention of the soul or the Deity in the
    analogy prior to the conclusion. Strong minus.

4. Although they are not stated in the exercise, there are
    many differences between the universe and animals

(beginning with the organic/inorganic chemistry of the two). Very strong minus.

5. If, as you did in point 1, you ignore the question of whether all animals do have souls, then the incredible variety of animals even on our realtively insignificant planet would seem to suggest about as much dissimilarity as you could ask for. Plus.

6. As had been hinted at in the earlier points, the real issue here must be the question of relevance. There are so many dissimilarities between animals and the universe and there is so little offered by Hume to show that they are alike in any important ways, that this argument surely fails the relevance test. Strong minus.

Overall, if this passage is read as an argument, it cannot be considered to be a very good one.

12.3   Refutation by Logical Analogy

Very commonly we use analogies, not to establish a point, but to show how it is that an idea that had sounded plausible reallly was not. What you are doing in such cases, in a fairly loose sense, is appealing to a sort of "semi-formal" criterion. Roughly the refuting argument you are offering is a **Modus Tollens:**

If an argument **like this** of this form is valid then another argument **like that** of the same form must also be valid.
That argument is clearly invalid.
Therefore this one must be invalid, too.

The refuting argument, then, serves to show that the argument it refutes is an invalid one.

But there are invalid arguments that we all want to use as good-but-not-valid. The entire range of inductive, analogical and hypothetical arguments is one of arguments we know not to be valid but which we can use effectively within restricted circumstances. Despite the non-deductive character of such arguments, we frequently choose to refute them by analogy. The key, then, to a refuting analogy in which the pivotal term is not "valid" but "good," where "good" is relative to the criteria for goodness **for that sort of argument.** The **Modus Tollens** argument becomes

If an argument **like this** of this form is good then another argument **like that** of the same form must also be good.
That argument is clearly bad.
Therefore this one must be bad, too.

The greatest difficulty you will encounter with refutation by logical analogy is coming up with them. Just as a given individual's inability to generate a formal proof of validity does not constitute any proof of the argument's invalidity, a given individual's inability to think of a refuting analogy is no significant proof of that argument's reliability. Again, however, practice helps, so you should try to work as many of the problems after 12.3 in Copi as you can.

(3)   The analogy claims that the original argument is roughly

All individuals who are allowed to fight are individuals
  who should be allowed to vote.
18-year-olds are allowed to fight.
Therefore, 18-year-olds should be allowed to vote.

But this is easily represented by a valid quantificational argument.

Fx =df x is allowed to fight
Vx =df x should be allowed to vote
Ex =df x is an 18-ear-old

(x)(Fx ⊃ Vx),   (x)Ex ⊃ Fx) ⊢ (x)(Ex ⊃ Vx)

The refuting analogy is the also-valid quantificational
argument

Fx =df x is allowed to fight
Vx =df x should be allowed to vote
Tx =df x is a trained fighting animal (mule or dog)

(x)(Fx ⊃ Vx),   (x)(Tx ⊃ Fx) ⊢ (x)(Tx ⊃ Vx)

The refutation **in this case** goes, the arguments are both
formally valid; the first premisses of the two arguments
are identical; the formal structure of the arguments is
also identical; and the second premisses of both arguments are indisputably true;   therefore the first premiss
must be false **in both arguments.**

(6)   This refutation is of a hypothetical argument

Animals eating grain without the hull grew sick.
Animals eating grain with the hull became well.
Therefore the hull is the crucial part of the grain and
  the heart is worthless.

The offered analogy is

Cars driven with a bad sparkplug ran poorly.
Cars driven with the bad plug fixed ran well.
Therefore the sparkplug is a crucial part of the car and
  the remainder of the car is worthless.

There is not the sort of formal analogy that occurred in
problem 2, but the refutation still seems to work. It's
interesting to see that, in both arguments, if the second
conjunct were discarded, the conclusion would seem plausible.

(11)   The argument to be refuted can be represented "semi-
formally" as

If non-violent protest is effective then it would work in
any political situation.
Non-violent protest would surely not have worked against
the Hitler Nazis.
Therefore non-violent protest is ineffective.

The refutation takes the form of two refuting arguments

If a car is an effective mode of transportation then it
would work in any driving situation.
Virtually any car you pick would not win the Indy 500.
Therefore virtually any car you pick is ineffective.

and

If a Cuisinart chops things effectively then it ought to
be able to chop any material.
A Cuisinart will not chop firewood.
Therefore a Cuisinart cannot chop things effectively.

The refutation here might be seen as semi-formally showing that the first premisses in each argument must be
false (since the arguments are all cases of **Modus Tollens**
and have true second premisses) or as simply suggesting
that there is a misinterpretation involved in understanding the first premisses, that each demands too much.
The sought conclusion of the refutation might be that a
"tool" does not have to be effective in **all** situations to
be useful.

CHAPTER TWELVE SUMMARY

I.   Analogies can be used to explain, describe, make a point vivid or to argue.

    A.   Explanations, descriptions and sharpening images are evaluated by how effective they are.

    B.   Arguments are evaluated by how much support their premisses provide for their conclusions.

II. Analogical arguments are judged to be reliable or not according to six criteria:

    A.   If the reference class contains a large number of individuals, then the argument is likely to be more reliable.

    B.   If the reference class and the claimed analog share a large number of characteristics, then the argument is likely to be more reliable.

    C.   If the conclusion is not too broad, if it allows a fairly wide range of events to count as acceptable, then the argument is more likely to be reliable.

    D.   If there are very many ways in which the claimed analog differs from its reference class, then the argument is less likely to be reliable.

    E.   If the memmbers of the reference class are fairly dissimilar to each other, except of course in the critical analogical ways, then the argument is more likely to be reliable.

    F.   If the ways in which the claimed analogy is like the reference class are significantly realted to the additional way in which we claim it resembles the others, then the argument is more likely to be reliable.

III. Analogies are effective ways of refuting arguments.

    A.   If you can offer an argument which strictly parallels the formal structure of the one you wish to refute but which has a premiss (or premisses) whose truth value matches the analogous premiss (or premisses) of the original argument and whose conclusion is obviously false, then the original is clearly bad.

    B.   If you can offer an argument whose "feel" parallels the original and whose premisses seem to match the analogous ones in the original, then the original is likely to be bad.

13

Casual Connections: Mill's Method of Experimental Inquiry

13.1 The Meaning of "Cause"

You may find the title of this section a bit misleading, for, as Professor Copi explains the word "cause" has several rather different meanings. Frequently what you mean by "cause" is a function of WHY you want to know what the cause is. A student who finds that she "clutches" on examinations, finding herself unable to fully demonstrate what she had learned, will surely wonder what the CAUSE of her behavior is. In all likelihood, her reason for wanting to know the cause is her desire to avoid the problem in the future. She seeks a necessary condition for her clutching, a condition which if eliminated would result in her no longer being unable to utilize her full knowledge. Necessary conditions are frequently symbolized (in a symbolic logic) as the consequents of conditions. In the implication "$p \supset q$," "q" is said to be the necessary condition for "p." The student's curiousity about that necessary condition is coupled with a desire to apply a **Modus-Tollens-**type effort to the situation. For example, our clutching student might find out that the "cause" of her freezing up on exams was her fear of being ridiculed by the teacher if she made a mistake. (Perhaps this fear was remotely caused by a teacher who HAD behaved in such an irresponsible manner.) In conditional terms the causal relationship would be expressed like this: if she clutches on the exam then she fears the teacher's scorn if she errs. Understanding this she reasons that if she can overcome the fear of ridicule then she won't clutch (a simple transposition). She comes to not harbor such a fear. Therefore, she will not clutch. In such a way one demonstrates the necessary condition view of causality based upon a desire to avoid certain undesirable occurrences.

A second view of causality, the sufficient condition one, is usually based upon a desire, not to avoid some consequence, but to achieve some end. For example, in Shulman's "Love is a Fallacy" Dobie Gillis notes that the successful lawyers he has notices are, almost without exception, married to beautiful, gracious, intelligent women. With that in mind he seeks to make the beautiful and gracious Polly Espy intelligent in order that she be a "fit wife" for him. Although Shulman is writing humor, Dobie is seeing such a wife as a cause of a lawyer's success, Obtaining such a wife, he seems to reason, will cause him to become a successful lawyer himself. The sufficient-condition causality that Dobie seems to use follows a pattern like the following: if Dobie marries a beautiful, gracious, intelligent woman then he will become a successful lawyer. Assume that his efforts with Polly are not, as they are in the story, wasted and that he subsequently marries her. In that event he ought to feel secure in his future. Thus this view of causality seems to be based upon the desire to attain some predetermined goal.

The third approach to causality would be to combine the two, treating causal explanation as requiring both a necessary and a sufficient condition in order to be satisfactory. The necessary and sufficient condition model of causation demands that there be one unique cause for a given event. For example, assume that a group of colonists landed on a distant planet and that their genetic makeup was accurately known. Further assume that there are two unique individuals among the colonists, fortunately a man and a woman, who respectively possess the genetic complexes for telepathy and telekinesis and that no combination of the genes of any other colonists could result in those powers. An appropriately timed union of the correct gametes from those two individuals would then be both a necessary and a sufficient condition for the production of a telepathic, telekinetic offspring. This approach satisfies some objections that could be raised relative to either the necessary or the

249

sufficient views of causation and also raises significant questions about the appropriateness of trying to approach a causal situation from more than one perspective at a time.

The greatest difficulties, however, with any attempt to clarify the concept of "cause" are that both our philosophical and our scientific conceptions of causation are vague and also that there is no consensus upon the meaning of "cause." In fact, the argument has been advanced that there is no such thing as causation, just regularly occurring conjunction of events. If, for example, you put a very powerful magnification device over the edge of a billiard ball and observed as the cue ball hit it, you would see both balls and the table, but you would not see a cause. At no time would a small figure wearing a jersey marked "Green Bay Causes" go leaping across from one ball to the other. If you think for a minute about the skills of the Hollywood special effects crews, then you would have little doubt that they could build a billiard table on which the **appearance** of a brilliant shot would occur without the cue or balls ever having made contact with each other. If their budget were sufficient, there is no question that they could do the whole sequence skillfully enough to have even close observers believe that htey had seen a skillfully executed shot when in fact they had not. The claim, then, is that the only evidence that we have for the existence of causality is the sequential occurrence of the supposed causally-related events. For our purposes, however, it makes little difference whether causality is a "real" property of events or an "impressed" quality which we read into our experience: our practical use of the idea and the term will be the same.

Inductive generalization by simple enumeration occurs when you observe that several instances of some event share some property or characteristic and infer that ALL such events will share it, too. It is a very short step from a simple enumeration to a generalization to a causual generalization. If you begin with such an enumeration, you will see how such steps occur:

John got married while in college and his grades improved.

Jeff got married while in college and his grades improved.

Gail got married while in college and her grades improved.

Thus all those who get married while in college will find that their grades improve.

Thus getting married while in college CAUSES one's grades to improve.

If you recall the fallacy of converse accident (hasty generalization) in chapter 3, then you will see that such inferences are not as reliable as you might hope. Obviously, some more sophisticated means of arriving at causal relationships is desirable. The next section will provide five such approaches.

13.2   Mill's Methods

John Stuart Mill was one of the finest minds of his century (the nineteenth) and, perhaps, of any century. His philosophic career spanned the middle forty years of the century, and his impact reaches until today. In the social-political sphere he defended Irish rights against England, radical freedom of speech, participatory religion, and the equality of women (among other unpopular positions). His **Autobiography** may be second only to Benjamin Franklin's in its candor and clarity. If you can find a copy in your local library, you should certainly take the opportunity to read it, if for no other reason than to see how the life of a full-blown genius develops.

In his massive (and influential) work **A System of Logic,** he laid out what he referred to as canons of inductive reason. What he wanted to do was find a way, based upon the work he had done in formal logic, to apply an at least partially-formed technique for handling inductive reasoning. In particular he wanted some method for generating hypotheses about what, among a set of events, could be identified as the cause of some subsequent event. The methods at which he arrived are simple and straightforward. That simplicity makes them relatively easy to learn and apply, but it also leads to some rather problematic conclusions. Ultimately, however, their ease of use and accuracy of hypothesis far outweighs any difficulties encountered in applying them to actual data. In any event, the fact that you know that they are sometimes problematic can forewarn you against such problems.

First indicated, and probably simplest, is the METHOD OF AGREE-MENT. Professor Copi's example of the students' becoming ill after a meal shows the format for examining a supposed candidate for applica-tion of Mill's Methods. In general, the key to such use is that the conclusion claims toh ave uncovered a **causal** relationship. For this method, like all the others, you begin by identifying the things that happened immediately prior to the event whose cause you are seeking. This collection of prior occurrences Professor Copi calls the "ante-cedent circumstances." The event whose cause you are seeking he calls the "phenomenon."

To identify a use of the Method of Agreement, you first check to see that all of the antecedent circumstances/phenomenon cases do have the same phenomenon; you then examine the antecedent circumstances to see if there is some one circumstance which is the only one to have occurred each and every time that the phenomenon occurred. If there is such an event, it is hypothesized to be the "cause" of the pheno-menon. The simplest occurrence would be the following two cases and their conclusion:

CASE	ANTECEDENT CIRCUMSTANCES	PHENOMENON
1	John Doe, injection of drug "a"	End of headache
2	Jane Doe, injection of drug "a"	End of headache

Therefore, the injection of drug "a" cures headaches.

This has minimal structure:

CASE	ANTECEDENT CIRCUMSTANCES	PHENOMENON
1	J_1 "a"	h
2	J_2 "a"	h

"a" causes   h

This is, of course, an argument based upon inadequate information: What else did they have in common? How long had they had the head-aches? What was the dosage of the drug each took? How quickly did the headache subside for each? The list could be extended without difficulty. Nevertheless, it does show in its simplist form how the Method of Agreement works.

Look at exercise 3 of the problems following Professor Copi's presentation of this method. It provides a real-life example to which this method can be applied. Jenner's cases are only listed in part, so the "formal" representation of the argument will have ellip-ses in it. (Ellipses are marks of omission. The are usually repre-sented by three periods--four if at the end of a sentence. They may occur horizontally, as in the discussion that follows, or vertically, to indicate the existence of additional cases that are not specified.) It is also the case that there is no detailing in the analysis of characteristics unique to each of the individuals involved: such individual properties are assumed and listed here in parentheses. Those characteristics could include age, health, height, weight, normal activity level, diet, etc. The pivotal occurrences are the infection with and recovery from cowpox (symbolized C), the infection with smallpox (S) and the failure to contract smallpox (F). Symbolically, then, the data looks like:

PERSON	ANTECEDENT CIRCUMSTANCES	PHENOMENON
Portlock	(A,B,D . . .E) C,S	F
Barge	(G,H,I . . .J), C,S	F
Wynne	(K,L,M . . .N), C,S	F
Nichols	(O,P,Q . . .R), C,S	F
Merret	(T,U,V . . .W), C,S	F
Rodway	(X,Y,A . . .AA) C,S	F
Phipps	(BB,CC,DD . . .EE) C,S	F

Therefore C is the cause of F.

There is an obvious problem with this formal representation of the situation--there are TWO antecedent circummstances which occur every time the effect occurs. Intuitively we might reject S as a cause of F, for infection with a disease would seldom be seen as a reason not to have the disease--quite the opposite. Mill's Method of Agreement does not, by itself, give us any reason for such a rejection of the data. Given the formal logic that you learned in Chapters 8-10, you may see that a better way to deal with the S-circumstance is to move it over to the phenomenon, but as an antecedent. This "conditional phenomenon" would then be "S − F" and would indicate that the occurrence of which you are seeking the cause is "failure to contract smallpox WHEN infected by it."

This sort of difficulty is relatively esily handled, but there are other cases that are more problematic. One sort is that where the antecedent circumstances are not well enough differentiated, as shown in the following:

A young man entered college and was away from parental supervision for the first time in his life. In order to appear more sophisticated than he was, he went out drinking every weekend. On the first Saturday evening he went to Barney;s and drank rum and cola. The next morning he had a terrible hangover. The second Saturday he went to The Golden Apple and drank bourbon and cola. He awoke the following morning with a terrible hangover. On the third Saturday he went to a private party and drank vodka and cola. Subsequently he spent Sunday morning terribly hungover. In the attempt to uncover the cause of his hangovers he applied Mill's Method of Agreement. It looked like the following:

CASE	ANTECEDENT CIRCUMSTANCES	PHENOMENON
1	Barney's, Rum, Cola	Hangover
2	G. Apple, Bourbon, Cola	Hangover
3	Private party, Vodka, Cola	Hangover

Therefore Cola is the cause of his hangovers.

While it may be that the sugar and caffeine could have some negative effect, no one would doubt that that the real cause of the hangovers was the alcohol in the various liquors he drank with the colas. The antecedent circumstances needed more detailing. Notice that, even had alcohol been separated out as another of the antecedents, Mill's Method of Agreement would not have provided a means for determining whether alcohol, cola, or the combination of the two was the cause of the hangover. That is the same sort of problem that was suggested in the analysis of problem 3, but it is not so easily resolved. Fear not, for a means of resolving it will be shown shortly.

The second sort of difficulty results when there is no ONE antecedent circumstance which causes some phenomenon. This would be shown in the case of several radio broadcasts which all suffered from a phenomenon known as feedback, a high-pitched whistle or squeal heard over the radio. If you laid out, say, half a dozen cases it would be very likely that you would find great variety in the antecedents; in fact there might be NO occurrence common to all the cases of feedback. Some of the cases would involve call-in broadcasts where the caller has his or her radio tuned into the show being broadcast and has the volume too high; the remaining cases would probably involve the broadcaster having the headset earphones too close to the microphone. Here, again, if you knew enough about the electronic principles involved, you might be able to sort out the detail that both types of case involved the broadcast somehow being looped back and being re-broadcast **almost** simultaneously. But if you couldn't find such a technical commonality, what you ought to be able to conclude is that there are **two** antecedent circumstances **either of which** can cause the phenomenon. This sort of complexity increases if there are two antecedents which cause the phenomenon when they occur together but neither of which is sufficient alone. Pregnancy is a great example of this sort of situation: ovulation and intercourse cause pregnancy (usually) when they occur together (without any intervening agents), but either alone is inadequate. The advent of computer-assisted searches of antecedent phenomena does much to eliminate this sort of problem.

The second sort of approach to causal hypotheses is the METHOD OF DIFFERENCE. When it is used, you lay out the antecedent circumstances of an initial case as you did with the method of agreement, but you seek as a second case circumstances which are almost identical to the first case. The sought-after difference is to be the absence of the phenomenon to which you seek a cause coupled with the absence of some one single antecedent. The inference runs that if the missing circumstance is the only difference in the antecedents, then it must be the reason the expected phenomenon did or did not occur.

The fourth problem among the exercises following Professor Copi's introduction of this method provides a good example of how to analyze an occurrence of the method of difference. As a matter of fact, this is an example of the method's having been used twice. The first case is based upon the germ-free laboratory work. The types of laboratory rats, the diet, etc., are all assumed to have been held constant. The difference is simply that one group of rats had normal oral bacteria while the others were kept germ-free. The latter had no cavities while the former averaged four apiece. Symbolically, using R, D . . . E for the common elements of being rats, having a standard diet, etc., and using G for the circumstance of having oral bacteria, and using c for having cavities, the argument looks like:

1. R, D, . . ., E, G ==> c

2. R, D, . . ., E, $\overline{G}$ ==> c

G ==> c (G causes c).

The second argument in the passage is absed on the feeding-technique research. The difference here is the method of feeding--oral or stomach. Using about the same symbols as above, with the addition of F for normal oral feeding (F being the symbol for the case of any other mode of feeding, including the direct stomach feeding suggested), the argument looks like:

1.   R, E, . . ., G, F   ==>   c

2.   R, E, . . ., G, $\overline{F}$ ==>   c

F ==> c

This case even includes the spectacular sub-case where the mutuality is extended to provide a case where the two rats share a circulatory system.

The greatest weakness of this method, like the previous one, comes when the "cause" is really some combination of circumstances. In the case, for example, of a fire, one could have the antecedents H=heat of combustion of some material, C=that combustible matter, and O=an oxydizing element, with f=the fire. Date supporting each of the three following arguments could be easily obtained.

1'   H, O, C   ==>   f

2'   H, O, $\overline{C}$ ==>   f

C ==> f

But   1"   O, C, H   ==>   f

2"   O, C, $\overline{H}$ ==>   f

H ==> f

And   1"' C, H, O   ==>   f

2"' C, H, $\overline{O}$ ==>   f

O ==> f

Here, by what seem to be proper uses of this method, there are three different things each claimed to be the "cause" of the fire. The truth, of course, is that all three are required for the fire.

One way to resolve the sort of difficulties mentioned with respect to the methods of agreement and difference is Mill's third method, the JOINT METHOD OF AGREEMENT AND DIFFERENCE. It is exactly what the title suggests, the simultaneous use of both of the first two methods. In the case of the inference derived by the method of agreement that cola drinks led to a hangover, all one would have to have would have been to have tried an evening drinking the rum , bourbon or vodka but NOT the cola. If the hangover had also absented itself (an unlikely occurrence) then you would have had the joint method at work. The fact that, probably, he would still have been hungover despite avoiding the cola would in itself provide incentive for him to have more carefully examined the antecendent conditions. Perhaps then he would have realized that all of the liquors contained alcohol. In the case of the requisite conditions for a fire, if you took cases 1', 1", and 1"' together as the agreemeent part of the inference, you would see that it is the triad of O,C and H that seem to yield fire.

Problem 6 in the exercises following Professor Copi's exposition of this method is a simple and clear demonstration of the method at work. Pasteur's experiement bgins by using the method of agreement upon the several chickens whose body temperatures were lowered and which proved susceptible to anthrax. Notice that the representation below utilizes a conditional effect like the one discussed above on pp. 236. The B,C and D characteristics are the assumed individual characteristics of the various hens; T is the use of the waterbath to lower the body temperature; A is the infection by the anthrax bacillus; f is the eventual death due to anthrax.

$$1 \quad B', C', D', T \quad ==> \quad A \supset f$$

$$2 \quad B'', C'', D'', T \quad ==> \quad A \supset f$$

.
.
.

$$n \quad B^n, C^n, D^n, T \quad ==> \quad A \supset f$$

$$\therefore \; T ==> (A \supset f)$$

Pasteur then picks another hen, which the experiment assumes is a reasonably good match for some one (or more) of the hens that died, and sets up the same conditions. The only variances are the return of the hen to normal temperature (basically the omission of T) and the subsequent return to health of the hen. This can be represented as:

$$1 \qquad B_i, C_i, D_i, T \quad ==> \quad A \supset f$$

$$2 \qquad B_{ii}, C_{ii}, D_{ii}, \overline{T} \quad ==> \quad A \& \overline{f}$$

These two instances, taken together, follow closely the pattern for the joint method.

A residue is a leftover, and that is the sort of material upon which the METHOD OF RSIDUES is based. In contrast to the methods discussed earlier, this method involves the occurrence of several phenomena together with their several antecedents. Once you have laid out the antecedent circumstances and the consequent phenoma, the approach of this method is to match them with each other, insofar as that is possible. If the example fits the method well, you will then be left with one antecedent and one phenomenon which you infer are causally related. Archimedes' famous example of using water displacement to determine the genuineness of the gold in a crown is a case of this method in about its simplest form. He had been ordered to determine whether the crown was truly gold, or just gilded lead, but with the added rpoviso that the crown was in no way damaged. He is said to have come upon the solution while bathing, whereupon Archimedes lept from his tub and nude (or clad only in a towel-- depending upon the modesty required by the storyteller) ran through the streets shouting "Eureka" (which is Greek for "I have found it"). What he had realized in the tub was that any material has a fixed weight/volume ratio. If you fill a spouted pitcher just to overflowing with water, then slowly lower the crown into it, catching the overflow water, then the volume of the water that overflows will be the volume of the crown. If you then remove the crown and weigh it you can calculate the weight/volume ratio. If you take known gold and measure out the same volume as was in the crown, then weigh it, you have both the weight/volume ratio for gold and the weight that the crown ought to weigh. Any variance between the weight of the crown and the weight of the same volume of pure gold (a left-over) or rsidue) must be accounted for by the presence of some non-gold material in the crown (another residue). THis example is valuable not only because it is so simple, but because it shows a slight variance from the "form" of the method. The "normal" way of showing the method of residues would be (for an adulterated crown):

```
G, L ==> g,l
G (the gold in the crown) is known to have weight g
-----------------------------------------
Therefore L (the lead in the crown) is known to have
    weight l.
```

But that is not really quite the way this inference (or many such method of residues inferences) took place. It really would have been more like this:

```
V (volume of the crown) has W (weight of the crown)
V (same) has G (weight of that volume of gold) IF the crown is
    pure gold.
W - G = x (some figure greater than l)
----------
Therefore there must be something heavier than gold accounting
    for part of W.
```

Since the only two elements commonly occurring in the third century B.C. (when Archimedes lived) that were heavier than gold were lead and mercury, it stood to reason that one of them had to be added to the crown to account for the excess weight. Given known weight/volume ratios for lead and mercury it would not be difficult to calculate what gold/mercury and gold/lead mixes would be required to produce a crown with that specific weight/volume ratio. Note that when Professor Copi discusses the discovery of Neptune he refers to "the (hypothesized) planet Neptune" as a causal antecedent. This is done in order to be able to add it to the list of antecedents in accord with the "normal" pattern for residues. In actuality, that inference, like the Archimedes one, follows the second pattern more closely than the first.

Example 5 after the discussion of this method provides a historical example of the use of the method. In a semi-formal fashion, the inference runs:

a. When body temperature rises, the hemoglobin count increases
      dramatically to level z.
b. The normal hemoglobin count is x.
c. The hemoglobin production rate for bone-marrow is y.
d. $(x + y) < z$ [or $\{z - (x + y)\} = k$]
e. Therefore k (the excess red blood cells) must be accounted
      for elsewhere.

Now--given this pattern--the whole can be transformed into the "normal" method of residues:

```
C,B,S ==> x,y,k
C (the circulatory system--a known red blood cell repository)
      accounts for x cells.
B (the bone marrow--a known red blood cell producer) accounts
      for y cells.
-----------------------------
Therefore S (the spleen--a known red blood cell repository) must
      account for the k cells which appear when body tempera-
      ture rises.
```

The last of the methods listed is the only one that takes into account the fact that most information that we encounter is not of the yes/no, off/on, necessary/impossible sort--most of it comes in many increments. It tends to be found in greater and lesser quantities. It is the pattern of variability that Mill identified as the METHOD OF CONCOMITANT VARIATION. ("Concomitant" is a six-bit word meaning "associated with.") Since many of the things that will be studied in science are quantified, this method utilizes the quantities, as they vary, as a means of recognizing causal relationships. The simplest sort of example is the conclusion one might draw after

reading a chart of recommended calorie intake for adult males.   The
chart would normally say that for a 30-year-old, 150 lb. man, it
takes 2700 calories/day to maintain health and body weight if he is
normally active, 2300 if he is sedentary and 3000 if he is active.
In a symbolic form with A - average activity level, B = 30-year-old
male, C = 150 lbs., a = calorie intake needed, b = weight maintenance, and c = health maintenance, this inference looks like:

$$A, \quad B, \quad C \quad ==> \quad a, \; b, \; c$$

$$A^-, \; B, \; C \quad ==> \quad a^-, \; b, \; c$$

$$A^+, \; B, \; C \quad ==> \quad a^+, \; b, \; c$$

Therefore A is the "direct" cause of a.   (Or the more
    active you are, the more calories you require.)

Note that reading another aspsect of the same sort of chart, the age
level, with O = age thirty, O = age forty, the inference would be:

$$O, \quad B, \quad C \quad ==> \quad a, \; b, \; c$$

$$O^-, \; B, \; C \quad ==> \quad a^-, \; b, \; c$$

$$O^+, \; B, \; C \quad ==> \quad a^+, \; b, \; c$$

Therefore O is the "inverse" cause of a.   (Or the older
    you get the fewer calories you require.)

The sixth problem following Professor Copi's discussion of this
method shows its use on a contemporary issue.   It is interesting, in
part, because it does not quite conform to the structures shown
above.   Although the passage does not spell out the individual cases
in any detail, what it surely intends to show is something like:

$$A, \; B, \; C \quad ==> \quad c \quad \text{(where A is the rate of alcoholism, B and}$$
                                     C are other constant factors, and c is
                                     rate of cirrhosis)
$$A^+, \; B, \; C \quad ==> \quad c^+$$

$$A^-, \; B, \; C \quad ==> \quad c^-$$

Therefore A is the causes of c (Or the increase in the rate of
                    alcoholism causes an increase in the
                    incidence of cirrhosis of the liver.)

In each of the uses of Mill's Methods shown above there is a
common element that is obvious: they are keyed to developing an
hypothesis about the causal relationships between sets of antecedent
circumstances and subsequent phenomena.   But there is another, more
subtle common element: being non-necessary inferences which could
have false conclusions, there is always additional information which
you would like to have before drawing the conclusion.   In the Jenner
/smallpox use of agreement, it would be nice to have more details
about the backgrounds of the individuals to see if there are other
common elements that might account for the smallpox immunity.   In the
rat/tooth-decay application of difference, there had to be added
assumptions about the diets of the various rats; it would have been
well to ccchave had them stated.   In the Pasteur/anthrax use of the
joint method, there surely were not enough cases tested, and it would
be informative to try to RAISE the body temperature of an anthrax-
susceptible animal to see if that would destroy the bacillus.   When
the spleen was inferred to be the locus of the additional hemoglobin,
it would have proven helpful had there been some atempt made to
"flag" the red blood cells in the spleen (radiologically, perhaps) to
se if they are the ones that flood into the system when body temperature rises.   And finally, in the alcoholosm/cirrhosis application of

conncomitatnt variation, there surely is evidence from other countries or of cases where the rate of alcohlism declined.

A significant part of the analysis of applications of Mill's Methods is such indication of areas in which the argument is weak, where the details are unclear (or even lacking), where additional research is necessary (or would be helpful), or where the same material might lead to different conclusions. This same material might lead to different conclusions. This last sort could often occur in applications of the concomitant variation method. Why, for example, was it conclulded that rise in alcoholism led to rise in cirrhosis? WHy not the reverse, that rise in cirrhosis led to increased alcoholism? Couldn't we hypothesize that the disease leads to an uncontrollable desire for alcohol? The "secret" (if there is any) to the application of Mill's Methods is to apply them cautiously and with an eye to further experiementation should the application yield a positive result.

13.3   Criticisms of Mill's Methods
13.4   Vindication of Mill's Methods

Profesor Copi indicates that there are two sorts of criticism that are leveled against Mill's Methods: They do not do what Mill claimed they do, and they donot supply a complete account of the scientific method. His discussion in 12.3, however, focuses only upon the first of these.

Mill's claims, stated simply, are that the methods (1) show how to make causal discoveries and (2) serve as a means of proving that causal connections exist. The Scientific Drinker example, either in Professor Copi's version or mine shows how use of the Method of Agreement can result in an incorrect conclusion. However, a bad conclusison could be reached using any inductive method, and, in this case, the difficulty is not with the method itself but with the application of it. It is, of course, a legitimate criticism to point out that a method is likely to be misapplied, but that seems not to be the point here.

Similarly, the criticism of the Method of Difference in showing that the description of the antecedent circumstances omitted a major, significant piece of evidence (the unfairness of the test) is not really a criticism of the method. Had the arguer done a respectable job of laying out the antecedent circumstances, there would have been no such erroneous argument. Thus neither of these criticisms is at all significant asa critiques of Mill's claims.

More importantly, such examples of weakness in the use of Mill's Methods ought to incline us to be more sensitive to their use and less reliant upon the "rule of the law" in applying Mill's Methods. In any event, the bulk of such criticisms ought to be directed toward Mill (or, since hs is dead, anyone who uncritically applies the Methods) rather than at the Methods themselves. It certainly would be nice if we had handed to us a set of teechniques that would guarantee us the ability to uncover causal relationships whenever we wanted to find them. The inability to find such a set of techniques, however, does not by itself suffice as a reason for scrapping the techniques. The fact that your Phillips head screwdriver is used seldom and, when erroneously used, causes damage is no reason for throwing it away. You may use it infrequently, but on those occasions when it does work it is irreplaceable. This would suggest that, if there are any circumstances at all in which Mill's Methods are useful, then they are justified.

Mill's Methods, then, are not applied within a vacuum. To be in a position to draw any sort of causal hypothesis, you must already know (or suspect or intuit) what is relevant. That is a preapplication necessity.

The second claimed failure to meet the claims for the Methods lies in the area of proof rather than discovery. As Professor Copi suggests, the mere fact that you could lay out the factual evidence in such a way as to match one of Mill's Methods does not constitute proof tht there is a causal relationship present. For example, if you were to look at women's hemlines since the First World War you would find that whenever hemlines go up or down the stock market goes up or down. Hemline highs in tht period would include the "Flapper" period of the late 20's, the knee-top skirts of World War II and the micro-miniskirts of the late 60's; corresponding market highs would be found, with the Dow-Jones averages finally braking 1000 during the micro-mini era. Low hemlines would be found in the 30's, the 50's anda the early 70's (with the ankle-length maxi being worn); of course, the great depression, the "rolling recession" of the Eisenhower years and the post-Vietnam economic woes correspond to the hemline lows with similar economic ones. If you actually bought into this inference, then you would be likely to claim that women who were truly patriotic would go back to the mini (or perhaps even resort to nudity) to heal the world's economic ills. While there are those who might wish to see such a move in the fashion industry, I have serious doubt about the economic nature of that preference. As a matter of fact, you could probably make a better case for the causality going the other way, claiming tht economic security would lead to more openess or exhibitionism in dress. In any event, it seems clear that Mill's Methods do not provide the sort of certainty either in discovery or proof that Mill claimed.

You may feel that you have missed Profesor Copi's discussion of the second charge against Mill's Methods, that they do not constitute a complete account of the scientific method. I do not believe that you will find that discussion as an issue separated from the discussion of Mill's claims for this Methods. It is a fairly straightforward inference from the inability of the Methods to discover all causal relationships or even prove their causal nature to the position that the Methods do not provide a complete explication of the scientific method (if, in fact, there is one). Thus, if there is any way to show how causal laws are discovered or proven, then, since Mill's Methods are inadequate to do either, Mill's Methods must also be an inadequate account of scientific method.

All of these criticisms, however, should seem to you to be a bit off-target. Their focus is not so much Mill's Methods themselves as it is the claims made for them. An analogy might be useful here. (Perhaps you should try to decide whether it is explanatory or argumentative.) In the last several years many brands of a kitchen device called a food processor have been widely advertised. The machine is essentially a motor which drives an assortment of blades which cut up (process) food in several ways, depending upon the design of the blade and of the housing. if you listen to the proponents of the machine and watch demonstrations done by the sales force of the processor manufacturers, you can be convinced that the device can do virtually anything you would ever want to do in a kitchen, that it can replace almost any other appliance. As a matter of fact, however, it falls short of specialized appliances in many of its functions. For example, a machine designed only to grind meat, say, to make hamburger turns out uniform, evenly-textured meat; the "ground" meat from many of the processors tends to be irregularly textured and more mashed than ground. Similarly, vegetables sliced by the machine tend to be tapered form one edge to the other while hand-sliced ones (if the slicer knows what he or she is doing) will be of uniform thickness. In fact, the products of the food processor tend generally to be inferior to the products of hand work or speci-

alized devices. On the other hand, the food processor does better
work at doing all these things than does any other device. The point
is, if you were evaluating the food processor, you would concentrate
on what **it can do**, not upon what someone may have claimed for it. By
analogy it seems reasonable to claim that criticisms of Mill's
Methods ought to be centered upon how well they do what they do and
upon how useful they are, not upon what Mill may have hoped they
would do. (Incidentally, the analogy **was** an argument.)

It turns out that Mill's Methods are quite useful when they are
used in the context of hypotheses which have already eliminated most
of the extraneous material from the antecedent circumstances. The
Methods, then, become devices for organizing evidence, for helping
show relationships in clear relief. If you were to find, as actually
happened, that some of the sensor readings in a laboratory devoted to
radiation research, occasionally but irregularly, were radically
different than you expected, then you would seek a cause for the
anomalous effects. It is almost certain that, among the hypotheses
you might consider, you would be quite unlikely to suspect the material of the shoes of the lab workers. In the actual case it turned
out that the artificial leather (plastic) of one person's shoes was a
sort that, when exposed to low level radiation, released a gas that
caused the sensors to malfunction. Without the hypothesis that the
material being carried into the laboratory was apparel of the workers, it is doubtful that Mill's Methods could do anything to suggest
that causal element. In the presence of that hypothesis, the Methods
will do a quite respectable job of **confirming** it. Mill's Methods,
then, can be seen as another tool to be maintained for the benefit of
the rest of society.

Examination of a few more of the problems relating to Mill's
Methods (at the end of chapter 13) may help clarify their use in
practice. Again it is far more valuable to you if you attempt the
problem on your own before looking at the answers either in Copi or
here.

(2)   It might help to draw a diagram of what Howell's plats
          might have looked like:

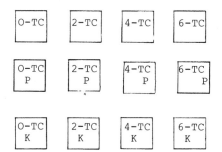

On any plat, "K" means
potassium was added, "P"
means phosphorus was
added and "C" (with a
number and "T") means
that some given number
tons of limestone (cal-
cium carbonate) was
added.

It seems clear that Howell had intended his research
to yield results under a concomitant variation type
model, else why would he have varied the concentrations of limestone? They seem clearly to be the joint
method of agreement and difference.

On the plats that contained potash, (the bottom row)
regardless of the additional factors (like limestone,
location, etc.), the common antecedent condition is
the occurance of potash and the common effect is the
strong, healthy corn. This fits the pattern of the
method of agreement:

```
First plat:    No added C,K, (A,B,...,N)    Good corn
Second plat:   2T added C,K, (D,E,...,M)    Good corn
Third plat:    4T added C,K, (F,G,...,H)    Good corn
Fourth plat:   6T added C,K, (I,J,...,L)    Good corn
```

Therefore K causes good corn

This seems a reasonable version of the method of agreement. There is, however, also the possibility of setting up several instances of the method of difference, too: there is such an instance corres ponding to each of the plats in the agreement argument above. At least on the assumption that Howell kept other variables resonably well under control, the plat shown being on the top row should be a good match for the corresponding plat on the bottom row. That would yield four instances of the method of difference:

```
First plat (t):   O added C, (A,B,...,N)    Bad corn
First plat (b):   O added C,K, (A,B,...,N)  Good corn
```

Therefore K causes good corn

```
Second plat (t):  2T added C, (D,E,...,M)   Bad corn
Second plat (b):  2T added C,K, (D,E,...,M) Good corn
```

Therefore K causes good corn

```
Third plat (t):   4T added C, (F,G,...,H)   Bad corn
Third plat (b):   4T added C,K,(F,G,...,H)  Good corn
```

Therefore K causes good corn

```
Fourth plat (t):  6T added C, (I,J,...,L)   Bad corn
Fourth plat (b):  6T added C,K, (I,J,...,L) Good corn
```

Therefore K causes good corn

Each of these is a reasonable use of the method of difference. Using all the arguments together, there is a substantial use of the joint method.

It would be possible, also, to perform a few tests on the Terra Ceia soil, based upon the inferences already drawn, and check to se that it is deficient in potassium. That might lead you to set up a series of agreement arguments for all of the non-potash-added plats which would conclude that potassium deficiency causes bad corn. Doing this, however, seems a bit foolish, for it really is only the complement (of sorts) of the original agreement argument.

Professor Copi does not ask it of you, but if you were to evaluate this argument in general, you would probably conclude that it is a pretty good one but not without defect. One would hope that Howell would repeat the experiment, this time varying the amount of potash added to the plats. It also would have been nice to have had him lay out the details of the location, soil and care of the plats in general. The differences in the quality of the corn **could**, of course, have been due to other variations not mentioned in the passage. All in all, however, the inference seems reliable enough to warrant significant further experimentation, and that actually is about all one ought to hope from the results of using one of Mill's Methods.

(6)   This seems clearly to be a use of the method of dif-
       ference. There are two groups of men, they are all
       patients at the veterans' hospital in Los Angeles, and
       the only supposed difference in the groups is in the
       amount of saturated fat in their diets. The argument
       in quasi-symbolic form has this form:

       (424 members) vets, men, unsaturated fats 31.3% c-v
          disease
       (422 members) vets, men, saturated fats 47.7% c-v
          disease
       _____
       Therefore the saturated fats cause the additional
          16.4% cardiovascular disease.

       There is an assumption that the subjects are men--not
       certain but likely. In this case there is a built in
       assumption that the elements common to the two cases
       cause the 31.3% cardiovascular disease.

       The fact that there are changes in percentages of c-v
       disease sufferers might have led you to suspect that
       the method of concomitant variation was being used,
       but you really don't have enough information for that
       method, you would really need at least one more group
       with some significantly different balance of saturated
       to unsaturated fats which led to some equally differ-
       ent result in rate of c-v disease. For example, if
       the third group consumed more saturated fats than the
       first group but less than the second and if that group
       had a c-v disease rate somewhere around 39 or 40%,
       then a variation would be apparent and concomitant
       variation could be claimed. Without the third case,
       however, it seems more accurate to describe this argu-
       ment as a case of the method of difference.

       Again, Professor Copi has not asked you to evaluate
       the argument, but it may be worth a little effort to
       think about problems that this argument has. The
       biggest difficulty that can be ascribed to this argu-
       ment is the inadequacy of the information presented.
       To properly evaluate this, you would need a good deal
       of in formation about the two groups, how similar the
       individuals in them are, how closely mtached the other
       elements in their lives and diets are, how closely
       their genetic makeups resembled each other, and so on.
       Even then, the proferred conclusion about the effect
       of saturated fats upon c-v disease rate would be on
       shakey ground. The groups selected for testing are
       certainly not representative of humanity in general,
       omitting (probably) women. It is also a reasonable
       suspicion that there might have been something in the
       service experience that might have made these subjects
       more sensitive to the saturated fats (perhaps a by-
       product of eating military food over an extended peri-
       od of time). Thus, it seems reasonable to claim that
       this is not a terribly good argument, even though you
       might believe (on other grounds) that the conclusion
       is correct. This ought to reinforce the idea that the
       quality of the argument may not have anything to do
       with the truth of the conclusion.

(11)   This argument, like the sixth one (discussed earlier),
       compares two groups: the juveniles who were given
       immediate parole and those locked up. The former
       group has a lower parole-revocation rate than the
       latter. As in exercise six, you might be tempted to

argue that this is a concomitant variation, but the
same arguments against that apply. Described as a use
of the method of difference, this argument would have
this form:

Juveniles, Criminals, Paroled,...   28% parole-revoked
Juveniles,Criminals,Imprisoned,... 52% parole-revoked

Thereforeimprisonmentcauseshigherparole-revocation rates.

Again, Profesor Copi does not ask for an evaluation,
but the argument fairly cries out to be criticized.
The question of what counts as "comparable" in the two
groups is certainly relevant. More violent, less
remorseful criminals would be less promising candidates for parole. Were the paroled group picked at
random for parole or were they selected very carefully? Were the "comparable" group who were initially
imprisoned given the same sort of follow-up observation and aid once they were paroled, that is, the
"intensive" care from parole officers, or were they
simply cast into the mill with dozens of other ex-
offenders? Were the experimental group put into better living environments than those they had left?
Were the imprisoned people returned to the same problematic circumstances? All these questions suggest
that the argument is quite inadequate.

(25)   It seems particularly appropriate to end the chapter
on Mill's Methods with an example drawn from Mill's **A
System of Logic**. It should not require much effort to
see the clue in the fourth line from the bottom of the
ex ample: "...a **residual** phenomenon appeared..."
[emphasis mine]. Clearly Mill sees this as a use of
the method of residues. The dangling needle stops in
a fixed length of time when it is not held over the
plate, but when it is held over the copper plate it
stops more rapidly. The analysis as a use of the
method of residues would look like this:

Needle, thread, vibration, plate ==> needle at rest in a
                                      fixed time period

Air resistance to the needle   ==> needle stopping in
                                      a given time

Incomplete elasticity of the thread ==> needle stop-
                                      ping in a given
                                      time

Therefore the copper plate causes the difference between
the expected stopping time of the needle and its actual
stopping time.

The interesting thing is that you could make a plausible
case for claiming that this, like several of the previous arguments, was a case of the methods of differences: the plate is the antecedent phenomenon that
occurs or not and the speeded stopping time is the
effect that occurs with the plate.

Whichever approach is taken to this argument, you ought
to see that there is a series of further experiments
that would make the inference much more reliable (if
they yielded the same conclusion). If you set up the
experiment where you were sure that there were no outside influences and where you could vary the distance

from the needle to the copper plate, then you should arrive at a reliable use of the method of concomitant variation. If your work were careful and if modern physics is correct, then you would find that the closer you got, the faster the needle would come to rest. As a matter of fact, the difference in stopping time should be inversely proportional to the square of hte distance between the needle and the plate.

CHAPTER THIRTEEN SUMMARY

I.   The meaning of "cause" is subject to significant dispute.

   A.   The **necessary-condition** view of "cause" identified "cause" with those things which, if eliminated, would also eliminate the event they are claimed to cause.

   B.   The **sufficient-condition** view of "cause" identifies "cause" with those events which, if they occur, will insure that the event they are claimed to cause will also occur.

   C.   The **necessary and sufficient condition** view of "cause" identifies "cause" with those things whose presence insures their effect and whose absence insures the nonoccurrence of their effect.

II.   Mill's method of agreement has the following form:

```
A, B, C, D  ==>  e
A, E, F, G  ==>  e
A, H, I, J  ==>  e
------------------
.˙.      A  ==>  e
```

III. Mill's method of difference has the following form:

```
A, B, C, D  ==>  e
A, B, C, D̄  ==>  ē
------------------
.˙.      D  ==>  e
```

IV. Mill's joint method of agreement and difference has the following form:

```
A, B, C, D  ==>  e
A, B, C, D̄  ==>  e
E, F, G, D  ==>  e
H, I, J, D  ==>  e
------------------
.˙.      D  ==>  e
```

V.   Mill's method of residues has the following form:

```
A, B, C, D  ==>  a, b, c, d
         A  ==>  a
         B  ==>  b
         C  ==>  c
---------------------------
.˙.      D  ==>  d
```

VI. Mill's method of concomitant variation has the following forms:

A. Direct:

$$A^+, B, C, D \implies e^+$$
$$A, B, E, F \implies e$$
$$A^-, C, D, F \implies e^-$$
$$\overline{\qquad\qquad\qquad\qquad}$$
$$\therefore \qquad A \implies e$$

B. Inverse:

$$A^+, B, C, D \implies e^-$$
$$A, B, E, F \implies e$$
$$A^-, C, D, F \implies e^+$$
$$\overline{\qquad\qquad\qquad\qquad}$$
$$\therefore \qquad A \implies e$$

VII. Mill's Methods are subjected to two basic criticisms.

A. They do not do what Mill claimed they did.

1. They seem unable to guarantee discovery of a casual relationship of which you do not already have suspicion.

2. They seem unable to prove that a claimed case of causality is not just a set of coincidences.

B. They are not a complete account of scientific method.

VIII. The criticisms of Mill's Methods can be answered on grounds apart from the claims made for the methods.

A. Mill's claims are independent from the functioning of the methods.

B. They show great value as a means to organize information.

C. They can be used to suggest routes for further investigation.

14

Science and Hypothesis

14.1 The Values of Science

Philosophers frequently describe values as being either instrumental or intrinsic. An object or action is said to be instrumentally good if its value is derived from its utility relative to somem goal apart from it. For example, under normal circumstances if you saw one person holding another down on a restaurant table and cutting at the "victim's" throat with a steak knife, you would probably suspect that that action was "bad." However, if you later found out that the victim had a blockage in his throat and that the "attacker" was actually a skilled surgeon who was performing an emergency tracheotomy to save the supposed victim's life, then you would surely believe the action had been "good." The point is that the action of cutting a person's throat cannot be judged apart from the context in which it is done. And the value it has, whether it is good or bad, is a function of whether or not it leads to or contributes to the achievement of some desired goal. The cutting of another's throat by someone who knows what he or she is doing in order to prevent strangulation is instrumentally good. Any action or thing, then, that aids us in achieving some sought-after goal will be called an instrumental good.

Those things that we claim are good (or bad) in and of themselves, without reference to any o ther occurrence or set of circumstances, are said to be intrinsically good (or bad). for example, we frequently justify an action by saying, "I felt good when I did it" or "I was happy when I did it." The action would be characterized as being an instrumental good, but the feeling good or happy was unjustified. In fact, to most of us, asking someone why they wanted to feel good or be happy would seem a pretty strange inquiry. Being happy seems to be "obviously" desirable. Try for a minute to think of how you would respond to someone who asked you why you wanted to be happy. Chances are that the only reply you can offer is that you like the way being happy feels. If the question were then shifted to ask why you should do what results in a way of feeling that you like, you would probably either shrug your shoulders and walk away or else suggest that the questioner might be best off in a well-padded room where he couldn't hurt himself. In either event, what you are doing is, in effect, asserting that being happy or feeling good is intrinsically good, that no justification is needed for claiming either is good.

The reason for this discussion of sorts of "goods" is its application to science. One of the common ways in which science is claimed to have value is the benefits it has brought to humanity. The lists of diseases conquered, consumer goods manufactured, living and farming space reclaimed, all are instrumental justifications of science. Any discussion of the practical applications of science is such a justification of the business of science as an instrumental good. The sorts of such arguments that you encounter are common, for example, in the defense of the government's spending large amounts of money on the space program. Defenders of the thrust into space will point as justification to the nonstick pans you use in your kitchen, to the digital watch that you wear and consult continually, to the Space-Invaders-type game into which Americans stuffed over **4 billion** quarters during 1980, and to the encyclopedia-book-size computer that you can buy for a couple thousand dollars but which can do more than the biggest computer on earth could have done twenty years ago. They can show that the extremely effective long-range telemetry needed for the outer planet fly-by's of *the* Voyager series is what led to the communications satellites that allow you to watch from fifty to one hundred television channels on your backyard "earth station." None of these defenses makes any claim for intrinsic merit for science, merely for its instrumental worth in bringing about the society that we think we want.

Alternative defenses of the scientific enterprise focus upon what is claimed to be humanity's native dsire for knowledge. On those accounts wanting to know what is currently unknown is a natural human drive and its satisfaction is seen to be good without any further justification. An example of htis sort of drive in people is the so-called Rubik's Cube fad. (If you have been in a Tibetan monastery for the last few years, or are too young to recall The Cube and don't know what the cube is, the description follows: the cube is actually composed of 24 small cubes and an internalspring and pivot arrangement. When new [or solved] each face displays nine small squares or a single color. Entire faces--top, bottom, front, back, left or right side--may be rotated as a unit. Once the colors have been scrambled, the object is to manipulate the cube in such a way as to restablish the original one-color-per-side arrangement.) With the occasional exception of persons driven to solve the cube as a means of bolstering their egos, there is no good reason for seeking to solve the cube except that it is there. The use of such an ability to solve the cube, except for the person who wrote and sold the solution book, is virtually impossible to justify on instrumental grounds. Nevertheless, millions of the cubes have been sold and probably hundreds of millions of hours of person-effort have been expended. Why? The challenge of trying to learn something that you did not previously know or of trying to accomplish a difficult goal.

Opponents of the intrisic value view of science have a persuasive attack: if there is an inborn human drive toward knowing, then the knowing itself is still good only instrumentally, as a release of the tension generated by unfulfilled desire. Knowing, they would claim, like eating, sleeping and keeping warm, derives its "goodness" from relieving you from an unpleasant state of want. Few people would offer scratching as an intrinsic good, preferring to identify it as instrumentally good in relieving an itch; similarly, couldn't you claim that knowledge is good because it "scratches" the "itch" of ignorance? If you'd like to explore this sort of position a bit further, you might look for "The Fixation of Belief" by Charles S. Peirce. It first appeared in the **Popular Science Monthly** in 1878 but is commonly reprinted in introductory philosophy texts.

No matter which view of the value of science that you take, you will surely see that one of hte most critical characteristics of science is its systematizatioan of the facts that it encompasses. The attempt by the scientist to place facts, usually derived from observation, into some order is directed at arriving at more than a mere record of data. In general the scientist hopes to understand what is happening and why it is happening. When Charles Darwin took his now-famous tour of duty on the H.M.S. Beagle, he gathered a great deal of information about the plants and animals that he observed. The science, however, in his efforts was his attempt to put all of the data together in some sort of coherent whole, so that he could UNDERSTAND how and why these organisms had come to be as they were. The theory of evolution at which he arrived was his attempt to EXPLAIN both the living organisms which he had encountered and hte fossil record that was just coming to light at mid-nineteenth century. Whether or not you choose to accept his work as accurate, it is important to understand that he ws trying to organize the data with which he was confronted in such a way as to explain both the similarities and the differences of living and fossilized organisms. The key was an attempt to arrive at a systematic prsentation of data in such a way as to explain the existent phenomena.

14.2   Explanations: Scientific and Unscientific

It is far beyond the scope of an introductory logic book to try to work out all the possible issues and problems that might be uncovered in trying to clarify the concept of "explanation." In everyday life you will encounter everything from a child's "explaining" a broken cookie jar by appeal to a mischievous imaginary friend to a cable-television operator "explaining" a bad picture in terms of sunspots, lines of magnetic force and ionospheric variation. The difficulty with trying to understand what explanation is comes from seeking common ground to account for both of these cases.

One school of philosophic thought suggests that a good way to identify and evaluate explanations is by thinking of them as resembling predictions. This means that the same thing that is acceptable as an explanation after the fact would have served well as a predictor before the fact. This parallel is not itself without difficulty, for the explanation always has the datum of the event's actually occurring while the prediction never has it. That is, you never explain the occurrence of an event which has not occurred (except in strange cases like the "explanations" that were printed before the votes were counted of Truman's defeat by Dewey in 1948) and you could scarcely claim to predict an event that you know has already occurred. Nevertheless, the sort of things that would seem acceptable as explaining one event would seem relevant as predictors, when they occurred, of another event of the same sort.

In general an explanation, whether scientific or not, has two kinds of elements: a description of the circumstances (like the antecendent phenomena of Mill's Methods) and the rules, laws or principles by which those circumstances are governed. When I try to explain why one child exposed to chicken pox caught the disease and another similarly exposed did not, I try to be sufficiently detailed in my investigation of the circumstances to show why, under the laws of contagion in our current medical science, circumstances were sufficient for the one child but not for the other. One obvious, and simple, explanation might have been to point out that the unaffected child had already had the disease, so was immune. Another explanation might refer to the basic health of both children. A third might appeal to probability laws and the Brownian motion of air molecules. The point is that, in any given set of circumstances, there are likely to be several possible explanations.

A critical issues will be to sort out the good explanations from the bad ones. A first step in doing htis usually is to separate the scientific and the unscientific explanations from each other. This is important because the unscientific ones, at least insofar as they are so identified by Profesor Copi, are not likely to be productive. They are almost always dogmatic. The attitude that they express is like the one which was such an unfortunate political slogan for Senator Barry Goldwater in his 1964 bid for the Presidency. His followers rallied to the cry "IN YOUR HEART YOU KNOW HE'S RIGHT!". Some of the more extrerme of them were heard to say things that amounted to saying, "I don't want to be bothered with the facts because I already am sure that I know the Truth" (and you could almost HEAR the capital T in "Truth"). A scientist acting as a scientist (or "qua scientist" as a philosopher might say), as opposed, say, to acting as a believer in a religious doctrine, has a different attitude toward facts. The scientist actually welcoms any new data, whether it supports a previously es tablished explanation or calls it into question. All scientific explanations, then, are taken to be provisional, subject to revision or rejection in the light of new information. This is never the attitude with dogma. Be aware, however, that something arrived at as science can degenerate into dogma. Ptolemy was doing the best science he knew how to do when he explained the positions and motions of the celestial bodies in terms of a geocentric (or Earth-centered) universe. His followers,

many generations removed, who opposed Galileo, Kepler, and Coperni-
cus, however, were operating dogmatically. They were so convinced of
hte truth of the geocentric theory that they wouldn't give supporters
of the heliocentric (or Sun-centered) theory a fair hearing.

This dogmatic attitude of nonscientific explanation is most
clearly indicated by the attitude toward evidence held by the unscientific explainer. To such a person the best evidence is a reference
to some authoritative source. The possibility of looking to the
world for evidence is largely unthinkable. In Isaac Asimov's book
Foundation the Encyclopedia Foundation is visited by Lord Dorwin, a
self-professed archeologist and representative of what Asimov takes
to be degenerate science. The following passage shows the authori-
tarian approach to science at its worst (or at least at its most
humorous). Note that for clarity I have altered spellings away from
the lisping accents that Asimov gives to Dorwin.

> "...I have done an awful amount of work in the
> science. Extremely well-read in fact. I've gone through
> all of Jordan, Obijasi, Kromwill...oh, all of them, y'know."

> "I've heard of them, of course," said Hardin,
> "but I've never read them."

> "You should some day, my dear fellow. It would
> amply repay you. Why, I certainly consider it well worth
> the trip here to the Periphery to see this copy of Lameth
> ... Lameth, you must know...presents a new and most inter-
> esting addition to my knowledge of the 'Origin Question.'
> ...Surely you must know that it is thought that originally
> the human race occupied only one planetary system."

> "Well Lameth goes off on a new trail completely.
> He tries to show tht archeological remains on the third
> planet of the Arcturian system show that humanity existed
> there before there were any indications of space-travel."

> "And that means it was humanity's birth planet?"

> "Perhaps. I must read it closely and weigh the
> evidence before I can say for certain. One must see just
> how reliable his observations are."

> Hardin remained silent for a short while. Then
> he said, "When did Lameth write his book?"

> "Oh--I should say about eight hundred years ago.
> Of course, he has based it largely on the previous work of
> Gleen."

> "Then why rely on him? Why not go to Arcturus
> and study the remains for yourself?"

> Lord Dorwin raised his eyebrow and took a pinch
> of snuff hurriedly. "Why, whatever for, my dear fellow?"

> "To get the information firsthand, of course."

> "But where's the necessity? It seems an uncom-
> monly round-about and hopelessly rigmarolish method of
> getting anywhere. Look here, now, I've got the works of
> all the old masters--the greatest archeologists of the
> past. I weigh them against each other--balance the dis-
> agreements--analyze the conflicting statements--decide
> which is probably correct--and come to a conclusion. That
> is the scientific method. At least"--patronizingly--" as I
> see it. How insufferably crude it would be to go to Arc-

turus, or to Sol, for instance, and blunder about, when the old masters have covered the ground so much more effectually than we could possibly hope to do." Isaac Asimov, **Foundation.** New York: Doubleday, 1951, pp. 58-60.

In contrast, the scientist takes any explanation as being hypothetical. This means that the scientist looks for proof in the world that we all share, the world of our senses.

In his paper, "The Fixation of Belief," the American philosopher and logician CHarles S. Peirce lays out what he takes to be the four possible ways of arriving at a belief. Simplest, he says, is the method of tenacity. It involves "grabbing" the nearest (or most available) belief and holding it regardless of the evidence that may appear. That sems quite close to the unscientific dogmatism that Professor Copi describes. Second, Peirce explains the method of authority. Its followers let some outside agency state what will and will not be believed, again without regard for experimental confirmation. This, too, seems to resemble what Professor Copi has called unscientific explanation. The third means "from the former" method. It claims that one arrives at beliefs by seeing if they are consistent with reason". Essentially this amounts to a reliance upon intuition as opposed to fact. This, too, seems closer to the position of dogmatism than that of science. The fourth method is, of course, the scientific method. Its value is tht it allows continual testing of your beliefs, permitting (or perhaps demanding) that beliefs be changed to keep them in line with the most current data available.

The key concept in the acceptance or rejection of a scientific explanation is TESTING. Those explanations which are not subject to test are, for the most part, to be rejected out of hand. Those that are testable are accepted or rejected in accordance with the outcomes of the tests. The most obvious, but least common, sort of testing in the sciences is direct testing. Most sciences, once they pass beyond a very primitive statge, are concerned with ideas, concepts and explanations which can only be verified indirectly. Direct verification, like putting a drop of **aqua regia** on a mineral suspected of being gold to verify (or falsify) the hypothesis that it IS gold, is seldom of crucial importance in modern theory--laden sciences. Direct verification is not terribly common, but at least has the benefit of being quite secure.

Indirect verification is never as secure an inference as direct but is used quite frequently in the sciences. An indirect test usually involves the use of both deductive and inductive reasoning. You begin by working out, deductively, some directly observable result of that which you wish to verify; then you perform the non-deductive testing of those results. A classic case of indirect verification occurred in Sir Arthur Conan Doyle's **A Study in Scarlet.** Sherlock Holmes hypothesizes that Irene Adler has secreted in her house the evidence of her former relationship with Holme's client. Holmes cannot directly search the house. He infers that if the house were imperilled that evidence would be among the first things she would wish to rescue. (The "deductiveness" of this inference depends upon several premises about the behavior of people toward endangered possessions which are held to be of value.) Holmes then conspires to be in her home when a fire appears to break out. By observing her actions, that is, where she looks, he locates what he takes to be the hiding place and later checks it for verification of that implicant of his original hypothesis. The confirmation that he receives is not quite what he had expected (to find out what it was, read the book), but he does receive such confirmation. This serves as indirect proof that his original hypothesis about her having the evidence hidden in her house was correct.

The question that this discussion should raise in your mind involves proper evaluation of these explanations, tests and verification procedures. That is the subject of the next section.

14.3   Evaluating Scientific Explanations

If the scientific enterprise were so structued as to provide only a single explanation for any given set of data, then the job of evaluation would seem pretty straightforward. Unfortunately the job is somewhat more complicated than the single-explanation situation would yield. In the same way that infinitely many lines may be drawn through a singel point, very many (if not infinitely many) explanations may be offered to account for the same set of facts. One of the most dramatic instances of htis sort of multiple-explanation situation can be found in the study of UFOs. The pivotal fact is that there is no reliable evidence, that is, evidence that we can put out on a table for us all to examine, of there being "stuff" from, for example, a flying saucer. Persons who deny the existence of flying saucers will claim that this lack of a crashed saucer, of their equivalent of beer cans strewn about, or of a smashed-up alien corpse all serve to prove the non-existence of flying saucers. On the other hand, persons who assert the existence of such vehicles take exactly that same data and use it as evidence that such things DO exist. Their argument is that any beings sophisticated enough to get here and not get caught yet will be beings who will have accepted their moral responsibility to clean up after themselves. THus the very lack of such alien refuse servess indirectly, to confirm the existence of such aliens. It is these sorts of conflicting hypotheses that tell us that some set of evaluative criteria are necessary to get the job of evaluating scientific explanations done. Professor Copi identifies and discusses five such criteria.

First is the criterion of **relevance**. If the proposed hypothesis does not account for the facts the explanation of which was the reason for developing said hypothesis, then we might as well forget the explanation. Explanations which do not relate to the issue at hand may be interesting, but they have no functional value unless they somehow tie into what you wish to explain. For example, a discussion of the sorts of ways in which the Egyptian pyramids were built may be interesting, true, and verifiable, but, barring a great deal of currently unavailable information, is not relevant enough to serve as a reasonable explanation of how (an author believes) the Mayas of Yucatan are descendants of the original inhabitants of Atlantis.

As was indicated earlier, **testability** is crucial to scientific hypothesis. If you and I have different hypothesis, for example, about why the Roman Empire fell, then we are going to have to agree at the beginning about what will "count" in our tests. If my hypothesis is that the Empire fell becuase its leadership suffered from lead poisoning due to the drinking of water which had passed through the lead pipes of Roman plumbing, then there are several elements of that hypothesis which could be indirectly tested. The tests which would have to be done would have to be such that both you and I would see their relevance to the hypothesis and that both of us would agree about the meaning of certain types of results. I might suggest that a test of lead pipe to se if the lead were sosluable in sufficient quantities to affect human functioning would be appropriate. If you deny that this test is of any great significance, pointing to a supposed lack of a general show if impaired function in those Romans as relevant, then we have little area for communication. It is only after such differences about relevance, reliability, and the conclusiveness are ironed out that the process of testing, which is a great part of the business of science, can take place.

The third criterion for the evaluation of a scientific explanation which Professor Copi suggests is **how well it "fits in"** with

other hypotheses which have themselves received previous favorable evaluation. This is a rather touchy means of evaluation, for it is evident that a new explanation which is intended to REPLACE an old one that had been thought to be fairly satisfactory will be incompatible with that earlier explanation. On the other hand, a new explanation which is intended to SUPPLEMENT establishsed explanations should be compatible with them.

The question of the nature of scientific progress is sone that has been of particular interest to philosophers of science, especially in the last couple of decades. In the early 1960's attention was drawn to this question by the book **The Structure of Scientific Revolutions** by Thomas Kuhn. In it Kuhn suggests that there are two quite different sorts of change in science. The first is the type to which this compatibility criterion applies, for this kind of change focuses upon the extension and clarification of existing ways of looking at the world. Kuhn calls this kind of science "normal science." The second type of change in science occurs when there is growing difficulty with getting observations and inferences to fit into normal science. When normal science finds itself patching itself up frequently, the time is right for a scientific revolution. Events that have been suggested as such revolutions include the Copernican revolution from geocentricity to heliocentricity, the Lavoissierian revolution from Phlogiston to oxygen, and the quantum revolution from classical to quantum mechanics. This criticism, then, is applicable only to normal scientific explanations, not revolutionary ones.

The fourth criterion for scientific explanations is **predictive** or **explanatory** power. If an explanation is used predictively, then the accuracy of such predictions can serve as a means of evaluating the original explanation. For example, in the last several years the statistically higher incidence of leukemia among those men who, as a part of their military service, were present at the testing of nuclear weapons in the early 1950s has been explained as being a long-term reaction to exposure to significantly higher than normal rates of radiation. Using that explanation predictively, one would expect to find similarly elevated leukemia rates among miners of radioactive ore, researchers into radioactive effects, medical personnel using radioactive substances, persons who painted "radium" dials on watches (to make their faces glow in the dark) and others similarly exposed. If, as a matter of fact, we were to find that these people **did** have significantly elevated rates of suffering leukemia (or even other radiation-related diseases), then we could consider the original explanation to have been confirmed.

Another application of this criterion involves what has traditionally been called the crucial experiment. You will frequently encounter two competing explanations; sometimes (but not as often as you would wish) these can constitute a crucial experiment. In such an event the two explanations, used predictively, imply strictly incompatible, that is, contradictory, results. Since one of a pair of contradictories must always be true and the other false, the crucial experiemnt set-up provides a mechanism for rejecting one of the alternate explanations. The inference in such a case looks like the inference form referred to in chapter nine as a destructive dilemma:

$$(H_1 \supset P) \cdot (H_2 \supset P)$$
$$\sim P \lor P$$
$$\overline{}$$
$$\therefore \sim H_1 \lor \sim H_2$$

The results of such crucial experiments is to provide DEDUCTIVE evidence against one of the hypotheses and INDUCTIVE evidence for the other. Of course it is important that you remember that a crucial experiment does provide only inductive evidence for that second hypothesis, for the assertion of "$\sim H_1 \lor \sim H_2$" does admit of the possibility that BOTH $\sim H_1$ and $\sim H_2$ are false.

The fifth criterion which Professor Copi suggests is **simplicity**. In the sciences this is frequently referred to as the "Principle of Parsimony"; in philosophy as "Occam's Razor." (The "Occam" to whose "razor" this refers was William of Occam, the fourteenth century philosopher who made one of the clearest early formulations of the idea.) Basically the assertion is that, given a choice, it is most reasonable to assume that the simpler of two (or more) possible explanations iss likely to be the correct one. For example, a child might explain to his teacher that the reason that he was late to school was because a minor earthquake caused a tee to fall, blocking the door to his home, in falling the tree tore out the telephone lines, and he had had to crawl out a window, go to the neighbor's home to call for help, and then wait until that help arrived to get back into the house to dress for school. The teacher might hypothesize that, given the child's previous tendency to daydream on the way to school, the boy had simply dawdled and had made up the story to avoid punishment. If the school's principal were to choose between the explanations, she might accept the teacher's explanation simply because the teacher had offered it. On the other hand, she might believe the teacher becaue his explanation was simpler. For the child's account to be true, there would have to have been a very long chain of coincidental occurrences. It seems unlikely that such a chain would have happened. There is, of course, no guarantee that such complex sequences don't occur, but they aren't very common.

The problem with trying to use the criterion of simplicity is that it frequently is hard to tell which of competing hypotheses, explanations or systems is really the simpler. And this criterion alone is not sufficient as a decision procedure. It is not terribly difficult to devise **ad hoc** explanations (ones designed to account only for a single present situation) which satisfy the simplicity criterion but fail all the others.

14.4   The Detective as Scientist
14.5   Scientists in Action: The Pattern of Scientific Investigation

These two sections are interesting parallels of each other. That is not terribly surprising, for Conan Doyle described Holmes as a **scientific detective**. Thus one would expect Holmess to use the tools of proper scientific investigation. It is particularly significiant that you realize that science is a **process**, a series of occurrences which lead from some initial point to some identifiable conclusion.

Whether in seeking the solution to a scientific or a criminal problem, the point of departure must always be the **problem**. Until you recognize the necessity of explaining or understanding some event, thing, or idea, there is nothing to do. If you did read Peirce's "The Fixation of Belief," you will recognize this as being in the situation which he calls doubt. When the situation is such that you are not comfortable, where you do not know how to act, when there is some difficulty felt, then there is motivation for investigating to try to become comfortable, to know how to act, to eliminate the difficulty. The point is that, although a detective could stumble upon the solution to a crime while investigating another, he couldn't try to solve a crime that he did not know had happened. Similarly, a scientist couldn't set out to investigate a phenomenon that he didn't realize was in need of investigation.

Once a problem is identified, the scientist and detective must begin by formulating some sort of **preliminary hypothesis**. This is necessary in order that the investigation may begin. This does not mean that you are going into the investigation with some preconceived conclusion at hand, but it does mean that, to do any research at all, you must have some idea of what sort of information is and what sort is not relevant. When the H.M.S. Beagle, with Charles Darwin aboard, visited the Galapagos Islands, the crew encountered an interesting

variety of finches. The several types of finches seemed to share a
basic coloration but not to share body, beak, foot and feather forms.
The similarity and differences could be seen as a problem: why are
these birds (later to be knows as "Darwin's finches") as they are? A
little pondering suggests that there are two fairly straightforward
preliminary hypotheses that Darwin, or others of the Beagle's crew,
might have offered: the birds constitiute several types of finch that
share the same coloration for some reason that is likely to be envi-
ronmental; or they are of a single type, but there is some environ-
mental factor that has led them to have varying body forms. Although
I can find no evidence to indicate that Darwin ever considered the
former hypothesis and rejected it, there would be good reasons for such
rejection: the most plausible reason for shared coloration would be
if it were of a protective nature (like a fawn's spotted coat), and
that would presuppose similar environments, which Darwin did not
find. The second suggested hypothesis, with which he did start,
could be explained by a common origin and subsequent differentiation.
The key thing, however, was that the preliminary hypothesis that the
finches were of a single type that had somehow differentiated into
the several forms gave him a starting point. There was no commitment
to it's ultimated truth, just a belief that it was the best possible
hypothesis about the phenomenon as it was then understood.

     Given a starting point for an investigation, the first step is
to **gather additional information**. It is, of course, always possible
that what you had thought was the case was merely the by-product of
chance circumstances. It is not hard to imagine a supposed psychic
claiming a means of seeing the future after he had made such a
prediction which had come to pass. It is also the case that such a
person would gain believers as the number of correct predictions
grew. Most of us, however, would remain skeptical unless the supposed mystic powers were put to rather severe tests.

     One leading psychic, for instance, claiming wondrous powers,
said she had predicted the assassinations of John and Robert Kennedy,
Martin Luther King, and George Lincoln Rockwell and the shootings of
George Wallace, Ronald Reagen and Pope John Paul II. Initial checks
with persons who had heard her predictions confirmed her claims. At
that point it was a reasonable hypothesis that she **did** possess some
sort of occult power, but additonal information was needed. In this
particular case the facts that were first sought were the times,
places and exact formulations of the claimed predictions. It turned
out, upon close examination, that the predictions had been made
anywhere from a couple of weeks before the shooting to more than
eleven years in advance. It was also the case that the predictions
had been made in varying circumstances ranging from the psychic's
newspaper column to informal chats with single individuals. But
worst of all was what had actually been said in the so-called prediction. Most detailed was her statement concerning Rockwell (he was
leader of the American Nazi party) that anyone who so strongly advo-
cated violence as a political tool should fear its being turned back
on him. Least detailed was her statement (made in 1969 supposedly
predicting the Pope's shooting in 1980) that the Roman Catholic
Church could expect to be under fire in the last quarter of the 20th
century. Her claims, then, that she had predicted specific events
were certainly open to question.

     More problematic with regard to her predictions was the record
found to indicate that the predictions which she had made that were,
more or less, correct were overshadowed by there really damning
facts. First it was found that she was in the habit of making
predictions which sounded very like the ones which she claimed to
have come to pass. When people say in January of each year that the
President of the United States will find himself in peril and are
willing to accept political, social, economic or physical peril as
"satisfying" the prediction, they don't find it hard to make correct
predictions. Second, it was easy to see that her predictions, for

the most part, were so vague as to be practically meaningless. And, third, when people are willing to ignore (and perhaps conceal) all of the occasions on which predictions have not been fulfilled, then her record tends to look better than it ought.

As you can see, then, the gathering of additional information which is relevant to thee preliminary hypothesis can be quite useful in disproving the hypothesis. If the added evidence does not seem to show the preliminary hypothesis to be wrong, then you are in a position to refine your original hypothesis (which may well have been little more than a hunch). The step of **formulating the hypothesis** in somewhat more detail is pivotal in the scientific enterprise. Unfortunately it also is the least understood element in the process of "doing" science. The developing of hypotheses is an act of creation no less mysterious (and womderful) than the painting of a picture or the composition of a symphony. Like paintings and symphonies, however, hypotheses may be amateurish, ill-conceived or sloppy. A well-done hypothesis takes into account all of the information available, ties it into a coherent package and suggests avenues for further investigation. (Of course such an ideal may not immediately present itself, and you may have to settle for a time for a "near miss," but you always hope for the best.)

Once you have a reasonably clearly formulated hypothesis is hand, you need to prepare for its evaluation. If you recall my discussion of indirect testing you remember that indirect tests usually involve checking to see if some expected rsult of that which you wish to test does, in fact, occur. To perform this sort of test, it is necessary that you decide waht those expectated results are. This is the point at which, if you are very careful, you can put your skills in deductive logic (the ones you learned while studying part Ii of this book and Copi) to work. You **deduce further consequences** of hte hypothesis which you have formulated. That there be such is very important not only for their value as testing devices but also for you to be confident to know that your hypothesis is something more than a collection of previously known facts. If there aren't areas which you can come to understand by means of your hypothesis, what good has it done you? In Moliere's play **The Doctor In Spite Of Himself**, the character Geronte, trying to tell whether the supposed doctor Sganarelle is medically knowledgeable, asks if he can explain morphine's ability to put people to sleep. Sganarelle's response, that it possesses a dormative property, is the sort of explanation that, as a hypothesis, would have no significantly different further consequences deducible from it. Hence, it would not be a terribly desirable explanation.

If you have generated a fruitful hypothesis based upon the facts available to you, then you will be able to deduce from it results which you would otherwise not have expected. Those results are the material for the sixth step for either a detective (at least of the Holmesean sort) or a scientist. Once you have deduced those consequences from your hypothesis, you need to **check to see if they actually occur.** If they do not occur, then you have a refutation of your hypothesis by means of **Modus Tollens:**

$$\text{Hypothesis} \supset \text{Expected Results}$$
$$\sim \text{(Expected results)}$$
$$\overline{\hspace{3cm}}$$
$$\therefore \quad \sim \text{(Hypothesis)}$$

If the results **do** happen, unfortunately you do not have a deductive proof that your hypothesis was true. What you have is support, confirmation, or corroboration for your hypothesis. The formal argument which you have is a case of what was called in chapter seven the fallacy of the affirmation of the consequent:

```
Hypothesis    ⊃   Expected Results
            Expected Results
----------------------------------
    ∴           Hypothesis
```

The argument is invalid, but if you find sufficient cases of the expected results of the hypothesis actually occurring, then you can consider the hypothesis confirmed. Confirmation, however, does not constitute proof, so you must always be ready to accept new tests, one of which could well disprove the hypothesis no matter how well-confirmed it had previously been.

The seventh step which Professor Copi lists in the procedure of the scientist and detective is **application**. In many ways it is not somuch an additon to the six earlier steps as it is the reward you derive from having done the earlier ones carefully. Once you have confirmed your hypothesis through testing, you have obtained a tool for your use. It is important, however, to keep in mind the possibility that each of the applications to which the confirmed hypothesis be prepared at any time to find that experience has proven your hypothesis not to be quite as good as you had thought it to be. The longer you go without a disconfirmation, the more secure you may feel, but always remember that Ptolmaic astronomy stood confirmed for 14 centuries, but that didn't stop the Copernican revolution from overthrowing it.

14.6   Crucial Experiments and Ad Hoc Hypothesis

The concept of a crucial experiment is a problematic one. As a process, science is not simply identified with a single idea or statement. As Professor Copi's example of the competing hypotheses of a flat and a spherical Earth shows, even the most straightforward-looking hypotheses usually turn out to be more complex than they originally appear.

The significance of this complexity for the understanding of the idea of a crucial experiment is most easily understood by looking at a formal representation of a hypothesis being refuted by showing one of the "deduced further consequences" not to occur. Begin by assuming that the hypothesis is composed of three elements; p, q, and r. The consequence that is deduced is s. Formally the following is what happens:

```
1.  [(p · q) · r] ⊃ s      Given (hypothesis ⊃ result)
2.  ~ s                    Given (result doesn't occur)
3.  ~ [(p · q) · r]        1,2, MT
4.  ~ (p · q) v ~ r        3, DeM
5.  ( ~ p v ~ q) v ~ r     4, DeM
```

As you can see, the conclusion results in a disjunction. A disjunction, however, has many ways of being true. The truth table for the last step of this proof is instructive:

p q r	~ p	~ q	~ p v ~ q	~ r	(~ p v ~ q) v ~ r
T T T	F	F	F	F	F
T T T	F	F	F	T	T
T F T	F	T	T	T	T
T F T	F	T	T	T	T
F T T	T	F	T	F	T
F T F	T	F	T	T	T
F F T	T	T	T	F	T
F F F	T	T	T	T	T

Here you see that there is only one situation in which the expression could be false: when all three propositions are true. Any situation in which at least one of the three is false will result in the overall expression's being true. In this case there were only three elements in the antecedent; in some of the more sophisticated theories and hypotheses of real-world science there could be dozens.

What Professor Copi wants you to understand is the difficulty of identifying a situation in which you can isolate the single antecedent hypothesis in order to claim that you have located a crucial experiment. Because science is such a complex interweaving of hypotheses, laws, theories and the like, it would seem that you always have the option of scrapping the bulk of established science rather than giving up some particular pet hypothesis. This possibility has sometimes been likened to the possibilities of rearranging things in a physical sense. Let's try one using magnetic monopoles made into marbles. A magnetic monopole is a body which has only a magnetic north or a magentic south polarity (and, in the realworld,does not exist). Assume that you are in space, away from any significant gravitational field, and that you have your bag of monopoles (all the same pole), a transparent nonmagnetic sphere with a trapdoor, and a set of nonmagnetic tongs with which you can grip a monopole. If you were to dump the monopoles into the sphere, quickly close the door and wait, then you would find, sooner or later, that they would come to rest, spaced throughout the sphere. If you suddenly realized that you had neglected to put one or two monopoles into the sphere and were then to inset them,then you would upset the established balance a bit. Most of the required adjustment, however, would be minor, involving very slight rearrangements of the previously located monopoles, But, if you decided that there was some one monopole whose position you particularly liked, then you could reach in with the tongs and, essentially, clamp it in place. That would very likely require a much more substantial rearrangement of the other monopoles in order to keep the one in its place. If you think of the original positions of the monopoles as representing the previously established hypotheses (laws, theories, etc.) of a science, the monopoles to be added as new data, and the use of the tongs as representing the decision to hold on to some one particular hypothesis no matter what, then the physical rearrangements would probably mirror the conceptual rearrangements necesary in the addition of the new facts: willingness to make small adjustments in anything yields little major alteration overall while stubbornly clingingg to some one pet hypothesis may enntail a radical adjustment of all the rest of your conceptual framework.

The other point that Profesor Copi wants you to understand from this section is the nature of ad hoc hypotheses. He traces the three possible (according to him) meanings of the term "ad hoc." If you trace the history of the meanings of the words, then you find that, roughly, calling a hypothesis ad hoc in the etymological sense merely means that it was developed in response to soem situation. But, in the two preceding sections you learned that the business of science proceeds by first identifying the problem and then setting forth hypotheses. It is virtually a definition of "hypothesis," then, that it be formulated in response to some occurrence. There would be no reason, however, for anyone to be at all distressed at having a hypothesis called ad hoc if this were the term's only meaning.

To account for the negative emotional reactions shown by scientists when their hypotheses are called ad hoc, Professor Copi suggests two other possible meanings for the term. The first would be toaccuse a theory of being rather like Sganarelle's "explanation" of morphine's actions: nothing is accounted for except the phenomenon under investigation. But even Sganarelle's explanation has a slight power of generalization attached to it, for it is not restricted to accounting only for the effect of morphine upon any one individual. Thus it seems unlikely that anyone who believed that he was doing something scientific would ever be guilty of an ad hoc hypothesis in the sense of accounting only for some particular fact. For example, one might want to account for the Star Wars phenomenon, including the movies, books, and all the auxillary merchandise. It is unlikely, however, that the analysis and discussion would be strictly limited to this one set of happenings. Discussion would surely include hypotheses about why **The Black Hole, Saturn 3, Galaxina, Battlestar Galactica**, and even **Star Trek** did not result in the same sort of reaction. One would also expect the analysis to include suggestions about how a repetition of the phenomenon could be achieved, at least approximately.

This sort of consideration leads Profesor Copi to the third possible meaning for **"ad hoc"**. If the generalization involved in a hypothesis were just a simple extension of the known data into very strictly analogous situations, then that hypothesis would not appear to be of very great scientific interest. There is some difficulty in understanding what would count as a "very strictly analogous" situation, but the example that Professor Copi uses, of Eijkman's experiments with chickens, suggests the sort of criterion that you ought to apply. Eijkman's generalization ran from his evidence that his chickens developed polyneueritis when deprived of rice polish to the generalized statement that any chickens so treated would become polineuritic. (Polyneuritis is a disease in fowl which is closely akin to beriberi in humans.) Generalization·from Eijkman's experimental chickens to all chickens is, at best, only slightly different from the second sort of **ad hoc** hypothesizing; after all, it is only vaguely possible that he had chickens with some sort of special that he had chickens with some sort of special susceptibility, that some othere breed would be resistant. Had he, however, generalized that elimination of rice polish in the diet of ducks, turkeys and other fowl would result in their also developing polineuritis, then he clearly has gone beyond the facts that he had discovered.

Professor Copi explains that such generalizations of empirical data **without some theoretical basis for the generalization** are the sorts of hypotheses that ought to be called **ad hoc** in the derogatory sense. Although this appears to be a pretty clear cut and reliable criterion, you must be quite cautious in applying it. After all, couldn't a reasonable case be made for the claim that either of the generalizations from Eijkman's research (to all chickens or to all fowl) contains a significant theoretical element: that chickens (or fowls) as a whole can be expected to react in roughly the same manner as some group of them selected as experimental subjects? Perhaps the point should be made that it will be quite difficult to specify what it takes for a hypothesis to be correctly accused of being **ad hoc**. It is clear that the third sense of the term is the one which Professor Copi takes to be the accurate one, but the above discussion shows that at least rasonable exception can be taken even to his example. In practice, it seems to me that the term **"ad hoc"** is used most frequently as an indicatiton of the user's dissatisfaction with a hypothesis for any of several reasons: lack of theoretical grounding, lack of generality, lack of simplicity, lack of testability or lack of other desirable properties. All too frequently the statement "this is an **ad hoc** hypothesis which I find flawed in a manner or manners which are difficult to specify" (or, perhaps more briefly, "this is a hypothesis with which I don't agree").

You may recall that Professor Copi's reason for invoking the concept of an **ad hoc** hypothesis was to show that the hypothesis that he added in the discussion of the possible crucial experiment between a flat and a curved Earth was not **ad hoc**. Moreover, he wanted to show that there is no need to resort to **ad hoc** hypotheses in order to point out difficulties in obtaining truly crucial experiments. The whole mass of assumed theories that underlie almost any scientific enterprise make it almost certain that the supposedly crucial experiment will in fact be likely to resemble the formal example that I laid out earlier.

The search for crucial experiments, however, is not a useless one. In the attempt to avoid ignoring hypotheses that were unstated as you formulated your own ideas, you are likely to discover assumptions which were necessary for your new hypothesis to be correct, assumptions of which you had not previously been aware. It is obviously a desirable result for such a search to uncover these "hidden" assumptions.

14.7   Classification as Hypothesis

The criticism offered against Eijkman's research with chickens might have been rephrased to accuse Eijkman of "mere" classification instead of theorization. It dos not take much of a scholar, however, to see that classification is a major stage through which all sciences pass. The mass of data that the world sends to us is so great that we could not function if we didn't have some means to classify it. For example, most of us find that there is some "type" of food of which we are particularly fond and another "type" (or "types") for which we do not care at all. If you had a particularly sensitive digestive system, you might find that you had best avoid so-called Mexican foods because they tend to be highly spiced. If you were to move to a new home in a large city with whose restaurants you were unfamiliar, then, without some system of classification, you would probably spend the rest of your life trying one restaurant after another in the attempt to find which cuisine you liked best. With a classification system, however, you could begin by eliminating all Mexican restaurants and all others that featured spicy foods. If you then sorted out the remaining possibilities according to the type of food served, you would be able to try one or two representatives from each group and to identify the general types of food you prefer. The process could then be refined by subclasses, sub-subclasses and so on until you had identified your very favorite place to eat. The critical point was the necessity of having some way of systematically sorting the phenomena with which you were confronted. Without some means of classification, you were left with a welter of sensations and no means to do science.

The example that Profesor Copi chooses to show how descriptive fields are theory-dependent is history. Many people would doubt that history ought even to be considered a science, but there is good evidence to show that history follows the same patterns as the more traditionally recognized sciences. Professor Copi suggests two approaches to history that obviously ought to be considered to be scientific: the identification of some overarching unity among the whole of history, and the identificatiton of historical laws from which we could also predict future events. Either of these would require explanations which would mirror the sort of explanations we use in physics, chemistry or any other "hard" science.

The more modest claim of more traditional historians is that they are merely trying to sort out a chronicle of past events. But even this group is dependent upon scientific considerations. It is a very naive view to think that the past is present for us to observe. One of the most fascinating tales of science and history is found in the quest of Troy by Henrich Schliemann. Although untrained in archeology, Schliemann was fanatically de voted to the search for the historical city which was the root of the tales of the **Iliad** and the **Odyssey**. The "professionals" in the field were inclined to ridicule his efforts, claiming that Homer's heroic fiction was just that-- fiction. Where the men trained as archeological investigators, using all the tools that the science had in the latter half of the nineteenth century, were inclined to ignore the details in the literary record, Schliemann chose to treat both the **Iliad** and the **Odyssey** as reasonably accurate historical records. Any good library can provide you with the story of Schliemann's discoveries, most of which read like "thrillers," but the most significant thing about his work was that he did discover, on the site described by Homer what he took to have been the ruins of Troy. As a matter of fact what he found was a site on which a dozen cities had been built and rebuilt. But one of them showed evidence of destruction by fire and of the main gate having been pulled down **as if to admit some object too large for the gate** (like a giant horse?). The point of all this account of Schliemann's work is to point out how a piece of theory gets used without anyone having noticed its use. In this case the theory is that literary documents provide details which ought to be treated as significant historical data. But, of course, all such literary allusions cannot be taken to be acccurate accounts of historical occurrences. Thus, for the historian to use the myriad sources of information available to him, it is necesary that there be some theory (or theories) which aid in the identification of the relevant fragments within whole mass of data.

The detective work used by the "field" historian is of very much the same sort as that used by the criminal detective or the practicing scientist. The pattern of steps which the historian follows in working out an explanation of a historical event is the same as those suggested as the scientist's or detective's method in sections 4 and 5 of this chapter. The historian must begin by identifying some problem, some event or sequence of events the occurrence of which needs to be explained. For example, the historian might begin by studying a map of the western United States, one that showed the locations of Indian reservations. One detail might catch his attention: Colorado is the only western state in which there are, for all practical purposes, no reservations. Given the fact that at least seven major tribes--Ute, Lakota, Kiowa, Comanche, Blackfoot, Arapaho and Apache--were known to have ranged across the state, it is strange that no reservations were located there. This would provide the historian with an interesting problem: why, historically, were there no reservations in Colorado?

I won't try to go through all of the seven steps in the scientific process here, but do want you to have some feel for where the investigation of this problem would lead. Relevant data which would be uncovered would include the newspaper accounts of anti-Indian sentiment, the Sand Creek massacre (in which unprotected Indian women and children were killed with the justification that "nits make lice"), and the domination of the state legislature by mining, ranching, and agricultural interests (which wanted no land to be placed out of their reach). Hypotheses would be developed suggesting that the tradition of anti-Indian feeling coupled with powerful economic forces which opposed having any land that might prove valuable set aside for the Indian would have spurred opposition to the formation of any reservations. Refinements would add facts about the impact of the silver-mining industry and its immensely wealthy owners upon national politics and would, thus, add to the earlier hypothesis the suggestion that the "powers-that-were" in Colorado had sufficient influence in Washington to prevent any significant rservation territory from being located within the state. Additional "testing" could be accomplished by examining presonal and Congressional memoirs of the period for corroborating data.

Professor Copi indicates that the process of classification in biology is, if anything, more clearly theoretical than it is in history. In particular, classification in biology is done for the purpose of aiding the scientist in the attempt to better understand the organisms which are being classified. The attempt, then, is always made to identify relevant similarities and differences between organisms. There is, however, a difficulty with this goal: the identification of what is relevant may well depend upon the classification which you are attempting to make. For this reason, the classifier will frequently be compelled to make preliminary groupings based upon whatever criteria seem handy at that moment. You see, once there is a hypotheis available for evaluation, you are in a position to perform research, examine further data and evaluate that hypothesis with an eye to refining it. Until you have the hypothesis, you are left just casting about for random data.

One of the strangest-seeming common classifications is that of trees. When you think of plants ranging from the hundred-year-old Bonsai which can be placed on a bookshelf to the California redwoods through which a car may be driven, you may find it difficult to identify what it is that counts as the criterion for being a tree. Bananas, for example, grow on things that look like trees but are classified as herbs; bamboo yields material that seems like wood (the product of trees), but bamboo is actually classed as a grass. The species **juniperus** contains both trees and shrubs, some of which are virtually indistinguishable to the untrained eye. The justification usually offerd for making such counterintuitive classifications is that there are characteristics shared by some sorts of plants--called trees--that not only set them apart from other sorts of plants but also provide models or structures according to which it is easier to understand what the plants are and how they function. But these models or structures which the botanist uses in order better to understand the class of plants which he calls trees constitute a theoretic approach to what it is to be a tree. Thee classification depends upon probably many but at least one theoretical construct, just like almost any other scientific explanation.

In the following exercises Professor Copi asks you to identify the data (the problem), the hypothesis, and those elements relevant to an evaluation of the hypothesis you discover. This is exactly the sort of thing you must do for yourself when you encounter supposedly scientific arguments which you cannot reduce to formal logic. Obviously, what you happen to know about the material in the argument will significantly affect your evaluation of that argument. When you encounter an exercise focused upon a subject about which you judge that you know virtually nothing, I would recommend that you make a quick trip to some reference material--an encyclopedia is often a good bet. This should at least put you in a position to understand what the argument is trying to say.

(2)   (a)   The problem that needs to be explained in this passage is the correlation between years of schooling and state of health, in particular why education seems to be the closest correlate to health.

(b)   Grossman's initial hypothesis is "the schooling increases the individual's efficiency in producing health."

(c)   The hypothesis is surely relevant because much of our past experience has shown the profound effect that education can have upon behavior. Who among us has not heard the story of the Pilgrims changing their entire approach to agriculture as a result of some demonstrative education by the Indians?

This hypothesis would seem to be testable both directly and indirectly. Most direct would be to identify two isolated groups which were quite similar in composition and general health, but whose members were ill-educated. One could then select one group for improved education and observe to see whether the general state of health of its members, in comparison with the unaided group, improved, too. If it did you would have a positive result from the test, that is, a confirmation of hypothesis; if there were no significant improvement, then this negative result would count as disconfirmatiton. (Such testing, of course, does not address the moral issues relative to using

people for such experiments.) More indirect testing
could be done by checking to see whether there were a
"washdown" effect in the event, for example, of improved education of only one member of a family or of
a fraction of a population.

This hypothesis would seem to be compatible with
previous hypotheses about the usefulness of education
in bringing about social change. After all, the programs of forced integration of schools were intended
to bring about social acceptance of racial differences
by education through acquaintance. (Incidentally,
there are conflicting conclusions about the reliability of this hypothesis). It has also long been the
practice of persons of some wealth but little family
background to send their children to rather exclusive
boarding schools with the intention of changing the
social attitudes and behavior patterns of their children so that they can better "fit in" with the so-
called upper classes.

This hypothesis would do very well as an explanation of the ill-health of peoples of the third world,
pointing to their woefully inadequate, and sometimes
nonexistent, eduations. It would also serve well to
predict, for example, increased need for health care
among the poor as a result of decreases in public aid
to schools. In fact, it might be offered as an argument against such budgetary cuts on the grounds that
the savings effected would only result in substantially greater necesary expenditures in the areas of
health care.

The explanation is simple. There is no great complexity in the hypothesis, even when given a more
detailed exposition pointing out the ways in which
more education could alter behavior relevant to the
obtaining or maintaining of good health.

Overall the hypothesis seems a reasonable, useful
and probably fruitful one.

(9) (a)   The problem to be explained is Dr. P's **lapsus
linguae** (slip of the tongue).

(b)   The basic hypothesis is that people tend to say
what is really on their minds, to speak truly, in
situations in which they are busy concentrating on
something other than the thing they wish to conceal.

(c)   The relevance of the hypothesis is a bit difficult
to confirm, but Dr. P's problem surely would be on his
mind and in the conversation with Brill there would be
little reason for him to be on his guard.

It would be difficult to set up specific tests for
this hypothesis. For the most part testing would have
to be in the form of checking out anecdotal accounts
of such slips. The difficulty with this sort of data
is that the correlation between such slips of the
tongue and the psychological state that is claimed to
cause them is largely a matter of interpretation.

The hypothesis seems compatible with the bulk of
Freudian theory. The only difficulty with this is
that there are several other competing models for the
underlying structure of the human mind. In fact,

persons who are unsympathetic with psychiatric theory in general have been known to claim that one oculd find some psychiatric theory that would be compatible with almost anything.

The hypothesis could explain other **lapsi linguae** and perhaps might be extended also to explain other behavioral quirks, like a dieter opening the refrigerator instead of the cupboard he had intended to open. It might also be used to predict that an individual who seemed troubled might let slip clues as to the source of her or his difficulty.

The hypothesis in itself seems pretty simple, unless you also consider the whole complex of Freudian theory. In the latter case you are dealing with a set of hypotheses that are not at all simple.

Overall the hypothesis seems plausible, but, as it is presented here, it is not terribly compelling.

(14) (a)   The phenomenon to be explained is the constancy of the location of several temperature-sensitive plants over the 1st 4000 years.

(b)   The hypothesis suggested is that the temperature of the earth has remained relatively constant for that period.

(c)   The hypothesis ought to be quite relevant to the data, since significant variations in temperature would appear to necessistate the nonsurvival of plants which are sensitive to such variation.

Testing could take several forms. Part of the test might be to take the supposedly temperature-sensitive plants and subject them to significant variations in temperature to see if they might be hardier than previously suspected. You might also check areas in which, for some reason, the climate has made a recent and radical change. If in such areas there was also a significant alteration in plant life, then you would have corroboration for the hypothesis. You might also look for parallel data in terms of constancy of architecture and weight of wardrobe. They would seem to imply that there had been no significant change in the backgound temperature.

The theory would be consistent with the basic "uniformitarianism" principles, claiming that things tend to remain as they are unless there are changes of a pretty significant kind in the background events.

In addition to explaining this data, the hypothesis would account for other periods of extended survival of some species of plants (perhaps animals that are temperature-sensitive too). It might also be used to predict the loss of some species in the event of climatic shifts. An analog to the hypothesis might be used to predict, for instance, that you wouldn't be able to transplant the citrus trees of the Rio Grande valley to the high mountain meadows of the Rockies, since the climates are too different.

This hypothesis is quite simple and straight-forward. It deals with the data without any twists, turns or complications.

The hypothesis seems quite good. It accounts for the data nicely and in a way consistent with intuition, too.

(19) (a)   The phenomenon to be explained is the occurrence of so-called balancing rocks.

(b)   The hypothesis offered is that the pressure of the capstone retards erosion under its center of mass, causing greater erosion on areas not under that point. The result is shifting of the center of mass and subsequent erosion in the area previously retarded. Ultimately it means gentle movement back and forth, but with the capstone staying generally atop the column.

(c)   The hypothesis is relevant to the phenomenon under question. It states a mechanism for symmetric erosion that correlates nicely with the curiosity of the rather common balancing rocks.

Testing this hypothesis could take a LONG time. You could probably construct physical models to simulate the columns that weather into shafts topped by the balancing rocks, but couldn't be sure that you had duplicated the natural conditions. Probably the best test you could apply would be indirect, based upon predictions of likely occurrences of the phenomenon in aeas in which they had not yet been discovered. This would be based upon knowledge of geologic structures where rivers had cut columns and where upper strata were more durable than lower ones, promoting undercut erosion.

The hypothesis fits in nicely with the theories of erosion, of dynamic forces, or pressures, and many more, It is, in fact, a very tidy application of many already well-accepted theories.

The hypothesis explains the phenomenon in question very persuasively. A variant of it might also be used to account for balancing rods, long cylindrical rock formations that look like logs balanced on ridges. To see possibilities for prediction, look back at the comments on testing.

Although the hypothesis as stated above appears rather complex, and is not as simple as many of the others that you have seen here, it does not bring into use any ideas outside the realm of accepted theories. It also has the benefit of doing a neat job of explaining. This seems to be as good a hypothesis about what appears to be a puzzling phenomenon as one could hope for.

(27) (a)   The phenomenon to be explained is the differential increase of induced radioactivity in silver when it is in different surroundings.

(b)   The hypothesis starts with the accepted theory that hydrogen nuclei are protons. It infers that when there is neutron bombardment of the silver through a medium that is rich in hydrogen the neutrons will be substantially slowed down and thus more easily captured by the silver. This would lead to increased radioactivity.

(c)   The hypothesis fits closely with the data, thus is obviously relevant to the data.

The account shows that the original hypothesis **was** tested by Fermi by altering the hydrogen-rich medium, using water in place of the paraffin. Other hydrogen-rich surroundings could be substituted for both of these to test further.

This theory fits well with the atomic physics of that period, and this one too.

This seems to be a good explanation, dealing well with the varying surroundings and the corresponding varyings of induced radioactivity. As a predictive tool it would suggest, for example, that one could anticipate greater radioactivity being induced during a rainstorm than in dry weather. It would also have the practical predictive value of suggesting how one could effectively irradiate material, as for example for medical use, with less energy needed.

The hypothesis isn't terribly simple, but it does serve to explain the phenomenon clearly.

Insofar as can be learned at this point in physics, the hypothesis seems to be the best available.

CHAPTER FOURTEEN SUMMARY

I. There are two sorts of value which science may be claimed to have.

    A. When science is justified by pointing to its values in achieving other goals, it is said to be instrumentally justified.

    B. When science is justified as an end in itself, it is said to be intrinsically justified.

II. Explanations can take many forms.

    A. Regardless of form, explanations include a statement of circumstances and the operative laws and/or principles in those circumstances.

    B. Unscientific explanations tend to be dogmatic.

    C. Scientific explanations are provisional, subject to revision in the light of changing information.

III. Scientific explanations are evaluated by five criteria.

    A. The hypothesis must be relevant to the data it explains.

    B. The hypothesis must be testable.

    C. The hypothesis must be compatible with previously established theorries, laws and hypotheses.

    D. The hypothesis must have some power of explaining things beyond the original data and/or must be usable as predictions.

IV. Investigation, detective or scientific, generally follows a pattern.

    A. First you must identify what the problem you wish to explain is.

    B. To begin investigating you need a provisional hypothesis to order data.

    C. Given a preliminary hypothesis, you must then begin to gather additional data.

    D. On the basis of that additional informataion, you then need to formulate a more detailed hypothesis.

    E. Given a full-blown hypothesis you then deduce further consequences of it.

    F. Once these consequences have been deduced, you must check to see if they actually occur.

    G. A confirmed hypothesis is ready to be applied in practice.

V.   A crucial experiment is one the completion of which will defin-
     itely confirm one of a set of competing hypotheses and dis-
     confirm all others.

     A.   Crucial experiments are rare.

     B.   Within a context of accepted science, the attempt to
          identify a crucial experiment may help clarify the
          context.

VI. An **ad hoc** hypothesis is one that is created to account only for
     a single phenomenon, without outside application.

VII. Classification is more than a recording of events, it is a
     hypothesizing about events and the records indicating their
     character and occurrence.

15

Probability

15.1 Alternative Conceptions of Probability

Professor Copi indicates several uses of the term "probability" and then focuses upon the **a priori** and relative frequency theories as the ones that are the basis of the calculus of probabilities. The **a priori** (called the theory of equally likely chances by its earliest significant devotee--Laplace) assumes that all outcomes of a set of circumstances are **equally likely** unless there is clear evidence to the contrary. The relative frequency theory is the one that you have probably encountered in previous classes that talked about probability. It uses "s" to represent the number of successful occurrences you have found, "p(a)" to represent the probability of event "a," and "f" to represent the number of unsuccessful occurrences you've encountered, yielding a symbolic representation of the probability of event "a":

$$p(a) = \frac{s}{s + f}$$

There is, however, a third approach to probability that is consistent with the **a priori** and relative frequency theories. It is called a propensity theory (sometimes a dispositional-relative-frequency theory). Its claim is that certain types of events or experimental arrangements have **as properties** certain propensities or dispositions. No one questions the disposition of crystal to shatter when severely impacted, or of lead to melt at relatively low temperatures, or of book paper to burn at 451° F. Why not, then, claim that homogeneous cubes with their centers of mass in their exact centers have a propensity when rolled to turn up each fact very, very slightly less than one-sixth of the time? (The other infinitesimal probability will be divided up among the edges and corners upon which--rarely--the cube will come to rest.) If that seems a reasonable position, then your sympathies may well lie with the propensity theorists. In general, however, the proponents of the various schools of thought about the "real" nature of probability are in substantial agreement about the use of probabilities, once they are known, in calculating other probabilities.

15.2 The Probability Calculus

At the outset, Professor Copi introduces the idea of independent events. Two (or more) events are said to be independent if the occurrence or nonoccurrence of one of them has no effect on the occurrence or nonoccurrence of the other(s). This means that drawing one card from a deck and NOT replacing it will mean that any other draw from that deck will not be independent of the first draw, since the first-drawn card is no longer a possible outcome of the second draw. Had you replaced the first card and shuffled the deck well, then the second draw, having all the same possibilities as the first, would be independent of the first. Unless you are given information that indicates otherwise, you should assume that events stated in the exercises in Copi are independent.

Joint Occurrences

Calculations of probabilities are based upon two fundamental relationships, conjunction and alternation. Virtually any complex event is the result of joint occurrences of simpler events [the occurrence of (a and b) is the conjunction of event a and event b], alternate occurrences of simpler events [the occurrence of (a or b) is the alternation of event a and event b], or some combination of the two. Joint occurrences are calculated by using the **product theorem** "P(a and b) = P(a) x P(b)." In this formula, the set of symbols "P(...)" is read "The probability of ...." And, normally, P(a and b) is written P(ab). As Professor Copi indicates, in the absence of contrary evidence, we take all possible events in a situation to be equally probable. Given the flipping of a coin twice, we consider the probability of getting heads (or ls) is 1/2. The following is what happens:

```
                                    ⎧1/2 of the time we get    H    a
1/2 of the time we get      {H  ⎨
                                    ⎩1/2 of the time we get    T    b

                                    ⎧1/2 of the time we get    H    c
1/2 of the time we get      {T  ⎨
                                    ⎩1/2 of the time we get    T    d
```

If you read across this structure you will see that

    a. 1/2 of 1/2 of the time we get H followed by H
    b. 1/2 of 1/2 of the time we get H followed by T
    c. 1/2 of 1/2 of the time we get T followed by H
    d. 1/2 of 1/2 of the time we get T followed by T

The nice thing about looking at the situation in this way is that it does not depend upon the equiprobable assumption. That means that is you should have the (mis)fortune to own a coin that had a probability of 1/3 of falling H and 2/3 or falling T, the diagram would look like this:

```
                                    ⎧1/3 of the time we get    H    a
1/3 of the time we get     {H  ⎨
                                    ⎩2/3 of the time we get    T    b

                                    ⎧1/3 of the time we get    H    c
2/3 of the time we get     {T  ⎨
                                    ⎩2/3 of the time we get    T    d
```

Reading across this you will see that

    a. 1/3 of 1/3 of the time we get H followed by H
    b. 2/3 of 1/3 of the time we get H followed by T
    c. 1/3 of 2/3 of the time we get T followed by H
    d. 2/3 of 2.3 of the time we get T followed by T

In numeric terms, we get HH 1/9 of the time, HT 2/9 of the time, TH 2/9, and TT 4/9 of the time.

    This calculation also indicates another very important characteristic of probabilities: the sum of the probability of an event and the probability of its complement (not-a is the complement of a) is always 1. More generally, the sum of the probabilities of any set of exhaustive and exclusive events always adds to 1. EXCLUSIVE EVENTS are events which CANNOT occur together; EXHAUSTIVE EVENTS are events at least one of which MUST occur. Thus in a set of events is exhaustive and exclusive, they cannot occur together but one of them must occur (more than one cannot occur since they are exclusive). In the examples above, a, b, c, and d are exclusive (since none of them can occur together) as well as exhaustive (there is no other event that can occur on the flip of two coins). The formal notation for complementarity is made by placing a bar over the event. Thus the complement of a (that is, not-a) is $\bar{a}$. Since the sum of the probabilities of an event and its complement add to 1, the formal statement is

$$P(a) + (P(\bar{a}) = 1$$

By subtracting P($\bar{a}$) from both sides we get

$$P(a) = 1 - P(\bar{a})$$

This means that if it is easier to calculate the probability of the complement of an event than that of the event itself, you have a choice of working the easy one and subtracting from 1. This will prove **very** useful later.

A few problems will make all of this easier to see. Look first at number 3 after Professor Copi's discussion of joint occurrences. There are a total of 67 balls, 27 white and 40 black. Thus on the inital draw there is a probability of 40/67 of drawing a black ball, 27/67 of drawing a white one. In the (a) case, since you replace after drawing, that same probability will be the case on all draws. If you figure that the event (complex) that you want is P(BBBB), then you could also figure that the event BBBB could be looked at as [(BB) (BB)], that is, blacks on the first two and blacks on the last two. Following the pattern for joint occurrence, we get

$$P[(BB)\ (BB)] = P(BB)\ x\ P(BB)$$

But since   P(BB)=P(B)xP(B), this becomes

$$P(BBBB) = P(B)\ x\ P(B)\ x\ P(B)\ x\ P(B)$$

This principle is generalizable so that the probability of the joint occurrence of any number of independent events is the product of the probabilities of those events. In the case of 3(a) all of this translates into

$$P(BBBB) = \left(\frac{40}{67}\right)^4$$

In the case of 3(b) there is no replacement of the balls, so the probability of each successive black ball is different from the preceding one. The (b) case, of course, takes you into the area of events that are **not** independent. There is no difficulty in using the probabilities of such events in calculating probabilities of joint occurrences of events, at least as long as you know what the probabilities are. Thus, for example, if you were to figure the probability of picking out a pair of black socks in the dark from a drawer containing 6 black socks and 7 non-black ones, you would get 6/13. The probability of picking out a second black sock from the same drawer (still in the dark) after having picked a black one the first time would be the same as the probability of drawing a black sock from a drawer with 5 black ones and 7 non-black ones. That is to say, some probabilities that depend upon the outcome of previous events can be calculated as if they were independent events, but where the circumstances in which they occur include the prior events already having happened. In a case like the one with the socks, if you wanted to know the probability of drawing a pair of black socks, you would figure p(ab) where a is the event of drawing a first black sock and where b is the event of drawing a second black one when one black sock has already been drawn. This p(ab) would be calculated just as any other:

$$p(ab) = p(a)\ x\ p(b)$$

In this particular case the result would be 6/13 x 5/12. The second probability would be 5/12 because there were 5 black socks and 7 non-black socks left in the drawer.

With the balls the initial probability is the same as (a), 40/67. After a black ball has been drawn, there are 39 black and the 27 white remaining, so P(B) = 39/66. The case where a white was

drawn first doesn't enter into the figuring, because it would have
been a failure and you'd be done already. By similar reasoning, the
probability of the third black ball would be 38/65 and the fourth
37/64. Putting them all together, 3(b) becomes

$$P(BBBB) = (\frac{40}{67}) \times (\frac{39}{66}) \times (\frac{38}{65}) \times (\frac{37}{64})$$

Problem 7 is straightforward. The probability of their having
such a celebration is P(he lives 25 years and she lives 25 years and
they are not divorced in 25 years). According to the formula, that
means

$$P(H \text{ and } S \text{ and } D) = P(H) \times P(S) \times P(D)$$
$$= .742 \times .801 \times .902$$

Note that the answer is **not** multiplied out. Since this is not a book
on arithmetic, there is no great value in multiplying out the answers. As a matter of fact, there are pretty good reasons for not
working out the arithmetic. Very few of us are capable of doing
flawless arithmetic, so multiplying out an answer adds another step
in which you could make an error. Even more significant is the fact
that an answer written out as the answers to problems 3(b) and 7 are,
gives an observer of your work, like a teacher, a better view of
what you have done. This is important, particularly when you have
made a mistake. In decimals, the sock-drawing problem discussed
earlier has the correct answer of .193. Had your answer been, for
example, (a) .178, (b) .213, or (c) .231, how would an outside observer know you had gone wrong? One possibility, of course, would have
been an arithmetic error. If your arithmetic is acceptable, then the
observer must try to guess what your error was and then check to see
if your math is correct for that error. The three incorrect answers
suggested earlier resulted from (a) assuming replacement, that is,
6/13 x 6/13, (b) realizing that you had one less black sock but
forgetting that you had one less total socks, too, that is 6/13 x
5/13, and (c) realizing that you had one less total socks but forgetting that you have one less black sock, too, that is, 6/13 x 6/12.
There is another possibility, too: you might have calculated from
(b) and then transposed the 1st two digits, yielding the results
appropriate to the error in (c). An instructor might choose to spend
a great deal of time "teaching" you to avoid an error that you
actually had not made. It seems clear, then, that the wisest course
is to leave the answer in its most helpful form, the one in which no
more arithmetic is done that necessary.

Problem 8 is another direct problem. What you want is P(right
closet and right carton and right can and right fruit and right
second fruit). If these events are represented as D(door), B(box),
C(can), F1(first fruit), and F2 (second fruit) you have

$$P(D \ B \ C \ F1 \ F2) = P(D) \times P(B) \times P(C) \times P(F1) \times P(F2)$$
$$= 1/2 \quad \times 1/3 \quad \times 6/24 \times 3/300 \times 2/299$$

Problem 10 is a bit tricky, the most evident answer would seem
to be to split the balls between the urns, getting 1/2 x 1/2 as the
answer. However, if you want to maximize the probability of getting
two white balls, you should insure getting one. To do that, you put
one white ball in one urn and the other 99 in the remaining urn.
Then,

P(W-1) = 1 and P(W-2) = 49/99, so
P(W-1 and W-2) = 1 x 49/99 = 49/99 (which is almost 1/2)

There are two approaches to solving problem 6. One way is to
figure that it makes no difference which door "a" (the first patient)
enters. What you want to know is what is the probability that "b"

and "c" (the second and third patients) came in the same door.   If
for each of them all five doors were equally probable, the probability for each of them that he or she entered the same door as "a" is
1/5.   Thus

$$P(bc) = P(b) \times P(c) = 1/5 \times 1/5 = 1/25$$

The second approach requires that you be able to calculate alternative occurrences, the next topic for discussion.

Alternative Occurrences

If you were playing roulette on a standard wheel, you would see
on the wheel 18 red numbers, 18 black numbers and two green ones (0
and 00).   If you could bet in such a way that the only failure was
green, you would have bet upon (red or black).   In this case, the
event (red or black) can be directly calculated as the sum of the
probabilities of (red) and (black).   Note that in this case you could
also have calculated on the basis of 1 - P(red or black)= P(red or
black).   Since the only way you could fail to get (red or black)
would be to get (green), you have

$$\begin{aligned} P(\text{red or black}) &= 1 - P(\text{green}) \\ &= 1 - 2/38 \end{aligned}$$

Calculated directly you had 18/38 + 18/38 = 36/38; calculated indirectly you have 1 - 2/38 = 36/38.   The two should always agree.

This is, however, an atypical example of alternative occurrences.
In most cases there is a possibility that the two events might both
occur, while in the roulette case you cannot get red and black at the
same time.   If you used the apparent formula that was applied to the
roulette case, which would have been

$$P(a \text{ or } b) = P(a) + P(b)$$

to the case of getting a head on the flip of a dime or a head on the
flip (made at the same time) of a penny, you would have

$$P(Hd \text{ or } Hp) = 1/2 + 1/2 = 1$$

But it is **not** certain that you would get at least one head; you could
get two tails.   What has happened?   You have accidently counted an
event twice.   The event "Hd" is actually a composite formed by the
above formula: P(Hd) = P(HdHp) + P(HdTp).   Now you cannot have those
events together, since you can't get both a head and a tail on the
penny at the same time.   Similarly you used P(Hp) = P(HdHp) +
P(TdHp).   When you added P(Hd) and P(Hp) you accidentally got the
following:

$$P(Hd \text{ or } Hp) = P(HdHp) + P(HdTp) + P(HdHp) + P(TdHp)$$

Notice that you counted the joint occurrence of heads twice.   That is
what led to the too-large number.   What needs to be done is to remove
one of them.   To do that you must alter the formula to be:

$$P(a \text{ or } b) = P(a) + P(b) - P(ab)$$

This formula will still work for cases like the roulette problem,
since the joint probability of exclusive events (such as red and
black in roulette) is always a zero.

Returning to that problem of the patients going to thee dentist
(which was promised above), you now have the tools necessary to try
the second appraoch.   That approach would say that the probability
that all three patients go through any given door is

$$\left(\frac{1}{5}\right)^3$$

This means that P(abcI), i.e., the probability that a, b, and c go in door I is $1/5^3$, as is the probability of all three going in each of the other doors. This means that the second approach would be to calculate on the basis of the five alternatives that would have counted as successes. What it becomes is

P[(abcI) or (abcII) or (abcIII) or (abdIV) or (abdV)] =

P(abcI) + P(abcII) + P(abcIII) + P(abcIV) + P(abcV) =

$$\left(\frac{1}{5^3}\right) + \left(\frac{1}{5^3}\right) + \left(\frac{1}{5^3}\right) + \left(\frac{1}{5^3}\right) + \left(\frac{1}{5^3}\right) =$$

$$5 \times \left(\frac{1}{5^3}\right) = \left(\frac{1}{5^2}\right)$$

Note that this is the same solution that was obtained on p. 287. The addition of alternatives here did not require any subtraction because the events were exclusive: they couldn't all come through different doors together simultaneously.

Coins provide simple examples for calculation of alternative occurrence probabilities. Problem 3 at the end of 14.2 is representative. What you seek is P(H-1 or H-2 or H-3). Recalling that you must take care to avoid double counting, you can look back to the general formula for alternative occurrences, but you will find that it is for two events, and this problem deals with three. As a first approach to this sort of problem it is wise to begin with a complete array of the events that could occur on three tosses of a coin. Each of the triads is exclusive of each other one, and the eight of them together are exhaustive. Here is the array:

	First Toss	Second Toss	Third Toss
a.	H	H	H
b.	H	H	T
c.	H	T	H
d.	H	T	T
e.	T	H	H
f.	T	H	T
g.	T	T	H
h.	T	T	T

Any of the exclusive events a-g would count as a success in seeking the probability of at least one head; only event h would be a failure. You may start by calculating the probability of each of the events a-g (they each happen to be 1/8) and then add them. That would give you the correct answer of 7/8 but wouldn't give you any insight into how the formula from p. 287 is generalized. You could also calculate 1 - failure (1 - 1/8) and get the same 7/8. Or you could take the events H-1, H-2, and H-3 apart. H-1 is a + b + c + d; H-2 is a + b + e + f; H-3 is a + c + e + g. Combined that means that P(H-1) + P(H-2) + P(H-3) = a + a + a + b + b + c + c + d + e + e + f + g. That counts "a" three times and "b," "c," and "e" twice each. Thus you try to apply the general formula, subtracting pairwise occurrences. Among three events there are three pairs: (H-1 H-2), (H-1 H-3), and (H-2 H-3). Taking them apart, as was done for H-1 and the others, you find that (H-1 H-2) is a + b, (H-1 H-3) is a + c, and (H-2 H-3) is a + e. If you subtract them from the earlier combination you will remove "a" three times and "b," "c," and "e" once each.

That leaves you with b + c + d + e + f + g. You have taken away one
too many of the "a" cases, so it must be added back in. Since "a" is
(H-1 H-2 H-3), the generalization of the alternative occurrences
formula for three events becomes

P(a or b or c) = P(a) + P(b) + P(c) - P(ab) - P(ac) - P(bc) + P(abc)

Applied to the coin toss problem (which was the problem under discussion) it becomes

$$P(H\text{-}1 \text{ or } H\text{-}2 \text{ or } H\text{-}3) = 1/2 + 1/2 + 1/2 - 1/4 - 1/4 - 1/4 + 1/8$$
$$= 3/2 - 3/4 + 1/8$$
$$= 7/8$$

It is comforting to see that each of the three approaches arrives at
the same numeric solution.

     Problem 8 in the same set offers a slightly different challenge.
Since you cannot choose both cases, each has an **a priori** probability
of 1/2 of being selected; one case (A) contains 6 soft drinks and 4
beers; the other case (B) contains 10 soft drinks and 2 beers. By
the joint occurrence formula, P(picking A and getting a soft drink)
is (1/2 x 6/10) or 3/10, and P(picking B and getting one) = (1/2 x
10/12) or 5/12. Since these are exclusive events, their probabilities add: either would be a success. Thus P (getting a soft drink
from one case or the other) = 3/10 + 5/12. Had you put all the
bottles in a single case you would have had 16 soft drinks and 6
beers. The probability of a soft drink then would be 16/22. The
difference resolves to: the first way you have a .717 probability of
a soft drink, while with all of the bottles in one case you have a
.726 probability of getting a soft drink. If you think about it,
there is something of problem number 10 (p. 286), where organization
has an effect, built into this.

     Problem 9 offers an opportunity to introduce another way to deal
with alternative success patterns. In the problem given, there are
47 cards remaining that you have not seen, so your two will be drawn
from them. (Any card you have not seen you should count as if it
were still available in the deck--that seems strange, but it's really
an averaging of the chances that any specific card is out, and thus
unavailable, with the higher chances of its being drawn if it is not
out, since the deck is smaller). For ease of reference, let us
assume that your original hand was J-J-J-x-y (where x and y are two
different small cards). Your possible successes after discarding the
x and y will be J-anything, anything-J, and a pair of non-J's. This
problem is short enough that you could solve it by generating all the
possibilities:

     P(J next) = 1/47
     P(anything else next, followed by a J) = 46/47 x 1/46
     P(a pair of x's) = 3/47 x 2/46 (since you discarded an x, three
                                    remain, then two)
     P(a pair of y's) = 3/47 x 2/46 (since you discarded a y, three
                                    remain, then two)
     P(a pair of z's) = 40/47 x 3/46 (once the first z is chosen,
                                    three remain)

Since these are exclusive, they add to give

 P(J or pair) = 1/47 + (46/47 x 1/47) + (3/47 x 2/46) + (3/47 x 2/46)
                 + (40/47 x 3/46)
              = 224/2162

The alternative structure, when you know that you are going to have
alternate ways of achieving success and where subsequent choices are
restricted by present ones, is to use what is called a PROBABILITY
TREE. In it you can "branch out" your choices, calculating the

probability of each branch.   One of the handiest characteristics that
this approach has is that it tends to be the easiest way to insure
yourself against omitting some options.   It also has the benefit that
each of the branches of the tree is an exclusive path which none of
the other paths overlap.   In problem 9 you begin with the hand as the
trunk, then branch to the successful draws:

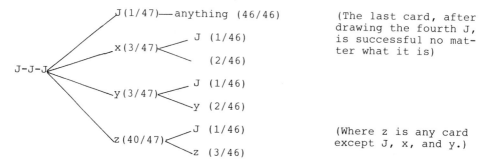

(The last card, after
drawing the fourth J,
is successful no mat-
ter what it is)

(Where z is any card
except J, x, and y.)

To calculate the probability of the tree as a whole, you mulitply out
the branches and add them together.   In this case you get

$$(1/47 \times 46/46) + (3/47 \times 1/46) + (3/47 \times 2/46) + (3/47 \times 1/46) +$$
$$(3/47 \times 2/46) + (40/47 \times 1/46) + (40/47 \times 3/46)$$

which is what you reached by the other method.   For this case the
tree structure was of no particular advantage, but, the longer the
problem, the greater the advantage.

    If, for example, you were asked to calculate the probability of
drawing a full house (three of one card and two of another), the
direct method is complicated and confusing while the tree is just a
large version of the above.   In it, "a" is the first card you draw
and "b" is the second unique card you draw.   You can't get any others
without failing to get a full house.   The tree for a full house looks
like this:

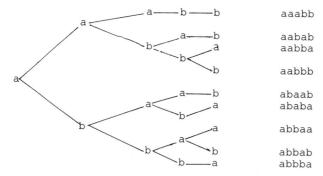

aaabb

aabab
aabba

aabbb

abaab
ababa

abbaa

abbab
abbba

At the right are the written-out forms of each of the branches.   The
probability of the first card drawn is always 52/52.   At the second
drawing of any card there are 3 of them left out of however many are
left in the deck; at the third there are 2 out of what remains.   At
the first drawing of the second unique card ("b") there are 48 of
them out of the remaining deck (52 - 4 a's).   The denominator with
the cards will always decrease one at a time--52 x 51 x 50 x 49 x 48.
In this problem, then, the first "a" is 52, the first "b" is 48, the
second "a" 3, the second "b" 3, and the third of a kind (whether "a"
or "b") is 2.   Thus the numerator for any branch of this tree will be
52 x 48 x 3 x 3 x 2.   Since there are ten exclusive branches on the
tree, they are all added, which means the entire fraction is multi-

plied by 10, yielding as the probability of drawing a full house from a fair poker deck as

$$10 \quad \times \quad \frac{52 \times 48 \times 3 \times 3 \times 2}{52 \times 51 \times 50 \times 49 \times 48}$$

15.3   Expectation or Expected Value

Expectation is a tool for deciding how "good" a choice may be. In the context of gambling, it's the way you tell whether or not you have a bet worth making. Essentially, it involves figuring out what results might occur, what the possibility of each is, and what you would win (or lose) on each of the possible outcomes. If you have been careful to insure that the possible results are exclusive, then the sum of the amounts that you could win on each of the given outcomes multiplied times the probabilities of the appropriate results is the expected value.

Professor Copi details the workings of a calculation of expected values as they apply to the game of chuck-a-luck. The only thing that might be confusing to you is the number of calculations that have to be used. Recently I encountered a carnival game that was a bit less complicated than chuck-a-luck but which also was an appropriate subject for a calculation of expected values. It involved the use of a regular dodecahedron. The one in the carnival must have been a foot thick at its widest, but you have encountered dice-sized dodecahedrons if you play Dungeons and Dragons: it is the 12-sided die. The carnival die had four red faces, three blue ones, two white ones, and a single face each in green, orange and gold. The wager was a quarter, and a roll of red paid nothing, of blue 10 cents, of white 25 cents, of green or orange 50 cents and of gold $1.00. The cost of playing was a quarter. The expectation for this bet can be seen in the following table:

Color	Probability (P)	Return (R)	Expectation (P x R)
Red	4/12 (1/3)	$ .00	$ .00
Blue	3/12 (1/4)	.10	.025
White	2/12 (1/6)	.25	.042
Green	1/12	.50	.042
Orange	1/12	.50	.042
Gold	1/12	1.00	.083
	Total Expected value		$ .234

This makes the dice roll game at that carnival a better game on which to bet than Professor Copi's game of chuck-a-luck. Why? Because the expected value in chuck-a-luck was 91.7 cents on the $1.00 bet while this game has an expected value of 93.6 cents on the same bet.

In a similar manner you could calculate the expected value in any gambling situation for which you knew the probabilities and the payoff. This lets you make an informed judgment on which "game of chance" you wish to put your money. Of course, you should always remember that gambling establishments are seldom in the business of losing money. One way that they try to insure against that possibility is by calculating expected values themselves. Since they set the payoffs, you can be confident that the expected value will be less than the entry cost. A good example of this sort of manipulation being done consciously is in the adjustment of slot machines. The working mechanism of a "one-armed bandit" is three wheels with pictures on their rims. By varying the number of lemons, cherries, bars and the like that are on each of the wheels, the owner can determine (within reasonable limits) what the probability of each possible combination of pictures is when all three wheels are set

into independent motion and are separately and independently brought
to rest. All the owner would have to do, then, would be to assign
such returns to each of the possible outcomes as to insure that the
expected value is less than the cost of playing. Barring a really
freak distribution of results, this gives the machine owner a way of
guaranteeing herself whatever level of profit she wished to have.
The only constraint will be having enough return to encourage the
player to come to the machine in the first place and to continue to
play once there. In fact, on rare occasions when the operator of a
gaming establishment sees business dropping, one machine might be
adjusted to pay off **above** the expected value. That would be done as
a form of advertising, to encourage others to play all of the available machines in the hope that others were also maladjusted. With
the advent of electronic hardware, the weighting of the wheels and
altering the distribution of pictures became unnecessary. The operator now simply programs payoff patterns into the machine and selects
the one that seems most appropriate at any given time. The pattern,
however, remains constant: with the exception of those rare times
when an unfavorable (to the house) expectation is acceptable as part
of the cost of advertising, the expected value of games of chance is
always lower than the cost of playing them.

The pattern for solving problems dealing with expected values is
actually quite simple. You must determine which of the possible
outcomes will bring you a return, what the return of each is, and
what the probability of each of these successful outcomes is. The
expected value of that situation (game, problem or whatever), then,
is the sum of the products of each of the returns and the probability
of its occurring. One value of thinking about the calculation of
expected values in this way is that it makes it easier to see how to
apply such techniques, for example, in the realms of investing and
employment. If you had a choice between two jobs, one of which was
likely to lead to advancement of a minor sort (say an 85% chance of
getting a 10% raise) and the other of which was less likely to lead
to advancement but where the advancement was more dramatic (say a 17%
chance of a 450% raise), which job should you choose? By calculating
the expected value of each option, you will find that the first job
has an expected value of .935 while the second has one of .935.
Curious, isn't it? Given such a wide disparity of the probability of
any increase at all, it seems likely that most of us would choose the
more secure option. However, when the expected values are the same,
there is no justification **in probability theory** for the choice of one
over the other. That choice must come from some other source: your
sense of luck, your self-confidence, your willingness to gamble, the
desperation of your need, or some other nonprobabilistic reason.

The job decision just discussed has an analog in the history of
probability theory. It involves an interesting wager. You pay me
$100.00 to start a game, and I agree to pay you on the basis of the
flips of a coin known to be reasonably fair. Your repayment, however, can take two different forms: I can agree to pay you $2.00 for
every head you flip in 100 flips of the coin, or I can agree to pay
you $2.00 if the first flip is heads, $4.00 is the first two are, and
so on doubling until you flip your first tail or until you reach 100
flips. The calculations of expected values are more complex than are
warranted here, but the result is like the one to the job decision
example; in the long run, each method of repayment has an expected
value of $100.00. There are significant differences between the
two--the first method is unlikely to vary much from a return of
$100.00 while the second is very likely to do so and the first cannot
yield a major profit while the second can--but the differences do not
involve expectation.

Problem 2 of the last set of problems in Copi is an interesting
attempt to insure yourself winning. To figure the expected value of
this sort of bet, you must follow the pattern identified above.

(2)   First you must identify the possible successful
           outcomes. In this case, since all numbers are bet,
           any outcome is a success. Since there are 216 pos-
           sible outcomes, there are 216 possible successes.
           Their probabilities and returns, however, are not all
           the same. You could solve the problem by making an
           exhaustive list of the possibilities, but that seems a
           rather inelegant approach. (It's also a bad precedent
           to set. What if the game were played with five dice?
           That would yield 7,776 possibilities, and I doubt that
           you have the time or energy to work all of them out.)
           There are three kinds of rolls that could occur: (i)
           all three dice could have the same number, (ii) two
           dice could share a number and the third be different,
           and (iii) all three dice could have different numbers.
           Let's consider the cases with their results and their
           probabilities separately.

           The probability of rolling three of any given number
           is an exercise in joint probabilities: p(abd) = p(a) x
           p(b) x p(c). The probability, for example, of rolling
           a 6 is 1/6, so the probability of rolling three sixes
           is (1/6) or 1/216.
           (i)
           You cannot get three of any two different numbers at
           the same time, so the probability of getting three
           matching numbers is an exercise in alternative EXCLU-
           SIVE probabilities: p(111 or 222 or ...or 666) =
           p(111) + ... + p(666). The probability, derived from
           the earlier calculation of the probability of three
           sixes, is (1/216) + (1/216) + (1/216) + (1/216) +
           (1/216) + (1/216), or 6/12.

           If you have $1 on each number and the roll turns up
           three of a single number, then you have both gain and
           loss. You lose each of the dollars wagered on the
           five numbers that did not appear; you get your $1 back
           that you bet on the number that did appear and you win
           $1 for each of the three instances of your winning
           number. This means that a roll of three of a single
           number has a return of $4.

           (ii) The probablity of rolling two of one number and
           a third different number is another joint probability
           exercise: p(aab) = p(a) x p(a) x p(b). The proba-
           bility for example, or rolling a 4 is 1/6, so the
           probability two fours and a nonfour is (1/6) x (1/6) x
           (5/6) or 5/216. You did not, however, have to get
           that nonfour in the third position, it could have been
           first or second. This means that the probability of
           two fours and a nonfour is three times as great, that
           is, 15/216. But four is not the only number that
           could be paired, so, as in the case of the three's of
           a kind in part i, the exclusive alternative probabili-
           ties can be added: p(11x or 22x or ... or 66x) =
           p(11x) + ... + p(66x), where, for example, 11x is
           taken to be the occurrence of two ones and a no one.
           The calculated probability, then, will be 90/216.

           If you have wagered $1 on each number and the roll
           turns up two of one number and one of another, then
           you again have both gain and loss. You lose each of
           the dollars wagered on the numbers which did not
           occur; you get your dollars back on the two numbers on
           which you had bet and $1 for the other number. This
           means that this sort of roll has a return of $5.

(iii)   The probability of rolling three different numbers is another joint probability exercise but one a bit simpler than the two previous. You calculate using the formula: p(abc) = p(a) + p(c). This time, however, any number could serve as a, so p(a) = 6/6. Anything but a could serve as b, so p(b) = 5/6. Anything but a or b could serve as c, so p(c) = 4/6. Thus the probability of three distinct numbers is (6/6) x (5/6) x (4/6) or 120/216.

If you have wagered $1 on each number then you again have both a gain and a loss. You lose each of the dollars that you wagered on the three numbers that did not occur; you get your dollars back on the three numbers that did appear; and you win $1 for each of the three winning numbers that you picked. This means that this sort of roll has a return of $6.

The calculation of the expected value in this approach to chuck-a-luck is straightforward:

Event	Return	Probability	R x P
xxx	$4	6/216	$ 24/216
xxy	$5	90/216	$ 450/216
xyz	$6	120/216	$ 720/216

The sum of the R x P column is $1194/216, or $5.53. The expected value of this approach to chuck-a-luck, then, is $5.53, which figures out to just about 92 cents on the dollar. 92 cents, of course, was the the return figure which Professor Copi showed was the expected value for any wager while playing the game.

(7)   The calculation done here is very like the example of the job decision on p. 291. You compare expected values for each investment. The expected value figure for the preferred stock is $93.50 (.85 x $110); for the common stock it is $93.80 (.67 x $140). Obviously the common stock is a slightly better investment.

(10)   In this case you have to approach the problem as you did some of the formal proofs in chapters 9 and 10, that is, backward. What you want to find out is how much money there must be in the pot for the expected value of your drawing to complete your straight to be worth the $2 you will have to bet in order to get that last card.   Since you hole 3-4-5-6 (the suits are irrelevant) and nothing you could draw except a 2 or 7 would let you beat the pair you believe him to have, you must draw either a 2 or a 7 to win. The exercise makes no mention of any of the other cards having been exposed, so you should assume that the two of you are the only players, and there is a 44-card deck left from which to deal, and that that deck contains four 2's and four 7's. That means that the probability of filling your straight is 8/44, or 2/11. Since the expected value is calculated as the product of the probability of successful outcome times the return for a successful outcome, the expected value of calling his bet would be P x (2/11), where "P" is the current contents of the pot. Your concern is that the expected value be at least $2, so you set the expected value of calling him equal to $2 if [(2P/11) = $2] then [P = $22/2 (or $11)]. This means that if there is $11 or more in the pot **before you wager the $2 to call him,** then you have a good bet.

CHAPTER FIFTEEN SUMMARY

I. There are many uses of the term "probability."

    A.   The commonest nonquantitative use of the term is as an indicator of evidential support, as in a **probable** hypothesis.

    B.   There are three quantitative uses of the term which compete as characterization of "probability."

        1.   The **a priori** theory assumes that all options are equally likely in the absence of evidence to the contrary.

        2.   The relative frequency theory identifies probability as the ratio of events judged to be successes to events judged to be either successes or failures.

        3.   The propensity (or dispositional relative frequency) theory holds that probabilities are properties belonging to events or circumstances and that they are approximated by relative frequencies.

II. Two (or more) events are independent if the occurrence or non-occurrence of one does not affect the occurrence or non-occurrence of the other(s).

III. If the probabilities of two events are known, then the probability of their joint occurrence can be calculated:

$$p(a + b) = p(a) \times p(b)$$

IV. If the probabilities of two events are known, then the probability of their alternate occurrences can be calculated:

$$p(a + b) = p(a) + p(b) - p(ab)$$

V. Probabilities always lie between 0 and 1.

VI. The probability of an event's occurring or its complement occurring always adds to 1.

VII. The expected value of an event is the sum of the products of the possibilities of its successful occurrences times the returns received for each of those occurrences.